VOYAGES
IN ENGLISH
GRAMMAR AND WRITING

Patricia Healey, I.H.M.
B.A., Immaculata University
M.A., Temple University
20 years teaching; 20 years in administration

Irene Kervick, I.H.M.
B.A., Immaculata University
M.A., Villanova University
46 years teaching

Anne B. McGuire, I.H.M.
B.A., Immaculata University
M.A., Villanova University
M.A., Immaculata University
*16 years teaching; 14 years as elementary
principal; 10 years staff development*

Adrienne Saybolt, I.H.M.
B.A., Immaculata University
Pennsylvania State Board of Education,
professional certification
M.A., St. John's University
40 years teaching

LOYOLA PRESS.

Loyola Press has made every effort to locate the copyright holders for the cited works used in this publication and to make full acknowledgment for their use. In the case of any omissions, the publisher will be pleased to make suitable acknowledgments in future editions. Continued on page 535.

Cover Design: Think Book Works   Cover Artist: Pablo Bernasconi
Interior Design: Maggie Hong/Loyola Press
Art Director: Judine O'Shea/Loyola Press
Editor: Nicola S. Caso/Loyola Press

ISBN-13: 978-0-8294-2817-9
ISBN-10: 0-8294-2817-8

LOYOLA PRESS.
3441 N. Ashland Avenue
Chicago, Illinois 60657
(800) 621-1008
www.loyolapress.com

Webcrafters / Madison, WI, USA / 04-10 / 1st Printing

Contents

PART 1 Grammar

PART 2 Written and Oral Communication

SECTION ONE
Sentences

1.1 Sentences

A **sentence** is a group of words that expresses a complete thought.

Every sentence has a subject and a predicate. The **subject** names a person, a place, or a thing. The **predicate** tells what the subject is or does. It expresses an action or a state of being.

SUBJECT	PREDICATE
The pretzels	were hard and salty.
Sue	ate two pretzels.
My friends and I	liked the pretzels.
The bag of pretzels	is now empty.

To find the subject, ask yourself *who or what is doing something or being some way?* To find the predicate, ask *what is the subject doing or how is the subject being?* To find a sentence, make sure there is a subject and a predicate.

Which of these word groups are sentences?

 A **The tall apple trees**
 B **The apple tastes good**
 C **My sister picked apples**
 D **Were left in the bowl**

You are right if you said that B and C are sentences. Each one expresses a complete thought. Each has a subject and a predicate.

A and D are not sentences. They do not express complete thoughts. A doesn't have a predicate. D doesn't have a subject.

EXERCISE 1 Tell which of these word groups are sentences. Tell which are not sentences.

 1. Our class enjoyed its visit to the zoo
 2. A huge gray elephant
 3. Eating food from a bucket
 4. A cub is a baby lion

5. The lion was chewing a bone
6. We couldn't count the leopard's spots
7. The giraffe's long legs
8. The keeper fed the seals
9. Swimming under the water
10. I liked the monkeys best
11. We enjoyed the striped zebras
12. Were swinging from branch to branch

EXERCISE 2 **Match each group of words in Column A with a group of words in Column B to make a sentence.**

Column A	Column B
1. At the circus, clowns	a. galloped around the ring.
2. Eight brown horses	b. wore funny costumes.
3. Several acrobats	c. raised its trunk.
4. A baby elephant	d. walked on their hands.

EXERCISE 3 **These groups of words are not sentences. Add subjects or predicates to make them sentences.**

1. went to the zoo last week
2. saw a tall giraffe
3. some children
4. counted the penguins on the rocks
5. gave the seals food
6. dove into the water after the food
7. slept on a rock
8. workers at the zoo
9. roared and walked back and forth
10. the chimps
11. laughed at the monkeys
12. studied a map of the zoo

APPLY IT NOW

Imagine you are at the zoo. Choose three of these topics. Write a sentence about each.

A. dolphins   D. popcorn
B. tigers   E. monkeys
C. crowd

1.2 Statements and Questions

A sentence begins with a capital letter and ends with a punctuation mark.

Some sentences tell things. A telling sentence is called a **statement.** A statement ends with a period (.).

There are many animals in the zoo.

The lions are sleeping under a tree.

Some sentences ask things. An asking sentence is called a **question.** A question ends with a question mark (?).

Do you like to go to the zoo?

What do the lions eat?

EXERCISE 1 Match each question in Column A with an answer in Column B. Then rewrite them. Add question marks at the end of questions. Add periods at the end of statements.

Column A

1. What is your favorite animal
2. When do you go to the zoo
3. Where do you see snakes
4. Who feeds the animals

Column B

a. I go there in the summer
b. I like snakes the best
c. Only the zookeeper feeds them
d. I see them at the reptile house

EXERCISE 2 Rewrite the sentences. Add periods at the end of statements. Add question marks at the end of questions.

1. Many people work at a zoo
2. What does a zoo veterinarian do
3. Veterinarians take care of sick animals
4. Do zookeepers feed the animals
5. They feed the animals and clean the cages
6. How do volunteers help at a zoo
7. Some volunteers lead tour groups through the zoo
8. Would you like to be a zookeeper

EXERCISE 3 Make statements or questions by matching the words in Column A with the words in Column B.

Column A

1. How many uses
2. Many people
3. A lot of food
4. Peanut shells

Column B

a. can be used to make kitty litter.
b. enjoy peanut butter.
c. are there for peanuts?
d. contains peanuts.

EXERCISE 4 Write an answer for each question. Make sure your answer is a complete sentence. Begin with *My* or *I* as shown after each question. Put a period at the end of each sentence.

EXAMPLE **Do you like corn on the cob?** (I)

I like corn on the cob.

1. How old are you? (I)
2. Do you have any brothers or sisters? (I)
3. What is your favorite sport or activity? (My)
4. What is your favorite kind of ice cream? (My)
5. Do you like baseball? (I)
6. Do you have a pet? (I)
7. How do you get to school? (I)
8. What is your favorite holiday? (My)

EXERCISE 5 Write a question for each answer. Make sure your question is a complete sentence. Begin each question with *What do you*. Put a question mark at the end.

1. I eat apples for snacks.
2. I put my books in my backpack.
3. I have pencils and paper in my desk.
4. I do my homework after school.

APPLY IT NOW

Write four sentences about yourself. Tell about these things. The sentences may be statements or questions.
1. your favorite TV show
2. a good book you've read
3. a food you like
4. a food you dislike

Grammar in Action.
Find the third question on page 211.

1.3 Question Words

A question—a sentence that asks for information—often starts with a **question word.** Some question words are *who, what, when, where, why,* and *how.*

Who is the president of the United States?

What did the president say in the speech?

When was the president elected?

Where does the president live?

Why is a president elected for four years?

How do we elect a president?

EXERCISE 1 Read each statement. Complete the question after each statement. Use *who, what, when, where, why,* or *how.*

1. The president lives in the White House.
   _____ lives in the White House?

2. The White House is located at 1600 Pennsylvania Avenue.
   _____ is the White House located?

3. The first wedding at the White House was in 1812.
   _____ was the first wedding held in the White House?

4. Central heating was installed in the White House in 1835.
   _____ was installed in the White House in 1835?

5. The White House needed to be repaired because it was in bad condition.
   _____ did the White House need to be repaired?

6. By fixing only the inside of the building, workmen around 1950 kept its original look.
   _____ did workmen keep its original look?

7. George Washington chose where the White House would be built.
   _____ chose where the White House would be built?

8. The White House burned down in 1814.
   _____ did the White House burn down?

George Washington

EXERCISE 2 Complete the questions with question words. Then match the questions in Column A with the answers in Column B.

Column A

1. _____ year was the White House named?

2. _____ named the White House?

3. _____ is it called the White House?

4. _____ can you get tickets to visit the White House?

Column B

a. Theodore Roosevelt named the White House.

b. You can write your member of Congress for tickets.

c. It is called the White House because of its color.

d. It was named in 1901.

Theodore Roosevelt

EXERCISE 3 Write a question for each statement. Begin with the word or words given in parentheses. Put a question mark at the end of each question.

EXAMPLE **The Vice President lives at Number One Observatory Circle.** (Where does)

Where does the Vice President live?

1. The president and the Cabinet meet in the Cabinet Room. (Where do)

2. John Adams and Abigail Adams were the first residents of the White House. (Who)

3. The White House was first called the President's House. (What was)

4. First Lady Abigail Fillmore started a library in the White House in 1850. (When did)

5. Presidents entertain important guests by holding state dinners. (How do)

6. Theodore Roosevelt hung moose heads in the State Dining Room. (What did)

7. Theodore Roosevelt built the West Wing. (Who)

8. The Oval Office was built in 1909. (When was)

9. The president's staff works in the West Wing. (Who)

10. President Franklin D. Roosevelt named his Scottish terrier Fala, a Scottish word. (What did)

Tech Tip With an adult, research your famous place online.

1.4 Commands

Some sentences tell people what to do. These sentences are called **commands.**

Directions for playing a game are examples of commands.

Take your turn.

Select a card.

Roll the number cube.

Go to the next green square.

The subject of a command is *you*. The subject is not stated in most commands. A command ends with a period (.).

When you give a command, it is polite to use a person's name and *please*.

Please do your homework, Katy.

Open the window, please.

Please have a seat right there.

Follow me, please.

Which of these sentences are commands?

A **Have some juice, Gilly.**

B **He finished the song.**

C **Unwrap your gift.**

D **Please blow out the candles.**

E **Are we going to play games?**

You are right if you said that A, C, and D are commands. They tell someone what to do. Sentence B is a statement. Sentence E is a question.

EXERCISE 1 Tell which of these sentences are commands.

1. I want to make bananas on a stick.

2. Do you have the recipe?

3. Please hand it to me, Brad.

4. I need a banana, a flat stick, honey, and granola.
5. First, peel the banana.
6. Then cut it in half.
7. Next, I need to put each half on a stick.
8. Finally, roll the banana in honey and granola.
9. Yum! It tastes good.
10. Please give me a piece.

EXERCISE 2 Change each sentence into a command.

EXAMPLE **You can learn how fast water evaporates from a fruit.**
Learn how fast water evaporates from a fruit.

1. You need to get three apples, a balance scale, and some weights.
2. You have to leave one apple whole.
3. You should peel one apple.
4. You have to cut the third apple into slices.
5. You should leave the three apples out on the table.
6. You need to weigh the apples every day for a week.
7. You will find out how much water evaporates.
8. You can try the experiment with other kinds of fruit.

EXERCISE 3 Write two commands for each of these scenes. Remember to start each sentence with a capital letter and end it with a period.

1. You are the owner of a pet store. Tell a customer how to care for a pet.
2. You are an art teacher. Tell the class how to draw a house.
3. You are a crossing guard. Tell the younger children how to cross the street safely.

APPLY IT NOW

Think of a game you like to play. Write four directions for playing the game. Use commands.

Grammar in Action. Find a command on this page.

1.5 Exclamations

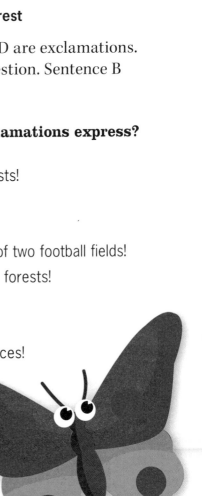

Boa constrictor

Some sentences express strong or sudden emotion. These sentences are called **exclamations.**

Exclamations express feelings such as wonder, respect, surprise, happiness, worry, or fear.

What a lovely butterfly that is!

How noisy the parrots are!

Those tangled vines look like snakes!

An exclamation ends with an exclamation point (!).

Which of these sentences are exclamations?

A **What lives in the rain forest**
B **Mammals such as monkeys and jaguars live there**
C **How amazing this rain forest is**
D **Wow, I'd love to live there**
E **Name two animals that live in the rain forest**

You are right if you said that sentences C and D are exclamations. Each shows strong feeling. Sentence A is a question. Sentence B is a statement. Sentence E is a command.

EXERCISE 1 What emotions do these exclamations express? More than one answer may be correct.

1. Wow, many plants and animals live in rain forests!
2. How beautiful the butterflies are!
3. Oh no, rain forests are disappearing rapidly!
4. Yikes, every second we lose an area the size of two football fields!
5. Great, many groups are trying to save the rain forests!
6. What important work they do!
7. How strange some rain forest animals are!
8. Gosh, rain forests are really hot and humid places!

EXERCISE 2 Tell which sentences need exclamation points. Tell what punctuation marks the other sentences need.

1. What a magical place the rain forest is
2. Please stay on the path
3. Kapok trees can grow 150 feet tall
4. Oh, snakes really scare me
5. Did you see that butterfly flutter
6. How colorful the flowers are
7. Can you hear the chirping birds
8. We must save the rain forest
9. Hurry, it's starting to rain
10. Do you have an extra umbrella
11. Ouch, I tripped on a root
12. Please help me up
13. Wow, I don't ever want to leave the rain forest
14. We have to visit the rain forest again soon

Toucan

EXERCISE 3 Change these statements to exclamations. Use the word *How* or *What* to begin each sentence. Use the correct punctuation mark at the end of each sentence.

EXAMPLE   **This bird is colorful.**

How colorful this bird is!

What a colorful bird this is!

1. These rocks are heavy.
2. The lizard is fierce.
3. Sophia quickly ran down the path.
4. It is very hot.
5. This is an old tree.
6. That monkey looks happy.
7. This part of the forest is dark.
8. These flowers have large petals.

APPLY IT NOW

Think of three things that caused you to have strong feelings. Write a statement describing the situation and an exclamation for your reaction.
Example:
I aced the math test.
I'm so happy!

1.6 Kinds of Sentences

What are the four kinds of sentences? A sentence can be a **statement**, a **question**, a **command**, or an **exclamation.** Let's review them.

KIND OF SENTENCE	WHAT IT DOES	END MARK
Statement	Tells something	Period (.)
Question	Asks something	Question mark (?)
Command	Gives a direction	Period (.)
Exclamation	Expresses a strong or a sudden feeling	Exclamation point (!)

Cocoa beans come from the fruit of the cacao tree.

Each of these four sentences is a different kind of sentence. Can you name what kind each is?

A **Do you like cake**

B **Chocolate comes from cocoa beans**

C **Mix the batter**

D **What a delicious cake you made**

You're right if you said sentence A is a question. It asks something. Sentence B is a statement. It tells about something (chocolate). Sentence C is a command. It tells what to do. Sentence D is an exclamation. It expresses a strong emotion (joy).

Cacao tree

EXERCISE 1 Tell what kind of each of the following sentences is.

1. Do you like to cook?
2. I sometimes help my parents in the kitchen.
3. What kinds of things do you do?
4. Karen, help me mix the dough.
5. How wonderful the bread tastes!
6. Wash the dishes, James.
7. Don't eat all the bread.
8. Mom's bread is better than store bread.

EXERCISE 2 Tell what kind each of the following sentences is. Tell what punctuation mark is needed at the end of each sentence.

1. I like to make cookies
2. Do we have chocolate chips
3. We have all the ingredients
4. What hard work stirring the dough is
5. Don't touch the hot stove
6. When will the cookies be done
7. How good the cookies smell
8. Please share the cookies with your sister

EXERCISE 3 Change each sentence to make it into a statement, a question, a command, or an exclamation.

1. The banana bread is in the oven.
   a. Question
   b. Command
2. Wash your hands.
   a. Statement
   b. Question
3. Can you eat that huge slice?
   a. Command
   b. Exclamation
4. Is it a delicious treat?
   a. Exclamation
   b. Statement
5. The dishes are in the dishwasher.
   a. Question
   b. Command

6. Put away the clean dishes.
   a. Question
   b. Statement
7. Can you set the table?
   a. Command
   b. Statement
8. Can you bake bread?
   a. Statement
   b. Command

APPLY IT NOW

You want to tell a friend how to make pancakes. Write four sentences, one of each type. Use the correct punctuation to end each sentence.

Tech Tip With an adult, find a pancake recipe online.

1.7 Subjects

A sentence has a subject and a predicate. The **subject** is who or what the sentence is about. The **simple subject** names the person, place, or thing that is talked about. The simple subject is usually a noun. A **complete subject** is the simple subject and words that describe it or give more information about it.

COMPLETE SUBJECT	COMPLETE PREDICATE
Mr. Liu	dived into the water.
The swim team	practices Tuesday.

In the first sentence, *Mr. Liu* is the simple subject and also the complete subject. In the second sentence, *team* is the simple subject. *The swim team* is the complete subject because *The* and *swim* tell more about *team*.

What is the complete subject in each of these sentences?

A **The boy did the breaststroke.**
B **Water splashed.**
C **The excited students cheered loudly.**
D **Our team's swimmers won the meet.**

If you said *The boy, Water, The excited students,* and *Our team's swimmers,* you are correct.

What is the simple subject of each of those sentences? If you said *boy, water, students,* and *swimmers,* you are correct. Each subject names a person or a thing.

EXERCISE 1 Tell what the complete subject is in each sentence.

1. The swim team practiced every day.
2. Sarub wanted to join the team.
3. The coach watched Sarub in the pool.
4. The determined boy finished his last lap.

5. Other swimmers patted him on the back.

6. The team members welcomed him.

7. Athletes need to train for meets.

8. The crowd roared for our team.

9. Our team won!

10. A win always feels good.

EXERCISE 2 **Tell what the complete subject is in each sentence. Then tell what the simple subject is.**

1. My brother swims every day.

2. Luke belongs to the swim team.

3. The coach chose my brother for the team.

4. The team practices in the morning.

5. The swimmers can swim very fast.

6. Meets take place every month.

7. The best swimmers go to the meets.

8. Many spectators watch the meets.

9. The people cheer the swimmers along.

10. All the winners receive a lot of applause.

EXERCISE 3 **Finish each sentence with a complete subject.**

EXAMPLE   **My friend** clapped for the other team.

1. _____ led the cheer.

2. _____ finished in first place.

3. _____ blew a whistle.

4. _____ looked nervous.

5. _____ was too close to call.

6. _____ swam two laps of the pool.

APPLY IT NOW

Imagine that you are at a swimming pool. Write five sentences that describe what you see. Underline the complete subjects.
Example: The children paddle in the shallow pool.

Grammar in Action. Find the complete subject in the first sentence of the page 214 excerpt.

1.8 Predicates

A sentence has a subject and a predicate. The **predicate** tells what the subject is or does. The **simple predicate** is a verb, which is the word or words that express an action or a state of being. A **complete predicate** is the simple predicate and any words that describe it.

COMPLETE SUBJECT	COMPLETE PREDICATE
The twins	cleaned their room.
Kate	folded all the laundry.

In the first sentence, *cleaned* is the simple predicate. In the second sentence, *folded* is the simple predicate.

What is the complete predicate in each of these sentences?

   A **Mom dusted the shelves.**

   B **Dad and Joseph washed the dishes.**

   C **Maggie put her toys away.**

   D **The house looked nice.**

If you said *dusted the shelves, washed the dishes, put her toys away,* and *looked nice,* you are correct.

What is the simple predicate of each of these sentences? You are correct if you said *dusted, washed, put,* and *looked.* These words tell what the subjects are or do.

EXERCISE 1 Tell what the complete predicate is in each sentence.

   1. Luis helps at home.

   2. His dad gives him a list of chores.

   3. Luis's sister has jobs too.

4. She makes the beds.

5. The vacuum cleaner broke.

6. Mom fixed it.

7. Luis dusts the furniture.

8. He finds coins under the couch sometimes.

9. The house smells of lemons.

10. The family cleans every week.

EXERCISE 2 Tell what the complete predicate is in each sentence. Then tell what the simple predicate is.

1. Luis's sister cleans her room every week.

2. Mom vacuums the rugs.

3. Luis sweeps the floor.

4. The house looks wonderful.

5. The children wash the car with their dad on the weekend.

6. Dad mows the lawn.

7. All the family members work in the garden.

8. The neighbors talk to the family.

9. Many vegetables grow in the garden.

10. The family picks tomatoes in August.

EXERCISE 3 Finish each sentence with a complete predicate.

EXAMPLE **I take out the trash.**

1. I _____.

2. We _____.

3. Grandmother _____.

4. My friends _____.

5. The neighbors _____.

6. Our kitchen _____.

APPLY IT NOW

Do you help with chores? Write five sentences about what you do. Underline the complete predicates.
Example: I wash windows.

1.9 Combining Subjects and Predicates

Two or more sentences in a paragraph may give information about the same subject. When this happens, you can often use the subject once and combine the predicates to make a single, smoother sentence. Two predicates joined by *and, but,* or *or* are called a **compound predicate.**

My tabby cat sits in the sun. My tabby cat purrs softly.

These sentences give information about the same subject—*My tabby cat.* The predicates, however, are different—*sits in the sun* and *purrs softly.* The two sentences can be made into one sentence by using the subject only once and combining the two predicates with the word *and.*

My tabby cat sits in the sun *and* purrs softly.

You can also combine two sentences when they have different subjects but the same predicate.

My tabby cat plays with string. My kitten plays with string.

These sentences have the same predicate—*plays with string.* They have different subjects, however—*My tabby cat* and *My kitten.* They can be combined by connecting the two subjects with *and* and by using the predicate only once. Two subjects joined by *and* or *or* are called a **compound subject.**

My tabby cat *and* my kitten play with string.

EXERCISE 1 Combine the predicates to make one sentence.

1. The dogs barked. The dogs howled.
2. The doctor petted Rex. The doctor spoke quietly.
3. Rex looked sick. Rex rested his head on his paws.
4. The dog looked out of its cage. The dog barked at the cat.
5. The vet examined Rex. The vet gave him a shot.
6. Rex barked. Rex put his head down.

EXERCISE 2 **Combine the subjects to make one sentence.**

1. Rex was sick. Sparky was sick.
2. Mom took Rex to the vet. I took Rex to the vet.
3. Two dogs were in the waiting room. Two cats were in the waiting room.
4. A boy held a big cage. A girl held a big cage.
5. Dr. Smith gave Rex a treat. I gave Rex a treat.
6. The vet looked at Rex. The vet's assistant looked at Rex.
7. The medicine helped Rex. Rest helped Rex.
8. The vet checked on Rex. I checked on Rex.
9. His treats pleased Rex. His new toy pleased Rex.
10. The vet felt happy about Rex. I felt happy about Rex.

EXERCISE 3 **Write complete sentences with these compound subjects.**

1. Veterinarians and vets' assistants _____.
2. Animal shelters and rescue groups _____.
3. Cats and dogs _____.
4. Food and water _____.
5. Gerbils and hamsters _____.
6. Canaries and parrots _____.

EXERCISE 4 **Write complete sentences with these compound predicates.**

1. _____ examine animals and give them medicine.
2. _____ feed the animals and clean their cages.
3. _____ walk and feed the dog every day.
4. _____ jumped onto the chair and fell asleep.
5. _____ flew to its perch and chirped.
6. _____ ran to the door and barked.

APPLY IT NOW

Use some of the words below to help you write two sentences. Each sentence should have two subjects or two predicates.

Subjects:

dog	cat
parrot	canary

Predicates:

growl	bark
purr	hiss
chew	sing
chatter	fly
perch	chirp
lick	sleep

1.10 Combining Sentences

Several short sentences in a row can be boring to read. Putting short sentences together into longer sentences can make your writing more interesting.

To combine two short sentences into one longer sentence, add a comma followed by *and, but,* or *or.* Two short sentences joined this way form a **compound sentence.**

Two sentences:	**Father read softly.** **The children listened.**
Compound sentence:	**Father read softly**, *and* **the children listened.**
Two sentences:	**Jim passes the library.** **Amy doesn't pass it.**
Compound sentence:	**Jim passes the library,** *but* **Amy doesn't pass it.**

What two sentences were combined to make this compound sentence?

I'll study music, or maybe I'll play ball instead.

The first word in the second part of the compound sentence does not begin with a capital letter unless it is *I* or the name of a person or place. For example, in the compound sentence above, *maybe* does not start with a capital letter.

EXERCISE 1 Match each sentence in Column A with a related sentence in Column B to make a compound sentence.

Column A

1. Nonfiction books have facts, but

2. Biographies are stories of people's lives, and

3. Adventure stories have lots of action, and

4. Folktales are old, but

Column B

a. people today still like to tell or read them.

b. fiction books are made up.

c. they are nonfiction books.

d. the action is often scary.

EXERCISE 2 Combine each pair of short sentences with a comma and the word *and* or *but* to form a compound sentence.

1. This book has many pages. I read it in a week.

2. Alex read *Super Fudge*. The funny story about two brothers made him laugh.

3. The mystery was exciting. Jenny couldn't stop reading it.

4. Katie likes horses. She would enjoy *The Black Stallion*.

5. Rosa likes reading mysteries. Cam Jansen is one of her favorite characters.

6. *Charlotte's Web* is a classic. I haven't read it yet.

7. The character Charlotte is a spider. She helps a pig.

8. Beverly Cleary created the funny character Ramona. I haven't read any books with Ramona.

9. I saw a book with the funny title *How to Eat Fried Worms*. I wanted to read it.

10. In a series of novels, Pippi Longstocking lives with a horse and a monkey. She doesn't live with her parents.

Jackie Robinson
Black Heritage USA 20c

EXERCISE 3 Complete the following to make compound sentences. Remember to include *and, but,* or *or.*

1. I might read a mystery, _____.

2. The novel was long, _____.

3. The story was interesting, _____.

4. The biography was about Jackie Robinson, _____.

5. I saw a film of the story, _____.

6. I found an exciting adventure book, _____.

7. I have a book of folktales, _____.

8. The library has a section of fiction books, _____.

9. Writers come to the library, _____.

10. The library is my favorite place, _____.

APPLY IT NOW

Think about a book you have read. Write four short sentences about that book. Then combine two short sentences into one compound sentence.

1.11 Run-on Sentences

A **run-on sentence** is one in which two or more sentences are put together without the proper connector.

Run-on sentences sometimes happen because two complete sentences are separated with only a comma.

A run-on is fixed easily by adding *and, but,* or *or* after the comma to make a compound sentence.

> Run-on sentence: **It rained, I wanted to play outside.**
>
> Compound sentence: **It rained, *but* I wanted to play outside.**

Which sentence is a run-on?

> A **The sun came out, and I went outside.**
>
> B **I have a raincoat, it is yellow.**
>
> C **My umbrella is large. It keeps me dry.**

You are right if you said B. Sentence B has two complete sentences run together and joined by only a comma.

Sentence A is two sentences linked together with a comma followed by the word *and*. Sentence A is correct because both the comma and the word *and* are included.

C is correct because there are two separate sentences that have proper punctuation. Each sentence ends with a period.

EXERCISE 1 Tell whether each sentence is a run-on or a correctly combined sentence.

1. Rain clouds rolled in, the sky turned dark.

2. The teacher looked out the window, she frowned.

3. The children must stay inside for recess, and they are sad.

4. There is more to do outside, it is more fun.

5. Most students play kickball, but some play basketball.

6. It's not raining hard, we have raincoats.

7. You will get wet, you might catch cold.

8. It will be sunny tomorrow, and we will go outside.

9. I like sunny days best, Eric likes rainy days.

10. Eric likes cold days, and he doesn't like warm days.

EXERCISE 2 Rewrite these run-on sentences. Add *and, but,* or *or* to make compound sentences.

1. The day was hot, we decided to go to the beach.

2. The beach was crowded, some people were sitting under umbrellas.

3. We wore hats, we put on sunscreen.

4. The water was cold, we still went swimming.

5. We played catch in the water, we played tag.

6. The lifeguard watched the swimmers, we felt safe.

7. We enjoyed the water, we had a great time at the beach.

8. We were tired, we were happy with our day.

EXERCISE 3 Rewrite the run-on sentences in Exercise 1 as compound sentences.

EXERCISE 4 Choose one group of run-on sentences. Then rewrite them as compound sentences.

A. The thunder clapped loudly, it shook the house, the little boy began to cry, his mom said it was only a storm, he didn't like the dark, she turned on a lamp, the boy fell asleep, the light kept his brother awake.

B. There was a big storm, the lights went out, trees had fallen, they had brought down the electrical wires, Dad made a fire in the fireplace, we played cards near the fire. We expected the lights to come on soon, they didn't come on until morning.

APPLY IT NOW

Think about what you did this morning. Write four sentences without any punctuation or connectors. Exchange papers with a partner. Then add correct punctuation and connectors to make the sentences complete.

Sentence Review

1.1 Tell which of these word groups are sentences. Tell which are not sentences.

1. Swimming with fins
2. A snorkel lets divers breathe
3. The snorkel sticks up out of the water
4. A cool way to see fish
5. Snorkeling is easy to learn

1.2 Rewrite the sentences. Add a period or a question mark to the end of each sentence.

6. Ana likes to dance
7. Her parents are teaching her dances from Guatemala
8. Do you know how to dance
9. When did you learn to dance
10. Square dancing is an American folk dance

1.3 Find the question word in each sentence.

11. Who is going to the party?
12. What are you going to wear?
13. Where is Stuart's house?
14. Why is he having a party?
15. When does it start?

1.4 Tell whether each sentence is a statement, a question, or a command. Then rewrite each sentence. Add a period or a question mark to the end of each sentence.

16. Please go shopping with me
17. I need juice and eggs
18. Where did I put my wallet
19. Bring me my keys
20. Thanks for your help

1.5 Rewrite the sentences. Add a question mark or an exclamation point to the end of each sentence.

21. Wow, I'm finally tall enough to ride the roller coaster
22. Do you want to ride with me
23. What an amazing view
24. Hang on tight
25. When does the park close

1.6 Tell whether each sentence is a statement, a question, a command, or an exclamation. Then tell what punctuation mark is needed at the end of each sentence.

26. Where is the newspaper
27. Please hand it to me
28. Wow, what a terrific article
29. My mom likes to read the city news first
30. What a great photo

1.7 Tell what the complete subject is in each sentence. Tell what the simple subject is.

31. My aunt is a vegetarian.

32. A vegetarian is someone who doesn't eat meat.

33. Sara doesn't eat beef, poultry, or fish.

34. Good food is important for everyone.

35. Sara's diet includes vegetables and tofu.

1.8 Tell what the complete predicate is in each sentence. Tell what the simple predicate is.

36. My parents own a business.

37. They make cowboy boots.

38. My mom selects the leather.

39. My dad creates the designs for the boots.

40. I have several pairs of these beautiful boots.

1.9 Combine the subjects or predicates to make one sentence.

41. Shawn rides bikes.
    Jo rides bikes.

42. We rode to the bike shop.
    We looked at helmets.

43. The bike shop sells bikes.
    The bike shop repairs bikes.

44. My sister took a class.
    My sister bought some tools.

45. We polish our bikes.
    We decorate our bikes.

1.10 Combine each pair of sentences with a comma and the word *and, but,* or *or* to form a compound sentence.

46. My family went to Colorado. We tried skiing.

47. I took a lesson. My parents already knew how to ski.

48. I could take the chairlift up the hill. I could use the rope tow.

49. I was nervous. The instructor helped me feel better.

50. I finished the lesson. I skied down a hill by myself.

1.11 Tell whether each sentence is a run-on or a correctly combined sentence. Rewrite the run-ons to make them correct.

51. We bought apples, Grandma sliced them.

52. I walked to the park, I saw Grandpa.

53. I watched him play chess, and I asked if I could play.

54. We went home, Grandma had an apple pie ready.

Tech Tip

Go to www.voyagesinenglish.com for more activities.

Sentence Challenge

Read the paragraph and answer the questions.

1. Do you like snow? 2. All the kids in my building love snow.
3. Most of the adults hate snow. 4. Last year we had 24 inches of
snow in one day! 5. People shoveled snow all day. 6. The city plowed
the streets and salted the sidewalks. 7. Then it got really cold!
8. Everything froze, and we all stayed inside. 9. What do you think
happened next? 10. In a few days, the sun came out, and most of
the snow melted. 11. The storm was a real challenge. 12. What a
big adventure we had!

1. What kind of sentence is sentence 1?

2. What kind of sentence is sentence 2?

3. Why is sentence 3 a statement?

4. What is the subject in sentence 5?

5. What is the complete predicate in sentence 5?

6. What kind of sentence is sentence 7?

7. What is the punctuation mark in sentence 7 called?

8. What two sentences were combined in sentence 8?

9. Which word is the question word in sentence 9?

10. What is the complete subject in sentence 11?

11. What kind of sentence is sentence 12?

12. What sentence has a compound predicate?

13. What sentences are compound sentences?

14. What is the simple subject in sentence 6?

15. What is the simple subject in sentence 11?

Nouns

2.1 Nouns

A **noun** is a word that names a person, a place, or a thing.

If you were taking a trip, you might see many different people, places, and things.

PEOPLE	PLACES	THINGS
passengers	runway	airplane
pilot	shop	tickets
Mrs. Garcia	Idaho	baggage
ticket agent	cockpit	seat belt

Which of these words names a person?

   A flight attendant

   B suitcase

   C East Coast

You are right if you said A. *Flight attendant* is a noun that names a person who works on an airplane.

Suitcase is a noun that names a thing. *East Coast* is a noun that names a place.

In the following sentence, can you tell whether each noun names a person, a place, or a thing?

   Arnold bought a ticket to Los Angeles.

You are right if you said that *Arnold* names a person, *ticket* names a thing, and *Los Angeles* names a place.

Can you think of other people, places, and things? The words you think of are nouns.

EXERCISE 1 Tell whether each noun is a person, a place, or a thing.

1. propeller	**5.** Hawaii	**9.** bus driver
2. travel agent	**6.** zoo	**10.** statue
3. restaurant	**7.** map	**11.** city
4. guidebook	**8.** Janine	**12.** tourist

EXERCISE 2 Use the nouns in the box to complete the sentences.

principal	children	Dallas	flowers
drum	camp	Jack	kitchen

1. The _____ play at the park.
2. _____ is a large city.
3. We learned to swim at summer _____.
4. He plays a _____ in the school band.
5. _____ is my younger brother.
6. The _____ bloomed in the garden.
7. Dad cooked his famous chili in the _____.
8. The _____ read the announcements over the loudspeaker.

EXERCISE 3 Tell what the nouns are in these sentences. The number of nouns in each sentence is in parentheses.

1. Paolo visited New York City. (2)
2. The Empire State Building was once the tallest skyscraper. (2)
3. The buildings were tall. (1)
4. Mom saw a celebrity and got an autograph. (3)
5. A guidebook has sights to see. (2)
6. The guide knew cool facts about the city. (3)
7. My lunch was a hot dog from a stand. (3)
8. A boat moved up the river. (2)
9. Margarita found the museum on the map. (3)
10. The stores were packed with shoppers. (2)
11. There were big crowds on the streets. (2)
12. Times Square had many signs and lights. (3)

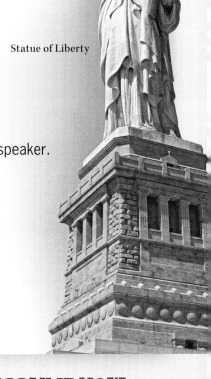

Statue of Liberty

APPLY IT NOW

Imagine you are going on a trip. Write one sentence for each of the following:
1. Name a person who would go with you.
2. Tell about a place you would visit.
3. Describe something you would take.

Underline all the nouns.

Type your sentences, using a computer.

2.2 Common and Proper Nouns

A **proper noun** names a particular person, place, or thing.
A **common noun** names any one member of a group of people, places, or things.

In these two lists, which are common nouns and which are proper nouns?

COLUMN A	COLUMN B
teacher	Mrs. Filippo
student	Javier
day	Monday
holiday	Labor Day
book	*The Giving Tree*
city	Chicago
planet	Jupiter

The nouns in Column A name one member of a group of people, places, or things. They are common nouns.

The nouns in Column B name specific people, places, or things. They are proper nouns. Many proper nouns have more than one part, such as *Elm Street* and the *Poppy Popcorn Company.* Generally, every part of a proper noun begins with a capital letter.

EXERCISE 1 Tell whether each of the following nouns is a common noun or a proper noun.

1. Benjamin Franklin
2. president
3. Atlantic Ocean
4. athlete
5. Amelia Earhart
6. river
7. Ireland
8. state
9. continent
10. Mickey Mouse
11. Abraham Lincoln
12. TV show
13. *Sesame Street*
14. country
15. inventor
16. Indiana

Amelia Earhart, first woman to fly solo across the Atlantic Ocean

EXERCISE 2 Name a proper noun for each common noun.

EXAMPLE **Common Noun**   **Proper Noun**
         neighbor   Mrs. Ahmed

1. friend
2. state
3. movie
4. grandmother
5. street
6. restaurant
7. song
8. country

9. singer
10. ocean
11. school
12. teacher
13. book
14. bicycle
15. store
16. mayor

EXERCISE 3 Tell what the nouns are in each sentence. Then tell whether each is a common noun or a proper noun. The number of nouns in each sentence is in parentheses.

1. Many writers create interesting, young characters. (2)
2. Ramona Quimby was created by Beverly Cleary. (2)
3. Ramona has a sister called Beezus. (3)
4. In the book *Ramona Quimby, Age 8*, the main character is a third grader. (4)
5. The story tells about her life at school and at home. (4)
6. Readers enjoy the funny events in the book. (3)
7. In *Third Grade Baby*, a young student has a problem. (3)
8. Polly Peterson still has her baby teeth. (2)
9. A student teases Polly about her situation. (3)
10. But Polly has friends who help. (2)
11. Jenny Meyerhoff is the author of the novel. (3)
12. The library has many wonderful books and magazines. (3)

APPLY IT NOW

Write sentences with nouns to answer these questions:

1. Where do you live? Tell a fact about your city or town.
2. On what street do you live? Describe how it looks.
3. What is the name of a neighbor? Tell one interesting fact about that neighbor.

2.3 Singular and Plural Nouns

A **singular noun** names one person, place, or thing.

A **plural noun** names more than one person, place, or thing.

> **I have one** *book*. (singular)
>
> **Our library has many** *books*. (plural)

The plural of most nouns is formed by adding -*s* to the singular.

SINGULAR	PLURAL
chapter	chapters
house	houses
Ford	Fords

The plural of a noun ending in *s, x, z, ch,* or *sh* is formed by adding -*es* to the singular.

SINGULAR	PLURAL	SINGULAR	PLURAL
glass	glasses	peach	peaches
box	boxes	wish	wishes
buzz	buzzes	stitch	stitches

Which of these nouns are plural nouns?

A bushes   B frogs   C bug

You are right if you said that *bushes* and *frogs* are plural nouns. *Bushes* means more than one bush. *Frogs* means more than one frog. *Bug* is singular and means one bug.

EXERCISE 1 Tell whether each underlined word is a singular or a plural noun.

1. The family went to the <u>ocean</u>.
2. They liked visiting <u>beaches</u>.
3. The <u>waves</u> were really big.
4. Mom read a <u>magazine</u>.
5. John built <u>castles</u> in the sand.

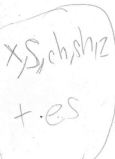

x, s, ch, sh, z
+ es

6. A <u>gull</u> flew overhead.

7. <u>Shells</u> washed up on the shore.

8. Lily put them in a <u>box</u>.

9. She put the box in her <u>room</u>.

10. The box sits by her jar of <u>coins</u>.

EXERCISE 2 Write the plural for each singular noun.

1. pencils
2. dishes
3. grapes
4. ditches
5. guesses

6. mixes
7. races
8. mittens
9. matches
10. patches

11. rings
12. pillows
13. Fridays
14. axes
15. watches

EXERCISE 3 Complete each sentence with the singular or plural of the noun in parentheses.

1. The _____ (beach) was filled with people on the weekend.

2. Many people were sitting under large _____ (umbrella).

3. There were many _____ (boat) on the water.

4. My sister and I played on some _____ (rock) near the ocean.

5. Our _____ (lunch) were in our cooler.

6. We ate our _____ (sandwich) in the picnic area.

7. Dad bought me a _____ (glass) of lemonade.

8. There was a _____ (lifeguard) near the water.

9. He was watching the _____ (swimmer).

10. Some _____ (teen) were playing volleyball.

APPLY IT NOW

Write four sentences about oceans. Underline all the nouns and tell if they are singular or plural. Write an *S* above each singular noun and a *P* above each plural noun. Example:

.P.   S.
<u>Oceans</u> contain salty <u>water</u>.

Grammar in Action. Find the plural noun in the first sentence of the page 248 excerpt.

2.4 More Plural Nouns

To make most nouns plural, you only need to add -s or -es to the singular form of the nouns. Some nouns that end in y are different. To form the plural of a noun ending in a consonant followed by y, change the y to i and add -es.

SINGULAR	PLURAL
baby	babies
country	countries
sky	skies
galaxy	galaxies

What is the correct plural form of the word *puppy*?

A **puppys**

B **puppies**

C **puppyes**

Stars of the Milky Way galaxy

If you said B, you are right. The word *puppy* ends in a consonant followed by y. To make *puppy* plural, change the y to i and add -es.

For nouns ending in a vowel and y, you just add -s, as with other nouns.

SINGULAR	PLURAL
monkey	monkeys
day	days
Kelley	Kelleys
boy	boys

EXERCISE 1 **Find the nouns in each sentence. Tell whether each noun is singular or plural.**

1. Puppies frequently try to catch their own tails.
2. My kitten likes to play with a mouse.
3. That bunny has a fluffy tail.

4. Guppies swim in the pond.

5. Our ferrets like to sit on the couch.

6. The bluebird eats wild blackberries.

7. Dad told stories about his many animals.

8. Jamie called the dog.

9. Gerbils play on the wheels in their cages.

10. Those canaries sing constantly.

11. The parrot with red and blue feathers can talk.

12. Toys for the cat are in the boxes.

EXERCISE 2 Write the plural for each singular noun.

EXAMPLE	Singular	Plural
	army	armies

1. country
2. hobby
3. Frey
4. key
5. pantry
6. play
7. daisy
8. melody

9. journey
10. way
11. duty
12. city
13. chimney
14. turkey
15. cry
16. valley

EXERCISE 3 Write a sentence for each word.

1. donkeys
2. ponies

3. cities
4. parties

APPLY IT NOW

Write two sentences using the plural of these words.
pastry cherry bakery quality

Grammar in Action

Tell the number of nouns in the second sentence of the page 248 excerpt.

2.5 Irregular Plural Nouns

The plurals of some nouns look somewhat different from their singular forms. These **irregular plurals** are not formed by adding -s or -es to the singular forms.

You should memorize these irregular plurals. If you forget how to spell an irregular plural, you can look it up in a dictionary.

SINGULAR	PLURAL
ox	oxen
child	children
tooth	teeth
foot	feet
mouse	mice
woman	women
goose	geese

Some nouns that have irregular plurals have the same form in the plural as in the singular.

SINGULAR	PLURAL
sheep	sheep
deer	deer
moose	moose
Chinese	Chinese

EXERCISE 1 Tell whether each noun is singular or plural. Some nouns may be both singular and plural.

1. geese
2. child
3. mouse
4. teeth

5. oxen
6. sheep
7. deer
8. women

EXERCISE 2 **Complete each sentence with the plural of the noun in parentheses.**

1. The _____ went to the nature center. (child)
2. They fed the _____. (goose)
3. Some animals had sharp _____. (tooth)
4. The _____ pulled a cart. (ox)
5. We saw _____ roaming in a field. (deer)
6. The _____ were white and woolly. (sheep)
7. The center also had reptiles such as _____. (turtle)
8. Black rat snakes are gray and six _____ long. (foot)
9. A dozen _____ shared a cage. (mouse)
10. Several _____ fed the animals daily. (woman)
11. There is a lovely garden with _____. (butterfly)
12. The center doesn't have any _____. (monkey)
13. There are four nature _____ in our city. (center)
14. When I grow up, I want to take care of _____ in my job. (animal)

EXERCISE 3 **Write the plural for each singular noun.**

1. class
2. moose
3. berry
4. brush
5. batch
6. mouse
7. wish
8. search
9. dress
10. tax
11. crutch
12. sky

APPLY IT NOW

Use these words to write a one-paragraph story about a make-believe situation.

mouse	mice
child	children

2.6 Singular Possessive Nouns

The **possessive form** of a noun shows possession, or ownership.

I walked to a *neighbor's* **house.**

Flowers grow in *Amy's* **garden.**

Neighbor's house means that the house belongs to a neighbor. *Amy's garden* means that the garden belongs to Amy.

To form the **singular possessive,** which is ownership by one person or thing, add an apostrophe and the letter *s (-'s)* to a singular noun.

SINGULAR	SINGULAR POSSESSIVE
friend	friend's
Pat	Pat's
bird	bird's
Mr. Storm	Mr. Storm's
Tess	Tess's

What is the correct way to show that the following things belong to Susan?

rake   hose   seeds

You are right if you said *Susan's rake, Susan's hose,* and *Susan's seeds.* By adding an apostrophe and *s (-'s)* to the noun *Susan,* you show that the rake, the hose, and the seeds belong to her.

EXERCISE 1 Write the possessive form of these singular nouns.

1. Nora
2. fox
3. cousin
4. Nicholas

5. passenger
6. student
7. mouse
8. book

EXERCISE 2 Rewrite each of the following to show possession.

EXAMPLE **The farmer owns a field.**

the farmer's field

1. The gardener planted a flower.
2. Mr. Shim has a rake.
3. The helper found a watering can.
4. The bee has a sting.
5. A butterfly has colors.
6. The rabbit was given a carrot.
7. The child has a hoe.
8. Gary bought roses.
9. Iris grew eggplants.
10. The girl has some seeds.

EXERCISE 3 Complete each sentence with the possessive form of the noun in parentheses. Then tell what the owner possesses.

EXAMPLE **Rabbits ate _____ lettuce.** (Mom)

Mom's lettuce

1. We helped dig _____ garden. (Peter)
2. I picked my _____ strawberries. (grandmother)
3. _____ vegetables grew quickly. (Derek)
4. The _____ rays beat down. (sun)
5. The _____ plants grew tall. (gardener)
6. Our _____ tomatoes are turning red. (uncle)
7. My _____ apples are still green. (brother)
8. _____ beanstalks are the tallest. (James)
9. _____ lettuce was eaten by rabbits. (Sarah)
10. My _____ yard has only flowers. (aunt)
11. My _____ flowers are colorful. (sister)
12. I like _____ birdbath. (Mr. Robinson)

APPLY IT NOW

Look around you. What things do you see? Write five sentences telling who owns those things or what they belong to. Use singular possessive nouns in your sentences.

2.7 Plural Possessive Nouns

A **plural possessive** shows that more than one person owns something. To form the plural possessive of most nouns, first make the singular noun plural. Then add an apostrophe after the *s* of the plural form.

Mom washed the *girls' bicycles.*

Dad tripped over the *babies' toys.*

Girls' bicycles means that two or more girls own two or more bicycles. *Babies' toys* means that the toys belong to more than one baby.

SINGULAR	PLURAL	PLURAL POSSESSIVE
girl	girls	girls'
baby	babies	babies'
Smith	Smiths	Smiths'

Which is the plural possessive of *sister*?

My _____ bedroom is full of toys.

A sister

B sister's

C sisters'

You are right if you said that C is the plural possessive. When an apostrophe is added to the word *sisters,* it means the bedroom belongs to two or more sisters.

EXERCISE 1 Complete the chart with the plural form and the plural possessive form of each noun.

Singular	Plural	Plural Possessive	
1. boy	_____	_____	pets
2. Mann	_____	_____	homes
3. student	_____	_____	books
4. gerbil	_____	_____	wheel
5. puppy	_____	_____	food
6. fox	_____	_____	cage

EXERCISE 2 Write the possessive form of each underlined plural noun.

1. The <u>fans</u> applause was loud.
2. The <u>players</u> uniforms were blue and gold.
3. The <u>runners</u> top speeds were amazing.
4. The <u>vendors</u> hot dogs were very good.
5. The <u>cheerleaders</u> voices could be heard throughout the gym.
6. All the marching <u>bands</u> performances were great.
7. The <u>drummers</u> drums were really huge!
8. The <u>singers</u> voices rang out clear and strong.

EXERCISE 3 Choose the correct meaning of each possessive phrase.

1. the girl's CDs
   a. One girl has one CD.
   b. More than one girl has some CDs.
   c. One girl has some CDs.

2. the boys' bikes
   a. Two or more boys have two or more bikes.
   b. One boy has many bikes.
   c. Two boys have the same bike.

EXERCISE 4 Rewrite each of the following to show possession.

EXAMPLE **The dogs have toys.**

the dogs' toys

1. George has a cat.
2. The two sisters have a dog.
3. The parakeets have a big cage.
4. The dogs have bones.
5. Samantha has three ferrets.
6. The puppies have a bed.

APPLY IT NOW

Write the plural possessive forms of the following nouns. Then use each possessive in a sentence.

astronaut   bee
swimmer   lady

2.8 Irregular Plural Possessive Nouns

The plural forms of irregular nouns do not end in *s*. Words such as *men, women,* and *children* are irregular plurals.

To form the plural possessive of irregular nouns, add an apostrophe and the letter *s (-'s)* to the plural form of the word.

SINGULAR	PLURAL	PLURAL POSSESSIVE
ox	oxen	oxen's
mouse	mice	mice's
man	men	men's
goose	geese	geese's
woman	women	women's

In the sentence below, which is the correct way to show that the children have warm mittens?

The _____ mittens are warm.

A **children**

B **childrens'**

C **children's**

You are right if you said that C is the answer. When an *-'s* is added to the word *children,* the word means that the mittens belong to the children.

EXERCISE 1 Complete the chart with the plural form and the plural possessive form of each noun.

Singular	Plural	Plural Possessive	
1. mouse	_____	_____	cheese
2. tooth	_____	_____	enamel
3. ox	_____	_____	tails
4. deer	_____	_____	tracks
5. policewoman	_____	_____	uniforms

EXERCISE 2 Write each group of words. Insert missing apostrophes to show plural possession. Be careful! Some words are regular plurals, and some words are irregular plurals.

1. womens purses
2. babies diapers
3. childrens backpacks
4. campers tents
5. scarves from sheeps wool
6. mens suits
7. jackets filled with geeses feathers
8. boys shoes
9. girls hats
10. ladies dresses
11. cooks pots
12. hikers boots

EXERCISE 3 Write the singular possessive and plural possessive form of each noun.

EXAMPLE **bunny**   **bunny's**   **bunnies'**

1. friend
2. child
3. lady
4. sheep
5. skater
6. snowman
7. country

8. giraffe
9. goose
10. coach
11. rose
12. fox
13. woman
14. lion

Giraffe

APPLY IT NOW

Draw a map of one floor of a department store. Put labels on the different sections. Use apostrophes in your labels. Use the phrases in Exercise 2 to help you.

Tech Tip Draw your map using an online drawing tool.

2.9 Collective Nouns

A noun that names a group of things or people is called a **collective noun.**

A *flock* of geese is flying overhead.

The collective noun *flock* names a group of animals considered together as a unit.

Here are some common collective nouns.

audience	club	flock	pack
army	crew	group	pair
band	crowd	herd	swarm
class	family	litter	team

A collective noun usually uses an action word that ends in *s* in the present tense.

The band *plays*.

Our club *runs*.

The class *takes* field trips.

Which sentences include collective nouns?

A My family is large.

B The judge spoke loudly.

C The crowd rushed forward.

You are right if you said sentence A and sentence C. *Family* and *crowd* are collective nouns. Each names a group. *Judge* names one person.

EXERCISE 1 Find the collective noun or nouns in each sentence.

1. The class wrote a play.
2. The drama club made some scenery.
3. A flock of birds was painted on a curtain.
4. A small band performed music before the play started.
5. A pair of violinists played beautifully.

6. In the play the family was lost in the woods.

7. A pack of wolves howled in the distance.

8. The crew was playing a recording of howls.

9. At the end a group of scouts led the family to safety.

10. What a great job the cast did!

11. The audience stood and applauded.

12. A crowd gathered at the stage door entrance.

EXERCISE 2 **Match each collective noun in Column A with a plural noun in Column B.**

Column A	Column B
1. band	a. members
2. class	b. soldiers
3. club	c. musicians
4. army	d. athletes
5. team	e. students

EXERCISE 3 **Complete each sentence with a collective noun. Use the list on page 44.**

1. The _____ of elephants roamed on the African plain.

2. The _____ played my favorite songs at the concert.

3. Our soccer _____ won its first game.

4. The _____ of horses pulled the wagon across the prairie.

5. A _____ of birds was traveling south for the winter.

6. A _____ of children wrote about animals.

7. The fourth-grade _____ read the book it wrote.

8. The _____ of bees was protecting its hive.

9. The _____ of the boat rowed together.

10. We chose one kitten from the _____.

11. Our math _____ meets once a week

12. A _____ of raccoons is living under the porch.

APPLY IT NOW

Choose three collective nouns from page 44 and write a sentence for each.
Example: The team won the race.

2.10 Nouns as Subjects

A noun may be used as the **subject** of a sentence. The subject tells what the sentence is about. It tells who or what does something.

> *Artists* **draw and paint pictures.**
> *Paints* **can be messy.**
> *Zoe* **is an artist.**

In the first sentence, *artists* is a noun that tells who draws and paints. In the second sentence, *paints* is a noun that tells what can be messy. In the third sentence, *Zoe* is a noun that tells who is an artist.

Which noun is the subject in this sentence?

> **Zack takes photos.**

You are right if you said that *Zack* is the subject of the sentence. *Zack* tells who takes photos. *Photos* is a noun, but it is not the subject.

What noun is the subject in this sentence?

> **His photos include animals.**

You are right if you said *photos. Photos* tells what includes animals. *Animals* is a noun, but it is not the subject of this sentence.

EXERCISE 1 Complete each sentence with a subject. Use these nouns.

> activity   class   markers   Mrs. Jones   students

1. The ___Class___ has art every week.
2. ___Mrs.Jones___ teaches art.
3. Some ___students___ are very good artists.
4. Our favorite ___activity___ is painting.
5. The ___markers___ come in many bright colors.

EXERCISE 2 **Find the subject in each sentence. Ask** *who* **or** *what* **is doing the action to help you.**

1. The teacher announced the start of the art class.
2. Sam looked happy.
3. Anita traced shapes on paper.
4. Many children used easels to support their drawing pads.
5. One unsteady easel fell over.
6. Paint spilled on the floor.
7. Towels soaked up the mess.
8. Clothespins hung the paintings to dry.
9. The children later displayed the paintings on the bulletin board.

EXERCISE 3 **Complete each sentence with a noun. You may use other words like** *a* **or** *the*.

1. _____ took us to the art museum.
2. _____ hung on the walls.
3. _____ told us about some of the paintings.
4. _____ had a chance to draw pictures.
5. _____ gave us some notebooks and pencils.
6. _____ did a lovely drawing of a tree in pencil.
7. _____ helped us with our drawings.
8. _____ is a good artist.
9. _____ liked my drawing.
10. _____ is my favorite thing to draw.

EXERCISE 4 **Write sentences using each noun as the subject.**

1. paints
2. brushes
3. friend

APPLY IT NOW

Write a sentence for each topic below. Use a noun as the subject of each sentence. Underline the subject.

1. a game to play
2. a movie to see
3. what to eat for lunch
4. a favorite color

2.11 Words Used as Nouns and as Verbs

Many words can be used both as nouns and as verbs. Check closely how a word is used in a specific sentence.

The word *walk,* for example, can be used as a noun or as an action word, a verb.

> **I *walk* to the store.**
> **Let's go for a *walk.***

In the first sentence, *walk* is used as a verb. It shows action. In the second sentence, *walk* is used as a noun. It is a thing.

Tell how the word *talk* is used in these sentences. In which sentence is it a verb? In which sentence is it a noun?

> **A Can we have a talk?**
> **B We talk on the phone often.**

You are right if you said *talk* is used as a noun in sentence A and as a verb in sentence B. In the first sentence, *talk* is a thing. In the second sentence, *talk* is an action.

The word *sails* is another word that can be used as a noun or as a verb. Can you tell which it is in these sentences?

> **A My uncle sails in the navy.**
> **B The sails filled with air.**

You are right if you said *sails* is used as a verb in sentence A and as a noun in sentence B.

EXERCISE 1 Tell whether the underlined word in each sentence is used as a noun or as a verb.

1. Will you <u>watch</u> the baby?
2. The <u>watch</u> has a leather band.
3. Birds <u>fight</u> over a worm.
4. The children had a <u>fight</u> over the game.
5. Joggers <u>run</u> every day.

6. He went for a <u>run</u>.

7. The class is putting on a <u>play</u>.

8. Some students <u>play</u> astronauts.

9. Please <u>ring</u> the doorbell.

10. Aunt Judy's <u>ring</u> has four rubies.

11. This letter needs a <u>stamp</u>.

12. Don't <u>stamp</u> your feet in the house.

EXERCISE 2 Complete each sentence with one of these words. Tell whether the word is used as a noun or as a verb.

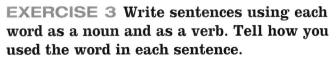

| blossoms | help | plant | practice | step |

1. We _____ volleyball after school.

2. Our soccer _____ is on Tuesday.

3. I can _____ you with the math homework.

4. Thank your for your_____ yesterday.

5. That's a pretty _____ in that pot.

6. Will you _____ those seeds in the garden?

7. That plant _____ once a year.

8. The plants have lovely red _____.

9. There is a toy on the _____.

10. Don't _____ on the cat's tail.

EXERCISE 3 Write sentences using each word as a noun and as a verb. Tell how you used the word in each sentence.

EXAMPLE **A *fly* buzzed around my head.** (noun)
Airplanes *fly* at hundreds of miles per hour. (verb)

1. play
2. cut

3. copy
4. drive

APPLY IT NOW

Think of other words that can be used as nouns and as verbs. Choose a word that hasn't been used in Exercise 1, 2, or 3. Write two sentences, one using the word as a noun and one using it as a verb.

Noun Review

2.1 Tell what the nouns are in each sentence. The number of nouns in each sentence is in parentheses.

1. Luke and his friends went to the big game at City Stadium. (4)

2. Crowds filled the stadium, and soon the two teams took the field. (4)

3. Luke sat next to his dad. (2)

4. Mike ate peanuts during the game. (3)

5. Our team won the game, and the fans cheered. (3)

2.2 Tell what the nouns are in each sentence. Then tell whether each is a common noun or a proper noun. The number of nouns in each sentence is in parentheses.

6. My older sister Amy lives in Philadelphia. (3)

7. My family sometimes goes to the city. (2)

8. My brother likes to visit the museum to see the dinosaurs. (3)

9. My mom likes to go to Independence Hall and other historic places. (3)

10. There is an old flag in the house where Betsy Ross lived. (3)

2.3 Write the plural for each singular noun.

11. dish

12. cave

13. song

14. class

15. speech

2.4 Complete each sentence with the plural of the noun in parentheses.

16. My grandmother has several _____. (hobby)

17. She volunteers at a school on _____. (Thursday)

18. She brings _____ to the food pantry. (grocery)

19. She also bakes pies with _____. (strawberry)

2.5 Complete each sentence with the singular or plural of the underlined noun.

20. Max caught one <u>mouse</u>, but Jenny caught six _____.

21. The <u>man</u> saw four other _____ waiting outside.

22. Yuan can balance on one <u>foot</u> as well as he can balance on both _____.

23. Mom said that <u>geese</u> can be mean, so I ran when I saw a _____.

2.6 Change the underlined noun to a singular possessive noun.

24. Henry helped organize his <u>neighborhood</u> annual party.

25. He borrowed his <u>friend</u> camera to take photos.

26. <u>Henry</u> sister Gloria painted faces all afternoon.

27. Henry got the photos published in the <u>newspaper</u>.

2.7 Rewrite each group of words to show plural possession.

28. the cleats of the girls

29. the mitts of the players

30. the scripts of the actors

31. the CDs of the boys

32. the bottles of the babies

2.8 Complete each of the following with the plural possessive form of the noun in parentheses.

33. _____ shorts (men)

34. _____ cage (mice)

35. _____ room (child)

36. _____ wool (sheep)

37. _____ blouses (women)

2.9 Find the collective noun in each sentence.

38. My family went to the circus.

39. A magician performed for the crowd.

40. A band played silly songs.

41. We laughed at a pair of jugglers.

42. Later, a group of acrobats performed.

2.10 Find the subject in each sentence.

43. My cousin rides a streetcar to work.

44. Streetcars were more common before World War II.

45. San Francisco has several old streetcars in use.

46. Many tourists ride them.

47. Downtown is a popular destination.

2.11 Tell whether the underlined word in each sentence is used as a noun or as a verb.

48. We <u>head</u> for the hills.

49. My <u>head</u> is too big for this hat.

50. Dion gave me funny <u>looks</u>.

51. The dog <u>looks</u> at his leash.

52. Why don't you <u>sketch</u> that apple?

53. Gina gave me a <u>sketch</u> of a boat.

Tech Tip Go to www.voyagesinenglish.com for more activities.

Noun Challenge

Read the paragraph and answer the questions.

1. Our aunt owns a farm. 2. Aunt Josie, Uncle Bueno, and my grandma live and work on the farm. 3. The farm has many cows. 4. It also has a flock of chickens. 5. The chickens' eggs are big and brown. 6. Grandma has a hive of bees. 7. There's grass for the herd of cows, and there's a vegetable garden for the family. 8. Aunt Josie sells the cows' milk to dairies. 9. The milk is used to make butter and different kinds of cheeses. 10. On our last visit, Dixie, Aunt Josie's pet dog, was tending six fat puppies. 11. I played with Dixie's puppies all afternoon. 12. There's always something interesting for me to see and do on the farm.

1. In sentence 1 which noun is the subject?

2. In sentence 2 find two common nouns and two proper nouns.

3. In sentence 3 find the plural noun.

4. In sentence 4 what kind of noun is *flock*?

5. In sentence 5 what kind of plural is *chickens'*? What does *chickens' eggs* mean in the sentence?

6. In sentence 6 how do you form the plural of *hive*?

7. In sentence 7 what are the collective nouns?

8. In sentence 8 what is the singular form of *dairies*?

9. In sentence 10 what is the singular form of *puppies*?

10. In sentence 11 what is the possessive noun? Is it singular or plural?

Pronouns

3.1 Pronouns

A **pronoun** is a word that takes the place of a noun. A **personal pronoun** refers to the person who is speaking or to the person or thing that is spoken to or about. Study the list of personal pronouns and read the sentences below them.

I	me	mine	we	us	ours
she	her	hers	they	them	theirs
he	him	his	you		yours
it		its			

Fred watches the bears.   **He watches the bears.**

In the second sentence, the pronoun *he* takes the place of the subject *Fred*.

Pronouns help avoid repeating nouns, and they make your writing sound smoother. Read this paragraph.

> **Black bears are one kind of bear. Black bears weigh about 300 pounds. The largest black bear ever sighted was in Wisconsin. The largest black bear weighed 802 pounds.**

Now read the paragraph with pronouns. What pronouns can you find? What word does each pronoun replace?

Black bear cub

> **Black bears are one kind of bear. They weigh about 300 pounds. The largest black bear ever sighted was in Wisconsin. It weighed 802 pounds.**

You are right if you said that *they* in the second sentence takes the place of *black bears* in the first sentence and that *it* in the fourth sentence takes the place of *black bear* in the third sentence.

Read the following pair of sentences. Which pronoun takes the place of the underlined word?

> **My <u>mother</u> was in Wisconsin. She saw a black bear.**

You are right if you said *she*. *She* takes the place of the noun *mother*.

EXERCISE 1 Find all the personal pronouns in these sentences. Some sentences have more than one pronoun.

1. You can see bears at Yellowstone National Park.
2. They are called grizzly bears.
3. I saw one grizzly bear when I was hiking.
4. I was with my friends.
5. We watched it from far away.
6. The park ranger told me that the bears could be dangerous.
7. He said to avoid them.
8. I listened to him.
9. A bear's strength is much greater than ours.
10. I told my teacher about the bear I saw.
11. I told her the bear actually wasn't near me.
12. We were all fascinated by it.

EXERCISE 2 Use personal pronouns to take the place of the underlined word or words.

1. Polar bears live in the Arctic.
2. My friends and I learned some facts about polar bears.
3. A polar bear can weigh more than 1,000 pounds.
4. Their fur is very thick and covers their feet.
5. Jessica, Juan, and Jeff saw polar bears at the zoo.
6. The zookeeper, Eva, gave a fish to the biggest bear.
7. Eva gave another fish to a baby bear.
8. Juan asked how much fish the polar bears ate daily.
9. The zookeepers give the polar bear four pounds of fish daily.
10. The bear also eats five pounds of meat and two pounds of apples.
11. Did you know that bears eat apples?
12. Jess and Juan did not know that either.

APPLY IT NOW

Tell about bears you have seen at a zoo, on TV, or in a movie. Write four sentences. Use a pronoun in each sentence.

Grammar in Action

Find the five different pronouns in the page 286 excerpt.

3.2 Subject Pronouns

Some personal pronouns may be used as the subject of a sentence. These are called **subject pronouns.**

> *I* dance.
>
> *He* dances.
>
> *We* dance.

In these sentences *I, he,* and *we* are subject pronouns. The subject tells what the sentence is about. It tells who or what does something.

Here is a list of the subject pronouns.

SINGULAR	PLURAL
I	we
you	you
he, she, it	they

Which of these sentences uses a pronoun as a subject?

A Jane is doing a square dance with Joe.

B She likes to square-dance.

C Wade watches them dance.

You are right if you said sentence B. *She* is a subject pronoun.

Tell which pronoun can take the place of the underlined words in this sentence.

> Jane and Joe learned how to square-dance.

You are right if you said *they.*

EXERCISE 1 Find the subject pronoun in each sentence.

1. Greta and I take jazz dance lessons together.
2. She dances on her toes.
3. We danced the Hokey Pokey.
4. It is a fun dance.

5. He taps his feet.

6. They clap to the music.

7. Does he dance well?

8. I like dancing.

9. Do you know this dance?

10. We can dance it together.

EXERCISE 2 **Tell whether the underlined subject in each sentence is a noun or a pronoun.**

1. Dogs are wonderful pets.

2. They are fun and loving.

3. The Jacksons bought a rescue dog from the animal shelter.

4. Danny Jackson picked out a cute brown and white puppy.

5. He named the dog Princess.

6. She followed Danny everywhere he went.

7. One day Princess followed Danny to the river near his house.

8. We laughed when Princess jumped into the water after Danny.

EXERCISE 3 **Use a subject pronoun to take the place of the underlined word or words.**

1. Mrs. Kim planned a dances-from-around-the-world day.

2. Max danced the csárdás, a Hungarian folk dance.

3. The students know many dances.

4. Margarita and I did the macarena for the class.

5. Christopher can do the polka.

6. Hannah showed an Indian dance called kathak.

7. Eileen and Patrick did a jig.

8. The jig was very well done.

9. Greta waltzed to pretty Viennese music.

APPLY IT NOW

Think about a time when you danced or saw people dancing. Write four sentences about dancing. Use subject pronouns in one or more sentences. Underline the pronouns.

3.3 Object Pronouns

Some personal pronouns may be used after an action verb in a sentence. They are called **object pronouns.**

> **The teacher asked *David* a question.**
> **The teacher asked *him* a question.**

The noun *David* comes after the action verb. It is an object in the sentence. It can be replaced with the object pronoun *him.*

Here is a list of the object pronouns.

SINGULAR	PLURAL
me	us
you	you
him, her, it	them

Ursa Major

Which of these sentences uses an object pronoun?

   A He is interested in the stars.

   B They are interesting.

   C The stars interest me.

You are right if you said sentence C. *Me* is the object of the sentence. It comes after the action verb, *interest. Me* is an object pronoun.

Which pronouns can take the place of the underlined words in these sentences?

   A The guide told <u>Jane</u> about the star map.

   B She hung the <u>map</u> on the wall.

You are right if you said *her* in sentence A and *it* in sentence B.

EXERCISE 1 Find the object pronoun in each sentence.

1. Mr. Kovach taught us about the features of the moon.

2. I lent you a telescope.

3. You borrowed it for the lunar eclipse.

4. Tell us about the eclipse.

5. The eclipse amazed him.

6. Jenna gave them a report on the eclipse.

7. The class liked it.

8. They told her about the nature of a lunar eclipse.

EXERCISE 2 Choose the correct pronoun or pronouns to complete each sentence.

1. Lunar eclipses are rare, and ancient people feared (they them).

2. Mr. Lin told (us we) that ancient Chinese people believed there was a dragon in the moon.

3. Eclipses fascinate (I me).

4. Mr. Lin showed (she her) a book with old Chinese legends.

5. The colorful pictures interested (she her) and (him he).

6. Fiona wants (I me) to teach (she her) about eclipses.

EXERCISE 3 Use an object pronoun to take the place of the underlined words in each sentence.

1. Tell Jonah and me about the moon landing.

2. Neil Armstrong reached the moon's surface.

3. A small ship took Neil Armstrong and Buzz Aldrin to the moon.

4. People watched the moon landing on TV.

5. People saw Neil Armstrong on the moon.

6. The astronauts' bravery amazed Maria and Jon.

Michael Collins,
Neil Armstrong,
and Buzz Aldrin

APPLY IT NOW

Write four sentences about a place you would like to explore. Use object pronouns in some of your sentences. Underline the object pronouns you used.

Tech Tip With an adult, do research on a science Web site.

3.4 Possessive Pronouns

A **possessive pronoun** shows who or what owns something. A possessive pronoun takes the place of a noun. It takes the place of both the person who owns the thing and the object that is owned.

Mine, yours, his, hers, its, ours, and *theirs* are possessive pronouns.

NOUN PHRASES	POSSESSIVE PRONOUNS
My bicycle is here.	*Mine* is here.
Our bicycle is here.	*Ours* is here.
Your bicycle is here.	*Yours* is here.
Brandon's bicycle is here.	*His* is here.
Nina's bicycle is here.	*Hers* is here.
Mom's and Dad's bicycles are here.	*Theirs* are here.
That is Leon's bicycle.	That is *his*.

In each sentence above, the noun and the person or thing that possesses it are replaced by a possessive pronoun. Possessive pronouns can be used as subjects, and they can be used in other parts of a sentence.

Mona admired *Lisa's bicycle.*   **Mona admired** *hers.*

Which of these sentences uses a possessive pronoun?

    A I ride my bicycle.

    B Sam rides his.

    C Stacy rides a bicycle.

You are right if you said sentence B. *His* means that the bicycle belongs to Sam.

EXERCISE 1 Find the possessive pronoun or pronouns in each sentence.

  1. Hers is the red one.

  2. What color is yours?

  3. Mine has a bell.

  4. Yours is bigger than my bicycle.

5. We keep ours at the bicycle rack during school.

6. Theirs are ten-speeds.

7. His is a mountain bike.

8. They rode theirs on the path.

9. That water bottle is hers.

10. Mine is the pink one next to yours.

EXERCISE 2 **Match the object owned in Column A with the correct possessive pronoun in Column B.**

Column A	Column B
1. my bike lock	a. his
2. her bike pump	b. theirs
3. Josh's and Min's flags	c. mine
4. Tom's handlebars	d. yours
5. our helmets	e. hers
6. your compass	f. ours

EXERCISE 3 **Change the sentences so that they have possessive pronouns. Use the pronoun in place of the underlined words.**

EXAMPLE **Malia's bicycle is missing.**

Hers is missing.

1. My bicycle has a basket.

2. The tandem is Mickey and Mary's bicycle.

3. Where is your lock?

4. My bicycle and my sister's bicycle have flags.

5. Jacob's bicycle is the fastest.

6. Is that Ana's helmet?

7. Did they ring their bells?

8. Your bike has a flat tire.

9. Keesha's bicycle has streamers.

10. My bike is yellow, and your bike is green.

APPLY IT NOW

Choose three different objects found either at school or at home. Write a sentence with possessive pronouns for each object. Underline the possessive pronouns.
Example:
My sister and I have raincoats.
Mine is red. Hers is blue.

3.5 Possessive Adjectives

An adjective is a word that describes a noun. Some adjectives show who owns something. *My, our, your, his, her, its,* and *their* are adjectives that go before nouns to show ownership. They are called **possessive adjectives.**

> **Our wagon has a broken wheel.**
>
> **Her wagon is in the garage.**

The words *our* and *her* are adjectives. They are used before the noun *wagon* to show who owns each wagon.

These are the possessive adjectives.

SINGULAR	PLURAL
my	our
your	your
his, her, its	their

Which of these sentences uses a possessive adjective?

A Her wagon is red.

B A wagon has four wheels.

C Hers is red.

You are right if you said sentence A. The word *her* shows that the wagon belongs to the girl. It comes before the noun *wagon.* In sentence C the possessive is a pronoun—it stands by itself and it points out both the owner and the thing that is owned.

Do not confuse possessive pronouns and possessive adjectives. Remember that possessive adjectives always come before nouns.

EXERCISE 1 Find the possessive adjective in each sentence.

1. Laura wants to play her new game.
2. Please be on my team.
3. Mark wants to make his own rules.
4. Take your turn, Phil.

5. May we play their game next?

6. Its rules are easy to follow.

7. Our game pieces are missing.

8. Ana and Kim, your pieces are mixed up.

EXERCISE 2 Complete each sentence with a possessive adjective.

1. The children played with _____ action figures.

2. Emily found _____ missing puzzle piece.

3. Brendan set up _____ game.

4. I said that this is _____ best sticker.

5. We played with _____ toy bricks.

6. Ed, are those _____ crayons?

7. Mom asked us to put away _____ games.

8. Christa and Brendan cleaned _____ play area.

EXERCISE 3 Find the possessive pronoun or possessive adjective in each sentence. Then tell whether it is a possessive pronoun or a possessive adjective.

EXAMPLE **Our** crayons are in the box. (possessive adjective)

The crayons in the box are ours. (possessive pronoun)

1. Those paints are mine.

2. Are these green beads hers?

3. My scissors are on the table.

4. The glue stick is his, isn't it?

5. Is that his construction paper?

6. The blue marker isn't yours.

7. The red clay sculpture is ours.

8. Where are their watercolors?

9. Your paintbrush has a blue handle.

10. Its bristles are thick and black.

APPLY IT NOW

Write four sentences about things, such as toys or sports equipment, that you and your friends like to play with. Use possessive adjectives before nouns.

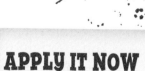

Grammar in Action Find the possessive adjective in the page 298 excerpt.

3.6 Agreement of Pronouns and Verbs

A subject and its verb must agree. A verb that shows an action is often in the present tense. Most subjects take the same form of the verb in the present tense. An -s is added to the verb only after *he, she,* or *it*—or the noun that each replaces.

SINGULAR SUBJECT	PLURAL SUBJECT
I sit.	We sit.
You sit.	You sit.
He sits.	They sit.
She sits.	
It sits.	

When a noun is used as a subject, -s is added to the verb form, just as it is for *he, she,* or *it.*

PRONOUN SUBJECT	NOUN SUBJECT
He sits.	Paul sits.
She sits.	Amy sits.
It sits.	The cat sits.

Which sentence shows correct agreement of subject and verb?

A It growl.

B It growls.

C They growls.

You are right if you said sentence B. The pronoun *It* is singular. It needs the verb *growls.*

EXERCISE 1 Choose the verb that agrees with the subject pronoun to complete each sentence.

1. She (work works) with animals.

2. We (walk walks) the dogs.

3. I (train trains) dogs.

4. It (jump jumps) on things.

5. They (chew chews) the furniture.

6. He (play plays) with the cats.

7. You (feeds feed) the cat.

8. It (chase chases) the ball.

9. She (make makes) the dog stay.

10. They (like likes) bones.

11. I (give gives) the dog commands.

12. It (obey obeys) me.

EXERCISE 2 Complete each sentence by adding a subject pronoun. Make sure the subject pronoun and verb agree.

1. _____ bring my dog to school.

2. _____ knows how to sit.

3. _____ does many tricks.

4. _____ speak by barking.

5. _____ teaches him to obey.

6. _____ watch the dog with interest.

7. _____ believes the dog is trying to speak.

8. _____ think that too.

EXERCISE 3 Complete each sentence with the correct form of the verb in parentheses.

1. He _____ with his dog after school. (play)

2. She _____ to teach her dog tricks. (like)

3. It _____ a lot of patience. (take)

4. We _____ them talking to their dogs. (hear)

5. You _____ your dog to behave. (want)

6. They _____ a lot when playing with the dogs. (laugh)

APPLY IT NOW

Write four sentences about an animal. Use subject nouns and subject pronouns. Make sure each subject agrees with its verb.
Example:
Max does tricks.
He gives a high five with his right paw.

Tech Tip Illustrate your sentences in a PowerPoint slideshow.

3.7 *I and Me*

I and *me* are used when you talk about yourself.
I is used as the subject of a sentence.

> **I like fruit.**
>
> **For a snack I prefer grapes.**

In both sentences *I* is the subject. *I* tells who does something.

Me is used as an object. It usually comes after an action verb.

> **Tell me about your favorite food.**
>
> **Mom gave me a new video game.**

Which sentence uses *I* or *me* correctly?

> A **Me slice the potato.**
>
> B **I eat the celery.**

You are right if you chose sentence B. The pronoun *I* is used before the verb.

Which pronoun, *I* or *me,* is correct in each of these sentences?

> A **Jasmine e-mailed (I me).**
>
> B **Can you send (I me) the message?**

Me is correct in both sentences because it is an object in both.

EXERCISE 1 Choose the correct pronoun or pronouns to complete each sentence.

1. Mom gave (I me) some vegetables for lunch.
2. (I Me) eat five pieces of fruit every day.
3. (I Me) usually have an apple for lunch.
4. My mother sometimes makes (I me) a salad for dinner.
5. Yesterday (I me) traded vegetables with Ty.
6. He gave (I me) some carrots.

7. (I Me) like blueberries and grapes.

8. She offered (I me) oranges, but (I me) prefer pears.

EXERCISE 2 **Use *I* or *me* to complete each sentence correctly.**

1. _____ picked apples from a tree.

2. My friend helped _____.

3. _____ climbed the ladder.

4. Grandma baked _____ a pie with fresh fruit.

5. _____ sprinkled sugar on the apples.

6. Then _____ waited for the pie to bake.

7. She cut _____ a huge piece.

8. _____ told Grandma that it tasted great.

9. _____ ate two pieces of apple pie.

10. She hugged _____ and said _____ am great!

11. _____ thanked her and smiled.

12. Grandma gave _____ some pie to take home.

EXERCISE 3 **Choose the correct pronoun to complete each sentence. Tell whether each pronoun is a subject pronoun or an object pronoun.**

1. Helen and (I me) are sisters.

2. She gave (I me) the best birthday present.

3. (I Me) like to skateboard.

4. The skateboard Helen gave (I me) is green with black stripes.

5. (I Me) fell the first time I rode it.

6. My friends want (I me) to compete in a skateboarding contest.

7. They think (I me) can do tricks better than other skateboarders.

8. (I Me) am excited about the contest next Saturday.

APPLY IT NOW

Use *I* and *me* to write four sentences about your favorite fruit. Choose from the following list or choose a fruit of your own.

blueberries   strawberries

pineapple   peaches

3.8 Compound Subjects and Objects

Pronouns can be used in compound subjects and compound objects.

SUBJECT PRONOUNS

I went to the park.
She went to the park.
She and I went to the park. (compound subject)

OBJECT PRONOUNS

Al told *me* about the team.
Al told *him* about the team.
Al told *him and me* about the team. (compound object)

Pronouns can be used with nouns in compound subjects and compound objects.

Jennie and I went to the park. (compound subject)

Sherry told *Larry and me* about them. (compound object)

In speaking and writing, it is polite to put *I* and *me* after words that refer to other people.

Which sentences use pronouns in compounds correctly?

A I want to play tag.

B You and I will play tag.

C Ben plays with Sherry and me.

You are right if you said sentences B and C. Sentence B includes compound subject pronouns. Sentence C includes a pronoun in the compound object.

EXERCISE 1 Choose the correct subject pronoun or pronouns to complete each sentence.

1. Pat and (I me) walked to the park.

2. Karen and (he him) swung from the monkey bars.

3. Martina and (her she) climbed the ladder.

4. Jim and (them they) played kickball.

5. (Her She) and I ran through the grass.

6. John and (they them) sat on the swings.

7. (He Him) and (me I) stayed until dark.

8. (Her She) and (them they) went home together.

EXERCISE 2 Choose the correct object pronoun or pronouns to complete each sentence.

1. Nancy invited Kevin and (we us) for a game of tag.

2. The team captains picked (she her) and (I me).

3. Kurt wants Jerry and (he him) on his team.

4. The fastest runners caught Carl and (me I).

5. Jess tagged Kathy and (I me).

6. The girls chased (they them) and (us we).

7. Derek tried to get Lily and (he him).

8. Nadia caught (she her) and (I me).

EXERCISE 3 Choose the correct subject or object pronoun to complete each sentence.

1. My friends and (I me) played statue tag.

2. Some classmates taught Jessica and (he him) the rules.

3. Jeff and (she her) explained that a tagged player stays frozen.

4. Jeff was it, and he tagged Ty and (I me).

5. Amy and (he him) were the last tagged.

6. Jeff then twirled my friends and (I me) around.

7. My friends and (I me) stayed in that position as statues.

8. Liz and (her she) were lying on the ground.

9. Jeff and (he him) chose the best statues.

10. The funniest statues were made by Luke and (she her).

APPLY IT NOW

Write four sentences about how you and your friends help other people at school, at home, or in your community. Write two sentences with compound subject pronouns and two sentences with compound object pronouns.

Pronoun Review

3.1 Find the personal pronoun in each sentence.

1. Did you snorkel in the ocean?
2. I saw many fish near the reef.
3. It is the best place to see fish.
4. The blue fish were not afraid of me.
5. We were amazed at the colorful creatures.
6. What are they called?
7. She told everyone about coral reefs.

3.2 Use a subject noun to take the place of the underlined word or words.

8. Coconuts grow on trees.
9. Tom found a ripe coconut.
10. Dad and I cracked the coconut open.
11. The coconut was tasty.
12. Mom drank some coconut milk.
13. Sherry and Georgia made a coconut cream pie.

3.3 Find the object pronoun in each sentence.

14. Mrs. Blair invited us to tea.
15. The guests helped her with the tea.
16. Mrs. Blair passed them the sandwiches.
17. Kara gave me a cup of tea.
18. Edward brought him a cucumber sandwich.
19. Many people enjoy it.
20. Mary and Isabel had never tasted them before.

3.4 Find the possessive pronoun in each sentence.

21. Mine has a tall sail.
22. Hers has a motor made from rubber bands.
23. Let's race ours across the pond.
24. Yours is sinking quickly.
25. His won the race by a yard.
26. Theirs finished second.

3.5 Find the possessive adjective in each sentence.

27. Our yard is full of leaves.

28. My chore is to rake the leaves.

29. Tabitha wants to jump in their piles of leaves.

30. Your tree is beautiful.

31. Linda wants to press her favorite leaf in a book.

32. There are some funny photos in his album.

3.6 Choose the verb that agrees with the subject pronoun to complete each sentence.

33. She (pick picks) the apples from the tree.

34. He (reach reaches) the high branches.

35. They (peel peels) apples for the pie.

36. You (make makes) the crust.

37. We (eat eats) the pie after dinner.

38. It (taste tastes) delicious.

3.7 Choose the correct pronoun to complete each sentence.

39. (I Me) like watching squirrels in the backyard.

40. (I Me) saw the squirrels bury acorns.

41. Squirrels interest (I me).

42. (I Me) laughed when a squirrel ran across the yard.

43. The squirrel surprised (I me) by digging in a flowerpot.

44. The squirrel saw (I me) and ran away.

3.8 Find the compound subject or the compound object in each sentence. Then choose the correct pronoun or pronouns to complete each sentence.

45. The other students and (I me) looked at the map.

46. The teacher asked (he him) and (I me) to find China.

47. I asked my partner and (she her) for help.

48. Kelly and (them they) are good at geography.

49. (He Him) and Javier located Antarctica.

50. I showed (he him) and (she her) where Australia is.

Go to www.voyagesinenglish.com for more activities.

Pronoun Challenge

EXERCISE 1 Read the paragraph and answer the questions.

1. Schools are different sizes. 2. Ours is rather big. 3. It has about 1,000 students. 4. The middle school in my town is even bigger. 5. It has 1,500 students. 6. My friends and I like our big school. 7. We all have lots of friends.

8. My dad went to a really small school. 9. The third-grade teacher taught him and only five other children. 10. She and he still see each other at school reunions. 11. My mom did not go to a regular school. 12. Mom's dad taught her at home. 13. She and her four brothers had class in their kitchen. 14. Theirs was a home school.

1. In sentence 2 what kind of pronoun is *ours?*

2. In sentence 3 what is the subject pronoun?

3. In sentence 4 is *my* a pronoun or an adjective?

4. In sentence 6 what is the compound subject?

5. In sentence 9 what is the object pronoun?

6. In sentence 10 what are the subjects?

7. In sentence 12 what is the pronoun? How is it used?

8. In sentence 13 how are *her* and *their* alike?

9. In sentence 14 find the pronoun. What kind of pronoun is it?

EXERCISE 2 Write a six-sentence paragraph about your school. Use at least three different kinds of pronouns and circle them.

Verbs

4.1 Action Verbs

Many verbs express action. An **action verb** tells what someone or something does.

These action verbs tell what a child does.

A child *plays*.
A child *runs*.
A child *laughs*.

These action verbs tell what water does.

Water *spills*.
Water *freezes*.
Water *bubbles*.

Which word is the action verb in the following sentence?

Arun jumps rope.

You are right if you said *jumps*. *Arun* is the subject. The verb *jumps* tells what Arun does.

Which word is the action verb in this sentence?

We studied about the rain forest.

You are right if you said *studied.* The verb *studied* tells what we did.

Which word is the action verb in this sentence?

The rain dripped down the window.

You are right if you said *dripped.* The verb *dripped* tells what the rain did.

EXERCISE 1 Find the action verb in each sentence.

1. Kurt and Elena joined the school science club.
2. They learn about the rain forest.
3. The world's largest rain forest grows in South America.
4. Many animals live in the rain forest.

New Zealand rain forest

5. Jaguars hunt for food.

6. Toucans pick fruit with their beaks.

7. The basilisk lizard walks on water.

8. Sloths move very slowly.

9. The trees grow tall and leafy.

10. More than 100 inches of rain fall in some rain forests each year.

EXERCISE 2 Use an action verb to complete each sentence. Use an action word from the word box.

calls	dribbles	drinks	shoots	play
shake	wears	wins	trips	block

1. Some students _____ on basketball teams.

2. Our school's team _____ red uniforms.

3. Kate _____ the basketball.

4. Avery _____ lots of water.

5. Eddie _____ running down the court.

6. The coach _____ time-out.

7. A player _____ the ball through the hoop.

8. Simon and Trevor _____ a shot.

9. The other team _____ the game.

10. The players _____ hands.

EXERCISE 3 Write a sentence using each action verb.

1. jump
2. run
3. talk
4. play
5. climb
6. throw

APPLY IT NOW

What do you do after school? Do you play sports, take lessons, practice band, or belong to any clubs? Write four sentences about activities you do. Use an action verb in each sentence.

4.2 Being Verbs

A **being verb** shows what someone or something is. Being verbs do not express action.

Here is a list of some being verbs.

BEING VERBS				
am	is	are	was	were
has been	had been	have been	will be	

Sentences That Show Action

Cindy *sings*.
The plants *grow*.
The bird *pecks*.

Sentences That Show Being

Cindy *is* happy.
The plants *are* green.
The bird *was* hungry.

The action verbs tell what Cindy, the plants, and the bird do. The being verbs do not express action.

Which one of these sentences has a being verb?

> A **Pedro is ready for school.**
>
> B **Angie ate a peach.**
>
> C **Kevin laughed at the movie.**

You are right if you said that sentence A uses a being verb. The word *is* is a being verb. In sentences B and C, *ate* and *laughed* are action verbs.

EXERCISE 1 Find the being verb in each sentence.

1. Many students are at home this week.
2. They have been sick with colds.
3. I was sick last week.
4. I am fine now.

EXERCISE 2 Find the verb in each sentence. Tell whether it is an action verb or a being verb.

1. Louie was sick.
2. He had a cold.
3. He will be home from school today.
4. Mom took Louie to the doctor.
5. They had been in the waiting room one hour.
6. Finally, the doctor was ready for them.
7. Dr. McGrath listened to Louie's cough.
8. The doctor gave Louie some medicine.
9. Louie is better.
10. Mom sent him to school.

EXERCISE 3 Complete each sentence with a verb from the list on page 76. More than one verb may fit.

1. Chicken pox _____ a virus.
2. I _____ four years old when I had it.
3. My brother and sister _____ sick then too.
4. I _____ glad I had it when I was little.
5. You _____ hot and tired.
6. Your skin _____ itchy.
7. Molly _____ ill now.
8. She _____ scratching her skin.
9. She _____ in bed.
10. I _____ sure Molly _____ better soon.

APPLY IT NOW

Tell about a time when you were not feeling well. Write four sentences about how you were feeling. Use being verbs.

Grammar in Action. Find the two being verbs in the third sentence of the letter on page 330.

4.3 Helping Verbs

A verb can have more than one word. A **helping verb** is a verb added before a main verb to make the meaning clear.

WITHOUT A HELPING VERB

We *sleep* **in a tent.**

WITH A HELPING VERB

We *will sleep* **in a tent.**
We *might sleep* **in a tent.**

Here are some helping verbs.

HELPING VERBS

am	was	have	can	do
is	were	had	might	does
are		has	will	did

A helping verb always comes before the main verb of the sentence.

Which sentences have a helping verb?

A **The family plans a trip.**
B **The family planned a trip.**
C **The family is planning a trip.**
D **The family has planned a trip.**

You are right if you said sentences C and D. In sentence C, *is* is a helping verb that is added before *planning*. In sentence D, *has* is a helping verb that is added before *planned*.

Can you find the helping verb and main verb in these sentences?

A **We have decided on Colorado for our vacation.**
B **We are thinking about a camping trip.**

In sentence A, *have* is the helping verb, and *decided* is the main verb. In sentence B, *are* is the helping verb, and *thinking* is the main verb.

EXERCISE 1 Find the helping verb in each sentence.

1. My family is going to Yellowstone National Park.
2. We might leave next week.
3. I had hoped to go tomorrow.
4. Mom will buy a tent.
5. Dad has planned the route.
6. I am hoping to see moose and bear.
7. We can see the geyser called Old Faithful.
8. It will shoot water high into the air.

EXERCISE 2 Find the helping verb and the main verb in each sentence.

1. Yellowstone has been a national park since 1872.
2. Many people have visited it.
3. You can camp in some areas of the park.
4. You might make reservations for a camping spot.
5. Some parts of the park will close in the winter.
6. We are going there this summer.

EXERCISE 3 Complete each sentence with a helping verb from the list on page 78. More than one verb may fit.

1. It _____ turn cooler tonight.
2. We _____ sitting around the campfire.
3. Dad _____ gone to get wood for the fire.
4. They _____ telling camp stories.
5. We _____ sing silly songs.
6. She _____ roast marshmallows.
7. I _____ sleeping in a tent.
8. The mosquitoes _____ biting me.
9. I _____ put on bug spray.
10. I _____ be awake all night.

Old Faithful

APPLY IT NOW

Imagine you are packing for a camping trip. What do you think you might need? Write five sentences. Use helping verbs. Underline them.
Example:
I might need some warm clothes tonight.
I will take a sweater.

4.4 Principal Parts of Verbs

A verb has four principal parts: **present, present participle, past,** and **past participle.**

PRESENT	PRESENT PARTICIPLE	PAST	PAST PARTICIPLE
learn	learning	learned	learned
walk	walking	walked	walked

The present participle is formed by adding *-ing* to the present. The past and the past participle of a verb are usually formed by adding *-ed* to the present.

My friends *play* **the drums.** (present)

My friends *are playing* **a march.** (present participle)

The band *played* **works by John Philip Sousa.** (past)

The band *had played* **a song before my arrival.**
(past participle)

Note these points:

- With a singular noun subject (and with *he, she,* or *it*), an *-s* is added to the present part of the verb: Kim *plays* in the band.
- The present participle is often used with forms of the helping verb *be* (*am, is, are, was,* and *were*).
- The past participle is often used with *has, have,* or *had.*

In this sentence what principal part is the underlined verb?

I never had <u>played</u> **in a band before.**

You are right if you said past participle. The verb *played* ends in *ed,* and it is used with *had.*

EXERCISE 1 **Tell whether each underlined verb is in the present, present participle, past, or past participle. Look for *be* verbs before present participles and for *have, has,* or *had* before past participles.**

1. I <u>like</u> classical music.
2. I was <u>listening</u> to a Mozart symphony last night.

3. Mozart <u>learned</u> to play piano when he was four years old.

4. He had <u>composed</u> his first symphony by the age of nine.

5. Mozart <u>produced</u> several other symphonies during his lifetime.

6. He <u>earned</u> little money from his music.

7. He <u>created</u> several famous operas too.

8. My collection <u>contains</u> a CD with songs from *The Magic Flute.*

9. I have <u>listened</u> to his music many times.

10. Mozart's popularity has <u>lasted</u> for hundreds of years.

11. People still <u>enjoy</u> his music today.

12. Leigh is <u>downloading</u> some music onto his MP3 player.

Wolfgang Amadeus Mozart, 1756–1791

EXERCISE 2 Complete each sentence with the form of the verb in parentheses.

1. The band _____ every Friday. (play—present).

2. The students are _____. (listen—present participle)

3. The band _____ many hours. (practice—past).

4. I am _____ to play the flute. (learn—present participle)

5. I have _____ the flute for six months. (study—past participle)

6. The band teacher has _____ me. (help—past participle)

7. My best friend also _____ flute lessons. (take—present)

8. I had never _____ onstage before. (perform—past participle).

9. People _____ us. (applaud—past)

10. Our teacher was _____. (cheer—present participle)

APPLY IT NOW

Write four sentences about a game you like. Write one sentence using each of the principal parts of a verb.

4.5 Regular and Irregular Verbs

The past and the past participle of **regular verbs** usually end in *d* or *ed*.

PRESENT	PAST	PAST PARTICIPLE
jump	jumped	jumped
wave	waved	waved

The past and the past participle of **irregular verbs** are not formed by adding *-d* or *-ed* to the present.

Here are some common irregular verbs.

PRESENT	PAST	PAST PARTICIPLE
begin	began	begun
do	did	done
feel	felt	felt
fly	flew	flown
give	gave	given
put	put	put
send	sent	sent
sing	sang	sung

Which sentence has an irregular verb?

A Paul Revere lived about 250 years ago.

B Paul Revere rode a horse.

C Paul Revere worked many jobs.

You are right if you said sentence B. The past of *ride* is not formed with the ending *d* or *ed*. That makes it an irregular verb.

Statue of Paul Revere

EXERCISE 1 Complete the chart with the correct parts of the verbs.

PRESENT	PRESENT PARTICIPLE	PAST	PAST PARTICIPLE
make			
	forgetting		
		told	
			ridden

EXERCISE 2 Tell whether each underlined verb is regular or irregular.

1. Paul Revere <u>lived</u> from 1735 to 1818 in Boston, Massachusetts.
2. He <u>became</u> a silversmith.
3. He <u>made</u> eating utensils and tea sets.
4. People <u>bought</u> his silver pieces.
5. He <u>joined</u> a secret group named the Sons of Liberty.
6. The members <u>opposed</u> British authority in the colonies.
7. The British <u>sent</u> soldiers against the colonists in Concord.
8. Revere <u>spread</u> that news to colonists on his famous ride.
9. The first battle <u>began</u> at Lexington and Concord.

EXERCISE 3 Complete each sentence, using one of the past tense verbs in the word box. Tell whether the verb is regular or irregular.

called	hated	put	threw

1. The British government _____ a tax on tea.
2. The colonists _____ the tax.
3. They _____ the tea into Boston Harbor.
4. People _____ this event the Boston Tea Party.

APPLY IT NOW

Think about things that you do with your family. Write four sentences, using regular and irregular verbs. Underline the verbs and label them.
Example:
I <u>built</u> a tree house with my dad. (irregular)
I <u>hammered</u> the nails. (regular)

4.6 Bring, Buy, Come, and Sit

Bring, buy, come, and *sit* are irregular verbs. The chart shows the principal parts of each. Remember that the present participle and the past participle are often used with helping verbs.

PRESENT	PRESENT PARTICIPLE	PAST	PAST PARTICIPLE
bring	bringing	brought	brought
buy	buying	bought	bought
come	coming	came	come
sit	sitting	sat	sat

I *buy* pens at the office-supply store. (present)

I *am buying* a purple pen now.
(present participle, with the helping verb *am*)

I *bought* a red pen yesterday. (past)

I *have bought* a green pen already.
(past participle, with the helping verb *have*)

Which choice correctly completes the sentence?

Marie (buy buys) pens at the stationery store.

You're right if you chose *buys.* Singular noun subjects in the present tense use the present verb with *-s* added. The subject is the singular noun *Marie.* Note that *-s* is also added to present verbs for the pronoun subjects *he, she,* and *it.*

EXERCISE 1 **Complete the chart with the correct parts of the verbs.**

PRESENT	PRESENT PARTICIPLE	PAST	PAST PARTICIPLE
		brought	
buy			bought
			come
		sat	

EXERCISE 2 Find the part of *bring, buy, come,* or *sit* in each sentence. Then tell whether the part is present, present participle, past, or past participle.

1. I was sitting outside on the stairs.
2. My grandmother came up the walk.
3. She had brought us some tomatoes from her garden.
4. She has come to take us to the antique store.
5. She often buys things there.
6. At the store my grandmother sat in an old rocking chair.
7. She liked the chair, and she bought it.
8. My dad has brought the chair to her home.
9. Grandma is sitting in the chair and talking to me on the phone.
10. She is coming to visit again next week.

EXERCISE 3 Complete each sentence with the correct part of *bring, buy, come,* or *sit.* Identify each verb as present, present participle, past, or past participle.

1. The mail carrier _____ the mail every day. (bring)
2. He is _____ a package today. (bring)
3. I _____ in the mail a few minutes ago. (bring)
4. I have _____ the package inside. (bring)
5. We _____ stamps at the post office. (buy)
6. Gail _____ some flag stamps yesterday. (buy)
7. Elliot has _____ envelopes at the store. (buy)
8. The mail carrier always _____, even in rain. (come)
9. The letter _____ from Max last week. (come)
10. A letter has _____ for you today. (come)
11. Josie _____ down and wrote a letter. (sit)
12. The mail carrier is _____ after walking all day. (sit)

APPLY IT NOW

Write a short letter to a friend. Include the verbs *bring, buy, come,* and *sit* in your letter.

Tech Tip Type your letter and highlight the verbs.

4.7 *Eat, Go, and See*

Eat, go, and *see* are irregular verbs. The chart shows the principal parts of each verb. Remember that the present and past participles are often used with helping verbs.

PRESENT	PRESENT PARTICIPLE	PAST	PAST PARTICIPLE
eat	eating	ate	eaten
go	going	went	gone
see	seeing	saw	seen

We *eat* potato pancakes every Friday. (present)

We *are eating* potato pancakes today. (present participle, with the helping verb *are*)

We *ate* potato pancakes last Friday. (past)

We *have eaten* all the potato pancakes on the platter. (past participle, with the helping verb *have*)

Which form of the verb correctly completes the sentence?

Have you ever (went gone go) to a deli?

You're right if you chose *gone.* The past participle is needed when the helping verb *have* is used.

Which form correctly completes the sentence?

My sister (go goes) to the deli after school.

You are correct if you chose *goes.* It is the present of *go.*

Note that to make *go* agree with a singular subject, you must add *-es* instead of *-s.*

EXERCISE 1 Complete the chart with the correct parts of the verbs.

PRESENT	PRESENT PARTICIPLE	PAST	PAST PARTICIPLE
		ate	
go			
	seeing		

EXERCISE 2 Complete each sentence with the correct part of *eat, go,* or *see*. Identify each verb as present, present participle, past, or past participle.

1. I often _____ to the deli on Saturday. (go)
2. I usually _____ a club sandwich there. (eat)
3. My father _____ there all the time. (go)
4. Sammy has _____ a bowl of noodle soup. (eat)
5. They are _____ all the pickles. (eat)
6. Jill _____ there yesterday. (go)
7. She has _____ there before. (go)
8. We have _____ our teacher at the deli. (see)
9. I sometimes _____ friends there. (see)
10. I _____ Louisa there last week. (see)
11. She _____ a corned beef sandwich for lunch. (eat)
12. I was _____ a bowl of chili. (eat)
13. Louisa _____ my father there last Friday. (see)
14. I have _____ her there too. (see)
15. She often _____ to the deli after school. (go)
16. I am _____ there with my father next week. (go)

APPLY IT NOW

Write four sentences, one each with the present, present participle, past, and past participle of *eat*.

4.8 *Take, Tear and Write*

Take, tear, and *write* are irregular verbs. The chart shows the principal parts of each verb. Remember that the present and the past participles are often used with helping verbs.

PRESENT	PRESENT PARTICIPLE	PAST	PAST PARTICIPLE
take	taking	took	taken
tear	tearing	tore	torn
write	writing	wrote	written

We *take* math. (present)

We *are taking* math. (present participle, with the helping verb *are*)

We *took* math. (past)

We *have taken* math. (past participle, with the helping verb *have*)

Which form of the verb correctly completes the sentence?

Sally has (took taken) the math test.

You're right if you chose *taken*. The past participle is needed when the helping verb *has* is used.

EXERCISE 1 Complete the chart with the correct forms of the verbs.

PRESENT	PRESENT PARTICIPLE	PAST	PAST PARTICIPLE
take			
	tearing		
		wrote	

EXERCISE 2 Find the part of *take, tear,* or *write* in each sentence. Then tell whether the part is present, present participle, past, or past participle.

1. We had written to the national park before our trip.
2. The park ranger wrote back with information.
3. We are taking the easier trail up the mountain.
4. We took backpacks with lunches and water bottles.
5. My bag was so heavy that the bottom has torn.
6. Jake had never taken a boat tour on a lake.
7. My net tore when I was catching fish at the pond.
8. We took photos of birds, including bald eagles.
9. I always take a lot of photos.
10. We are writing a thank-you letter to the park rangers.

EXERCISE 3 Complete each sentence with the correct part of *take, tear,* or *write.* Identify each verb as present, present participle, past, or past participle.

1. Our class _____ a field trip every spring and fall. (take)
2. Last year we _____ a trip to the planetarium. (take)
3. This year we are _____ a trip to a forest. (take)
4. The strap of my backpack has _____. (tear)
5. Many students have _____ cameras with them. (take)
6. I _____ my jacket sleeve in the forest. (tear)
7. We each are _____ a letter to thank our guide on the trip. (write)
8. The teacher always _____ some ideas on the board. (write)
9. Mary is _____ a sheet of paper out of her notebook for me. (tear)
10. Sanjay has _____ a report on ants. (write)

APPLY IT NOW

Write four sentences, one each with the principal parts of *write*: present, present participle, past, and past participle.

4.9 Simple Present Tense

The tense of a verb shows when the action takes place. A verb in the **simple present tense** tells about something that is always true or about an action that happens again and again.

> **Frogs** *live* **in or near water.**
>
> **A frog** *catches* **flies.**
>
> **Flies** *stick* **to a frog's tongue.**

The verbs *live, catches,* and *stick* are in the simple present tense. The verbs tell things that are true about frogs. They tell about actions that happen again and again.

Use the present part of a verb for the present tense. In simple present tense, *-s* (or *-es*) is added to the verb when the subject is a singular noun or *he, she,* or *it.*

> **Crickets** *make* **a good meal for my frog.** (plural subject)
>
> **It** *lives* **in a tank.** (a singular noun subject, *frog,* so the present tense verb ends in *s*)

For verbs ending in *y* following a consonant, change the *y* to *i* and add *-es: fly—flies.* For verbs ending in *s, z, ch,* or *sh,* add *-es: buzz—buzzes.*

Which present tense verb form is correct in this sentence?

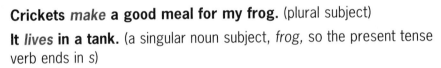

> **My friend (want wants) a pet frog.**

The correct answer is *wants.* The subject *friend* is a singular noun, so the present tense verb should end in *s.*

EXERCISE 1 Choose the correct verb to complete each sentence.

1. Frogs (belong belongs) to a group called amphibians.
2. An amphibian (live lives) in water and on land.
3. Frogs (like likes) warm weather.

Bullfrog

4. Their sticky tongues (trap traps) insects.

5. Their skin (protect protects) frogs from enemies.

6. A frog's color (match matches) the surroundings.

7. Frogs (burrow burrows) in mud if they are cold.

8. A tree frog (hide hides) from its enemies.

9. Leopard frogs (plays play) dead.

10. Poison dart frogs (tastes taste) bad to other animals.

EXERCISE 2 **The subject in each sentence is underlined. Tell if it is singular or plural. Then choose the verb that correctly completes each sentence.**

1. A <u>frog</u> (lay lays) eggs in water.

2. Each <u>egg</u> (hatch hatches) into a tadpole.

3. The <u>tadpole</u> (swim swims) underwater.

4. <u>People</u> also (call calls) tadpoles pollywogs.

5. A <u>tadpole</u> (develop develops) legs and lungs.

6. <u>Lungs</u> (help helps) frogs breathe on land.

7. Frogs' hind <u>legs</u> (make makes) them good jumpers.

8. Some <u>frogs</u> (leap leaps) 20 times their body length.

Poison dart frog

EXERCISE 3 **Rewrite each sentence with the singular subject shown. Be sure the verb goes with the subject.**

1. Tadpoles live in water. (a tadpole)

2. Pollywogs eat plants. (a pollywog)

3. They seem more like a fish. (It)

4. Tadpoles grow hind legs and short arms. (a tadpole)

5. The tails go away. (the tail)

6. The young frogs hop out of the pond. (the young frog)

7. Frogs communicate by croaking. (a frog)

8. Croaks sometimes signal danger. (a croak)

Tadpoles

APPLY IT NOW

Write four sentences about the habits of frogs or another type of animal. Use the simple present tense.

4.10 Simple Past Tense

A verb in the **simple past tense** tells about something that happened in the past.

> **Our class** *studied* **history.**
> **We** *learned* **about colonial America.**
> **Everyone** *wrote* **a report.**
> **Maria** *drew* **a map.**
> **Our teacher** *talked* **about the American Revolution.**
> **I** *asked* **a question about the Boston Tea Party.**

The verbs *studied, learned, wrote, drew, talked,* and *asked* are in the simple past tense.

Most past tense verbs end in *ed*. Remember that irregular verbs do not end in *ed*.

> **We** *discussed* **colonial life.** (regular verb)
> **I** *read* **a book on colonial life.** (irregular verb)

If a regular verb ends in *e*, just add *-d*. If a verb ends in *y* following a consonant, change the *y* to *i* and add *-ed*.

> **name + -d = named**   **try + -ed = tried**

Thomas Jefferson

Which sentence shows simple past tense?

> A **We learn about Thomas Jefferson.**
> B **We are learning about Thomas Jefferson.**
> C **We learned about Thomas Jefferson.**

You are right if you said that sentence C shows simple past tense. The *ed* ending on *learned* signals the past tense.

Monticello

EXERCISE 1 Write the simple past tense of each verb. Be careful! Some verbs are irregular.

Verb	Simple Past		Verb	Simple Past
1. help	_____		6. win	_____
2. talk	_____		7. try	_____
3. raise	_____		8. listen	_____
4. take	_____		9. offer	_____
5. serve	_____		10. grow	_____

EXERCISE 2 Complete each sentence with the verb in parentheses. Use the simple past tense.

1. Thomas Jefferson _____ in Charlottesville, Virginia. (live)

2. He _____ a plantation. (own)

3. Jefferson _____ the law. (study)

4. He _____ a home called Monticello. (build)

5. Martha Wayles Skelton _____ Thomas Jefferson. (marry)

The signing of the Declaration of Independence

6. Jefferson _____ the Declaration of Independence. (write)

7. He _____ freedom for the colonies. (want)

8. He _____ Ben Franklin and George Washington. (know)

9. Jefferson _____ liberty and people's rights. (support)

10. He _____ to France as an ambassador. (go)

11. He _____ help from France to fight the war against Britain. (get)

12. He _____ in President Washington's first Cabinet. (serve)

13. Jefferson _____ for president of the United States. (run)

14. He _____ the third president of the United States. (become)

15. The United States _____ the Louisiana Territory while Jefferson was president. (purchase)

APPLY IT NOW

Write four sentences about a historical figure you have been studying. Use the simple past tense in your sentences.

Tech Tip With an adult, research a historical figure online.

4.11 Future Tense with *Will*

The word *will* is one way to express something that will take place in the future. The helping verb *will* is used with the present part of a verb to form a future tense. For example, *will + help = will help.*

> I **will help** on the project.

The sentence tells what you will do in the future.

What do these sentences tell?

> Our youth group **will organize** an activity.
> The activity **will raise** money for charity.
> Our advisor **will help** us in our decision.
> We **will decide** on a project soon.

Will organize, will raise, will help, and *will decide* are in the future tense.

Which sentence expresses the future?

> **A** I worked on the fund-raising project.
> **B** Marti worked on the fund-raising project.
> **C** Patrick will work on the fund-raising project.

You are right if you said sentence C expresses the future. *Will* means that Patrick has agreed to work on the project at a later time.

EXERCISE 1 Complete each sentence with the verb in parentheses. Use the future tense with *will*.

1. Our class _____ our fund-raising project. (discuss)
2. Our teachers _____ the discussion. (lead)
3. Some students _____ presentations. (make)
4. I _____ a clothing drive. (suggest)
5. Lily _____ a car wash. (recommend)
6. We all _____ on the best project. (vote)
7. The winning project hopefully _____ a lot of money. (raise)

EXERCISE 2 **Change each sentence to the future tense by using *will*.**

1. We help with the clothing drive.
2. They collect more clothes than usual.
3. You put the items on tables.
4. Monica gets the tables.
5. The teachers decide the prices.
6. I write the price tags.
7. Darnell hands out flyers.
8. Jasmine makes signs.
9. We take turns working at the clothing drive.
10. People buy the items.
11. We give the money to charity.
12. They appreciate our donation.

EXERCISE 3 **Find the verb in each sentence and tell its tense: future, simple present, or simple past.**

1. Marcie helps with the project.
2. Kevin collected old clothes.
3. I will take the clothes to school.
4. I asked my family for old items.
5. My brother will give me some old CDs.
6. My mom will find some old clothes.
7. Dad will donate a winter coat.
8. We will put the clothes in the school basement.
9. The teachers put some tables there.
10. Our fund-raisers are very successful.

APPLY IT NOW

How would you like to help other people? Write five sentences about what you would like to do. Use the future tense with *will*.

4.12 Future Tense with *Going To*

Like *will,* the phrase *going to* is used to express future tense. A form of the helping verb *be* must go in front of *going to.*

Use *am going to, is going to,* or *are going to* followed by the present part of the verb. For example, *is going to + make = is going to make.*

> **Nina** *is going to make* **breakfast.**

This sentence tells what Nina is going to do at some time in the future.

What does each of these sentences tell?

> **I** *am going to cook.*
> **You** *are going to cook.*
> **We** *are going to cook.*
> **They** *are going to cook.*

Each sentence describes something that will happen in the future.

Which sentence uses the future tense with *going to*?

> **A** **Nick made pancakes.**
> **B** **Nisha is going to make scrambled eggs.**
> **C** **Nellie makes French toast.**

You are right if you said sentence B uses the future tense with *going to.* Sentence A uses the past tense. Sentence C uses the simple present tense.

EXERCISE 1 Find the verb in the future tense in each sentence.

1. What are you going to eat for breakfast?
2. Mary Jo is going to eat oatmeal.
3. She is going to toast a bagel.
4. I am going to have an omelet.
5. Idalia is going to drink a smoothie.

6. We all are going to go to a restaurant.

7. Roberto is going to order pancakes.

8. They are going to make grits.

9. He is going to try something new.

10. It is going to cook quickly.

EXERCISE 2 Change each sentence to use the future tense with *going to.*

1. We made brunch.

2. I was squeezing the oranges.

3. Freddy toasts the bread.

4. Mom is scrambling the eggs.

5. Santiago set the table.

6. You had poured the juice.

7. Brody is flipping the pancakes.

8. I put blueberries on my cereal.

9. Michael cut some melon.

10. They did the dishes.

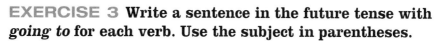

EXERCISE 3 Write a sentence in the future tense with *going to* for each verb. Use the subject in parentheses.

1. grill (he)

2. chop (they)

3. bake (she)

4. boil (it)

5. wait (we)

6. taste (you)

7. clean (they)

8. sweep (I)

APPLY IT NOW

Tell what you are going to have for breakfast, lunch, or dinner tomorrow. Write three sentences. Use the future tense with *going to.*

4.13 **Present Progressive Tense**

A verb in the **present progressive tense** tells what is happening now. This tense is formed with *am, is,* or *are* and the present participle. For example, *is + fishing = is fishing.*

	PRESENT FORM OF *BE*	PRESENT PARTICIPLE OF *FISH*
Bob	*is*	*fishing.*

The sentence tells what Bob is doing right now. What does each of these sentences tell?

I *am fishing.*
You *are fishing.*
She *is fishing.*
We *are fishing.*
They *are fishing.*

Which sentence uses the present progressive tense?

A I am using worms for bait.
B I will use bread for bait.

You are right if you said sentence A. Sentence A tells about an action that is happening now. It has the verb *am* and the present participle of a verb: *am using.* Sentence B tells something about the future and is in the future tense.

To form the present participle, for verbs ending in *e*, drop the *e* and add *-ing: use + ing = using.* For many verbs ending with a consonant following a vowel, double the consonant before adding *-ing: grab + ing = grabbing.*

EXERCISE 1 Write the present progressive tense of each verb. Use the subject in parentheses.

EXAMPLE take (I)   I am taking

1. try (you)
2. look (we)
3. steer (he)
4. dive (they)
5. bubble (it)
6. swim (they)
7. sink (it)
8. paddle (I)

EXERCISE 2 Change the verb in each sentence to the present progressive tense.

1. Bob rows the boat.
2. He hopes to catch a big fish.
3. The sun shines.
4. Lynn helps him row.
5. They drop the anchor.
6. Something tugs the line.
7. Bob hooks a big fish.
8. Lynn takes a picture.
9. The fish gets away.
10. People laugh at Bob's fish story.

EXERCISE 3 Complete each sentence with a verb in the present progressive tense.

1. Jessica _____ a blanket on the grass.
2. We _____ on the blanket.
3. Mom _____ the picnic basket.
4. They _____ chicken salad.
5. I _____ an apple.
6. You _____ a glass of water.

APPLY IT NOW

Imagine you are at a lake. Write five sentences that tell the things you are doing. Use the present progressive tense. Try to use some of these verbs: *row, swim, dive, build, run, float.*

4.14 Past Progressive Tense

A verb in the **past progressive tense** tells what was happening in the past. This tense is formed with *was* or *were* and the present participle. For example, *was + clapping = was clapping.*

	PAST FORM OF *BE*	PRESENT PARTICIPLE OF *CLAP*
The clown	*was*	*clapping.*

The sentence tells what the clown was doing in the past. What does each of these sentences tell?

I *was clapping.*

It *was clapping.*

You *were clapping.*

We *were clapping.*

They *were clapping.*

Which of the following sentences uses the past progressive tense?

A We are petting the seal.

B We could pet the seal.

C We were petting the seal.

You are right if you said sentence C. *Were petting* is in the past progressive tense. It tells about something that was going on in the past.

EXERCISE 1 Write the past progressive tense of each verb below. Use the subject in parentheses.

EXAMPLE **think (I) I was thinking.**

1. climb (you)

2. stand (we)

3. swing (he)

4. throw (they)

5. hang (it)

6. play (they)

7. sing (we)

8. cheer (I)

9. step (she)

EXERCISE 2 Find the verb in each sentence. Change the verb to the past progressive tense.

1. We waited for the show to start.
2. We sat in the bleachers.
3. The man sold peanuts.
4. Acrobats flew through the air.
5. Penguins jumped out of a tiny car.
6. Lions roared.
7. A man juggled.
8. A woman twisted balloons into animal shapes.
9. We ate popcorn.
10. People applauded.
11. Horses trotted around the ring.
12. I watched three things at once.

EXERCISE 3 Find the verb in each sentence. Tell whether the verb is in the present progressive tense or the past progressive tense.

1. The children are attending a summer circus camp.
2. Eliza is twirling a plate on a stick.
3. Mike was walking on a low tightrope.
4. The instructors were teaching different tricks.
5. Performers are demonstrating the tricks.
6. I am swinging on a trapeze.
7. Everyone was having fun.
8. We are returning next year.

APPLY IT NOW

Imagine that you have just come home from a circus. Write five sentences that tell about the things that were happening and what you were seeing and doing. Use the past progressive tense. Try using some of these words: *eating, swinging, falling, jumping, dancing, juggling.*

4.15 *Is and Are, Was and Were*

Is, are, was, and *were* are being verbs. These words do not express actions.

- *Is* and *was* are always used with singular subjects.
- *Are* and *were* are always used with plural subjects.

SINGULAR SUBJECT	VERB
A *tiger*	*is* a cat.

PLURAL SUBJECT	VERB
Tigers	*are* the biggest cats in the world.

Which verb correctly completes the sentence?

This tiger (was were) the biggest in the zoo.

You are right if you said *was.* The subject *tiger* is singular. The past tense verb *was* is used with a singular subject.

Which verb correctly completes the sentence?

The Siberian tiger (is are) endangered.

You are right if you said *is.* The subject *Siberian tiger* is singular, so the verb form *is* is needed.

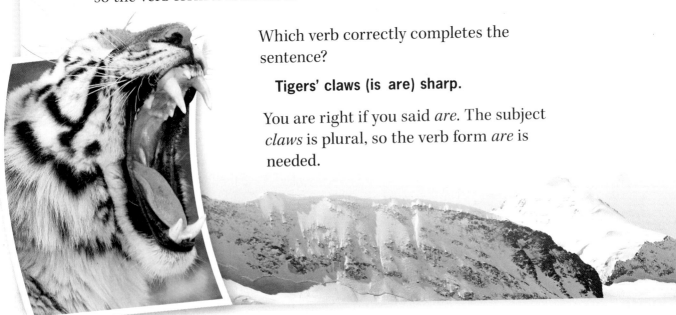

Which verb correctly completes the sentence?

Tigers' claws (is are) sharp.

You are right if you said *are.* The subject *claws* is plural, so the verb form *are* is needed.

EXERCISE 1 Choose the verb that correctly completes each sentence.

1. Tropical jungles (is are) the home of some tigers.
2. The cold forest (is are) the home of other tigers.
3. Asia (is are) the native home of all tigers.
4. Tigers (was were) once widespread in Asia.
5. A tiger's coat (is are) striped.
6. The stripes (is are) different for each tiger, just as fingerprints are for humans.
7. A tiger's teeth (is are) between two and three inches long.
8. The ancient saber-toothed tiger (was were) not a direct ancestor of the modern-day tiger.
9. The bite of the saber-toothed tiger (was were) deadly.
10. A tiger (is are) a solitary hunter.
11. Tigers (is are) nocturnal, which means they move around at night.
12. At a year old, a tiger cub (is are) already a good hunter.

Siberian tiger

EXERCISE 2 Complete each sentence with *is, are, was,* or *were.* Use the tense shown in parentheses.

1. Hunters _____ a danger to tigers. (present)
2. Tiger fur _____ a valuable product. (present)
3. The sale of tiger fur _____ illegal. (present)
4. Tiger bones _____ sometimes used in Asian folk medicine. (present)
5. Iran _____ once home to tigers. (past)
6. At one time tigers _____ plentiful there.
7. Now tigers _____ gone from the area. (present)
8. Protected parks _____ important to help save tigers.

APPLY IT NOW

Write four sentences about an animal. Use *is, are, was,* and *were* in your sentences.
Example:
My cat is white and brown.
My cat was the tiniest in the shelter.

4.16 Contractions with Not

A **contraction** is a short way to write some words. An apostrophe (') marks the place where one or more letters have been left out of the words.

The word *not* is often part of a contraction. The letter *o* in *not* is left out, and an apostrophe is used in its place.

> Caroline *is not* going to the movie.
>
> Caroline *isn't* going to the movie. (contraction with *not*)

Here are some other contractions with *not*.

aren't = are not   don't = do not

wasn't = was not   doesn't = does not

weren't = were not   didn't = did not

The following contractions with *not* are different in form.

can't = cannot   won't = will not

Which of these sentences does not use a correct contraction with *not*?

A The movie wasn't really funny.

B The theater does'nt sell popcorn.

C The children didn't like the movie.

You are correct if you chose sentence B. The correct form is *doesn't*.

EXERCISE 1 Make a contraction from each word group.

1. were not
2. did not
3. is not
4. will not

5. do not
6. are not
7. does not
8. cannot

EXERCISE 2 Rewrite each sentence with a contraction for the underlined words.

1. Henry <u>was not</u> in front of the theater when I arrived.
2. The movie <u>did not</u> start on time.
3. I <u>do not</u> want to sit in the front row.
4. Lynn <u>is not</u> sitting with her friends.
5. I <u>cannot</u> see the screen because of the tall person in front of me.
6. The children <u>are not</u> laughing much.
7. We <u>were not</u> talking during the movie.
8. The movie <u>does not</u> have a happy ending.
9. It <u>was not</u> my favorite movie.
10. Sydney <u>does not</u> understand why I <u>did not</u> like the movie.
11. I <u>will not</u> recommend the movie to my friends.
12. Most of my friends <u>do not</u> plan to see it.

EXERCISE 3 Change each sentence using a contraction with *not*.

1. I like scary movies.
2. I will go see scary movies.
3. I saw a scary movie last Friday.
4. My sister likes scary movies.
5. We sit in the back of the theater.
6. You can bring in your bottled water.
7. The ticket line was long.
8. We bought popcorn.
9. The theater was filled.
10. The actors in the movie were very good.
11. My friends stayed for the whole movie.
12. We were surprised by the ending.

APPLY IT NOW

Tell about a time you could not do something or go somewhere. Write four sentences that tell what you missed. Use a contraction with *not* in each sentence.
Example:
I didn't go to the beach last weekend because the weather wasn't good.

Grammar in Action. Find the contraction with *not* on page 325.

Verb Review

4.1 Find the action verb in each sentence.

1. The girls often drink hot chocolate.
2. Shelly likes whipped cream.
3. Erin adds marshmallows.
4. The marshmallows melt in the hot chocolate.

4.2 Find the being verb in each sentence.

5. I was hungry at breakfast.
6. The cartons of orange juice were empty.
7. Mom and Dad are tired in the morning.

4.3 Find the helping verb and the main verb in each sentence.

8. The family is eating dinner.
9. The roast has cooled enough to eat.
10. We will clear the table.

4.4 Tell if the underlined verb part is present, present participle, past, or past participle.

11. The farmer <u>grew</u> pumpkins.
12. He has <u>stacked</u> them.
13. We <u>pick</u> pumpkins every fall.
14. Gail is <u>choosing</u> her pumpkin.

4.5 Tell whether each underlined verb is regular or irregular.

15. We <u>planned</u> a toy drive.
16. Trina <u>colored</u> posters.
17. I <u>brought</u> blocks to donate.
18. Justin <u>donated</u> puzzles.

4.6 Complete each sentence with the correct part of the verb in parentheses.

19. I am _____ in the park. (sit)
20. My friends _____ late. (come)
21. They have _____ the kites. (bring)
22. I _____ some ice cream, and I ate it. (buy)

4.7 Complete each sentence with the correct part of the verb in parentheses.

23. Joy and her mom always _____ grocery shopping. (go)
24. They are _____ samples from the trays. (eat)
25. Now Joy _____ cake, shrimp, and fruit. (see)
26. She had _____ home with a stomachache. (go)

4.8 Complete each sentence with the correct part of the verb in parentheses.

27. Max _____ his clothes to the cleaners every week. (take)

28. The cleaners _____ his shirt. (tear)

29. Yesterday Max _____ a letter of complaint. (write)

4.9 Choose the correct verb to complete each sentence.

30. Birds (build builds) nests.

31. They (gather gathers) twigs.

32. Maya (watch watches) them.

4.10 Change each sentence to the simple past tense.

33. Clouds drift in the sky.

34. The forecast calls for rain.

35. We button our raincoats.

4.11 Change each sentence to the future tense using *will*.

36. Our group plans the party.

37. Jean made the decorations.

38. Bill is bringing some food.

4.12 Change each sentence to use the future tense using *going to*.

39. My grandma made lasagna.

40. She boils the noodles.

41. I helped Grandma.

4.13 Change each sentence to use the present progressive tense.

42. A sidewalk artist sketches.

43. Her customer sits still.

44. I wait in line for my portrait.

4.14 Change each sentence to use the past progressive tense.

45. My friends played tennis.

46. Connie served the ball.

47. Tanner returned the ball.

48. Lin and I watched the game.

4.15 Choose the verb that correctly completes each sentence.

49. A quilt (is are) pretty.

50. Quilt makers (is are) patient.

51. The quilt's squares (was were) colorful.

52. The quilt (was were) warm.

4.16 Write a contraction for the underlined words in each sentence.

53. I did not want to eat corn.

54. Corn was not my favorite vegetable.

55. Kai is not eating corn either.

56. The dog will not eat the corn.

Tech Tip Go to www.voyagesinenglish.com for more activities.

Verb Challenge

Read the paragraph and answer the questions.

1. Tim and Tina were excited about the field trip to the dinosaur museum. 2. Each student brought lunch and wore old clothes. 3. A bus took the class to the site of the museum. 4. Everyone was talking about the dinosaur pit there. 5. In the pit children sift through soil. 6. They look for dinosaur bones. 7. Tina hoped she might find something. 8. She had dug in the pit last year. 9. Scientists are learning more and more about dinosaurs all the time. 10. The museum will provide a great experience to any student with an interest in dinosaurs.

1. In sentence 1 is the verb *were* an action verb or a being verb? How do you know?

2. In sentence 2 what form is the verb *brought*? Name its other principal parts. Is it a regular or an irregular verb?

3. In sentence 3 what tense is the verb?

4. In sentence 4 what tense is the verb?

5. In sentence 6 what tense is the verb?

6. In sentence 7 what tense is the verb *hoped*? Is it a regular or an irregular verb?

7. In sentence 7 what is the helping verb?

8. In sentence 8 what is the helping verb? What part of the main verb follows the helping verb?

9. In sentence 9 what tense is the verb? Is it a regular or an irregular verb? Give its principal parts.

10. In sentence 10 what is the verb? What is its tense?

Adjectives

5.1 Identifying Adjectives

An **adjective** tells more about a noun. Adjectives describe nouns. They can tell how something looks, tastes, sounds, feels, or smells.

LOOKS	TASTES	SOUNDS	FEELS	SMELLS
tired	sour	loud	rough	smoky
huge	sweet	quiet	hard	fragrant
pink	tasty	silent	oily	stinky
happy	bitter	musical	smooth	fresh

Adjectives tell such things as size, number, color, shape, and weight.

That cactus has *red* flowers.

In this sentence *red* is an adjective. It tells more about the noun *flowers*. Red tells what color the flowers are. Here are some other adjectives you could use to describe a flower: *small, beautiful, round, fragrant, delicate,* and *fresh.*

What is the adjective in this sentence?

The cactus was in a large pot.

A was

B large

C pot

You are right if you said B. The word *large* describes the noun *pot. Large* tells about the size of the pot.

EXERCISE 1 Find the adjective that describes the underlined noun in each sentence.

1. Deserts are dry <u>areas</u>.
2. Deserts usually have hot <u>days</u>.
3. Cold <u>nights</u>, however, follow them.
4. Deserts are difficult <u>places</u> to live because of the lack of water.
5. Animals in the deserts are usually small <u>creatures</u>.
6. Colorful <u>flowers</u> bloom quickly after rains.

EXERCISE 2 Add an adjective to describe each noun. Choose a word from the word box.

broken	funny	good	happy	heavy	loud
pretty	sad	soft	spicy	tired	warm

1. the ~~sad~~ girl
2. a ~~funny~~ joke
3. a *heavy* backpack
4. the *broken* window
5. a _____ blanket
6. a _____ coat
7. the _____ music
8. the _____ food

EXERCISE 3 Find the adjective in each sentence. Tell the noun it describes.

1. The cactus is an unusual plant.
2. Cactuses have sharp spikes.
3. The spikes are good protection against animals.
4. Cactuses can survive for long periods without water.
5. Waxy stems help them hold in water.
6. Cactuses can produce sweet fruit.

EXERCISE 4 Add an adjective before each noun. Use the kind of adjective in parentheses. Use the chart on page 110 for help.

1. _____ baby (looks)
2. _____ sandpaper (feels)
3. _____ flower (smells)
4. _____ horn (sounds)
5. _____ peach (tastes)

Prickly pear and dragon fruit

APPLY IT NOW

Write five sentences about plants and animals that you are familiar with. Use an adjective before a noun in each sentence.
Example:
Robins are <u>common</u> birds in my area.
<u>Pink</u> roses are my favorite flowers.

Grammar in Action. Find three adjectives in the first sentence of the page 367 excerpt.

5.2 Adjectives Before Nouns

Most adjectives describe various features of nouns. They are called **descriptive adjectives.** Descriptive adjectives generally come before the nouns they describe.

> **The town has a *shady* park.**
>
> **There are *old* statues in the park.**

Shady and *old* are adjectives. In the first sentence, *shady* describes the noun *park.* In the second sentence, *old* describes the noun *statues.* In both sentences the adjectives come before the nouns they describe.

What are the adjectives in this sentence? What are the nouns they describe?

> **A large statue shows a man with a long beard.**

You are right if you said *large* and *long. Large* tells about the size of the *statue. Long* describes the noun *beard.* Both adjectives come before the nouns they describe.

EXERCISE 1 Find the descriptive adjectives in each sentence. The number of adjectives is in parentheses.

1. Benjamin Franklin was an extraordinary leader. (1)
2. Franklin was a talented writer who wrote a popular book. (2)
3. The famous book contains clever sayings. (2)
4. Franklin also produced useful inventions and did scientific experiments. (2)
5. His tireless work helped build an early library in Philadelphia. (2)
6. He was an able statesman who supported independence. (1)
7. His political ideas contributed to the Declaration of Independence. (1)

Benjamin Franklin

EXERCISE 2 Find the descriptive adjective in each sentence. Tell the noun the adjective describes. N ville Aundertine

1. Philadelphia has interesting sights.
2. An old building is Independence Hall.
3. The famous hall was built in 1732.
4. Leaders held long meetings there in 1787.
5. It was where they wrote an important document—the U.S. Constitution.
6. One great leader there was George Washington.
7. He had a reputation as an honest man.
8. Washington was a brave leader during the Revolutionary War.
9. His troops survived a difficult winter at Valley Forge.
10. George Washington lived on a beautiful estate in Virginia called Mount Vernon.

EXERCISE 3 Complete each sentence with a descriptive adjective. Tell the noun the adjective describes. Choose from the adjectives in the word box.

important	cracked	curious	helpful
historic	blue	interested	large

Replica of the Liberty Bell

1. In Philadelphia Julie saw the _____ Liberty Bell.
2. The _____ visitors asked questions about the bell.
3. She learned about the bell's history from the _____ guide.
4. Independence Hall is where the _____ bell once hung.
5. The _____ bell no longer rings.

APPLY IT NOW

Write three sentences about a place you have visited or would like to visit. Use a descriptive adjective in each sentence.

Example:
San Francisco has a pleasant climate. I couldn't wait to see the famous Golden Gate Bridge. A noisy bus stopped at the corner near our hotel.

5.3 Subject Complements

Some descriptive adjectives come after a being verb. They are called **subject complements.** An adjective used as a subject complement tells more about the subject of the sentence. Some being verbs are *is, are, was,* and *were.*

> **The ocean is** *salty.*
>
> **Fish are** *scaly.*

In the first sentence, *salty* is the subject complement. It follows the being verb *is. Salty* tells about the subject, *ocean.* In the second sentence, *scaly* is the subject complement. It follows the being verb *are. Scaly* tells more about the subject, *fish.*

Which sentence has a subject complement?

A **Brown trout live in lakes.**

B **The sunfish were colorful.**

C **Guppies eat plants.**

You are right if you said sentence B. *Colorful* is a subject complement. It describes *sunfish,* and it comes after *were,* a being verb.

EXERCISE 1 Find the adjective used as a subject complement in each sentence.

1. The aquarium in my city is big.
2. A visit to the aquarium is enjoyable.
3. The area near the shark tank is always quiet.
4. The sand tiger sharks are really scary.
5. Their teeth are sharp.
6. Their skin is brown.
7. They are not dangerous to humans, however.
8. To me, the divers feeding the sharks are extremely brave.

EXERCISE 2 Find the adjective used as a subject complement in each sentence. Tell the noun the subject complement describes.

1. The tank in the center of the aquarium is large.
2. The view from the staircase is great.
3. The seahorses in the tank are tiny.
4. The stingray's fins are wide.
5. The sea turtle is gigantic.
6. The eel's skin is green.
7. Eels are really ugly.
8. Our visit to the aquarium was wonderful.
9. The guide was helpful.
10. Her information was interesting.

EXERCISE 3 Write five sentences with adjectives used as subject complements. Use a noun from Group A and an adjective from Group B in each sentence.

EXAMPLE **The fish was colorful.**

Group A	Group B	
aquarium	cloudy	dirty
fish	quick	brave
scuba diver	colorful	big
shark	beautiful	scary
tank	new	shiny

Stingray

APPLY IT NOW

Imagine you are looking into a fish tank. Write four sentences describing what you see. Use an adjective as a subject complement in each sentence.
Example:
Some fish are yellow.

Grammar in Action. Find the subject complement in the second sentence of the third paragraph on page 362.

5.4 Compound Subject Complements

Some sentences have more than one adjective used as a subject complement. Two adjectives joined by *and* or *or* after a being verb form a **compound subject complement.** Both adjectives tell more about the subject.

Some dinosaurs were *big* and *scary*.

The adjectives *big* and *scary* come after the being verb *were*. Both *big* and *scary* tell more about the subject, *dinosaurs*. *Big* and *scary* form a compound subject complement joined by *and*.

Dinosaurs might be *large* or *small*.

In this sentence the adjectives *large* and *small* come after the being verb *be*. *Large* and *small* form a compound subject complement joined by *or*.

Which sentence has a compound subject complement?

A **Dinosaurs are extinct.**

B **Some dinosaurs were small and fast.**

C **Dinosaurs ate plants or meat.**

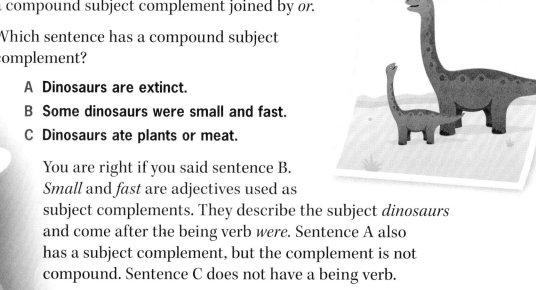

You are right if you said sentence B. *Small* and *fast* are adjectives used as subject complements. They describe the subject *dinosaurs* and come after the being verb *were*. Sentence A also has a subject complement, but the complement is not compound. Sentence C does not have a being verb.

EXERCISE 1 Find all the adjectives used as subject complements in these sentences. Tell which are compound subject complements.

1. *T. rex* was big and fierce.
2. Many plant-eating dinosaurs were huge and heavy.
3. Their necks were long.
4. Their back legs were strong and thick.

5. The teeth of meat-eating dinosaurs were long and sharp.
6. The teeth of plant-eating dinosaurs were flat.
7. Some predator dinosaurs were intelligent and quick.
8. A few dinosaurs' skin was hairy or feathery.
9. Dinosaurs are unusual and fascinating.
10. The disappearance of dinosaurs is mysterious and puzzling.

EXERCISE 2 Complete each sentence with a compound subject complement. Choose from the adjectives in the word box.

amazing	ancient	complete	crowded	excited
happy	huge	interested	interesting	tall

1. The dinosaur exhibit is _amazing_ and _huge_.
2. The dinosaur skeleton was _tall_ and _____.
3. The children are _happy_ and _interested_.
4. The visit was _complete_ and _crowded_.

EXERCISE 3 Use these adjective pairs to write four sentences with compound subject complements.

1. hungry and tired
2. pleased and delighted
3. tall and skinny
4. slow or fast

APPLY IT NOW

Write four sentences about dinosaurs. The sentences can be about a particular dinosaur, a TV program, a book, or a museum exhibit. Use a compound subject complement in each sentence.
Example:
T. rex was <u>mean</u> and <u>scary</u>.

 Videotape or podcast a dinosaur fun-facts program.

5.5 Adjectives That Compare

Adjectives can be used to make comparisons. To compare two people, places, or things, *-er* is often added to an adjective. To compare three or more people, places, or things, *-est* is usually added to the adjective.

Earth is a *large* planet.

COMPARE TWO NOUNS

Earth is *larger* than Mars.

COMPARE THREE OR MORE NOUNS

Jupiter is the *largest* planet.

Note that the *-er* form is often used with *than* to compare two nouns.

Here are some spelling rules for adding *-er* and *-est* to make comparisons.

- If an adjective ends in *e,* drop the final *e* and add *-er* or *-est.*

  safe   safer   safest

- If the adjective ends in *y* following a consonant, change the *y* to *i* and add *-er* or *-est.*

  sunny   sunnier   sunniest

- If a short adjective ends in a consonant that follows a vowel, double the final consonant before adding *-er* or *-est.*

  big   bigger   biggest

EXERCISE 1 Complete the chart.

ADJECTIVE	COMPARE TWO NOUNS	COMPARE THREE OR MORE NOUNS
short	shorter	shortest
hot	hotter	hottest
wide	wider	widest
windy	windier	windiest
small	smaller	smallest
scary		
brave		
tiny		
sad		

EXERCISE 2 Find the adjective that compares in each sentence.

1. Mercury is the closest planet to the sun.
2. The planet Venus has longer days than any other planet.
3. Do you know what the hottest planet is?
4. The sandiest desert is the Arabian Desert in Africa.
5. Australia is a smaller continent than Antarctica.
6. The warmest continent is Africa.
7. Antarctica is the emptiest continent.
8. The Pacific Ocean is deeper than the Atlantic Ocean.
9. The Amazon River is shorter than the Nile River.
10. The Amazon is called the mightiest river because of the amount of water it carries.
11. Mount Everest is higher than Mount McKinley.
12. The deepest lake in the world is Lake Baikal.

APPLY IT NOW

Write four sentences about places you know. Use an adjective that compares in each sentence.
Example:
The park near school is the largest park in town.

Grammar in Action
Find the adjective that compares in the excerpt on page 367.

5.6 Irregular Adjectives That Compare

Some adjectives that compare are irregular. They are not formed by adding -er or -est. Two common irregular adjectives are *good* and *bad*.

	COMPARE TWO NOUNS	COMPARE THREE OR MORE NOUNS
good	better	best
bad	worse	worst

A *good* snack is a cookie.

Cheese is a *better* snack than candy. (compares two nouns)

The *best* snack of all is fruit. (compares three or more nouns)

Which sentence uses an irregular adjective that compares?

A A tasty fruit for a snack is an apple.

B My favorite fruit is grapes.

C The best fruit for lunch is a pear.

You are right if you said sentence C. *Best* is part of the irregular adjective *good*.

Which choice correctly completes the sentence?

The purple jelly bean tastes even (worse worst) than the yellow jelly bean.

The correct answer is *worse*. It is used to compare two things. Note that *better* and *worse* are often used with *than*.

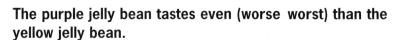

EXERCISE 1 Choose the correct adjective to complete each sentence.

1. Water is a (good better) drink than lemonade.

2. Fruit smoothies are (good better) for you than soda.

3. Potato chips are a (worse worst) snack than carrots.

4. Apples are the (better best) snack of all.

5. A (good best) snack is raisins and celery.

6. This is the (bad worst) pizza I've ever eaten.

7. Candy is (bad worst) for your teeth.

8. Fried foods are (worse worst) for your health than grilled foods.

EXERCISE 2 Use *good, better,* or *best* to complete each sentence.

1. _____ food contributes to a person's health.

2. Strawberry is the _____ ice cream flavor.

3. Chocolate pudding is _____ than vanilla.

4. The runner gave his _____ effort.

5. We had a _____ time at the fair.

6. Fairs are _____ than zoos.

7. Dogs are _____ than cats.

EXERCISE 3 Use *bad, worse,* or *worst* to complete each sentence.

1. I have the _____ cold I've ever had.

2. I am _____ today than yesterday.

3. She has the _____ luck of all.

4. Ken was in trouble for his _____ behavior.

5. His project was _____ than mine.

6. The weather today is _____ than yesterday.

7. The pool was closed during _____ weather.

APPLY IT NOW

Think about something you do regularly. Write three sentences about it. Use an adjective that compares in each sentence. Choose from *good, better, best, bad, worse,* and *worst*.

Example:

The best sport at school is soccer.

I am a worse player than Myra.

5.7 Adjectives That Tell How Many

Adjectives can tell how many or about how many.

Adjectives that tell how many include numbers, such as *one, two, five, ninety.*

> Derek has *two* brothers and *one* sister.
> I'm taking *four* classes this semester.
> *Sixteen* people are coming to the party.

Adjectives also include words that tell numerical order; for example, *first, second, fifth, ninetieth.*

> Her house is the *third* one on the right.
> The alarm sounded for the *second* time.
> That was my *fourth* trip to California.

Some adjectives tell about how many; for example, *few, several, many, some.* They do not tell exact numbers.

> **Exactly how many**   *Six* hikers went down into the canyon today.
> **About how many**   *Several* people went to the visitor's center to see the film.

Which sentence has an adjective that tells about how many?

> A   The Grand Canyon is in Arizona.
> B   Some trails are quite steep.
> C   The canyon is a natural wonder.

You are right if you said sentence B. The adjective *Some* tells about how many trails. *Some* is not an exact amount.

EXERCISE 1 Find the adjectives. Tell whether each tells about how many or exactly how many.

1. many tourists
2. ten mules
3. third trail
4. some rocks

5. few people
6. twenty miles
7. several schools
8. two guides

EXERCISE 2 Find the adjective that tells how many in each sentence. Tell whether the adjective tells about how many or exactly how many.

1. Ten people were in our tour group to the Grand Canyon.
2. I became friendly with two students from Mexico.
3. Many visitors to the canyon make the hike.
4. Some visitors prefer to ride on mules.
5. The first settlers in the area were the Pueblo.
6. Some Native Americans still live in the area.
7. My family has made a few trips to the Grand Canyon.
8. Many friends of mine have also visited there.
9. It took us several hours to make the hike.
10. We spent three nights camping in the Grand Canyon.
11. My cousin's trip through the Grand Canyon lasted four days.
12. Millions of people see the Grand Canyon every year.
13. The Grand Canyon is one mile deep in places.
14. There are some mountain lions in the park.

Grand Canyon

EXERCISE 3 Complete each sentence with an adjective that tells how many. Use the directions in parentheses.

1. _____ students have visited the Grand Canyon. (exactly how many)
2. We spent _____ days at the canyon. (exactly how many)
3. We saw _____ sunrises over the Grand Canyon. (exactly how many)
4. Our family took _____ photos. (about how many)
5. There were _____ tourists in the canyon. (about how many)

APPLY IT NOW

Write four sentences to tell about an adventure you have had or would like to have. Use adjectives that tell how many in each sentence.
Example:
I swam in a lake that was <u>twenty</u> feet deep.

5.8 Articles

The, an, and *a* point out nouns. They are called **articles.**

I saw *an* airplane in *a* museum.
There were many old airplanes in *the* museum.

- *A* and *an* point out any one of a class of people, places, or things. This sentence tells about one of several guides.

  A guide took us around and told us interesting facts.

- Use *a* before a word that begins with a consonant sound.

  a glider   a plane   a uniform

- Use *an* before a word that begins with a vowel sound.

  an airplane   an inspection   an hour

- *The* points out a specific person, place, or thing. This sentence tells about one specific museum.

  The aircraft museum was interesting.

Which one of these sentences uses an article?

A **My family flew to Orlando.**
B **Our flight was on time.**
C **An attendant showed us to our seats.**

You are right if you said sentence C. *An* is an article. Because *attendant* begins with a vowel sound, the article *an* is used.

EXERCISE 1 Find all the articles in each sentence.

1. Orville and Wilbur Wright were the first inventors to make a successful flight in an airplane.
2. First they tested a glider at Kitty Hawk, North Carolina.
3. The early test flights failed.
4. They finally flew a glider they could control.
5. The Wright brothers were in a race to build a powered aircraft.

6. In 1903 the Wright brothers successfully flew an aircraft that had an engine.

7. Someone took a picture of the first flight, but it received little attention.

8. Eventually, someone wrote an article about the flight.

EXERCISE 2 Add *a* or *an* before each noun.

1. __an__ event
2. __a__ pilot
3. __an__ adventure
4. __a__ wing
5. __a__ runway

6. __a__ hangar
7. __an__ aisle
8. __a__ passenger
9. __a__ helicopter
10. __an__ instrument

EXERCISE 3 Choose the correct articles to complete the sentences.

1. Working with machines was (a an) interest of (a the) Wright brothers.

2. Orville and Wilbur worked to build (an a) airplane with (a an) engine.

3. They spent much time studying (a the) flight of birds.

4. They built (a an) wind tunnel to test different designs of wings.

5. (The A) first flight of the Wright brothers lasted only 12 seconds.

6. But it was (a an) amazing moment in history.

7. After (a the) first flight, the Wright brothers kept experimenting.

8. (An The) plane the Wright brothers used in their first flight is at (an the) National Air and Space Museum in Washington, D.C.

APPLY IT NOW

Have you flown on a plane, been to an airport, or seen a plane in the sky? Write five sentences about airplanes. Underline each article you use.
Example:
I saw <u>an</u> airplane with <u>a</u> propeller.

5.9 Demonstrative Adjectives

This, that, these, and *those* are called **demonstrative adjectives.**
They point out or tell about a specific person, place, or thing.

SINGULAR

Near: *This* swim mask fits me.
Far away: *That* swim mask is too big.

PLURAL

Near: *These* swim masks are on sale.
Far away: *Those* swim masks are too costly.

This and *these* point out something that is near. *That* and *those*
point out something that is farther away.

Which sentence has a demonstrative adjective?

A The locker room is to the left of the pool.

B My swimming gear is in this bag.

C I have a new swim mask.

You are right if you said sentence B. *This* tells
about a bag that is nearby.

EXERCISE 1 Add *this* or *these* to show that
the things are near.

1. _This_ pool
2. _These_ backpacks
3. _These_ keys
4. _This_ sweater
5. _These_ chairs
6. _This_ air mattress

EXERCISE 2 Add *that* or *those* to show that the things are
far away.

1. _That_ swimsuit
2. _____ kickboard
3. _____ lanes
4. _____ sunglasses
5. _____ diving board
6. _____ goggles

EXERCISE 3 Find the demonstrative adjective in each sentence. Tell whether the adjective tells about something that is near or far away.

1. This swimming pool is deep.
2. Those children are having fun.
3. These flippers are mine.
4. Is that towel yours?
5. Those flip-flops are Sarah's.
6. Mike is playing with that pool float.
7. Give me that swim vest.
8. I like these mermaid swim fins.
9. Come and sit down under this umbrella.
10. Don't slip on that puddle of water.

EXERCISE 4 Complete each sentence with a demonstrative adjective. Use the directions in parentheses to tell whether the thing is near or far away.

1. _____ part of the pool is fairly deep. (near)
2. _____ children are great swimmers. (far)
3. _____ man is my swimming teacher. (far)
4. _____ shoes are mine. (near)
5. Use _____ red towel. (near)
6. _____ beach ball is Jackie's. (far)
7. Please hand me _____ swim goggles. (far)
8. Is _____ diving ring yours? (near)
9. _____ bottles of sunscreen are full. (near)
10. _____ sun hat is for my baby sister. (near)

APPLY IT NOW

Write five sentences describing the people and things at a beach or swimming pool. Use a demonstrative adjective in each sentence.
Example:
That woman is the lifeguard.
These shells are orange.

5.10 **Proper Adjectives**

A proper noun names a particular person, place, or thing. Some adjectives are formed from proper nouns. These adjectives are called **proper adjectives.** A proper adjective always begins with a capital letter.

> **The world's largest country is** *China.* (proper noun)
>
> **I like to eat** *Chinese* **food.** (proper adjective)

Here are some proper nouns and their proper adjectives.

PROPER NOUN	PROPER ADJECTIVE
Mexico	Mexican
Canada	Canadian
Spain	Spanish
Japan	Japanese

Which of these word groups include a proper adjective?

   A the trip to Japan

   B a Polish dish

   C a Vietnamese doll

You're right if you said B and C. *Polish* and *Vietnamese* are proper adjectives. They are formed from the proper nouns *Poland* and *Vietnam.*

EXERCISE 1 Choose the proper adjective from each pair of words.

1. America	American	**4.** Jamaica	Jamaican
2. Romania	Romanian	**5.** Texan	Texas
3. Chilean	Chile	**6.** Korean	Korea

Moai statues on Easter Island (Chile)

EXERCISE 2 Find the proper adjective in each sentence. Then tell the noun the adjective describes.

1. My mom has a Swiss watch.
2. Have you ever had French cheese?
3. That Italian car is fast!
4. Diego Rivera was a famous Mexican artist.
5. My grandparents went on a trip to see the Alaskan coast.
6. The Egyptian pyramids are amazing.
7. Russian winters are very cold.
8. Portuguese beaches are very beautiful.
9. The handmade Peruvian sweaters were colorful.
10. Shish kebab is a Turkish food.
11. Laila is a Moroccan name.
12. A kangaroo is an Australian animal.

EXERCISE 3 Complete each sentence with the proper adjective for the proper noun in parentheses. Use a dictionary if you need help.

1. I have a _____ e-mail pal. (Russia)
2. The _____ subcontinent is huge. (India)
3. How rare is a _____ tiger? (Siberia)
4. He reads about _____ history. (Iceland)
5. An _____ sweater makes a nice gift. (Ireland)
6. I like _____ food. (Italy)
7. She is fascinated by _____ culture. (Greece)
8. Tigers are _____ animals. (Asia)
9. We ate _____ meatballs. (Sweden)
10. Trevor visited a _____ rain forest. (Brazil)

Vases from Greece

APPLY IT NOW

Write four sentences about special things from other countries.
Example:
Pierogi are a kind of Polish dumpling.
Tomie dePaola's book retells an Italian tale.

Tech Tip With an adult, find facts about countries online.

Adjectives • 129

5.11 Nouns Used as Adjectives

Sometimes a noun can be used as an adjective. When two nouns are used together, the first noun often acts as an adjective. It tells more about the second noun.

All the *strawberry* jam is gone.

Put it on our *grocery* list.

In these sentences the nouns *strawberry* and *grocery* act as adjectives. *Strawberry* tells more about *jam. Grocery* tells more about *list.*

What are the two nouns in this sentence? Which noun acts as an adjective?

I often go to the hobby shop.

You are right if you said *hobby* and *shop* are nouns. *Hobby* acts as an adjective. It tells more about *shop.*

Which sentence has a noun that acts as an adjective?

A It has hundreds of model planes.

B I like to build miniature airplanes.

C My dad bought me a new kit.

You are right if you said sentence A. *Model* tells more about the noun *planes.*

EXERCISE 1 Tell if the underlined word is used as a noun or as an adjective.

1. We go on a <u>class</u> trip every year.
2. This year our <u>class</u> is going to a farm.
3. The farm has an <u>apple</u> orchard.
4. I picked an <u>apple</u> from a tree and ate it.
5. We went to a <u>pumpkin</u> patch.
6. We each got a <u>pumpkin</u> to take home.
7. A <u>bus</u> took us back to school.
8. We sang during the <u>bus</u> trip.

EXERCISE 2 Find all the nouns in each sentence. Tell which noun acts as an adjective.

1. Our school has many student activities.
2. There is a computer lab.
3. My math teacher runs it.
4. I take music lessons after school.
5. We have an art fair in the spring.
6. We also have a science fair.
7. In the fall we go on a class trip.
8. Once we went to the city aquarium.
9. Our history teacher gives us a lot of homework.
10. He wants to try out for the baseball team.

EXERCISE 3 Write six phrases by using the nouns in Group A as adjectives before the nouns in Group B.

EXAMPLE   movie star

Group A	Group B	
movie	holder	star
apple	pie	theater
pencil	sharpener	tree

EXERCISE 4 Write two sentences with each word. Use it once as a noun and once as an adjective. Tell how you used the word in each sentence.

1. spring
2. library
3. garden
4. orange
5. mud

APPLY IT NOW

Look around your classroom. What do you see? Make a list of noun pairs in which the first noun acts as an adjective.
Example: trash can
          chalkboard eraser
          math book

Adjective Review

5.1 Find the adjective that describes a noun in each sentence.

1. Poodles are fluffy dogs.
2. The white dog was the color of a cloud.
3. She wore a sparkly collar.
4. The black poodle is barking.
5. My dog sleeps near the sunny window.

5.2 In each sentence, find the descriptive adjective. Tell the noun it describes.

6. A rusty plow sat in the field.
7. The old rooster crowed.
8. The farmer planted an early crop.
9. Sweet corn grows in rows.
10. Cows grazed by the red barn.

5.3 In each sentence, find the adjective used as a subject complement. Tell the noun it describes.

11. Geodes are interesting.
12. These rocks are hollow, with crystals inside.
13. Geodes are dull on the outside.
14. The inside of a geode is glittery.
15. Tanya is careful with her geode collection.

5.4 In each sentence, find the adjectives used as compound subject complements.

16. Many ladybugs are red or orange.
17. Their backs are spotted or unspotted.
18. The spots are usually black and round.
19. A ladybug is useful and valuable in gardens.
20. A gardener is lucky and thankful for ladybugs.

5.5 Find the adjective that compares in each sentence.

21. Wear the warmest coat you have.
22. The temperatures will be colder today than yesterday.
23. That is the longest scarf I have ever seen.
24. It is the windiest day of the year.
25. Her hat is cuter than mine.

5.6 Use *good, better,* or *best* to complete each sentence.

26. Chris and I had a _____ time at the park.
27. He thinks the slides are _____ than the swings.
28. The monkey bars are _____ of all.

Use *bad, worse,* or *worst* to complete each sentence.

29. There was a _____ storm last night.

30. The storm last April was the _____ our state has ever had.

5.7 Find the adjectives that tell how many in each sentence. Tell if the adjective tells exactly how many or about how many.

31. Many people were waiting for the bus.

32. Two buses arrived.

33. Most seats were taken.

34. The bus drove twenty blocks to the train station.

35. Some passengers got off the bus there.

5.8 Find all the articles in each sentence.

36. The rainy days kept the children inside.

37. Let's find a project we can work on.

38. We used the magazines and a glue stick to make a collage.

39. Gilda learned how to make collages in an art class.

40. Mom hung the collages on the refrigerator.

5.9 Find the demonstrative adjective in each sentence.

41. This truck is full of boxes.

42. Those movers must be tired from the heavy lifting.

43. Take these boxes upstairs.

44. The dishes are in that box.

45. Those plates are broken.

5.10 Find the proper adjective in each sentence. Name the noun the adjective describes.

46. My family took a European vacation.

47. We ate German sausages.

48. We drove through the French countryside.

49. We visited many Italian towns.

50. We saw old Roman ruins.

5.11 Find the noun that acts as an adjective in each sentence.

51. Dad made beef stew.

52. What kind of salad dressing do you like?

53. Use the can opener to open the soup.

54. I put apple butter on bread.

55. Please hand me the pepper mill.

Tech Tip Go to www.voyagesinenglish.com for more activities.

Adjective Challenge

EXERCISE 1 **Read the paragraph and answer the questions.**

1. Some places on Earth are cold, and some places are hot.
2. The North Pole is one of the coldest spots on Earth. 3. This frozen place is home to polar bears, not people. 4. As you move south toward the equator, the climate becomes warmer. 5. You begin to see many trees, green grass, and colorful flowers. 6. As you travel south from the equator, temperatures get cooler again. 7. Finally, you get to the South Pole in Antarctica. 8. The South Pole is even colder than the North Pole. 9. Antarctic temperatures are icy.
10. They go down to 129 degrees below zero!

1. In sentence 1 find the adjectives that tell about how many.
2. In sentence 1 what are the two descriptive adjectives?
3. In sentence 2 find an adjective that compares.
4. In sentence 3 does the adjective *this* refer to one place or more than one place?
5. In sentence 5 find three adjectives. Which two are descriptive adjectives?
6. In sentence 7 find an article.
7. In sentence 8 find the adjective that compares.
8. In sentence 9 find the subject complement.
9. Find the proper adjective in the paragraph.

EXERCISE 2 **Write a five-sentence paragraph about one of the hottest places on Earth, such as the equator or a desert. Use at least four different kinds of adjectives.**

Adverbs and Conjunctions

6.1 Adverbs

An **adverb** tells more about a verb. Some adverbs tell when, where, or how something happens. Many adverbs end in *ly*.

When: I walked in the park *today*.

Where: The leaves were colorful *there*.

How: I *happily* gathered some red leaves.

In the first sentence, *today* tells when about the verb *walked*. In the second sentence, *there* tells where about the verb *were*. In the third sentence, *happily* tells how about the verb *gathered*.

Each of these sentences has an adverb. Can you find it?

A We listen for the weather report daily.

B We go outside in warm clothes.

C We all listen carefully.

You're right if you said *daily, outside,* and *carefully. Daily* tells when. *Outside* tells where, and *carefully* tells how.

Study this list of common adverbs.

WHEN	WHERE	HOW
yesterday	far	quickly
always	nearby	noisily
soon	upstairs	easily
first	up	nervously
last	beneath	slowly
never	there	anxiously
sometimes	inside	colorfully

EXERCISE 1 Find the adverb in each sentence.

1. In the fall the weather suddenly gets cool.

2. Colorful fall leaves appear everywhere.

3. They glow brilliantly in the warm sun.

4. We are studying plants now in class.

5. In the fall, trees slowly stop making chlorophyll.

6. Then the green color disappears from their leaves.

7. The colors yellow and orange were always in the leaves.

8. Without the green, we see the other colors clearly.

EXERCISE 2 Complete each sentence with an adverb from the word box.

| carefully | inside | later | outside | yesterday |

1. We did an experiment on leaf color _____ in class.

2. We went _____ and got some green leaves and crushed them.

3. We put the leaves and some rubbing alcohol _____ a jar.

4. We _____ put a piece of special filter paper into the jar.

5. _____ we looked at the strip and saw the colors green, yellow, and orange.

EXERCISE 3 Complete each sentence with an adverb. Have the adverb tell what is in parentheses.

1. Our class was assigned a science project _____. (when)

2. Mr. Gonzalez _____ showed us pictures of trees common in our area. (when)

3. We studied them _____. (how)

4. Today our class went _____. (where)

5. We _____ walked to the park. (how)

6. _____ we looked for trees. (where)

7. We _____ found four common types of trees. (how)

8. We _____ recognized the trees by their leaves. (how)

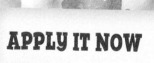

APPLY IT NOW

Write five sentences about a recent class project or field trip. Use at least one adverb in each sentence. Then underline all the adverbs.

6.2 Adverbs That Tell When or How Often

An adverb tells more about a verb. Some adverbs tell when or how often something happens.

When: **Our teacher read a great story** *yesterday*.

How often: **He** *always* **reads after lunch.**

Here are some adverbs that tell when or how often.

always	ever	never	then
again	first	now	today
after	forever	often	tomorrow
before	frequently	sometimes	weekly
early	later	soon	yesterday

Which of these sentences have adverbs that tell when?

A Mr. Marsh read us a story about Harriet Tubman.

B Before I did not know much about her.

C Now I know some facts about her life.

You are right if you said sentence B and sentence C. *Before* and *now* are adverbs that tell when.

EXERCISE 1 Find the adverb or adverbs that tells when or how often in each sentence.

1. I have often heard stories about Harriet Tubman.

2. First, she was a slave.

3. Then she escaped to the North.

4. She was soon traveling to the South and leading slaves to freedom in the North.

5. She went to the South again and again.

6. She never lost any of the hundreds of slaves she guided.

7. Later she campaigned for women's rights.

8. We now consider her a great hero.

Harriet Tubman

EXERCISE 2 Complete each sentence with an adverb from the word box that tells when.

| later | now | today | yesterday | tomorrow |

1. _____ I looked for a book on Harriet Tubman at the library.
2. I read the book _____.
3. I _____ know a lot about Harriet Tubman.
4. _____ I will write a report on what I learned.
5. I will present my report to class _____.

EXERCISE 3 Complete each sentence with an adverb that tells when or how often.

1. Sojourner Truth was _____ a slave, and her original name was Isabella.
2. _____ escaping to freedom, Isabella moved to New York City.
3. She _____ changed her name to Sojourner Truth.
4. Sojourner _____ spoke at antislavery meetings.
5. People _____ came to hear her powerful words.
6. Sojourner _____ decided to be a traveling preacher.
7. We _____ remember her as a strong voice against slavery and for women's rights.

EXERCISE 4 Complete each sentence with an adverb that tells how often.

1. I _____ read biographies.
2. I _____ go to the library.
3. I _____ watch history programs on TV.
4. I _____ read fiction books.

APPLY IT NOW

Look at the list of adverbs on page 138 that tell when or how often. Choose five adverbs and write a sentence using each one. Underline the adverbs you use.

Grammar in Action. Find the adverb in the first sentence on page 401. Does it tell when or how often?

6.3 Adverbs That Tell Where

Some adverbs tell where something takes place. These adverbs answer the question *where*.

> **Where:** **The bear scampered** *inside*.
>
> **We stayed** *there* **and watched it go** *in* **and** *out*.

Here are some adverbs that tell where.

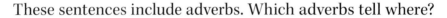

above	downstairs	inside
alongside	everywhere	nearby
away	far	nowhere
back	farther	out
backward	forward	outside
below	here	there
down	in	up

These sentences include adverbs. Which adverbs tell where?

> **The leaves fell swiftly down after the storm.**
>
> **The hawk came back to the nest yesterday.**

Did you choose *down* and *back*? You are right. *Down* and *back* are adverbs that tell where. *Swiftly* is an adverb that tells how, and *yesterday* is an adverb that tells when.

EXERCISE 1 **Find the adverb that tells where in each sentence.**

1. We rode everywhere in the zoo on a tram.
2. The guide told us to look up.
3. We moved forward to get a closer look at the great apes.
4. A mother panda with a baby slept nearby.
5. Then we heard a noise above.
6. A flock of noisy geese flew away.
7. Did they live here at the zoo?
8. No, the geese just come here to get food.

9. If you look <u>down</u>, you can see two bear cubs.

10. The bear stayed <u>inside</u>.

11. I think the elephants are <u>there</u>.

12. The tigers were walking <u>outside</u>.

13. We jumped <u>back</u> when the lion roared.

14. The park attendant was pointing <u>backward</u>.

EXERCISE 2 Complete each sentence with an adverb from the word box that tells where.

above	back	below	far	outside

1. We stayed <u>outside</u> all day.

2. We hiked <u>far</u>.

3. We could see the mountaintop <u>above</u>.

4. <u>below</u> we could view the green valley and the rivers.

5. We didn't want to come <u>back</u> home.

EXERCISE 3 Complete each sentence with an adverb that tells where.

1. My family and I often go to the zoo <u>nearby</u>.

2. We always have a good time <u>outside</u>.

3. Sometimes we watch the monkeys <u>above</u>.

4. We took a chairlift <u>up</u> the African area.

5. Our chairlift went _____.

6. _____ we saw lions, zebras, and wildebeest.

7. Dad rented a canoe, and we all got _____.

8. Soon the canoe went _____ the river.

9. We saw dingoes _____ the river bank.

10. The river took us _____ in the zoo.

APPLY IT NOW

Choose one of these places: amusement park, mall, or library. Then write four sentences about it, using adverbs from the list on page 140.

Grammar in Action ✏ Find the adverb that tells where in the second sentence of the second paragraph on page 401.

6.4 Adverbs That Tell How

Some adverbs tell how an action takes place. These adverbs answer the question *how*.

How: **My pizza maker rolls out the dough *fast*.**

My mother makes pancakes *expertly*.

Here are some other adverbs that tell how.

carefully	gently	kindly	sadly
cleverly	gingerly	lightly	safely
clumsily	gracefully	loudly	slyly
coolly	happily	quickly	softly
frivolously	hard	quietly	sweetly

These sentences include adverbs. Which adverbs tell how?

The waiter always carries the dishes carefully.

The dishwasher here operates noisily.

Did you choose *carefully* and *noisily*? You are right. *Always* is an adverb that tells when, and *here* is an adverb that tells where.

EXERCISE 1 Find the adverb that tells how in each sentence.

1. The day started <u>perfectly</u>.
2. Both mom and dad were sleeping <u>peacefully</u>.
3. I crept <u>noiselessly</u> into the kitchen.
4. The sun was rising <u>slowly</u>.
5. I <u>carefully</u> stirred the batter for the pancakes.
6. My sister and I worked <u>quietly</u>.
7. We <u>eagerly</u> went upstairs to wake our parents.
8. Our parents ate their surprise breakfast <u>happily</u>.
9. We spoke <u>softly</u> so as not to wake up our younger brother.
10. We <u>quickly</u> ate all the pancakes.

EXERCISE 2 Find the adverb in Column B that best answers the question in Column A. Write your answer as a sentence.

EXAMPLE **How does a baby sleep?**
A baby sleeps peacefully.

In 1876 Maria Spelterini crossed the gorge below Niagara Falls on a tightrope, blindfolded, and with weights attached to her feet.

Column A   Column B

C **1.** How does a tightrope walker walk?   loudly

G **2.** How does a ballerina dance?   fast

F **3.** How does a jet plane fly?   gracefully

S **4.** How do turtles walk?   carefully

L **5.** How does a band play?   slowly

EXERCISE 3 Complete each sentence with an adverb from the word box that tells how.

softly	safely	gently	~~fast~~	~~sadly~~
quickly	loudly	frivolously	sweetly	~~cleverly~~

1. I _gently_ placed the locket in the jewelry box.
2. Jamie called _loudly_ to wake up the campers.
3. Martine _quickly_ spent her entire allowance on baseball cards.
4. The pilot _sadly_ landed the damaged plane in a nearby field.
5. When the fire drill started, everyone _frivolously_ left the classroom.
6. Joanie _sweetly_ waved good-bye to her friends and got on the bus.
7. The yellow bird sang _softly_.
8. My brother and I cleaned the room _fast_.
9. The fox _cleverly_ outwitted the crow.
10. The rain fell _gently_ on the spring flowers.

APPLY IT NOW

Make a list of things you like to do. Think of one or more adverbs that tell how you do each thing. Write four sentences with those adverbs.
Example:
I play the piano.
I play loudly, fast, and happily.

Tech Tip   Make a PowerPoint slide with art for each sentence.

6.5 Negative Words

A negative idea is formed in several ways.

- Add *not* to the verb.
- Add *not* as part of a contraction: *didn't, can't, won't.*
- Add *never* before the verb.

Because these words tell more about verbs, they are adverbs. Study these negative sentences.

The cage *was not* clean.

She *didn't* feed the canary.

She *never* feeds the class pet.

Which of these sentences expresses a negative idea?

A I never let my cat outside.

B She is always in the house.

If you chose sentence A, you are right. Sentence A uses *never.*

Be careful to use only one negative word in a sentence. Is this sentence correct? Why or why not?

I don't never forget to walk my dog.

The sentence is incorrect because it has two negative words: *don't* and *never.* To correct it, remove one of the negative words: *I don't forget to walk my dog* or *I never forget to walk my dog.*

EXERCISE 1 Find the negative word in each sentence.

1. Wild animals never make good pets.
2. People can't provide a good home for a tiger.
3. A yard isn't big enough for animals that like to roam.
4. Even a gentle wild animal should not be kept as a pet.
5. Parents shouldn't let young children play with wild animals.

EXERCISE 2 Rewrite each sentence that incorrectly expresses a negative idea. Not all sentences have errors.

1. My parents won't never let me have a pet.
2. They don't like cats.
3. They don't never want to walk a dog.
4. I can't even get a bird.
5. I don't want a goldfish.
6. It isn't no trouble to care for a bird.
7. My sister doesn't want no dog.
8. We don't have no room in our house.
9. We have no garden or yard.
10. My mother didn't have no pets as a child.
11. My father never had pets either.
12. I never pass a pet shop without looking at the dogs.
13. I didn't see no black cats in the pet shop.
14. I haven't given up on my wish for a pet.

EXERCISE 3 Rewrite each sentence so that it expresses a negative idea.

1. Snakes are my favorite animals.
2. I like the way they move.
3. For my parents a boa is a good choice for a pet.
4. Mom really does like most reptiles.
5. My sister is scared of snakes.
6. Some snakes are poisonous.
7. I have seen a boa at the zoo.
8. Many people fear snakes.
9. Some owners feed frogs to their snakes.
10. Snakes get sick often.

APPLY IT NOW

Write five negative sentences about animals that should not be kept as pets.

Grammar in Action. Find the two negative words in the page 408 excerpt.

6.6 *Good and Well*

Good is an adjective that describes a noun. It tells what kind. *Well* is an adverb that tells about a verb. It tells how. Be careful to use *good* and *well* correctly.

Adjective:	We saw a *good* game last night.
	Our family had *good* seats in the front row.
Adverb:	Ryan hit the ball *well*.
	The home team played *well*.

Tell why *good* and *well* are used correctly in these sentences.

A The new coach is good.

B He works well with young players.

In sentence A *good* is an adjective. It is a subject complement that tells more about the noun *coach*. In sentence B *well* is an adverb that tells how he works.

Which word completes the sentence correctly?

We could see (good well) from our seats.

You are correct if you chose *well*. *Well* is an adverb that describes the verb *see*.

EXERCISE 1 Add *good* or *well* to each group of words.

> EXAMPLE   can spell *well*
> *good* grades

1. swimming teachers
2. swimmers
3. can swim
4. does dive
5. basketball players
6. can dribble
7. plays basketball
8. point guards

EXERCISE 2 Complete each sentence with *good* or *well*.

1. a. The new catcher is quite __good__.

   b. She has been playing __well__ all season.

2. a. Brad doesn't bat very __well__.

   b. That's OK because he's a __good__ pitcher.

3. a. Your field has __good__ seats.

   b. Everyone has a __good__ view of home plate.

   c. Yes, everyone speaks __well__ of it.

4. a. Baseball is a __good__ game.

   b. You need to throw, catch, bat, and run to play it __well__.

5. a. The shortstop is a __good__ fielder.

   b. Does she bat __well__?

   c. She was hitting __well__ until she hurt her shoulder.

6. a. The center fielder made a __good__ catch.

   b. Then he made a __good__ throw to home plate.

   c. It's fun to see someone play __well__.

7. a. The team doesn't play __well__ on the road.

   b. They played __good__ last week, however.

8. a. Mark throws the ball __well__.

   b. I think that he would be a __good__ pitcher.

EXERCISE 3 Use each word in a sentence with *good* or *well*.

1. sing   **3.** plays   **5.** draw

2. dancer   **4.** reader   **6.** musician

APPLY IT NOW

Write four sentences about your schoolwork. Use *good* in two sentences and *well* in two sentences.

6.7 *To, Too, and Two*

To, too, and *two* sound alike. Each word means something different, however. Be careful to use the words correctly.

- *To* means "in the direction of" or "until."
- *Too* means "also" or "more than enough."
- *Two* means "the number 2."

To: Chickadees come *to* the bird feeder from dawn *to* dusk.

Too: Squirrels come *too.* They eat way *too* much seed.

Two: Yesterday I saw *two* blue jays.

Can the same word complete each of these sentences? Why or why not?

A Bees fly _____ the hive.

B There are _____ kinds of bees—social bees and solitary bees.

C Sometimes a hive has _____ many bees.

Each sentence needs a different word to make sense. Sentence A needs *to,* sentence B needs *two,* and sentence C needs *too.*

EXERCISE 1 Choose the word from the word box for each definition.

to	too	two

1. in the direction of
2. more than enough
3. also
4. toward a place
5. more than one
6. until

EXERCISE 2 Choose the word that correctly completes each sentence.

1. Chris and I went (to two) the park.
2. We saw butterflies, and we saw bees (to too).
3. The bees flew (to two) the pretty spring flowers.
4. The gardener spoke to the (too two) of us.
5. She gave interesting information about bees (to two) us.
6. She told us about the flowers (to too).
7. It got (to too) cold for us to stay in the park very long.

Honeybees carry pollen
on their back legs.

EXERCISE 3 Complete each sentence with *to*, *too*, or *two*.

1. There are _____ groups of honey bees in a hive—worker bees and drones—as well as a queen.
2. Worker bees leave the hive and fly _____ flowers.
3. They gather nectar and carry it back _____ the hive.
4. If there are _____ many bees, the queen stops laying eggs.
5. The queen and some workers move _____ a new place.
6. Bees can sting one another _____ death.
7. Some people can die from bee stings _____.
8. Bees make _____ important products—honey and beeswax.
9. Bees collect nectar from morning _____ night.
10. Nectar from _____ million flowers makes one pound of honey.
11. Bees are important in pollination _____.
12. They carry pollen from one flower _____ another.
13. The queen may live three _____ five years.
14. Settlers from Europe brought bees _____ North America in the 17th century.

APPLY IT NOW

Choose a subject from the list below. Write three sentences about it, using *to*, *too*, and *two*.

school	fishing
video games	reading
horses	skateboards
a mall	reptiles

6.8 *Their and There*

Their and *there* sound alike. Each word means something different, however. Be careful to use the two words correctly.

- *Their* tells who owns something. *Their* is an adjective.
- *There* usually means "in that place." *There* is an adverb.

Their: **The children let go of *their* balloons.**
(*Their* tells that the children own the balloons.)

There: **We went *there* to watch the many balloons.**
(*There* tells where we went.)

Can the same word complete each sentence? Why or why not?

A _____ **paintings are hanging in the library.**

B **Mine is** _____, **near the door.**

Each sentence needs a different word to make sense. Sentence A needs *their* to show whose paintings are hanging. Sentence B needs *there* to show where the speaker's painting is.

EXERCISE 1 Add *their* or *there* to complete a word group that makes sense.

1. crayons
2. over
3. scissors and tape
4. up
5. scrap paper
6. standing
7. art projects
8. stay
9. drawings
10. go
11. mural
12. sit

EXERCISE 2 Choose the correct word or words to complete each sentence.

1. The children's art area is (their there).
2. The art supplies are kept (their there).
3. (Their There) art supplies include paints and markers.
4. You can see (their there) artwork on the walls.
5. Look (their there) on the walls.
6. Those are (their there) watercolor pictures of flowers.
7. Do you see that big blossom (their there)?
8. (Their There) pictures are very colorful.
9. Which of (their there) drawings do you like best?
10. I like (their there) artwork over (their there).

EXERCISE 3 Complete each sentence with *their* or *there*.

1. The art teacher put the paint jars _____.
2. The young children will work on _____ projects.
3. They will make a big mess _____.
4. _____ painting skills aren't too good.
5. They will get paint on _____ clothes.
6. They can use the smocks hanging _____.
7. They can wash the paint off _____ faces.
8. Some paint remained on the wall _____.
9. I don't really mind _____ messes.
10. _____ paintings are such fun to look at.
11. We can hang the paintings over _____.
12. Put the paintbrushes _____.
13. The children are proud of _____ work.
14. _____ creativity is amazing.

APPLY IT NOW

Write four sentences about another grade or class in your school. Use *their* in two sentences and *there* in two sentences.

6.9 Coordinating Conjunctions

A **coordinating conjunction** joins two words or groups of words. The words *and, but,* and *or* are coordinating conjunctions. Use them when you want to join words or groups of words that are similar.

And: Canaries *and* parakeets are good pets.

But: My parakeet sings *but* does not talk.

Or: Put the cage near a window *or* on a shelf.

In these sentences the conjunctions join similar words or groups of words: *canaries* and *parakeets, sings* but *does talk, near a window* or *on a shelf.*

These sentences have coordinating conjunctions. What do the conjunctions join?

A Give your pet fresh food and clean water.

B My dog often jumps and licks my face.

C Our cat is usually sleeping in the yard or on the porch.

D Our cat is independent but cute.

E My dog likes to sleep in my bed or on the sofa.

F Our cat sometimes scratches but rarely bites.

In sentence A *and* connects *fresh food* and *clean water.*
In sentence B *and* connects *jumps* and *licks.*
In sentence C *or* connects *in the yard* and *on the porch.*
In sentence D *but* connects *independent* and *cute.*
In sentence E *or* connects *in my bed* and *on the sofa.*
In sentence F *but* connects *sometimes scratches* and *rarely bites.*

EXERCISE 1 Find the coordinating conjunction in each sentence.

1. Baby otters are called cubs or pups.

2. Otters can live in fresh water or in the ocean.

3. Otters are good swimmers and divers.

4. They hold and toss small objects.

Sea otter pup with mother

Sea otter

5. Otters eat fish or shellfish.

6. They also sometimes eat frogs or snakes.

7. Otters often play and romp.

8. They slide down muddy slopes and icy riverbanks.

9. I think otters are funny-looking but cute.

EXERCISE 2 Find the coordinating conjunction in each sentence. Name the words or groups of words that the conjunction joins.

1. Otters have thick fur but no layer of fat.

2. Otters and birds are among the few animals that use tools.

3. Otters use rocks or other small objects as tools.

4. They get and open shellfish with the tools.

5. Oil spills and pollution are dangers to otters.

6. All otters have slim bodies and webbed claws.

7. You can see otters in zoos or nature centers.

EXERCISE 3 Complete each sentence with a coordinating conjunction from the word box that makes sense.

and	but	or

1. Beavers have long front teeth _____ a flat tail.

2. Beavers build dams _____ lodges to store food.

3. Beavers live in water _____ don't eat fish.

4. Beavers cut down _____ eat trees.

5. Otters are not found in Australia _____ Antarctica.

6. Otters usually eat fish _____ will also eat crayfish and crabs.

Beavers

APPLY IT NOW

Choose an animal common to your area. Write three sentences telling about the animal. Write one sentence with *and*, one with *but*, and one with *or*.

Tech Tip With an adult, find facts about your animal online.

Conjunctions • 153

Adverb and Conjunction Review

6.1 Find the adverb in each sentence.

1. To play a song, hum loudly into the kazoo.
2. We practiced yesterday and learned the songs.
3. The group gathered quickly to play their kazoos.
4. We happily played the new songs.
5. Mr. Bell asked us to play quietly.
6. We moved away from the window.

6.2 Find the adverb that tells when or how often in each sentence.

7. I see an opossum in the backyard frequently.
8. The animal was on the deck today.
9. Then I saw it in the yard.
10. The opossum never comes out before dark.
11. I did not know before that opossums have trouble seeing in the day.
12. I now know that it is a nocturnal animal.

6.3 Find the adverb that tells where in each sentence.

13. We climbed inside to see the hot-air balloon basket.
14. Other hot-air balloons floated above.
15. Our balloon went up.
16. We could see far into the distance.
17. We headed back, returning to the launch pad.
18. A red and blue balloon landed nearby.

6.4 Find the adverb that tells how in each sentence.

19. Sheila acted perfectly at the dinner table.
20. Her baby brother chewed noisily.
21. He clumsily shoved peas into his mouth.
22. Then he laughed loudly as the mushy peas ran down his chin.
23. His mother quickly wiped his face with a napkin.

6.5 Rewrite each sentence to express a negative idea.

24. Riding a bike at night is a good idea.
25. Drivers can see bike riders in the dark.

26. She rides her bike without a helmet.

27. Some bike riders follow the rules of the road.

28. Ride your bike into oncoming traffic.

6.6 **Complete each sentence with *good* or *well*.**

29. Storytelling is a _____ skill to have.

30. The storyteller told the story _____.

31. The audience listened _____ to the story.

32. We had a _____ time.

33. The story had a _____ ending.

6.7 **Complete each sentence with *to, too,* or *two*.**

34. The mail carrier brings us _____ packages.

35. He rings the doorbell if a package is _____ big for the mailbox.

36. Mail delivery is easier than going _____ the post office for mail.

37. The mail carrier brings us letters and cards _____.

38. Some packages need _____ stamps.

6.8 **Complete each sentence with *their* or *there*.**

39. _____ favorite hobby is stargazing.

40. Did the group members bring _____ telescopes?

41. The Big Dipper is _____, to the left.

42. Thick fog makes it difficult to see the stars _____.

43. The planetarium is where people can learn about space, so we often go _____.

44. _____ tour is fun and educational.

6.9 **Find the coordinating conjunction in each sentence.**

45. Sunflowers and daisies are pretty flowers.

46. The houseplant has leaves but no blossoms.

47. Put the vase of flowers on the table or on the desk.

48. The petals wilted and fell off.

49. Those flowers are beautiful but don't last long.

50. I will pick more flowers from the yard or from the garden.

Go to www.voyagesinenglish.com for more activities.

Adverb and Conjunction Challenge

Read the paragraph and answer the questions.

1. Our class eagerly planned a special field trip. 2. The third-grade class always goes on a field trip. 3. We decided to go to a children's hospital and to take gifts. 4. First, we planned a fund-raising project for the gifts—making T-shirts. 5. Next, students designed and sold T-shirts. 6. The fund-raising went well. 7. We raised $500 for gifts. 8. We then bought DVDs and CDs for the children. 9. Yesterday we eagerly took our gifts to the hospital. 10. We were warmly welcomed there. 11. We played games with the children. 12. Now we plan to go again in the spring.

1. In sentence 1 find the adverb that tells how.
2. In sentence 2 find the adverb that tells how often.
3. In sentence 4 what is the adverb? What kind of adverb is it?
4. In sentence 5 what is the coordinating conjunction? What words does it connect?
5. In sentence 6 what is the adverb?
6. In sentence 8 what is the adverb?
7. In sentence 8 what is the coordinating conjunction? What words does it connect?
8. In sentence 9 what are the two adverbs?
9. In sentence 10 what adverb tells where?
10. In sentence 12 what are the two adverbs? What kind of adverbs are they?

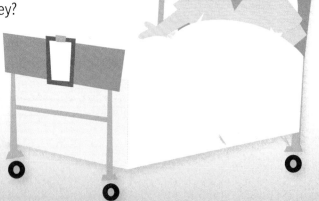

Punctuation and Capitalization

7.1 End Punctuation

End punctuation makes your sentences clear. It lets readers know where one sentence ends and the next one begins, and it signals the kind of sentence you are writing.

- A sentence that tells something ends with a **period.**

  Baseball is a sport.

  A baseball team has nine players.

  The two leagues in baseball are the American League and the National League.

- A sentence that asks a question ends with a **question mark.**

  Do you like baseball?

  Have you ever been to a major league baseball game?

  Do you play baseball?

- A sentence that expresses strong or sudden feeling ends with an **exclamation point.**

  I love baseball!

  My team won the championship!

  I hit a home run!

Which punctuation mark goes at the end of this sentence?

Who was Jackie Robinson

A a period (.)

B a question mark (?)

C an exclamation point (!)

You are right if you said B. The sentence uses a question word *(Who)* and asks a question. It needs to end with a question mark.

EXERCISE 1 Tell whether each sentence tells something, asks a question, or expresses a strong feeling.

1. Jackie Robinson was a baseball player.
2. Why is he famous?
3. He was the first African American in major league baseball.
4. What an amazing athlete he was!
5. When did he join the major leagues?
6. He helped his team win the World Series.
7. He was voted the National League Most Valuable Player in 1949.
8. What position did he play?
9. Is he in the Baseball Hall of Fame?
10. Robinson is also famous for his commitment to civil rights.

Jackie Robinson

EXERCISE 2 Rewrite the sentences, adding the correct punctuation at the end of each sentence.

1. In 1947 Robinson played his first major league game
2. What team did he play for
3. He played for the Brooklyn Dodgers
4. Robinson's talent and pride won him respect
5. He was really awesome
6. Robinson became the first African American in the Baseball Hall of Fame in 1962
7. When did he get a postage stamp in his honor
8. The Post Office honored him with a postage stamp in 1982

APPLY IT NOW

Think about a famous person who is brave. Write three sentences about that person. Use all three kinds of end punctuation.

With an adult, research your famous person online.

7.2 Capitalization

Certain words always begin with a capital letter.

- The first word in a sentence
- Names of people and pets

Jennifer	Luis	Lucky
Min	Tom	Rover

- Names of streets, cities, states, and countries

Elm Avenue	Chicago	Ohio
First Street	New Orleans	Canada

- Names of days, months, and holidays

Monday	September	Labor Day
Friday	June	Memorial Day

- The personal pronoun *I* is a capital letter.

Which word group needs capital letters?

- A last weekend with my sister
- B holiday shopping in town
- C valentine's day party on february 12

You are right if you said C. Both *Valentine's Day* and *February* need capital letters. *Valentine's Day* names a holiday, and *February* names a month.

Which word groups need capital letters?

- A my sister holly
- B houston, texas
- C my birthday

You are right if you said A and B. *Holly* is a person's name. *Houston* is a city, and *Texas* is a state.

EXERCISE 1 Tell why each word or word group uses a capital letter.

1. Matthew
2. England
3. Maple Lane
4. New Year's Day
5. Florida
6. Rachel
7. Monday
8. Thanksgiving
9. October
10. our dog, Whiskers

EXERCISE 2 Rewrite each sentence, adding capital letters where they are needed.

1. the last day of school is thursday, may 28.
2. sam and his family leave for denver the next day.
3. there are high mountains in colorado.
4. my family and i are going to new york on vacation.
5. we are going to visit karen, my mother's sister.
6. she lives near central park in manhattan.
7. her address is on fifth avenue.
8. we'll be back home for independence day on july 4.
9. in august we are going camping.
10. we camp at a state park in northern wisconsin.
11. my cousin lorenzo is coming with us.
12. my favorite part of camping is sitting around the campfire.

EXERCISE 3 Complete each sentence. Use capital letters correctly.

1. _____ is a place I would like to visit.
2. If I had a snake, I'd name it _____.
3. _____ is the capital of my state.
4. The Golden Gate Bridge is in _____.
5. _____ is my favorite day of the week.
6. We celebrate Presidents' Day in _____.

APPLY IT NOW

Write three sentences about your favorite holiday. Use capital letters correctly.
Example:
My favorite holiday is Thanksgiving.

7.3 Abbreviations

A short form of a word is called an **abbreviation.** Abbreviations often end with periods.

DAYS OF THE WEEK

Sunday—Sun.	Thursday—Thurs.
Monday—Mon.	Friday—Fri.
Tuesday—Tues.	Saturday—Sat.
Wednesday—Wed.	

MONTHS OF THE YEAR

January—Jan.	September—Sept.
February—Feb.	October—Oct.
March—Mar.	November—Nov.
April—Apr.	December—Dec.
August—Aug.	

May, June, and *July* are not abbreviated.

ADDRESSES

Street—St.	Avenue—Ave.	Road—Rd.	Boulevard—Blvd.
North—N.	South—S.	East—E.	West—W.

UNITS OF MEASURE

inch—in.	foot—ft.	yard—yd.
pint—pt.	quart—qt.	gallon—gal.

Abbreviations for units of measure do not begin with capital letters.

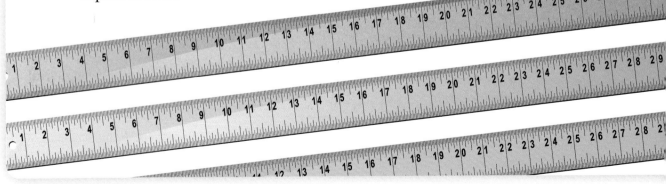

EXERCISE 1 Rewrite each word group, using the abbreviation for each underlined word.

1. Logan Boulevard
2. West 57th Street
3. one quart of paint
4. Mulberry Street
5. one foot of rope
6. one gallon of gasoline
7. one yard of fabric
8. North Oak Road
9. Prairie Avenue
10. Tuesday, October 10
11. one inch of rain
12. Sunday, March 21

EXERCISE 2 Write the word for each abbreviation.

1. Sun.
2. qt.
3. W.
4. in.
5. Sept.
6. yd.
7. S.
8. Thurs.
9. gal.
10. Wed.

EXERCISE 3 Rewrite each of the following. Use abbreviations where you can.

1. Monday, December 22
   Buy mom a yard of ribbon at Edwards Fabric Store on East 25th Street. Buy a pint of strawberries at the supermarket.
2. Tuesday, December 23
   Remind Dad to buy a gallon of milk. Go to Gina's house. Her address is 781 West Jefferson Avenue.

APPLY IT NOW

Write today's day and date, your birthday, and your address. Rewrite them, using abbreviations where you can.
Example: Monday, January 19
Mon., Jan. 19

7.4 Personal Titles and Initials

The titles *Mr., Mrs., Ms., Dr., Gov.,* and *Capt.* are abbreviations.
Each one begins with a capital letter and ends with a period.

TITLE	USE FOR	EXAMPLE
Mr.	a man	Mr. Sam Doherty
Mrs.	a married woman	Mrs. Mai Nguyen
Ms.	an unmarried or a married woman	Ms. Cathy Whalen
Dr.	a doctor	Dr. Ramon Ramirez
Gov.	governor, a state's leader	Gov. Anton Jones
Capt.	captain, a group leader	Capt. Joy Sears

A person may use an initial instead of his or her first or middle name. An initial is a capital letter followed by a period.

Martha Alice Russo   **Martha A. Russo**

M. Alice Russo   **M. A. Russo**

Which name is written correctly?

A **dr Marc Wood**

B **Mrs Kris Chow**

C **Mr. A. P. Smith**

You are right if you said C. Both A and B have mistakes. In A *dr* should be capitalized and followed by a period. In B *Mrs* needs a period.

EXERCISE 1 Rewrite these names, using periods and capital letters.

1. dr richard p dean
2. ms elizabeth a young
3. mrs nisha n barimi

4. mr patrick r monocelli

5. ms mary m reilly

6. a n fiorito

7. gov thomas willner

8. capt barbara laboure

9. mrs emily d maggio

10. mr michael e lewis

EXERCISE 2 **Rewrite these sentences. Use periods and capital letters where they are needed. Use abbreviations where you can.**

1. doctor kerry murphy is our family dentist

2. mr n patel is a pharmacist

3. mrs lee balbo runs the local flower shop

4. ms kathy heedum is an artist

5. governor j p weinstein is visiting our school

6. ms nadiah alizadeh is in college

7. mrs a r taylor works at the bank

8. captain c j smith is a police officer

9. ms sandra rasche is a lawyer

10. mrs susan p taylor works in the school library

11. ms janet jefferies is a science teacher

12. the leader of the state is gov james w quinn

13. the city council is led by mr michael m olson

14. mr richard j martinez is the mayor of our town

APPLY IT NOW

Write five sentences with names of people from your neighborhood or people who help you, such as doctors, teachers, or firefighters. Use abbreviations where you can.

7.5 Titles of Books and Poems

There are special rules for writing the titles of books and poems.

- Each important word in a title begins with a capital letter. The first word and the last word of a title always begin with a capital letter. Short words such as *of, to, for, a, an,* and *the* are not capitalized unless they are the first or last word in the title.
- Underline the title of a book.
- Put quotation marks around the title of a poem.

Book: <u>The Chocolate Touch</u> by Patrick Skene Catling
<u>The Little House on the Prairie</u> by Laura Ingalls Wilder

Poem: "Nine Mice" by Jack Prelutsky
"The Pork" by James S. Tippett

Which of the following is a poem? How do you know?

A <u>**The Giving Tree**</u> **by Shel Silverstein**
B **"The Barefoot Boy" by John Greenleaf Whittier**
C <u>**Babe, the Gallant Pig**</u> **by Dick King-Smith**

You are right if you said B. "The Barefoot Boy" has quotation marks around it. It is the title of a poem. <u>The Giving Tree</u> and <u>Babe, the Gallant Pig</u> are books. They are underlined.

EXERCISE 1 Rewrite the titles. Use capital letters where they are needed. Tell whether each is a book or a poem.

1. "by myself" by Eloise Greenfield
2. <u>where the sidewalk ends</u> by Shel Silverstein
3. <u>the cat in the hat</u> by Dr. Seuss
4. <u>ramona's world</u> by Beverly Cleary
5. "louder than a clap of thunder" by Jack Prelutsky
6. <u>the watsons go to birmingham</u> by Christopher Paul Curtis
7. <u>mr. popper's penguins</u> by Richard Atwater and Florence Atwater

8. <u>the hundred dresses</u> by Eleanor Estes and Louis Slobodkin

9. "evangeline" by Henry Wadsworth Longfellow

10. <u>chasing vermeer</u> by Blue Balliett

11. <u>little house in the big woods</u> by Laura Ingalls Wilder

12. "my hippo has the hiccups" by kenn nesbitt

EXERCISE 2 **Write the titles correctly. Underline book titles. Put quotation marks around poem titles. Use capital letters where they are needed.**

1. kate and the beanstalk (book)

2. sarah, plain and tall (book)

3. there's an owl in the shower (book)

4. you've no need to light a nightlight (poem)

5. horrible harry and the purple people (book)

6. a fly and a flea in a flue (poem)

7. commander toad and the planet of the grapes (book)

8. keep a poem in your pocket (poem)

9. the bears on hemlock island (book)

10. until i saw the sea (poem)

11. sing a song of people (poem)

12. the lion, the witch and the wardrobe (book)

13. i dreamed i was riding a zebra (poem)

14. my robot's misbehaving (poem)

15. abel's island (book)

16. stuart little (book)

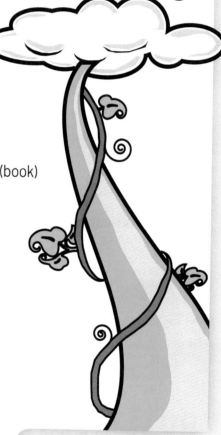

APPLY IT NOW

Write the titles of five books or poems that you have read. Remember to underline book titles and to put quotation marks around poem titles.

Grammar in Action. ✎ Write the title of the book from the excerpt on page 438.

7.6 Commas in a Series

Commas separate words and groups of words so that they are easier to read. Three or more words or groups of words of the same kind written one after another are called a **series.** Often part of the series is connected by the coordinate conjunction *and* or *or.* Commas are used to separate words in a series.

I play football, soccer, *and* baseball.

I hit, pitch, *and* catch for my baseball team.

Ping, Ana, *or* Carl will bring a soccer ball.

I will play midfielder, forward, *or* goalie.

Which sentence uses commas in a series correctly?

A We need helmets, footballs, and uniforms.

B We need helmets footballs and uniforms.

C We need helmets, footballs and uniforms.

You are right if you said sentence A. There are commas between the words in the series.

Which sentences use commas in a series correctly?

A I am bringing balloons candles and streamers to the party.

B We still need to buy cake, ice cream, and milk.

C Don't forget the wrapping paper, bows, and ribbons.

You are right if you said sentences B and C. There are commas separating the words in the series.

EXERCISE 1 Rewrite the word groups. Use commas to separate the words in a series.

1. quarterbacks mascots and fans
2. referees coaches and players
3. socks shoes and shoulder pads
4. popcorn peanuts or pretzels
5. balls jerseys and helmets

6. Monday Wednesday and Thursday

7. run catch and throw

8. first place second place or third place

9. touchdown field goal or safety

10. black red and white stripes

EXERCISE 2 Rewrite the sentences. Put commas in each sentence to separate the words in a series.

1. Olympic Games were held in Beijing Athens and Sydney.

2. We watched swimming track and gymnastics.

3. We saw gymnasts from China Russia Sweden and Romania.

4. The gymnasts jumped tumbled and leaped.

5. The audience watched waited and applauded.

6. Winter Olympics sports include skiing snowboarding and ice-skating.

7. The ice-skater jumped twirled and landed.

8. Cycling gymnastics and running have been sports at all the modern Olympic Games.

9. The three Olympic medals are gold silver and bronze.

10. Running biking and swimming are part of the triathlon.

11. Swimming diving and water polo take place at a pool.

12. Water polo players swim throw and score goals.

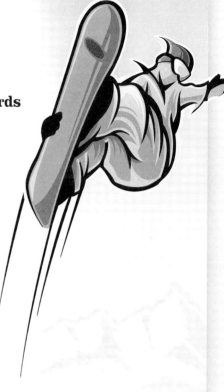

EXERCISE 3 Complete each sentence with at least three words. Put commas in each sentence to separate the words in a series.

1. My favorite sports are _____.

2. Some famous athletes are _____.

3. I like to play _____.

4. At recess we _____.

APPLY IT NOW

Use the two groups of words below to write two sentences. Each sentence should contain a series.

1. soccer baseball tennis
2. shorts shirts sneakers

7.7 Commas in Direct Address

Speaking directly to a person and using that person's name is called **direct address.** Commas are used to set off the name of the person spoken to from the rest of the sentence. Use one comma to separate the name if it is at the beginning or the end of a sentence. Use two commas to separate the name if it is in the middle of a sentence.

Ben, **let's build a playhouse.**

We'll put it behind the garage *, Ben.*

Do you think *, Callie,* **we can build it in a day?**

Which sentences are correct?

A **I think we can Ben.**

B **I think we can, Ben.**

C **Ben, I think we can.**

You are right if you said sentences B and C. The name *Ben* is in direct address. It comes at the beginning or the end of a sentence and is separated from the rest of the sentence by a comma.

Which sentence is correct?

A **Please, Bernie, draw a plan.**

B **Please Bernie, draw a plan.**

C **Please, Bernie draw a plan.**

You are right if you said sentence A. The name *Bernie* is in direct address. It comes in the middle of a sentence. Two commas separate it from the rest of the sentence.

EXERCISE 1 Find the name in direct address in each sentence. Rewrite the sentences, using commas where they are needed.

1. Paula tell us where to build the playhouse.
2. I think Mark it should go near the fence.

3. Give me the plans Ellen.

4. Help us with this hammering Mr. Ashton.

5. Felix let's paint the playhouse red.

6. Be careful kids the paint is wet.

7. We are almost done Jamie.

8. Dad will you help us clean up?

9. It seems to me Ken that the kids will really like it.

10. Put the sign up over there Jackie.

11. Olivia put the chair inside the playhouse.

12. Leigh have you chosen a name for your playhouse?

13. I want to hang some of my paintings on the wall Mom.

14. The inside of the playhouse Jake is tiny.

15. Come over David and see our playhouse.

EXERCISE 2 **Rewrite the sentences, using commas correctly.**

1. Mom will, you, make us some sandwiches?

2. Tell me Bob and Claire, what kind would you like?

3. Kevin here is, your ham and cheese sandwich.

4. Please pass, the mustard Evan.

5. Hand, me, a napkin Maddie.

6. Pam clear the table.

7. I'd like, some potato salad Mom.

8. I want some lemonade Diane, and some pickles too.

9. Is there, any more milk Kate?

10. Oh, Mom I dropped my fork.

11. Give, me, another fork Mom please.

12. Here is a plastic, fork, Luke.

13. This lemonade, Dad tastes great!

14. Sam help us clean up.

APPLY IT NOW

Imagine that you are cooking or building something with friends. Write three sentences that ask or tell your friends to do things. Use their names in direct address.

7.8 Commas in Compound Sentences

A comma is used when two short sentences are combined into one longer sentence. This longer sentence is called a **compound sentence.** Compound sentences can make writing easier to understand and more enjoyable to read.

> *Wagon Wheels* by Barbara Brenner is set in the Old West, *and* it tells the story of three brothers.
>
> The brothers faced a hard winter, *but* they survived.
>
> Ryan and Tim may read this story in class, *or* they may borrow it from the library.

To make a compound sentence, use a comma followed by *and, but,* or *or* to join two sentences.

Which of these choices makes a compound sentence from the two short sentences?

> The brothers faced dangers.
> They survived in the wilderness.
>
> A The brothers faced dangers in the wilderness.
>
> B The brothers faced dangers, but they survived in the wilderness.
>
> C The brothers faced dangers and the wilderness.

You are right if you said sentence B. This sentence joins two shorter sentences with a comma and the word *but* to make one longer compound sentence.

EXERCISE 1 Rewrite the sentences, adding commas where they are needed.

1. Laura Ingalls Wilder was born in Wisconsin in 1867 but she grew up mostly in the prairie states.

2. Her family traveled west in a covered wagon and they lived in several different places.

3. Her father tried to earn a living by farming but the family faced many problems.

4. Wilder later wrote about her childhood experiences and people enjoyed her *Little House* books.

5. You may have read Wilder's stories or you may have seen some of them on TV.

EXERCISE 2 Join the sentence from Column A with the one in Column B to make a compound sentence. Add a comma and the word *and* or *but* when joining the sentences.

Column A	Column B
1. Tomie de Paola writes books, *and*	He draws the pictures too.
2. I looked for *Baseball Saved Us*.	It was checked out of the library.
3. Alma Flor Ada writes in English, *and*	She writes in Spanish too.
4. *Stone Fox* tells about dogsled racing,	It has a lot of action.

EXERCISE 3 Rewrite the sentences. Add commas for a series, names in direct address, and compound sentences.

1. Alice please tell about me about your favorite books.

2. My favorite authors are Louis Sachar Ann Cameron and E. B. White.

3. I like detective stories and Encyclopedia Brown is my favorite detective.

4. Do you read detective stories Robin?

5. I like mysteries tall tales and nature books.

6. Aliki's books include *Feelings Dinosaur Bones* and *Mummies Made in Egypt*.

7. Rick Elaine and Pat like books about science.

8. I have read the book but I haven't written my report yet Mr. Jones.

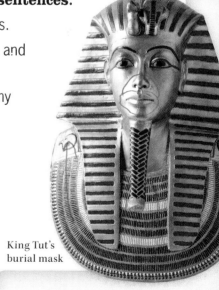

King Tut's burial mask

APPLY IT NOW

Write three compound sentences about books that you have read.

With an adult, read an online book review.

7.9 Apostrophes

The **apostrophe** is a punctuation mark used in several ways.

- An apostrophe is used to form the possessive of a noun.

   The lunch box belongs to Jason.

   It is *Jason's* **lunch box.** (possessive noun)

- An apostrophe can replace letters left out in a contraction. Common contractions are *isn't, aren't, wasn't, weren't, don't, doesn't, didn't, can't, won't,* and *shouldn't.*

   Jason cannot find his lunch box.

   Jason *can't* **find his lunch box.**

Which sentence uses an apostrophe to show possession?

   A **Kathy's lunch is missing.**

   B **I didn't eat her lunch.**

   C **She doesn't know where her lunch is.**

You are right if you said sentence A. The apostrophe and *s* added to the name *Kathy* show that the lunch belongs to her. Sentences B and C use apostrophes to form contractions.

Which sentences use an apostrophe to replace letters left out in a contraction?

   A **I didn't eat breakfast today.**

   B **Paul's bag is on the counter.**

   C **I can't stay after class today.**

You are right if you said sentences A and C. Sentence B uses an apostrophe to show possession.

EXERCISE 1 Tell whether the apostrophe in each sentence shows possession or forms a contraction.

1. Jane wasn't in the cafeteria line.
2. Matt can't save that seat for you.
3. That is Brian's seat.
4. We aren't able to sit together.
5. There aren't any seats at that table.
6. Erin won't be able to sit with us.
7. George's coat is on the back of that chair.
8. Karin's tray is at the end of the table.
9. Macaroni and cheese is Carrie's favorite food.
10. Tamara's choice was soup.
11. I don't like carrot soup.
12. Stacy's snack was a kiwi.

EXERCISE 2 Rewrite the sentences, adding apostrophes where they are needed.

1. Isnt it the day for pizza in the cafeteria?
2. Jimmy cant decide what kind of pizza to have.
3. Pepperoni is Alicias favorite.
4. She doesnt like mushrooms.
5. Pattys pizza slice has sausage.
6. Malcolm wont eat green peppers.
7. That is Valeries second slice.
8. I dont like pizza with just cheese.
9. Pete doesnt like some toppings.
10. He wont eat pizza with onions.
11. Pizza wasnt on the menu last week.
12. Marks sandwich looks good, doesnt it?

APPLY IT NOW

Write three sentences about your lunch and your friends' lunches at the cafeteria or in the lunchroom yesterday. Use a word with an apostrophe in each sentence.

Grammar in Action. How is an apostrophe used in the first sentence on page 439?

7.10 Addresses

Capital letters and commas are used in writing addresses. An address is written like this.

Name
Street Address, Apartment Number
City, State Abbreviation Zip Code

In an address capitalize the first letter of every word and abbreviation. Capitalize both letters of a state abbreviation.

Ms. Kathleen Connor
313 N. Melrose St., Apt. 3
Chicago, IL 60657

A comma always separates the city and the state, but there is no comma between the state abbreviation and the zip code. If there is an apartment or a floor number, it is separated from the rest of the address by a comma.

Is this address written correctly?

James Jones
215 Broadway, 15th Floor
Minneapolis, MN 55413

You are right if you said yes. The first letter of each word is capitalized. Commas are used between the street address and floor number and between the city and state.

EXERCISE 1 Rewrite each address, using capital letters where they are needed.

1. ms. carolyn walters
   2232 s. main st., apt. 334
   ann arbor, mi 48103

2. mr. ron harty
   44 hillvale rd.
   westport, ct 06880

3. mrs. sarah jemielity
   418 benton court
   south bend, in 46615

4. ms taylor thomas
   35 queens blvd.
   new york, ny 10001

EXERCISE 2 Rewrite each address, using commas and capital letters where they are needed.

1. mr. hector perez
   1220 oak ave. apt 3
   salem or 97302

2. mrs. jackie kim
   115 w. 101st st. apt. 4D
   jefferson mo 50025

3. dr. charles mattes
   341 e. irving park rd.
   las vegas nv 80503

4. ms rose whitelaw
   2110 w. orchard avenue
   philadelphia pa 19129

5. mrs jennon bodini
   600 19th st. apt. 301
   denver co 80202

6. the city company
   1209 market parkway 9th floor
   st. louis mo 63103

7. mr. peter sabarsky
   5990 w. loomis rd. apt. 10
   greendale wi 53129

8. mrs. michelle mccarthy
   870 w beach blvd.
   jacksonville fl 32246

APPLY IT NOW

Address an envelope. Use your name and address in the upper left corner for the return address. Use your teacher's name and the school address for the mailing address.

7.11 Direct Quotations

A **direct quotation** contains the exact words a person says. Use quotation marks before and after the words of a speaker. Use a comma to set off what is said from the rest of the sentence.

Cargo ships entering
the Gatun Locks

> **Javier said, "I know a lot about the Panama Canal."**
>
> **"You are smart," replied Lucy.**

Which sentence tells Mrs. Becker's exact words?

> **A Mrs. Becker said, "We will learn about the canal."**
> **B Mrs. Becker said that the canal is important.**
> **C Mrs. Becker said that ships sail on the canal.**

You are right if you said sentence A. This sentence tells Mrs. Becker's exact words. Her exact words are inside the quotation marks. A comma sets off what she said from the rest of the sentence.

EXERCISE 1 Rewrite each sentence. Use a comma to separate what is being said from the rest of the sentence.

1. Mrs. Becker said "Tell me about the Panama Canal."

2. Rick replied "The Panama Canal joins the Atlantic Ocean and the Pacific Ocean."

3. Casey exclaimed "That's a long canal!"

4. Suzanne added "It is more than 50 miles long."

5. Miguel said "The canal was opened in 1914."

6. Mrs. Becker asked "Who was president when the Panama Canal was built?"

7. "It was Theodore Roosevelt" answered Iris.

8. "The Panama Canal has been called the eighth wonder of the world" said Ana.

Gatun Lake

EXERCISE 2 Rewrite each sentence. Put quotation marks around each person's exact words.

1. It takes my ship eight to ten hours to travel through the canal, said the ship's captain.

2. He said, Without the canal we would have to travel around South America to go from New York to California.

3. The canal's locks are like giant stairs, the teacher said.

4. She explained, Locks let water in and out to raise and lower ships.

5. I read that a new canal may be needed, said Mr. Michaels.

6. Yolanda asked, Why do people want a new canal?

7. Modern ships are much larger, answered Robin.

8. Robin continued, They cannot fit through this canal.

9. There may be a new canal in Mexico, reported Fernando.

10. We can research the topic of a new canal, suggested Madison.

EXERCISE 3 Rewrite each sentence. Use a comma to separate what is being said from the rest of the sentence. Put quotation marks around each person's exact words.

1. We found some interesting facts about the canal said Louis.

2. Anita said The canal has three sets of locks.

3. Thirty ships go through the canal every day reported Edward.

4. A man once swam across the canal began Jake.

5. Jake continued He had to pay a toll for using the canal!

6. I said A hydrofoil ship went through it in under three hours.

7. Mrs. Ricci asked Do you know the nickname for the canal?

8. It's called the Big Ditch replied Emma.

9. Mrs. Ricci continued By how many miles did the canal shorten the trip?

10. Inez quickly responded A boat cuts about 8,000 miles off the trip from east to west.

APPLY IT NOW

Imagine you are talking with a few friends about what you did last weekend. Write four sentences that contain your friends' exact words.

Grammar in Action.

Find the second direct quotation on page 439.

Punctuation and Capitalization Review

7.1 Rewrite the sentences. Put the correct punctuation at the end of each sentence.

1. How do we get to the park
2. We will take the subway
3. What fun the subway is
4. Why is it called the subway
5. The train runs underground

7.2 Rewrite the sentences, adding capital letters where they are needed.

6. thanksgiving is always on a thursday in november.
7. pilgrims held the first celebration in massachusetts.
8. my family travels to denver, colorado, for the holiday.
9. we drive through pueblo, fairplay, and littleton.
10. we will return on sunday.

7.3 Rewrite each word group, using an abbreviation for each underlined word.

11. one <u>quart</u> of oil
12. <u>Monday</u>, <u>August</u> 7
13. <u>1</u> <u>yard</u> of rope
14. <u>North</u> Waterford <u>Street</u>
15. <u>February</u> 14, 20–

7.4 Rewrite the sentences, using capital letters and periods where they are needed.

16. mrs hilbert hurt her knee.
17. dr kerry suggested surgery.
18. mr hilbert came to visit.
19. gov jim f tan was also there.
20. capt hidalgo had the flu.

7.5 Rewrite the titles correctly.

21. it's a fair day, amber brown by Paula Danziger (book)
22. big anthony by Tomie de Paola (book)
23. the purple cow by gelett burgess (poem)
24. holes by Louis Sachar (book)
25. fireflies in the garden by Robert Frost (poem)

7.6 Rewrite the sentences, using commas to separate the words in a series.

26. Please set the table with forks spoons and knives.
27. Do you want milk water or juice?
28. We ate turkey potatoes and peas for dinner.
29. The family talked laughed and ate at the table.

7.7 Rewrite the sentences, using commas for direct address where they are needed.

30. Daren please walk on the pool deck.

31. I think Shauna that the water is too deep.

32. It's your turn Kevin to go down the water slide.

33. Be careful on the stairs Liz.

34. Watch your sister Jo.

7.8 Rewrite the compound sentences, adding commas where they are needed.

35. Kate ate spaghetti and she spilled some on her shirt.

36. She wiped the shirt with a napkin but it made the mess worse.

37. Her dad quickly washed the shirt or the stain would never have come out.

38. Kate went shopping and she bought a new shirt anyway.

39. Kate still eats spaghetti but she's more careful now.

7.9 Rewrite the sentences, adding apostrophes where they are needed. Then tell whether each apostrophe is used to show possession or forms a contraction.

40. People arent the only ones who get sick.

41. My pet bunny wasnt well.

42. Tys dog had a broken leg.

43. The vets office was open.

44. The doctor didnt turn any animal away.

7.10 Rewrite each address, using commas and capital letters where they are needed.

45. mr stan moore
123 boxcar st apt 3B
wysox pa 18854

46. mrs georgia molder
500 flat river lane
pickering oh 43147

47. ms maria e garcee
34 w oak ave
ann arbor mi 48103

7.11 Rewrite each sentence, adding quotation marks and commas where they are needed.

48. Mr. Davis said I grew up on a farm.

49. We grew corn he continued.

50. Tell me if you have a story to share about a farm the teacher said.

51. My grandparents have a farm in Iowa Lena said.

52. She exclaimed They wake me up at 4 a.m. to milk the cows!

 Tech Tip Go to www.voyagesinenglish.com for more activities.

Punctuation and Capitalization Challenge

Read the paragraph and answer the questions.

1. On Thursday the third graders were going to make Thanksgiving turkey decorations. 2. They needed feathers, paper, and a school picture. 3. Kelly was so excited! 4. She thought she would send the turkey to her grandparents in Miami. 5. If she mailed it by Wednesday, November 8, the turkey would arrive in time for Thanksgiving. 6. The day finally came to make the turkeys. 7. "Does everyone have materials?" asked Ms. Talbot. 8. She told the class to draw his or her hand on the paper, and then she said to cut it out. 9. Each student glued a feather to the finger of each hand. 10. "Kelly, can you guess where you will put your picture?" asked Ms. Talbot.

1. In sentence 1 why does *Thursday* begin with a capital letter?
2. What is the abbreviation for *Thursday* in sentence 1?
3. In sentence 2 why is a comma used after *feathers* and after *paper*?
4. What kind of sentence is sentence 3? How do you know?
5. In sentence 4 why is the first letter in *Miami* capitalized?
6. What is the abbreviation for *November* in sentence 5?
7. In sentence 7 why are quotation marks used before *Does* and after *materials*?
8. In sentence 7 why do *Ms.* and *Talbot* begin with capital letters?
9. What is the punctuation after the direct quotation in sentence 7?
10. In sentence 8 what does *and* connect?
11. In sentence 10 what name is in direct address?

SECTION 8

Diagramming

8.1 Subjects and Predicates

A **sentence diagram** is a drawing that shows how the parts of a sentence go together.

The most important parts of a sentence are the subject and the predicate. The **simple subject** of a sentence is usually a noun, a word that names a person, a place, or a thing. It may also be a subject pronoun, a word that takes the place of a noun. The **simple predicate** of a sentence is a verb.

In a sentence diagram, the simple subject and the simple predicate go on a horizontal line (a line that goes across). The subject is at the left, and the predicate is at the right. A vertical line (a line that goes up and down) separates them.

subject (noun or pronoun) | predicate (verb)

Let's do an example: **Birds fly.**
1. Draw a horizontal line.
2. The verb in the sentence is *fly.* Write it on the line at the right.

fly

3. Think: *What can fly?* The answer is *Birds. Birds* is the simple subject. Write it to the left. Draw a vertical line to separate the subject and the predicate.

Birds | fly

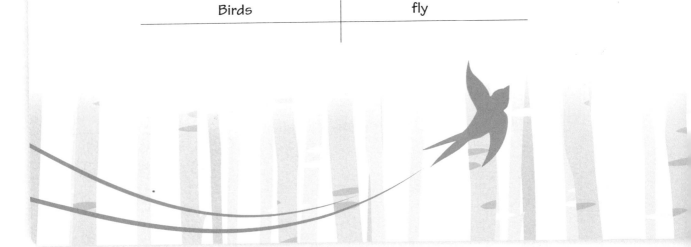

EXERCISE 1 Copy each diagram. Finish it by adding a subject or a predicate. Choose a word from the word box.

> bees   cats   talk   bark

1. _____ | meow

2. Dogs | _____

3. _____ | buzz

4. People | _____

EXERCISE 2 Diagram each sentence.

1. Eva cooks.
2. Globes spin.
3. Bees sting.
4. Len swims.
5. Wolves howl.
6. Keith writes.
7. Lions roar.
8. I sew.
9. He reads.
10. We hike.
11. Balls bounce.
12. She swims.
13. They dance.
14. Lightning strikes.
15. Popcorn pops.

Wolf pup

APPLY IT NOW

Write three sentences about people you know and something that each person does. Use only a simple subject and a simple predicate. Diagram each sentence.

Examples: Mom works.
Sarah skates.

8.2 Possessives

The **possessive form** of a noun shows who possesses or owns something. Possessive nouns end in *'s* or just in an apostrophe: the *cat's* food, the *cats'* food. The noun that follows a possessive noun names what is owned.

In a sentence diagram, a possessive noun is written on a slanted line under the noun it goes with. The possessive adjectives *my, your, his, her, its, our,* and *their* are diagrammed the same way.

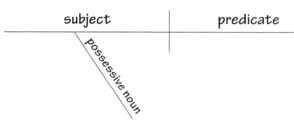

Let's do an example: **Jeff's bird sings.**

1. Write the simple subject and the simple predicate on the horizontal line.

2. Think: *Who owns the bird?* Jeff owns the bird. It is *Jeff's* bird. Write *Jeff's* on a slanted line under *bird.*

Here's another example: **Mom's vase broke.**

1. Write the simple subject and the simple predicate on the horizontal line.
2. Think: *Who owns the vase?* Mom owns the vase. It is *Mom's* vase. Write *Mom's* on a slanted line under *vase.*

EXERCISE 1 Copy each diagram. Finish it by adding the possessive noun.

1. Dogs'

tails	wag

2. Dad's

computer	froze

EXERCISE 2 Diagram each sentence.

1. Mark's sister skis.

2. Our plane landed.

3. Fireflies' bodies glow.

4. Cinderella's coach disappeared.

5. Your phone rang.

6. His brother runs.

7. Kate's watch stopped.

8. Their robot talks.

9. Jack's beanstalk grew.

10. Amy's mother teaches.

11. Her backpack tore.

12. Elephants' ears flap.

13. Its pocket ripped.

14. Chris's kite flew.

15. My seeds sprouted.

APPLY IT NOW

Write two sentences about people you know and things they own. Use a possessive in each sentence. Then diagram each sentence.

Examples:

Grandma's rocker squeaks.

Wally's hamsters play.

Grammar in Action. Find a possessive in the page 476 excerpt.

8.3 Adjectives

An **adjective** tells more about a noun. An adjective tells how something looks, tastes, sounds, or smells. Adjectives can also tell how many. The articles *a, an,* and *the* are adjectives; they point out nouns.

Add an adjective to a sentence diagram by writing it on a slanted line under the noun it tells more about.

Let's do an example: **Colorful flags flew.**

1. Write the simple subject and the simple predicate on the horizontal line.

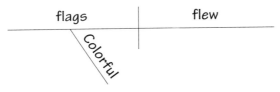

2. Think: *What kind of flags flew?* The answer is *colorful. Colorful* is an adjective that tells more about the noun *flags.* Write *colorful* on a slanted line under *flags.*

What does the adjective tell more about in this sentence diagram?

drums | boomed

Big

You are right if you said *drums.*

EXERCISE 1 Copy each diagram. Finish it by adding the adjective under the subject.

1. Dark

clouds	gather

2. Bright

lightning	flashed

3. Loud

thunder	booms

EXERCISE 2 Diagram each sentence.

1. Heavy rain fell.

2. Good students study.

3. Happy babies smile.

4. Many children swim.

5. The fans cheered.

6. Strong winds blew.

7. A bird sings.

8. Sharp pencils break.

9. Red lights flashed.

10. Some people danced.

11. The rabbit disappeared.

12. A balloon burst.

13. Tiny insects buzzed.

14. Tired babies cry.

15. Busy people rush.

APPLY IT NOW

Write two sentences to describe things around you. Use an adjective that tells about the simple subject in each sentence. Then diagram each sentence.
Examples:
Beautiful flowers bloom.
Busy students write.
Fluffy clouds float.

Grammar in Action. Name the adjectives in the fourth sentence on page 477.

8.4 Adverbs

An **adverb** tells more about a verb. An adverb tells when, where, or how about a verb.

Add an adverb to a sentence diagram by writing it on a slanted line under the verb it tells more about.

subject | predicate

adverb

Let's do an example: **Juan hummed loudly.**

1. Write the simple subject and the simple predicate on the horizontal line.

   Juan | hummed

2. Think: *How did Juan hum?* The answer is *loudly. Loudly* is an adverb that tells how about the verb *hummed.* Write *loudly* on a slanted line under *hummed.*

   Juan | hummed

   loudly

EXERCISE 1 Copy each diagram. Finish it by adding the adverb under the verb.

1. beautifully

   Clara | paints

2. fast

   Neil | runs

3. yesterday

Tom	sang

4. bravely

Serena	acted

EXERCISE 2 Diagram each sentence.

1. Ballerinas dance gracefully.
2. Toddlers walk clumsily.
3. Careful students write neatly.
4. Safe drivers drive attentively.
5. The monkey chattered nearby.
6. Carol's bird sang loudly.
7. The librarian spoke quietly.
8. The doctor operated yesterday.
9. Wet paint dries slowly.
10. Good teachers explain patiently.
11. The boys laughed upstairs.
12. She tripped accidentally.
13. The bell rang suddenly.
14. We arrived late.
15. Jennifer answered confidently.

APPLY IT NOW

Write three sentences about getting ready for school. Use an adverb to tell when, where, or how in each. Diagram your sentences.
Examples:
I wake early.
I dress quickly.
I eat downstairs.

Tech Tip Use a computer program to create a sentence diagram.

Diagramming • 191

8.5 Adjectives as Subject Complements

A **subject complement** comes after a being verb. Some being verbs are *is, are, was,* and *were.* A subject complement tells more about the subject of the sentence. An adjective can be a subject complement.

In a sentence diagram, an adjective used as a subject complement is placed on the horizontal line to the right of the predicate. A slanted line that points back to the subject separates the adjective from the being verb.

subject	being verb \ subject complement

Let's do an example: **Giraffes are tall.**

1. Write the subject and the being verb on the horizontal line.

Giraffes	are

2. Think: *What are giraffes?* Giraffes are *tall. Tall* is a subject complement. It is an adjective that tells more about the subject, *giraffes.* Draw a slanted line after the being verb that points back to *giraffes.* Write *tall* after the verb.

Giraffes	are \ tall

EXERCISE 1 Copy each diagram. Finish it by adding the adjective as a subject complement.

1. sweet

| Sugar | is |

2. dark

| Caves | are |

3. funny

| Monkeys | are |

EXERCISE 2 Diagram each sentence.

1. Teachers are helpful.

2. Sherri's bike is new.

3. Poodles are cute.

4. Dad's bread is delicious.

5. The library was quiet.

6. The ride was scary.

7. The pumpkin is huge.

8. Dolphins are smart.

9. Jessica's joke was silly.

10. Ted's hamster is asleep.

11. His backpack is empty.

12. The peaches were ripe.

13. Ida's cat is black.

14. The water is cold.

15. Oatmeal is lumpy.

APPLY IT NOW

Write two sentences about places you know. Use adjectives as subject complements in your sentences. Then diagram the sentences.

Examples:
The beach is noisy.
The sand is hot.

Grammar in Action. Diagram the third sentence in the fourth paragraph on page 477.

8.6 Compound Subjects

A sentence may have more than one subject.

SIMPLE SUBJECT	CONJUNCTION	SIMPLE SUBJECT	SIMPLE PREDICATE
Eagles	and	hawks	soar.

In a sentence diagram, each subject goes on a separate line. The conjunction that connects the subjects goes on a dashed line.

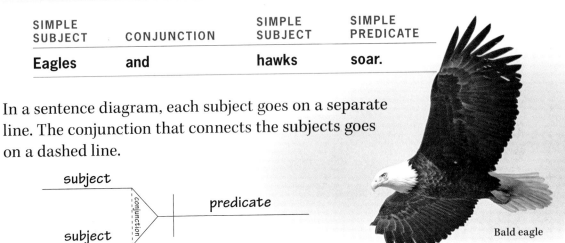

Bald eagle

Let's do an example: **Eagles and hawks soar.**

1. Draw two short horizontal lines. Write a subject on each line. Connect the subjects as shown. Write *and* on the dashed vertical line.

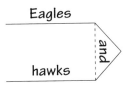

2. What do eagles and hawks do? They *soar*. *Soar* is the predicate. Write *soar* on a horizontal line after the subjects. Draw a vertical line to separate the verb from the subjects.

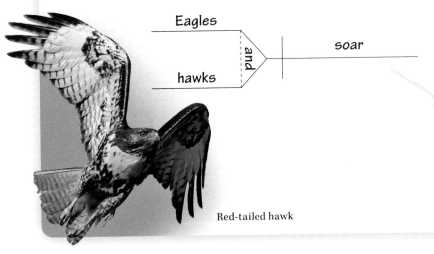

Red-tailed hawk

EXERCISE 1 Copy the diagram. Finish it by adding the compound subject.

Bats and bees

EXERCISE 2 Diagram each sentence.

1. Lions and tigers growl.
2. Lily and Hope sail.
3. Flowers and trees grow.
4. Carrots and celery crunch.
5. Fingers and toes wiggle.
6. Nurses and doctors help.
7. Sarah and Ben write neatly.
8. Airplanes and helicopters fly.
9. Horses and zebras run swiftly.
10. Mom and Dad clean carefully.
11. Apples and cherries taste sweet.
12. Diamonds and emeralds sparkle.
13. Rabbits and kangaroos hop.
14. Whales and porpoises swim.
15. Molly and Alicia laughed.

APPLY IT NOW

Write two sentences with compound subjects. You might use the names of friends as the subjects of your sentences. Diagram your sentences.
Example:
Don and Marco race.

8.7 Compound Predicates

A sentence may have more than one predicate.

SIMPLE SUBJECT	SIMPLE PREDICATE	CONJUNCTION	SIMPLE PREDICATE
Jason	bats	and	catches.

In a sentence diagram, each verb goes on a separate line. The verbs are connected by a dashed line for the conjunction.

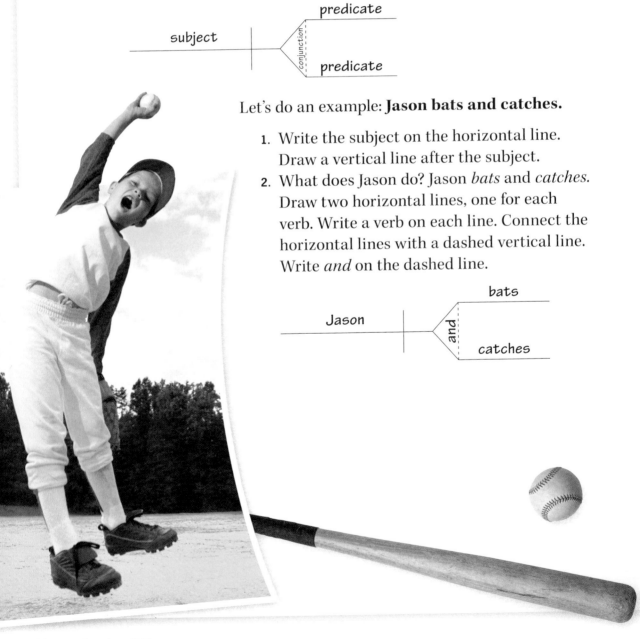

Let's do an example: **Jason bats and catches.**

1. Write the subject on the horizontal line. Draw a vertical line after the subject.
2. What does Jason do? Jason *bats* and *catches*. Draw two horizontal lines, one for each verb. Write a verb on each line. Connect the horizontal lines with a dashed vertical line. Write *and* on the dashed line.

EXERCISE 1 Copy the diagram. Finish it by adding the compound predicate.

kicks and passes

EXERCISE 2 Diagram each sentence.

1. Bob's horses trot and gallop.
2. Farmers plant and harvest.
3. The kite rose and fell.
4. Sean dusts and irons.
5. The audience stood and applauded.
6. Our teachers instruct and explain.
7. Monkeys climb and swing.
8. George reads and writes.
9. Artists imagine and create.
10. The students listened and discussed.
11. The flowers bloomed and faded.
12. Cats purr and meow.
13. Stars twinkle and glow.
14. Our hearts beat and pump.
15. Good friends call and e-mail.

APPLY IT NOW

Write two sentences with compound predicates about playing a sport. Diagram your sentences.
Examples:
I swim and dive.
The player shoots and scores.

8.8 Compound Subject Complements

Some sentences have more than one adjective used as a subject complement.

SIMPLE SUBJECT	BEING VERB	TWO ADJECTIVES AS SUBJECT COMPLEMENTS
Bats	are	scary but helpful.

To diagram a compound subject complement, you will need a line for each adjective and a place to write the conjunction.

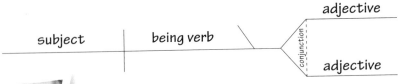

Let's do an example:

Bats are scary but helpful.

1. Diagram the subject and the being verb.
2. *Scary* and *helpful* are adjectives used as subject complements that tell more about bats. Draw a slanted line that points back to the subject. Then draw a horizontal line for each adjective. Use a dashed vertical line to connect these horizontal lines. Write *but* on the dashed line.

The Indian flying fox is one of the world's largest bats.

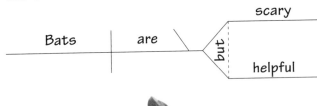

Grey long-eared bat

EXERCISE 1 Copy the diagram. Finish it by adding the compound subject complement.

sharp but useful

```
    Scissors    |    are    \
                |            \
```

EXERCISE 2 Diagram each sentence.

1. Popcorn is tasty but salty.
2. The movie was long and boring.
3. Lions are big and fierce.
4. The children were happy but tired.
5. The street was dark and quiet.
6. The marathon was long and tiring.
7. The doctor is concerned but hopeful.
8. Judy's blanket is warm and cozy.
9. The soup is hot but bland.
10. Her vase is beautiful and expensive.
11. The cat is black and white.
12. Michael was exhausted but happy.
13. The roses were large and fragrant.
14. Jaime's story was weird and scary.
15. My sneakers are old but comfortable.

APPLY IT NOW

Write a sentence about summer, winter, spring, or fall. Use a compound subject complement. Choose from the list below. Diagram your sentence.

cool but sunny
hot and humid
crisp and colorful
cold and snowy

8.9 Compound Sentences

Compound sentences—sentences that are made up of two smaller sentences—can also be diagrammed.

SIMPLE SUBJECT	SIMPLE PREDICATE	CONJUNCTION	SIMPLE SUBJECT	SIMPLE PREDICATE
Jane	watered,	and	Joe	weeded.

To diagram this sentence, put two sentence diagrams together. Connect the sentences with a dashed vertical line. Write the conjunction on the dashed line.

```
              subject    |    predicate

  conjunction
              subject    |    predicate
```

Let's do an example: **Jane watered, and Joe weeded.**

1. Diagram each smaller sentence. Put one above the other.
2. Draw a dashed vertical line to connect the sentences. Write the conjunction on the dashed line.

```
              Jane    |    watered

  and
              Joe     |    weeded
```

EXERCISE 1 Copy each diagram. Finish it by adding the second sentence.

1. Bart sings.

2. My brother wrote.

EXERCISE 2 Diagram each sentence.

1. Dogs bark, and cats meow.

2. The wind howled, and the lightning flashed.

3. The weather was cold, but we played outside.

4. The cartoon was funny, and the children laughed.

5. Some pretzels are hard, and some pretzels are soft.

6. The test was difficult, but I passed.

7. The game was exciting, but our team lost.

8. My brother painted, and my sister cleaned.

9. Carmen ran, and Mike walked.

10. Sophie sang, and Michelle danced.

11. My cousin called, and we chatted.

12. Watermelon is sweet, but lemons are sour.

13. The wind blew suddenly, and the door slammed.

14. The concert ended, and the performers bowed.

15. We hiked, but we rested often.

APPLY IT NOW

Write two compound sentences. Trade your sentences with a partner. Diagram each other's sentences.

 Tech Tip Diagram a compound sentence from a popular song.

8.10 Diagramming Practice

You have learned to diagram different kinds of sentences. Can you match the correct diagram with each of these sentences?

1. Jake snowboards fast.
2. We skated.
3. The lake is beautiful.

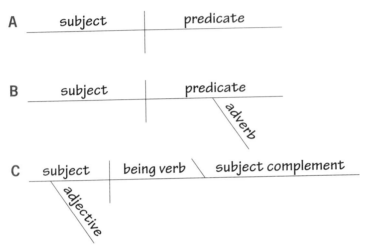

You are right if you matched sentence 1 with B, sentence 2 with A, and sentence 3 with C. Notice that in sentence 3, the article *the* goes with the noun *lake*.

EXERCISE 1 Match each sentence with one of the diagrams above—A, B, or C.

1. The milk is cold.
2. Parades move slowly.
3. Bands played.
4. Drummers drummed loudly.
5. People cheered.
6. The dogs are hungry.
7. Corinna answered last.
8. The car is old.
9. Musicians practice.
10. Authors write.

EXERCISE 2 Write out the sentences.

1. Roses | smell

2. Mom | works
   late

3. snakes | slither
   Shiny *swiftly*

4. grapes | are \ sour
   The

5. eggs | are \ brown
   Some

6. Flowers | wilt

7. Ice | melts
   slowly

8. Julie | practices
   often

9. Tara | paints
   well

10. Antelopes | run
    fast

11. peanuts | are \ salty
    The

12. Fire | burns
    rapidly

APPLY IT NOW

Write one sentence for each diagram pattern on page 202. Then diagram the sentences.

8.11 More Diagramming Practice

You have learned to diagram sentences that have compound parts. Can you match the correct diagram with each of these sentences?

1. Mom shops and cooks.
2. Jim and Chloe bake.
3. Papayas are orange, and strawberries are red.

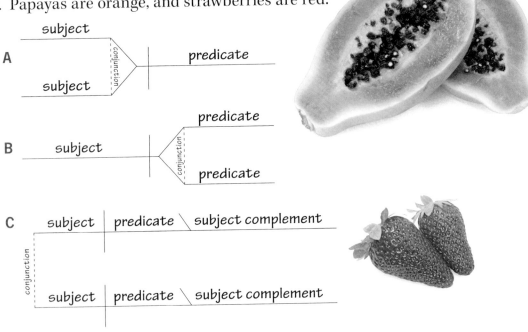

You are right if you matched sentence 1 with B, sentence 2 with A, and sentence 3 with C.

EXERCISE 1 Match each sentence with one of the diagrams above—A, B, or C.

1. Planes land and depart.
2. Bands and choirs practice.
3. Cherries are sweet, and lemons are sour.
4. Mom is busy, and Dad is tired.
5. Scientists study and discover.
6. Tops and pinwheels spin.
7. Class was hard, but I was successful.
8. Diamonds shine and sparkle.

EXERCISE 2 Write out the sentences.

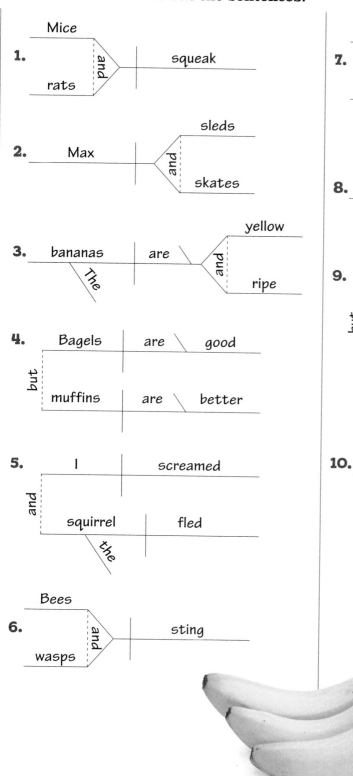

1. Mice and rats squeak

2. Max sleds and skates

3. The bananas are yellow and ripe

4. Bagels are good but muffins are better

5. I screamed and the squirrel fled

6. Bees and wasps sting

7. Teachers and coaches explain carefully

8. The car is old and rusty

9. The book was long but I finished quickly

10. Dex skied and skated

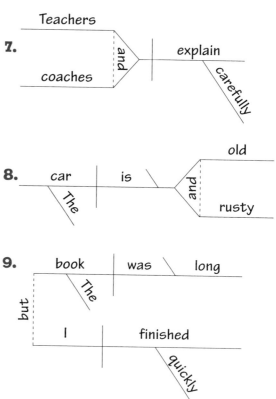

APPLY IT NOW

Write one sentence for each diagram pattern on page 204. Then diagram the sentences.

Diagramming Review

Diagram the sentences.

8.1
1. Clocks tick.
2. Motors hum.
3. Water flows.

8.2
4. Tommy's sister paints.
5. My friends sculpt.
6. Marcy's painting disappeared.

8.3
7. Healthy people exercise.
8. Good skiers practice.
9. A skater fell.

8.4
10. Turkeys gobble loudly.
11. Hens cluck constantly.
12. Jays squawk often.

8.5
13. Seals are sleek.
14. Jake's turtle was slow.
15. Sheep's wool is fluffy.

8.6
16. Cheetahs and leopards run.
17. Rabbits and hares hop.
18. Bats and birds fly fast.

8.7
19. Babies eat and sleep.
20. Toddlers crawl and walk.
21. Sue's brothers play and laugh.

8.8
22. Carrots are orange and crunchy.
23. Jam is sweet and sticky.
24. The crackers are old and stale.

8.9
25. Thunder clapped, and rain fell.
26. The cat hid, and the dog barked.
27. The storm ended, and the sky cleared.

Write out the sentences.

8.10

28.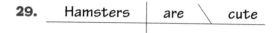

hamster | runs

Tom's / constantly

29. Hamsters | are \ cute

30.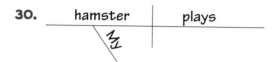

hamster | plays

My

8.11

31.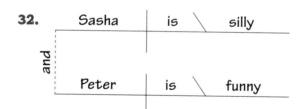

Snow

and > fell

rain

32.

Sasha | is \ silly

and

Peter | is \ funny

33.

simmered

soup | and

The / bubbled

Diagramming Challenge

EXERCISE 1 **Study the diagram and answer the questions.**

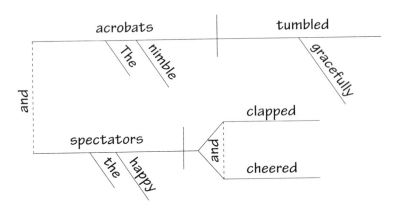

1. What kind of sentence is the diagram?
2. What compound sentence part is there?
3. What are the simple subjects? What are the simple predicates?
4. What are the articles and the adjectives? What noun does each describe or point out?
5. What is the adverb? What verb does the adverb tell more about?
6. Write out the sentence.

EXERCISE 2 **Diagram each sentence.**

1. The enormous elephant ate slowly, and the lazy lions dozed and played.
2. The colorful fish swooped and darted, and the busy penguins hunted skillfully.

PART 2

WRITTEN AND ORAL COMMUNICATION

Chapters

Personal Narratives

LiNK

Water Buffalo Days
Growing Up in Vietnam
by Huynh Quang Nhuong

I was born in the central highlands of Vietnam in a small hamlet on a riverbank that had a deep jungle on one side and a chain of high mountains on the other. . . . Like all farmers' children in the hamlet, I started working at the age of six. I helped look after the family herd of water buffaloes. Someone always had to be with the herd, because no matter how carefully water buffaloes were trained, they were always ready to nibble young rice plants when no one was looking.

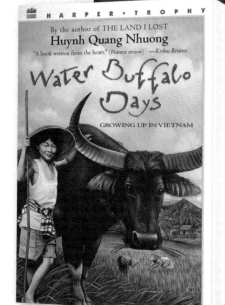

> In *Water Buffalo Days*, a man recounts his childhood in Vietnam, a country in Southeast Asia. *Water Buffalo Days* has many characteristics of a personal narrative. It is a true story, told from the writer's point of view, and it tells about events in the order they happen.

210

CHAPTER 1

Bad, Bad Mud

by Charlotte Eaton

I come to you today with some good advice: DON'T WALK IN MUD! It all started when Melissa and I were walking outside, with umbrellas, rainboots, rain jackets, and no fear of the rain. We were set for anything. At least that's what we thought.

Then Melissa asked, "Can we go into the cow pasture?" "Sure," I said. We ran to the edge of the barn and came to a halt. There before us was a pasture full of mud. Melissa said, "What are you stopping for?" I said, "MUD!" She said, "Look, just follow me. You won't get stuck. I promise." Before I could say yes or no, she was off. My heart was pounding. A little voice in my head kept saying, "Don't do it" over and over again.

Melissa was going deeper and deeper into the cow pasture. She wasn't sinking, so why would I? It's just a bunch of dirt, I said to myself. So I took one step, then another, and there I was in the middle of the pasture, actually, standing there in mud. "Melissa," I said. "This isn't so bad."

Wait, what am I feeling? Thick, cold, gooey, watery, mud. I was sinking as fast as a lightbulb burns out. I felt like someone was pushing and pulling me under. My fear was coming true! I started yelling for help.

Melissa heard me and came running over to see what my problem was. I told Melissa, "The ground is sucking me under!" "Quick, pull me out!" She tugged and tugged at my boots, but the mud was winning. We both started screaming for help.

Finally, my sister Jennie and my cousin Natasha came to the rescue. They grabbed ahold of me and all pulled. Out I popped, but my boots remained. I stepped on my umbrella and then pulled my boots out. My feet were now black and freezing. I put my boots back on and made a mad dash, barely touching the ground, and I was out of the gate. I said, "Melissa, score one for mud and I'm out!"

What Makes a Good Personal Narrative?

The story on page 211 is about Melissa and Charlotte's muddy adventure. Because Charlotte tells this true story about herself, it is a personal narrative. The interesting details of the events, people, and things make this personal narrative fun to read.

A well-written personal narrative has the following things.

Topic

What is the topic of a personal narrative? The topic of a personal narrative is you, the writer. A personal narrative might be about something that you did or something that happened to you. It might also tell how you feel about something.

A personal narrative can be about almost anything, but it should be a true story. When you write a personal narrative, you should tell what happened just as you remember it.

Point of View

Personal narratives are always told from the writer's point of view. Did you notice how Charlotte is always part of the story? Go back and count the number of times you see the word *I*.

The words *I, we, me, us, my,* and *our* signal that you might be reading a personal narrative. When the audience reads these words, they know the story is told from the writer's point of view.

Time Order

When you write a personal narrative, tell about the events in the order that they happened. Use time words such as *first, next, after that, then, finally,* and *last* to show how one event comes after another.

ACTIVITY A Read the personal narrative "Bad, Bad Mud" on page 211. Work with a partner to answer the following questions.

1. What is the topic?
2. What interesting details are included?
3. What words in the story tell you that it is a personal narrative?
4. What words in the story show the order that the events happened?

ACTIVITY B Work in groups to draw a comic strip of "Bad, Bad Mud." The pictures in the comic strip should follow the order of the story. Then write a sentence about what is happening in each picture.

ACTIVITY C Read this excerpt from a personal narrative. Then answer the questions.

Clubhouse Surprise

My friends and I thought it would be fun to build a clubhouse. First, we chose a secret spot in the back of my yard. We put boards on the ground under a big, old pine tree. We were sure no one could see us hidden under the branches. But then we were surprised when a little skunk waddled into the clubhouse.

1. What words show the point of view?
2. What is the topic?
3. What interesting details are there in the story?
4. What words show the order of the story?

WRITER'S CORNER

Think about a personal narrative that you would like to write. Then write a sentence that tells the topic.

LiNK

Water Buffalo Days

Some of the best times of my life were spent roaming the rice field, riding on the young buffalo's back. . . . The calf's time was not yet in demand, so we were free to explore all the nooks and corners of the field or leisurely catch all kinds of living creatures for food or for fun.

Huynh Quang Nhuong

ACTIVITY D Read the following topics. Which ones are good topics for personal narratives? Why?

1. teaching your dog to wave
2. the day I got lost at the mall
3. grandma and I go skating
4. what I want to be when I grow up
5. our winter camping trip
6. how to ride a horse
7. my favorite character in a book
8. the life of a famous person
9. the day I met my best friend
10. how I learned to ride a bike

ACTIVITY E Each sentence comes from a personal narrative, but the time words are missing. Complete each sentence with a time word from the word box to show when things happened. More than one answer may be correct.

after	before	during	finally	first
then	today	until	when	while

1. _____ I cleaned my room, I went to the park.
2. I could smell breakfast cooking _____ I woke up.
3. _____ I played my soccer game, I put on my shin guards.
4. _____ will be the first day of my summer vacation.
5. Those people would not stop talking _____ the movie.
6. _____ we ate dinner, we went outside.
7. I never went fishing _____ one day last June.
8. Tommy says he can snap his fingers _____ singing "Row, Row, Row Your Boat."
9. I worked and worked, and I _____ finished the jigsaw puzzle.
10. We bought our tickets for the movie, _____ we bought popcorn.

ACTIVITY F Complete the personal narrative with the time words from the word box. More than one answer may be correct.

> after that   finally   first   next   then

An Easy Choice

It was going to be a special day. My parents and I had decided to adopt a cat from a local animal shelter.

At the shelter we told the volunteers that we were looking for a cat. (1)_____, they gave us a form to fill out. (2)_____, the volunteers took us to a room with several cats. Some were playing in the center of the room, and some were sleeping on shelves in the wall.

I just stood and looked around. (3)_____, I took a piece of string out of my pocket and begin to twirl it. A little calico cat came up to me. She batted the string with her paw. I knelt down. She kept hitting the string. Slowly I petted the back of her head. She started to purr loudly. (4)_____ she rubbed her body against my leg.

(5)_____, I knew that this was the cat for me. Cali (short for calico), has become a member of the family. She is sitting on my lap as I write this.

ACTIVITY G Here is a personal narrative. The order of the sentences is mixed up. Put the sentences in the correct order.

1. He picked me up.
2. I was having fun until I reached the top of a hill.
3. I tried to steer, but I was going too fast.
4. I never went near that hill again.
5. Zoom, I flew down the hill!
6. A man ran to help me.
7. One Saturday I went for a ride on my new bike.
8. I hit the curb and tumbled over the handlebars.

WRITER'S CORNER

Tell a personal narrative about a pet or other animal to a partner. Use time words. Be sure you tell the narrative in the correct order. Have your partner write the time words you used.

Beginning, Middle, and Ending

A personal narrative is a story. Because it is a story, it should have a beginning, a middle, and an ending.

Beginning

The beginning of a personal narrative tells the reader what the story is about. A good beginning grabs the reader's attention and makes the reader want to read more.

The beginning of the story is also where you let the reader know why you're telling the story. For example, the beginning of a narrative might say, "Let me tell you the funny story about how I learned to ride a bike." The reader will be interested because everyone wants to read a funny story.

Middle

The middle of a narrative is important because this is where you tell the story. The middle is usually the longest part of a narrative.

The middle tells the events in the order they happened. It also has details that help the reader paint a picture in his or her mind about what happens.

You need to think carefully about all the parts of the story. Be sure the middle includes everything important to your story so that the reader doesn't get mixed up.

Suppose you were telling a story about learning to ride a bike. While you were learning, the bike tipped over and you scraped your knee. The reader would want to know what you were doing before and after your bike tipped over. The reader would also want to know why the bike tipped over. Did it hit a big rock, or did it slide in a puddle of water?

Ending

The ending tells how the story comes out. A good ending might leave readers with a smile or a new idea to think about. The ending can tell something you learned or how you felt about what happened.

The ending is where you tell the reader what the story means to you and why the story is important. Suppose you are telling about a time that your baseball team won a game. The middle of the narrative might tell about all the time you spent practicing. The ending might tell how proud you were that your hard work helped win the game.

ACTIVITY A Answer the questions about the personal narrative "Bad, Bad Mud" on page 211.

1. Which paragraph is the beginning?
2. Which paragraphs are the middle?
3. What are some details in the personal narrative?
4. Which paragraph is the ending?

ACTIVITY B Answer the questions about the personal narrative "An Easy Choice" on page 215.

1. Which paragraph is the beginning? What information is in that paragraph?
2. What information is in the middle paragraphs?
3. Do you think that the ending is interesting? Why or why not?

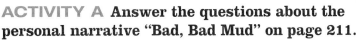

Grammar in Action. Circle the subject in both sentences.

Title

The title should give readers a hint about what the story is about. A funny or an interesting title can make people want to read your narrative.

ACTIVITY C Read this personal narrative. Copy the chart below. Then use your own words to fill in the chart. Use the information in the chart to think of a title for the narrative.

LiNK

Water Buffalo Days

It was very tiring to walk in the mud, so I rode on the calf's back when I wanted to catch land lobsters. When I spotted a nest, I poured salt water into it, and the land lobsters jumped out like crazy.

Huynh Quang Nhuong

What a horrible morning! My pet snake, Snerdly, was missing. Where could he be?

First, I looked in the living room. I checked under the couch and behind the cushions. I thought I heard soft, shooshing noises, but I couldn't find my little snake.

After that, I looked in the hall closet. I saw something long and slithery behind the coats. Was it Snerdly? No, it was just some ribbon.

Then I went to the laundry room. There was Snerdly, fast asleep on top of the warm dryer. I've never been so happy to see him!

Title	
Topic	
Beginning	
Middle	
Ending	

ACTIVITY D Below are parts of personal narratives. Which parts are they? Tell which part of a personal narrative they come from: the beginning, the middle, or the ending. Explain your answers.

1. Just then the roaring of the wind stopped. Was the tornado over? Dad crept up the stairs. He looked out the back door. He saw something and ran back down into the basement really fast.

2. Everyone asks how I got such a strange first name. The story of my name began a long time ago when my mom was a little girl.

3. It was such a hard way to learn that words can really hurt a person's feelings. After what happened to me, I'll never again say mean things about someone just to get a laugh.

4. Things were going fine. I was walking in time to the music. I was holding my basket of flowers and smiling. But when I heard our dog barking outside, I forgot everything I had practiced

5. I want to tell you about the first time I rode a roller coaster. It was not a good idea to have a lunch of three chili dogs before climbing aboard.

6. I enjoyed all the applause. I can't believe I was ever nervous about going on the stage. Now I'm planning to try out for the lead in the next school play.

ACTIVITY E Work with a partner. Choose one of the parts from a personal narrative in Activity D. Think of ideas for the two missing parts. Make up interesting details. Share your ideas for the personal narrative with the class.

WRITER'S CORNER

Look at the sentences you wrote for the previous Writer's Corner. Then write three sentences for the middle of your personal narrative. Save your work.

Strong Verbs

A verb is often the action word in a sentence. It tells what the subject does. In this sentence *Jan* is the subject. The verb *jumped* tells what Jan did.

Jan *jumped* off the diving board.

Some action verbs are stronger than others. They can tell the reader more clearly what the subject does. Use strong verbs when you write. Strong verbs make clear pictures in the reader's mind.

Which of these sentences creates a clearer picture in your mind?

The mouse *went* into its hole.

The mouse *ran* into its hole.

Ran is a stronger verb than *went* because it tells how the mouse moved. *Went* is a weaker verb because it tells only that the mouse did move. *Ran* makes a clearer picture in the reader's mind than *went* does.

Read the following pairs of sentences. In each pair the second sentence uses a stronger verb or verbs than the first sentence does.

I *asked* my brother to teach me.

I *begged* my brother to teach me.

I *went* off the skateboard as soon as I *got* on.

I *tumbled* off the skateboard as soon as I *stepped* on.

With a little practice, your writing will soon be full of strong, clear verbs.

ACTIVITY A Which sentence in each pair has the stronger verb or verbs? Explain why.

1. a. The dog <u>walked</u> down the street.
   b. The dog <u>trotted</u> down the street.

2. a. Celia <u>cleaned</u> her dog before the show.
   b. Celia <u>bathed</u> her dog before the show.

3. a. Jason was late, so he <u>hurried</u> to the bus stop.
   b. Jason was late, so he <u>went</u> to the bus stop.

4. a. People <u>come</u> to the beach to <u>see</u> the sunset.
   b. People <u>drive</u> to the beach to <u>gaze</u> at the sunset.

5. a. Suze <u>whispered</u> softly into her dog's ear.
   b. Suze <u>talked</u> softly into her dog's ear.

6. a. Shawn <u>made</u> a model ship out of toothpicks.
   b. Shawn <u>built</u> a model ship out of toothpicks.

7. a. The snake <u>slithered</u> away from the campfire.
   b. The snake <u>moved</u> away from the campfire.

8. a. A kangaroo <u>hopped</u> behind the hill.
   b. A kangaroo <u>went</u> behind the hill.

9. a. The class <u>did</u> the school project on time.
   b. The class <u>finished</u> the school project on time.

10. a. Is it too cold to <u>go</u> across the river?
    b. Is it too cold to <u>wade</u> across the river?

LiNK

Water Buffalo Days

Sometimes . . . I would just stretch myself on the calf's back and let him carry me where he liked. I gazed at the sky and forgot everything around me. I felt as if the sky moved, but not the calf and I.

Huynh Quang Nhuong

WRITER'S CORNER

Look at the beginning and middle that you wrote in previous Writer's Corners. Then write a two-sentence ending. Tell the reader what the story means to you.

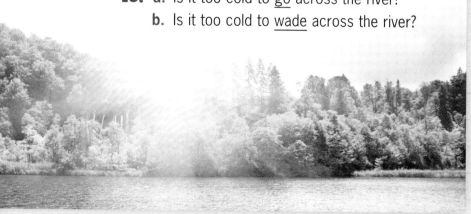

ACTIVITY B Read the following sentences. Replace each underlined verb with a stronger verb.

1. I <u>went</u> down the hill on my new sled.
2. I <u>go</u> to school on the bus every day.
3. The penguin <u>walked</u> toward me.
4. I <u>looked</u> at the rows of colorful sneakers in the window.
5. Our cat <u>likes</u> his cat food.
6. My little brother <u>looked</u> everywhere for his shoe.
7. We <u>put</u> one block on top of the other.
8. Leandro <u>put</u> his sister into the crib.
9. We <u>go</u> the same way to the gym every time.
10. The dish <u>broke</u> into tiny pieces.

ACTIVITY C Read each set of sentences. How does the verb in each sentence create a different picture? Add two more sentences to each set. Use strong verbs to show other actions the animals might do.

1. The dragon snorts.
   The dragon breathes.
   The dragon sneezes.
2. The eagle flies.
   The eagle soars.
   The eagle swoops.
3. The rabbit hopped.
   The rabbit leaped.
   The rabbit jumped.
4. The horse strutted.
   The horse galloped.
   The horse ran.
5. The cat meows.
   The cat hisses.
   The cat purrs.

ACTIVITY D Choose a verb from the word box to complete each sentence. Use each verb only once.

dialed	roamed	sprayed	leaped
limped	swim	peered	sold
spun	barked	drives	flew

1. The volleyball _____ through the air.
2. Some alligators _____ above the water's surface.
3. The dogs _____ at the mail carrier.
4. Dad _____ to his office every day.
5. Spiders _____ webs under the eaves.
6. Dean _____ four subscriptions last week.
7. Wild buffalo once _____ across the Great Plains.
8. I _____ Toby on my cell phone.
9. The skunk _____ its startled enemies.
10. She _____ from the barge.
11. With a twisted ankle, Tad _____ away from the field.
12. The tigers _____ on hot days.

ACTIVITY E Write strong verbs for each blank to complete the paragraph.

The fans _____ as the players _____ onto the field. The cheerleaders _____ as they _____ up and down. Music _____ through the stadium. Everyone _____ when the game ended.

WRITER'S CORNER

Look at the beginning, middle, and ending that you wrote in previous Writer's Corners. Replace the verbs with strong verbs to help paint a picture in the reader's mind.

Colorful Adjectives

Adjectives are words that tell something about nouns. Colorful adjectives are like strong verbs. They can paint clear pictures in the reader's mind.

A *gentle* wind blew through the oak grove.

A *fierce* wind blew through the oak grove.

The adjectives *gentle* and *fierce* both tell something about the wind. Which kind of wind blows harder—a gentle wind or a fierce one? How is the picture that *gentle* makes in your mind different from the picture that *fierce* makes?

Colorful adjectives make clearer pictures.

a *nice*, *cute* puppy

a *wrinkled*, *black* puppy

Which set of adjectives makes a clearer picture—*nice* and *cute* or *wrinkled* and *black*? Adjectives like *nice* and *cute* are not exact. Many people have different ideas about what is nice or cute. *Wrinkled* and *black* are colorful, exact adjectives. Good writers put just one idea in the reader's mind. That idea is the one they are writing about.

ACTIVITY A Which set of adjectives makes a clearer picture? Explain why.

1. a sweet, little kitten a tiny, playful kitten
2. a steep, winding road a long, narrow road
3. slender, golden stalks thin, yellow stalks
4. a large, bright fire a gigantic, glowing, orange fire
5. a tall, steel skyscraper a towering, glass skyscraper

ACTIVITY B Which sentence in each pair has a more colorful adjective? Give reasons for your answer.

1. **a.** The big boat sailed on the lake.
   b. The huge boat sailed on the lake.
2. **a.** I bit into a good apple.
   b. I bit into a crispy apple.
3. **a.** Will you wear your worn jeans?
   b. Will you wear your old jeans?
4. **a.** That dog has stinky breath.
   b. That dog has bad breath.
5. **a.** Ryan had a great time yesterday.
   b. Ryan had a thrilling time yesterday.
6. **a.** Aunt Jane gave me a yummy treat.
   b. Aunt Jane gave me a nice treat.

ACTIVITY C Describe a park. Write two adjectives for each noun.

1. _____ _____ trees
2. _____ _____ pond
3. _____ _____ picnic tables
4. _____ _____ flowers
5. _____ _____ squirrels

Describe your classroom. Write two adjectives for each noun.

6. _____ _____ room
7. _____ _____ desks
8. _____ _____ windows
9. _____ _____ floor
10. _____ _____ lights

Water buffalo working in rice paddies in Vietnam

WRITER'S CORNER

Write three sentences to describe an object in your classroom. Use three colorful adjectives.

ACTIVITY D Replace each underlined adjective with a colorful adjective from the word box.

terrified	vast	hilarious	packed

1. The scared rabbit bolted into the trees.
2. I couldn't find a seat in the crowded theater.
3. We laughed at the funny movie.
4. Wheat grows on the large plain.

ACTIVITY E Add a colorful adjective to tell something about each underlined noun.

1. Balloons floated in the air.
2. The puppy played with the children.
3. Rain poured from the clouds.
4. The girl picked a bunch of flowers.
5. We ate yogurt for a snack after practice.
6. Kwame got a suit and shoes for his birthday.
7. Dad likes to try foods from many countries.
8. The museum was built in 1898, and the library went up in 1909.
9. The pig that Shannon raised weighed nearly 1,000 pounds.
10. Tara decided to have her hair cut.
11. We saw the White House on our trip.
12. Where did the rabbit go?
13. The actor shouted her lines to the crowd.
14. Frank wanted to see that movie.
15. I watched the sun set over the river.

ACTIVITY F Add colorful adjectives to the paragraph about a room. Use the list after the paragraph to help you. The way the room you describe looks, feels, and even smells will depend on which adjective you choose.

I walked slowly into the (1)_____ room. (2)_____ flowers rested on the (3)_____, (4)_____ table in the corner. Next to the table was a (5)_____ chair. A (6)_____ book was lying by the chair on the (7)_____ floor. (8)_____ light streamed through the (9)_____ window. I shut the (10)_____ curtains and strolled out of the room.

1. stuffy	dark	small
2. Colorful	Drooping	Fake
3. old	shaky	polished
4. broken	dusty	white
5. velvet	wooden	soft
6. torn	new	thick
7. spotless	tile	sticky
8. Golden	Bright	Dim
9. cracked	large	open
10. dirty	heavy	red

ACTIVITY G Write colorful adjectives to complete the paragraph.

It was a _____ day. _____ clouds moved across the _____ sky. The _____ trees swayed in the _____ wind. Then a _____ rain began to fall on the _____ grass. I got on my _____ bicycle and rode home.

WRITER'S CORNER

Work in groups to use adjectives to tell a story. Write an adjective on a slip of paper. Place the slips in a box. Each person chooses a slip and uses the adjective on it in a sentence. When your group has used all the adjectives, the story is done.

Dictionary

Do you know what an English horn is? What about a joist? Every day we read words that we may not know. A dictionary is a book we use to look up these kinds of words.

A dictionary is a book of words and their meanings. In a dictionary you can find these things:

- how words are spelled
- the way words are pronounced
- what words mean

> **A**   **B**   **C**
> **quest** (kwest) **1.** A hunt or search [a quest for gold] **2.** A journey in search of adventure [the quests of medieval knights]
>
> **A.** Entry word
> **B.** Pronunciation
> **C.** Word definition(s)

Each word listed in a dictionary is called an entry word. The entry word is followed by the pronunciation and the definition of the word. The pronunciation is the way to say the word correctly. The definition is what the word means. Many words have more than one definition.

Alphabetical Order

Entry words are listed in alphabetical order. When more than one word begins with the same letter, the words are alphabetized by the second letter. When more than one word begins with the same two letters, the words are alphabetized by the third letter. What order would the words *account, absolute,* and *accept* be in?

ACTIVITY A Put each group of letters in alphabetical order.

1. s, v, y, t
2. k, h, i, j
3. r, t, e, o
4. n, l, g, q

5. f, k, d, b
6. m, c, h, i
7. w, m, q, r
8. j, t, h, k

ACTIVITY B Put each list of words in alphabetical order.

1. space
   planet
   rocket
   moon

2. Saturn
   Jupiter
   Mars
   Pluto

3. Earth
   enormous
   explore
   encounter

4. astronaut
   asteroid
   adventure
   atmosphere

ACTIVITY C Rewrite the scrambled letters to make a word. Then put the words in each list in alphabetical order.

1. yocp
   tac
   tosc
   enac

2. mfil
   rofu
   wlfe
   aflg

3. tset
   het
   doat
   ite

4. roup
   trpo
   moep
   cophr

WRITER'S CORNER

Reread the excerpt from *Water Buffalo Days* on page 225. Then look up *monotonous* in a dictionary. Write the definition. How does the meaning of the word change your understanding of the story?

Tech Tip With an adult, explore an online dictionary.

Guide Words

To save time when you're looking up a word in a dictionary, you can use guide words. Guide words tell the first and last words found on a dictionary page. The guide words are located at the top corner of the page.

When you look for a word in a dictionary, you should follow these steps.

1. Decide whether the word can be found at the beginning, middle, or end of the dictionary. (Think of where the first letter of the word comes in the alphabet.)
2. Look at the guide words at the top of the pages.
3. Decide whether you can find the word between the two guide words.
4. If so, look for the word on that page.

Fawn-colored lark

ACTIVITY D Where in the dictionary would you find the following words—toward the beginning, the middle, or the end?

1. batter
2. staff
3. maiden
4. dowel
5. afghan
6. lark
7. vine
8. jump
9. exile
10. undo
11. rural
12. cinder

ACTIVITY E Below are three sets of guide words with a page number for each. Tell the page number where you would find each word.

> linger—list 430   listen—liven 431   liver—loan 432

1. liter
2. load
3. livery
4. lisp
5. little
6. lipstick
7. lint
8. lizard
9. lip

ACTIVITY F Tell if each word comes before, after, or between each pair of guide words.

Word	Guide Words
1. double	door—dove
2. rug	ruby—rule
3. gravel	grasp—gull
4. spruce	sponge—square
5. power	practice—praise
6. watch	wallet—warmth
7. kitchen	knife—koala
8. normal	nomad—noon
9. movie	multiply—mumps
10. electric	elbow—empty
11. shave	sharpen—sheepdog
12. latitude	larva—lateral
13. bowl	bought—bow
14. profile	probe—produce
15. certain	ceremony—chairperson

ACTIVITY G Write a word that comes between each of the following pairs of guide words.

1. land—life
2. shallow—sky
3. background—balance
4. crawl—crusade
5. pack—penny
6. train—trout

Nomad and camels in the Sahara

WRITER'S CORNER

Use a dictionary to find where your first name would appear if it were an entry word. Write the entry word just before and just after where your name would appear. Then write the guide words for that page of the dictionary.

Grammar in Action. What does *hamlet* mean in the page 210 excerpt?

Oral Personal Narratives

An oral personal narrative is a story about you. You tell personal narratives every day. Have you ever told your family about your day? Have you ever told a friend about learning to ride a bike? These are personal narratives.

Get Ready

Telling a story to the class can be like telling a story to your friends. Try to choose a story that your classmates would like. It can be about almost anything, but it should be true.

Just like stories that you write, oral personal narratives use time words to show the order that things happened. Personal narratives are told from your point of view.

A good personal narrative should also include something that you learned or how you felt. You should share what you learned or how you felt with your audience.

Plan Your Story

Just like a personal narrative that you write, a personal narrative that you tell has a title, a beginning, a middle, and an ending. A good beginning opens the story and gives the audience a clue about what they will find out.

The middle is the main part of your story. It tells what happened in the order the events took place.

The ending finishes your story. It tells what you learned or how you felt. Many endings give listeners something extra to think about. An ending might show a new way to think about something.

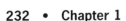

ACTIVITY A Choose two of these ideas and write a beginning sentence for each. Read aloud the sentences to a partner.

1. Saturday fun
2. My first time to . . .
3. A special trip
4. An accident
5. A pet gets into trouble
6. My last birthday
7. A big success
8. A dream I've had
9. A scary experience

ACTIVITY B Read aloud the following sentences from personal narratives. Use the feelings given in parentheses.

1. I had never had an experience as scary as this before, or ever again. (frightened)
2. My aunt Sarah was coming to stay with us for a visit. (happy)
3. The day our dog Max was lost was a day I won't forget. (sad)
4. It was another rainy day—the third in a row. (disappointment)
5. So I learned the hard way that I should always lock my bike. (sad)
6. My dad announced one Saturday morning that we were going ice-skating, which we had never done before. (surprise)
7. I always put away my homework in a special folder after I finish it. I never want to repeat the experience I had last fall. (determination)
8. Harry is my best friend, and we do lots of things together. (happy)

SPEAKER'S CORNER

Think of an idea for an oral personal narrative. You can use an idea you had during this chapter or a new idea. Write your idea and save it.

Write and Practice

Write your personal narrative on note cards. Write the beginning on the first card. Write the middle on two or three cards. Write the ending on the last card.

Practice your personal narrative by telling it aloud. First, tell it aloud to yourself in front of a mirror. Then tell it to a partner. Ask your partner to tell you any parts of your story that were confusing or too long. Fix those parts. Ask your partner for help on how to tell your story better. For example, should you speak louder or slower?

Present

Here are some tips for presenting your story.

- Look at the audience as much as you can. Move your eyes from person to person.
- Speak up so everyone can hear you, but do not shout.
- Use your voice, your face, and your body movements to share the feelings the people in your story were showing.
- Be sure to breathe when you tell your story.

Listen

Listening to a speaker is almost as important as telling the story. Here are some tips for listening to your classmates when they tell their stories.

- Look at the speaker. Try not to move your arms or legs or tap your feet.
- Picture in your mind what the speaker is talking about. Think about how the story will end.
- Save your questions until the speaker has finished.

ACTIVITY C Use the idea for a personal narrative that you wrote in the Speaker's Corner on page 233. Ask yourself what happened.

Think about the order that things happened. Then draw a set of pictures. Draw one picture for each thing that happened.

Think about what the people in your story said. Write what they said in "word balloons" above each person. Leave some space to write about your pictures at the top of your paper. Save your work.

ACTIVITY D Take the set of pictures you drew for Activity C. Write a sentence that tells what happens in each picture.

ACTIVITY E Practice your oral personal narrative. Ask a family member or a classmate to give you ideas to help make your story better. Tell your story to the class.

SPEAKER'S CORNER

Listen to a classmate's oral personal narrative. Write anything that you like or that you think is funny. Think about ways the speaker could make the story better. Share your notes with the speaker. Remember to make positive suggestions for improvement.

Tech Tip Record a podcast of your personal narrative for review.

Writer's Workshop

Prewriting and Drafting

The story you tell in a personal narrative can be about anything that happened to you, as long as it is true. Has something funny happened to you? Do you remember a time when you learned an important lesson? These things can be topics for personal narratives.

Prewriting

Ivan was assigned to write a personal narrative for class. Before he could start  writing, he needed an idea. He took time to do some prewriting. Ivan knew that this was the time when he could plan out the ideas that would go into his narrative.

Choosing a Topic

Ivan remembered that the topic of his personal narrative should be something that happened to him. He sat in a quiet place and began to think about a topic. However, Ivan didn't know where to begin. So he made a list to help him choose a topic. Here is part of Ivan's list.

> Possible Topics
> a trip I'll never forget—the time I visited Uncle Max in Florida
> I've never laughed so hard—when my older sister Isabel and I pretended to be monkeys
> an experience with an animal—when I was scared of dogs but became friends with Britney's dog, Shadow
> my proudest moment—when my painting won the district art contest

Ivan decided to write about becoming friends with the dog, Shadow. He thought this would be a good topic because it was about how he overcame a fear.

Your Turn

Use the following list to help you think of ideas for your personal narrative. After you finish the list, circle the topic that you are the most excited to write about. Remember that the topics have to be about something that really happened to you.

- a trip I'll never forget
- I've never laughed so hard
- an experience with an animal
- my proudest moment
- an event I'll never forget
- my biggest surprise
- the hardest thing I ever did
- the most excited I've ever been

Storyboarding

Now that Ivan had a topic, he started to plan for his first draft. Ivan drew pictures of three

 **Organization**

major events from his topic.

After he drew each picture, he wrote a sentence about what was happening in each one.

In Ivan's first picture, he drew himself sitting in his desk next to the dog and its owner. The second picture showed Ivan watching Shadow kick his legs while dreaming. The third picture showed Shadow using Ivan's foot as a pillow.

Ivan knew that personal narratives were written in time order. He drew the pictures and wrote the sentences in the order they happened.

Your Turn

Think about the three most important events that happened during the story you have chosen to tell. Draw each event on its own sheet of paper. Write a sentence about the picture at the bottom of the sheet. Then put the pictures in the order that the story happened.

Drafting

It was now time for Ivan to write a draft. First, he wrote the beginning. It told what his narrative was going to be about. Then Ivan used his pictures to help him write the middle. He finished with an ending that told how his story turned out. Here is Ivan's draft.

When I was three years old, I was biten by a German shepherd. The bite made me scared of big dogs, but I'm not anymore. It all changed last year when Britney was in my class. She is blind. Brings her helper dog. His name is Shadow, and he is a German Shepherd. When I saw him, I was so scared!

One day Ivan sat next to Britney and Shadow. It was the day everybody had to give a speech about the state they studied. Mine was Iowa. Shadow slept under Britney's desk. I looked at him. He was on his side, and he kicked his legs. He must have been dreaming. he didn't look as scary when he was asleep. I felt something on my foot. I looked under my desk. Shadow was using my foot as a pillow! He must have liked me and trusted me. I am still a little nervous when I meet new dogs, but I am not as scared as before.

Thanks, Shadow

While Ivan wrote, he tried to use what his class had talked about. He knew that he had to use his own point of view. He also knew that he had to write the narrative in the order it happened. He gave the story a beginning, a middle, and an ending. Ivan left extra space between lines so that he had room to make changes later.

Your Turn

Now you will write a draft of a personal narrative.

- Write your personal narrative from your point of view. Use words such as *I*, *me*, and *we*.
- Make sure your draft has a beginning. Tell the reader what the narrative will be about in the beginning.
- Write the middle of the draft. The middle is where you tell the story. Write the story in the order that it happened. Use the pictures you drew in storyboarding to help.
- Don't forget to tell in the ending how the story turned out. You might also want to tell why the story is important to you.

Prewriting

Drafting

Content Editing

Revising

Copyediting

Proofreading

Publishing

Content Editing

Now that Ivan had a draft, he wanted to make it better. He knew that he could if he edited the content. Content editors make sure the writing and the ideas make sense. They also check that the writing stays on the topic.

Ivan thought it would be a good idea to ask a friend to content edit his personal narrative. He asked Sal. Sal was in the class with Ivan and Britney. He knew about Shadow. Sal used the Content Editor's Checklist below.

Content Editor's Checklist

- ☐ Does the writing stay on the topic?
- ☐ Is the story told from the writer's point of view?
- ☐ Are the events described in time order?
- ☐ Are time words used to explain the order?
- ☐ Does the story have a title, a beginning, a middle, and an ending?

Sal read Ivan's personal narrative a few times. He used the Content Editor's Checklist to help him. Sal wrote his ideas for making Ivan's draft better. When he was finished, he had a meeting with Ivan.

Sal first told Ivan what he liked about the personal narrative. Sal liked how the narrative was told in time order. Nothing happened out of place. He also liked how Ivan was honest with his feelings. Then Sal told Ivan these ideas:

- The writing gets off the topic when you talk about the state reports.
- You used your name instead of the word *I* at the start of the second paragraph.
- Maybe you could use some time words to show the order. The second paragraph doesn't tell how much time took place between the different things that happened.
- I had trouble understanding where the middle stopped and the ending started.

Ivan thanked Sal for his help. Ivan wasn't sure if he was going to use all of Sal's ideas. He wanted to take time to think about how to use the ideas to make his narrative better.

Your Turn

- Read your first draft. Use the Content Editor's Checklist to help you improve the draft.
- Work with a partner and read each other's narratives. Pay attention to only one question from the checklist at a time. Take notes about your partner's draft. Then take turns talking about each other's drafts.
- Write your partner's ideas about your draft. Think about each one. The personal narrative is made up of your own ideas. Make the changes that seem right to you.

Writer's Tip When meeting with your partner about his or her draft, remember to start with something you liked.

Prewriting

Drafting

Content Editing

Revising

Copyediting

Proofreading

Publishing

Revising

This is how Ivan revised his draft.

Scared of Shadow

When I was three years old, I was biten by a German shepherd. The bite made me scared of big dogs, but I'm not anymore. It all changed last year when Britney was in my class. She is blind. Brings her helper dog. His name is Shadow, and he is a German Shepherd. When I first saw him, I was so scared!

One day, ~~Ivan~~ I sat next to Britney and Shadow. ~~It was the day everybody had to give a speech about the state they studied. Mine was Iowa.~~ Shadow slept under Britney's desk. I looked at him. He was on his side, and he kicked his legs. He must have been dreaming. he didn't look as scary when he was asleep. A little later, I felt something on my foot. Then I looked under my desk. Shadow was using my foot as a pillow! ¶ That's how Shadow and I became friends. He must have liked me and trusted me. I am still a little nervous when I meet new dogs, but I am not as scared as before.

Thanks, Shadow

Here are some of the things that Ivan did to improve his personal narrative.

- He agreed with Sal that he got off the topic. There was no need to tell his readers what was happening in school that day. Do you agree? Why or why not?
- He changed *Ivan* to *I* at the start of the second paragraph. Why?
- What did Ivan add to show how much time passed between the actions?
- Ivan agreed that the middle and ending ran together. What did he do to fix this?
- Ivan added a new sentence. What did it tell?

As Ivan looked at his paper again, he saw that he had forgotten to add a title. He tried

Voice

to think of a catchy title. He decided to use *Scared of Shadow.* Ivan thought it was a good title because people are sometimes scared of shadows. He was scared of Shadow, the dog.

Your Turn

Use your ideas and the ideas from your partner to revise your draft. Take your time making your draft better. Then look at the Content Editor's Checklist again. See if you can answer yes to each question.

Grammar in Action

Ivan found that he had an incomplete sentence. Can you find it? (Hint: It is in the first paragraph.)

Prewriting

Drafting

Content Editing

Revising

Copyediting

Proofreading

Publishing

Copyediting and Proofreading

Copyediting

Ivan knew that his ideas made more sense now. He also knew that he could make his personal narrative even better by copyediting it. When you

Sentence Fluency

copyedit you check that all the sentences work. You also check if you used all the words correctly. Ivan used this checklist to copyedit his personal narrative.

Ivan wanted to use stronger verbs. Since

Word Choice

Shadow was sleeping in the middle of the day, Ivan used *napped.* Ivan remembered how he was afraid to look at Shadow. He changed *looked* to *peeked.*

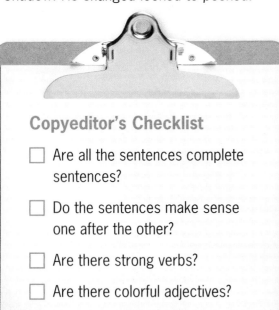

Copyeditor's Checklist

☐ Are all the sentences complete sentences?

☐ Do the sentences make sense one after the other?

☐ Are there strong verbs?

☐ Are there colorful adjectives?

Ivan also thought that he used *scared* or *scary* too often. He decided to use the word *frightening.*

Your Turn

Now it's your turn to copyedit your personal narrative. You might add stronger verbs. Make sure the new words you use don't change the meaning of the sentence.

Writer's Tip Be sure to look for only one type of mistake at a time.

Proofreading

Ivan decided to ask his friend Nate to proofread his draft. Look at the checklist that both Ivan and Nate used.

Nate found one misspelled word. He also

 Conventions

found a sentence that didn't start with a capital letter and one that didn't end with a punctuation mark. Can you find these three errors in Ivan's draft?

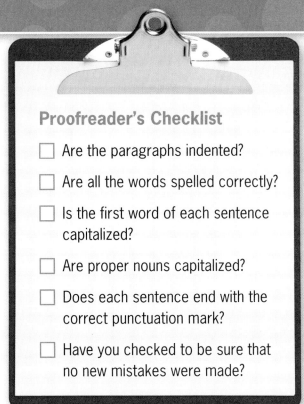

Proofreader's Checklist

☐ Are the paragraphs indented?

☐ Are all the words spelled correctly?

☐ Is the first word of each sentence capitalized?

☐ Are proper nouns capitalized?

☐ Does each sentence end with the correct punctuation mark?

☐ Have you checked to be sure that no new mistakes were made?

Ivan found a capitalization problem too. He saw that he capitalized *shepherd* one of two times he used the word. Ivan looked in the dictionary and found that *German shepherd* was correct.

Your Turn

Use the Proofreader's Checklist to proofread your draft. Then ask a partner to use the checklist to check your work.

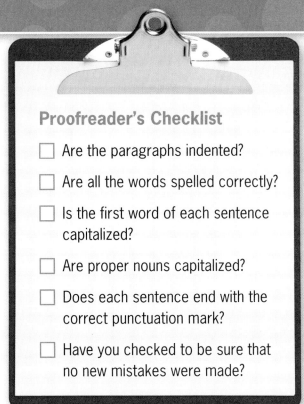

Common Proofreading Marks

Symbol	Meaning	Example
¶	begin new paragraph	over. ¶Begin a new
⌒	close up space	close u͡p space
∧	insert	students∧think *should*
ℒ	delete, omit	that the ~~the~~ book
/	make lowercase	Mathematics
∼	reverse letters	reveᴙse letters
≡	capitalize	washington
⌄" ⌄"	add quotation marks	⌄"I am,⌄" I said.
⊙	add period	Marta drank tea⊙

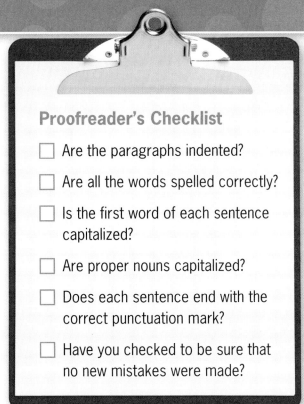

Publishing

Presentation Ivan carefully typed the final draft of his personal narrative. He slowly added the proofreading changes. Ivan knew that publishing is sharing work with an audience. Ivan drew a picture and shared the picture and narrative with the class. The picture was of Shadow sleeping on Ivan's foot.

Scared of Shadow

When I was three years old, I was bitten by a German shepherd. The bite made me scared of big dogs, but I'm not anymore. It all changed last year when Britney was in my class. She is blind and brings her helper dog. His name is Shadow, and he is a German shepherd. When I first saw him, I was so scared!

One day I sat next to Britney and Shadow. Shadow napped under Britney's desk. I peeked at him. He was on his side, and he kicked his legs. He must have been dreaming. He didn't look as frightening when he was asleep. A little later I felt something on my foot. Then I looked under my desk. Shadow was using my foot as a pillow!

That's how Shadow and I became friends. He must have liked me and trusted me. I am still a little nervous when I meet new dogs, but I am not as scared as before.

Thanks, Shadow!

Eventually, a professional writer submits his or her personal narrative to a magazine or book publisher. Whenever you publish your work, your goal is to share your thoughts and experiences with other people. There are many ways you can publish your personal narrative.

 Create a classroom book. Include classmates' photos, drawings, or other souvenirs of their experience.

 Have your class book on hand for Parents' Night. You might wish to present it as a PowerPoint presentation or a video.

 Make a classroom newsletter. Use a digital camera to add photos of your classmates.

 Post it to a Web site that publishes student writing. Work with an adult to find an appropriate site.

 Draw one part of your story on a separate sheet of paper. Then play a guessing game. Put all the narratives on one bulletin board and all the pictures on another board. Have everyone read the narratives and try to match each picture to its story.

Your Turn

- Make a final copy of your personal narrative. You can use a pencil and paper or a computer. Include the proofreading corrections.
- Take plenty of time finishing your work. You are going to share it with your audience. Be careful not to make any new mistakes while writing or typing.

Prewriting

Drafting

Content Editing

Revising

Copyediting

Proofreading

Publishing

How-to Articles

LiNK

The Kids' Multicultural Cookbook
by Deanna F. Cook

Cheesy Quesadillas

If you're a fan of grilled cheese sandwiches, then you will love this Mexican version. Instead of melting the cheese between sliced bread, northern Mexicans melt cheese in a flour tortilla. You can buy tortillas in the refrigerator section of most grocery stores.

What You Need

Pat of butter	1/4 cup grated cheese
1 flour tortilla	Salsa

1. In a frying pan, melt the butter over medium heat.
2. Set the tortilla in the pan and sprinkle half of it with the grated cheese. Fold the other half over the cheese to form a half circle.
3. Cook for about 2 minutes or until the tortilla browns. Then, use a spatula to flip the tortilla over. Cook it for another 2 minutes or until it browns. If you want, you can dip the quesadilla in salsa.

Makes 1 Mexican grilled cheese sandwich.

> This recipe has the characteristics of a how-to article. It has an introduction that tells what you will make or do, directions in step-by-step order, and a conclusion.

CHAPTER 2

Paper Stained Glass

by Steffi Anderson

Does your room need some color? Stained glass is a pretty decoration to hang in a window. This project uses black paper as the background. You cut holes in it and then put colored tissue paper in back of the holes. Just follow these steps.

What You Need

one piece of black construction paper

pieces of tissue paper in different colors

a sheet of paper and a pencil

scissors

glue or tape

1. Draw a design on white paper with shapes for the stained glass. Look at the sample drawing for ideas.
2. Copy your design on the black paper.
3. Cut out holes in the black paper for the shapes.
4. Cut out pieces of colored tissue paper to fit behind the shapes.
5. Glue or tape the pieces of tissue paper behind the shapes.

When you finish your stained glass, hang it in a window. Let the sun shine through!

What Makes a Good How-to Article?

A how-to article tells how to do something. A how-to article might be a recipe for how to make peanut butter cookies. A how-to article might be directions to a party or rules for a game. A how-to article might teach you how to do something, like braid your hair or fly a kite. A how-to article might teach you how to make something, like the how-to article on page 249. Here are some things to remember when you write a how-to article.

Topic

Before you write a how-to article, you need to decide what the article will be about. The topic of a how-to article is what the reader will learn to make or do.

It is important to pick a topic that you can explain in a few short steps. It is also important to pick a topic that you know about. A how-to article about how to build a real-life castle would be too long and difficult. A better topic might be how to build a sandcastle.

Try to pick a topic that you think people will want to learn about. What topics interest you?

ACTIVITY A Read each topic. Tell whether it is a topic for a how-to article and explain how you know.

1. decorating a pet rock
2. types of dinosaurs
3. my Uncle Lewis
4. why kids need to study math
5. teaching a dog to sit
6. making a fruit salad
7. how to get to the skate park
8. what I did last winter
9. searching for information online
10. how I found my lost homework

ACTIVITY B Read each topic. Is it a topic you would like to learn more about? Explain why or why not.

1. how to build the best paper airplane
2. how to underline a sentence
3. how to turn the page in a book
4. how to make waffles
5. how to turn on a light switch
6. directions for finding pirate treasure
7. how to build a clubhouse
8. how to peel a carrot
9. how to win at your favorite video game
10. directions for growing an herb garden

WRITER'S CORNER

What are some snacks you like to eat at home? Which ones do you know how to make? Write a list of at least three snacks that you know how to make.

Order

A how-to article gives directions in step-by-step order. When you write a how-to article, put the steps in the same order that you want the reader to do them. Then number your steps, starting with 1.

Here are the steps for growing marigolds in an egg carton.

1. Put plastic wrap in each cup of an egg carton.
2. Fill the cups with soil.
3. Plant a marigold seed in each cup.
4. Pour a little water on the soil.
5. Close the egg carton to keep the seeds warm.
6. Give the seeds time to sprout. Then plant them outside.

Be sure that you put the steps in the right order before you number them. Imagine if steps 1 and 2 were in the wrong order. The reader might put the soil in the egg carton before putting in the plastic wrap. What a mess! You also have to be careful not to leave out an important step. Imagine if step 4 was left out. The plants wouldn't grow because they had no water.

ACTIVITY C **These steps for making colored noodles are out of order. Copy the steps in the right order. Then number the steps 1, 2, 3, 4, 5, and 6.**

- Swish the noodles in the bag until they are colored.
- Repeat the above steps with other colors.
- Place the noodles on paper towels to dry.
- Pour some food coloring and a few drops of rubbing alcohol into a plastic bag.
- Add some noodles and zip the bag closed.
- Use the different-colored noodles in a craft project.

ACTIVITY D Imagine you have to explain how to do something simple to an alien creature. Pick a topic. Write the steps you would need to explain the topic to the alien creature.

1. how to make chocolate milk
2. how to do laundry
3. how to study spelling words
4. how to climb a tree
5. how to make a bed
6. how to play dodgeball
7. how to care for a hamster
8. how to use a digital camera

LiNK

Happy Pop-Up Card

1. Fold [a sheet of] paper in half to make a card.
2. Cut a thin strip of paper. Fold it back and forth to make the pop-up spring.
3. Use markers to make a decoration. Cut it out.
4. Paste one end of the spring to the inside of the card. Paste the other end to your decoration.
5. Write your message in the card.

Jill Frankel Hauser

ACTIVITY E There is something missing in these steps for how to set a dinner table. Read the steps and tell what is missing.

1. Get a plate, a fork, a knife, a napkin, and a glass for each person.
2. Put a plate at each place.
3. Put a fork to the left of the plate.
4. Fold the napkin and put it next to the fork.
5. Put a glass to the top right-hand side of the plate.
6. Do this for each person.

WRITER'S CORNER

Choose a snack from the list you made for the Writer's Corner on page 251. Write three steps for making that snack.

Grammar in Action. Circle all the nouns in your snack recipe.

Parts of a How-to Article

A how-to article has five parts: the title, the introduction, the What You Need list, the steps, and the conclusion. Read what each part does in the example below.

Title
The title tells what the article is about.

What You Need
What You Need is a list of all the things the reader will need. Sometimes this part is called Materials.

Conclusion
The conclusion tells what readers made or did. You might give tips for other ways to do the activity. You might tell readers why what they learned will help them.

Make a Banana Milk Shake

A banana milk shake is tasty. It's so easy to make, you can enjoy it any time!

What You Need
1 scoop of vanilla ice cream
1/2 cup of milk
1 ripe, peeled banana
blender

Steps
1. Ask an adult to help you slice the banana.

2. Put ice cream in the blender. Add milk and the banana.

3. Place the lid on the blender. Have an adult turn on the blender.

4. When the ingredients are mixed, have an adult turn off the blender.

5. Pour the milk shake into a glass.

You've now made a tasty banana milk shake. Try using other fresh fruit to come up with flavors of your own!

Introduction
The introduction tells what you will make or do. It might also give a reason to make or do something.

Steps
The steps list what to do. Numbers show the order of the steps.

ACTIVITY A This how-to article is mixed up. Copy the parts of the how-to article. As you copy the article, put the parts where they belong.

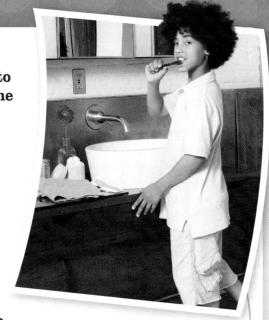

What You Need

toothbrush
toothpaste
water

Conclusion

Remember to brush at least twice a day. Try to brush after eating sugary snacks. And remember to floss!

Title

How to Brush Your Teeth

Introduction

Healthy teeth help you chew. They help you look your best. Follow these steps for healthier teeth.

Steps

1. Wet the toothbrush.
2. Squeeze the toothpaste onto the toothbrush.
3. Brush your teeth for three minutes. Use gentle strokes.
4. Rinse with cool water.

ACTIVITY B Read the how-to article "Paper Stained Glass" on page 249. Work with a partner to answer the following questions.

1. What will the readers learn to make?
2. Which part is the introduction?
3. What items are listed in the What You Need part?
4. How many steps are there?
5. Which part is the conclusion?

WRITER'S CORNER

Imagine that you are writing a how-to article about playing checkers. Write what you would list in the What You Need part.

Including What You Need

When you write a how-to article, be sure to include everything needed to do the steps. Try doing the activity yourself to make sure you haven't left out any materials.

Unneeded Information

Adding unneeded information to a how-to article can confuse the reader. Look at these steps about how to make a penny bank.

How to Make a Penny Bank

Steps
1. Clean an old coffee can.
2. Cover the outside with white paper.
3. Use markers or paint to decorate it.
4. Don't ever tell your brother or sister where you keep your pennies.
5. Ask an adult to cut a slit in the center of the lid. Place the lid on the container.
6. Use your bank to collect spare pennies or other coins.

Do you see an unneeded step? If you said step 4, you are right. It might be a good idea to keep your penny bank secret, but this information is not needed to make a penny bank.

Always check that you have included only the information you need in your steps.

ACTIVITY C **Read this What You Need list. Then read the steps. What is missing from the list?**

What You Need	Steps
bowl	1. Pour cereal into the bowl.
spoon	2. Add milk to the cereal.
cereal	3. Use a butter knife to slice the banana.
banana	4. Drop the sliced banana into the cereal.
butter knife	5. Stir and eat.

ACTIVITY D Read these steps for making a peanut butter and jelly sandwich. Tell which step is not needed.

Making a Peanut Butter and Jelly Sandwich

1. Spread peanut butter on one slice of bread.
2. Spread jelly on the other slice of bread.
3. Some people call this a PB and J sandwich.
4. Place the slices together so that the peanut butter and the jelly are inside the sandwich.

ACTIVITY E The following sentences are from a how-to article about making a bird feeder. Decide which sentence is the introduction and which is the conclusion. Then arrange the steps in order.

1. Enjoy watching birds flock to your bird feeder.
2. Steady the pinecone by holding it from the loop and spread cream cheese or soy butter on it.
3. Making a bird feeder is simple and fun.
4. Loop a piece of yarn around the top of the dried pinecone.
5. Roll the covered pinecone in birdseed.
6. Get a large pinecone and let it dry.
7. Hang the finished pinecone on a tree branch.

Grammar in Action. Circle all the common nouns and underline all the proper nouns in your directions.

Dictionary Meanings

A dictionary is a book of words and their meanings. A word is listed in the dictionary in an entry. An entry lists the word, its pronunciation, and what it means. If a word has more than one meaning, each different meaning is listed with a number.

Learning new meanings for words can be fun. Learning new meanings can also help you become a better reader, writer, and speaker.

In this entry the word *quill* has three meanings. Can you find them?

quill (kwil) **1.** a large, stiff feather. **2.** a writing pen made from the hollow stem of a feather. **3.** one of the sharp, stiff spines of a porcupine.

ACTIVITY A Use guide words and alphabetical order to find these words in a dictionary. Tell how many meanings each word has.

1. find
2. grade
3. steam
4. safe
5. phantom
6. family
7. drive
8. trunk
9. land
10. character

ACTIVITY B These words have more than one meaning. Under each word there are three meanings. Two meanings are correct. Use a dictionary to choose the two meanings of each word.

1. safe
   a. a steel box for storing money or jewels
   b. in baseball, reaching a base without being out
   c. the dried leaves of a plant

2. crane
   a. a large box made of wood
   b. a machine for lifting heavy objects
   c. a large bird with long legs

3. flurry
   a. a brief, light snowfall
   b. a type of musical instrument
   c. a sudden burst of activity

4. cinch
   a. a strong strap for fastening a saddle on a horse
   b. something that is easy to do
   c. a cup-shaped object used to store water

5. substantial
   a. underwater
   b. strongly made
   c. large or important

6. stock
   a. a large fort
   b. a share in a company
   c. items in a store that people can buy

WRITER'S CORNER

Open a dictionary to any page. Find a word that you do not know. Read the meanings of the word. Then write a sentence that shows one meaning of the word.

ACTIVITY C Write one meaning you know for each word below. Then look up each word in a dictionary. Tell how many other meanings there are.

1. blank
2. land
3. sharp
4. shell
5. double

6. pocket
7. party
8. train
9. rule
10. brand

ACTIVITY D Look up each word in a dictionary. Write one meaning of the word.

1. appliance
2. knoll
3. demolish
4. nocturnal

5. heron
6. cleaver
7. grime
8. bard

9. glacier
10. hush
11. pace
12. quest

ACTIVITY E Use a word from Activity D to complete each sentence.

1. The soldiers walked up the _____ to the castle.
2. Ziggy built a special _____ for making fruit smoothies.
3. It was difficult to keep up with the runner's fast _____.
4. The rain washed the _____ off the sidewalk.
5. I watched a wrecking ball _____ the old dance hall.
6. My dad uses a _____ to chop steaks.
7. The bell rang and a _____ fell over the entire auditorium.
8. Bats are my favorite _____ animals.
9. The _____ sang a beautiful song for the king.
10. Scientists tell us that a large _____ created the Great Lakes.
11. The knight went on a _____ to kill the dragon.
12. A large _____ crossed the pond.

ACTIVITY F Look carefully at the meanings for *press*. Tell which sentence goes with each meaning.

> **press** (w) *verb* **1.** to push something with steady force. **2.** to make something smooth with a hot iron. **3.** to hold someone or something close to you; hug. **4.** to keep asking somebody to do something.

1. My dad presses his shirts every morning so that he doesn't go to work with wrinkled clothes.

2. Dahlia pressed a tack into her wall.

3. Theodore pressed his teddy bear to his chest.

4. Mrs. Brown pressed her students to stop talking during the film.

ACTIVITY G Look up the names of the planets in our solar system in a dictionary. Use the definitions to put the planets in order from the sun. The first planet has been done for you.

EXAMPLE **1. Mercury**

Mars	Jupiter
Saturn	Neptune
Uranus	Earth
Venus	

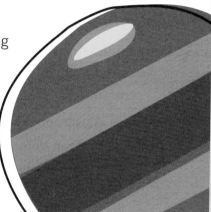

With an adult, use an online dictionary.

The Four Kinds of Sentences

Writers can use sentences to say just about anything. There are four kinds of sentences. Each of them has a different purpose. The four kinds of sentences are statements, questions, commands, and exclamations.

Statements

Some sentences tell. Telling sentences are called statements. Statements end with a period. Here are four statements.

Mushrooms grow in warm, soggy places.

A clean dog is a healthy dog.

Your skateboard looks new.

Many students enjoy music class.

Questions

Some sentences ask. Asking sentences are called questions. Questions often begin with words such as *who, what, when, where, do,* and *is.* Questions end with a question mark. Here are four questions.

Do you like to paint?

Where can I buy wind chimes?

Is it going to rain today?

What did you do over summer vacation?

 LiNK

Learning How: Karate

As a beginning karate student, you will learn four basic blocks. A *rising block* blocks a punch to the face. With your right fist facing up and resting on your right hip, raise your right arm in a bent position above your head. This upward motion deflects an opponent's punch to the face.

Jane Mersky Leder

ACTIVITY A Read each sentence. Tell whether the sentence is a statement or a question. Put the correct punctuation mark at the end of each sentence.

1. Is that a brown bear outside the tent
2. This tire would make a good swing
3. Where can I find a ring like that
4. Kiki likes to watch the fish in the pond
5. That apple has a worm in it
6. Did that spy escape
7. Puppets scare my little sister
8. Did you say he lives in the jungle
9. What is a diamond
10. A can of blue paint was spilled on the grass

ACTIVITY B Read each question. Write a statement that answers the question. Put the correct punctuation mark at the end of each sentence.

1. What kinds of books do you like to read?
2. What is your favorite food?
3. When did you start going to school?
4. What do you like to do on the weekends?

ACTIVITY C Read each sentence. Write a question about the statement. Begin each question with a question word. Put the correct punctuation mark at the end of each question.

1. Charlotte and Wilbur are characters in *Charlotte's Web.*
2. Police officers help protect us.
3. Mumbai is in India.
4. We celebrate Memorial Day on the last Monday in May.

WRITER'S CORNER

Here are some other words that begin questions. Choose three words. Use each to write a question.

Has	Are	Did
Does	Was	Am
How	Which	Why

Commands

Sentences that tell or ask readers to do something are called commands. Game directions and steps in a how-to article direct people to do something. Many commands begin with a verb. Here are three commands.

> **Go to the red square.**
> **Glue the yarn to the mask.**
> **Unwrap your gift.**

Exclamations

Sentences that express strong feelings are exclamations. Exclamations end with an exclamation point. Here are three exclamations.

> **What a great party!**
> **There's a spaceship over my house!**
> **I'm so happy to see you!**

Can you name the four kinds of sentences?

> A **George Washington was our first president.**
> B **Who was our second president?**
> C **Think about it for a minute.**
> D **It was John Adams, of course!**

You are right if you said that A is a statement, B is a question, C is a command, and D is an exclamation.

ACTIVITY D Tell which sentences are commands. Put a period at the end of each command. If the sentence is not a command, put the correct punctuation mark at the end.

1. Listen to the whistle
2. Sprinkle sugar on the berries
3. Can you hear the crickets
4. Wash the dishes

5. How scary that was

6. Are there going to be clowns

7. Show me your new bike

ACTIVITY E Read the how-to article "Paper Stained Glass" on page 249. Work with a partner to find a statement, a question, a command, and an exclamation. Write the four sentences you find. Then write which part of the how-to article each sentence comes from.

ACTIVITY F Read these statements about things that Keri said. For each statement write a sentence telling what you think Keri actually said. Use questions, commands, and exclamations as your answers.

EXAMPLE **Keri asked if I wanted to go to the park.**

Do you want to go to the park?

1. Keri asked what time it is.

2. Keri told me to take out the garbage.

3. Keri shouted for me to shut the door.

4. Keri told me to take the dog for a walk.

5. Keri asked what I had learned at school.

6. Keri yelled that she was glad it was Friday.

7. Keri told me to turn off the TV and read a book.

8. Keri asked when Mom would be home.

9. Keri asked if I had heard a noise upstairs.

10. Keri said she was excited to be going to California.

WRITER'S CORNER

Read the steps for making a penny bank on page 256. Write three sentences for an introduction. Make at least one sentence a statement and one a question.

Grammar in Action, Include one possessive noun in your introduction.

Compound Words

A compound word is one word that is made by putting two words together. Look at these compound words. Can you name the two words in each compound word?

lighthouse	**bluebird**
fingernail	**bookcase**
raincoat	**watermelon**
hairbrush	**junkyard**

The compound word *lighthouse* is made by putting together the words *light* and *house*. Each part of a compound word tells something about what the whole compound word means. A lighthouse is a kind of house built to shine a bright light. A hairbrush is a brush made for your hair.

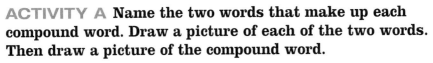

ACTIVITY A **Name the two words that make up each compound word. Draw a picture of each of the two words. Then draw a picture of the compound word.**

1. horseshoe
2. houseboat
3. goldfish
4. ladybug

5. football
6. wheelchair
7. handshake
8. flowerpot

ACTIVITY B Make a compound word by choosing the correct word from each list.

1. book_____
   a. stare
   b. mark
   c. check

2. camp_____
   a. tree
   b. burger
   c. fire

3. shoe_____
   a. lace
   b. stone
   c. shirt

4. ship_____
   a. horn
   b. wipe
   c. wreck

5. door_____
   a. hand
   b. mat
   c. hammer

6. sand_____
   a. plan
   b. floor
   c. storm

7. tug_____
   a. boat
   b. rope
   c. coast

8. steam_____
   a. cup
   b. rabbit
   c. ship

9. arrow_____
   a. bow
   b. grass
   c. head

10. black_____
    a. bird
    b. tire
    c. bend

11. mail_____
    a. card
    b. box
    c. paper

12. sky_____
    a. light
    b. near
    c. stick

WRITER'S CORNER

Make a new compound word by putting two words together, such as *noseball*. Tell a partner what your new compound word means. Write a sentence that uses your new word.

ACTIVITY C Make compound words by matching each word in column A with a word in column B.

Column A   Column B

1. junk_____   room
2. bird_____   ball
3. table_____   storm
4. class_____   yard
5. air_____   house
6. thunder_____   guest
7. night_____   water
8. house_____   gown
9. basket_____   cloth
10. under_____   plane

ACTIVITY D Answer each question with a compound word. Each compound word is started for you.

1. I am at the end of a fishing line. What am I? a fish_____

2. I bring printed news and information to people every day. What am I? a news_____

3. I leave my mark on wet sand. What am I? a foot_____

4. I work at beaches and swimming pools, and I save lives. Who am I? a life_____

5. I make your dishes clean and sparkling. What am I? a dish_____

6. I hold your clothes when you go on vacation. What am I? a suit_____

7. I am the place where you play or watch a baseball game. What am I? a ball_____

8. I am a red and black-spotted insect. What am I? a lady_____

ACTIVITY E **Choose the words from each box to complete the compound words.**

1. earth_____, earth_____

worm	fly	fighter	rig
heart	quake	plane	front

2. fire_____, fire_____, _____fire

button	fighter	weather	card
road	vine	cracker	wild

3. air_____, air_____, air_____, air_____

craft	beep	port	line
trail	fruit	plane	paper

4. water_____, _____water, water_____, water_____

under	wave	melon	fall
color	car	dip	wind

5. _____bird, bird _____, bird_____, bird_____

play	ball	house	bath
seed	room	blue	line

WRITER'S CORNER

Read a page from a book with a partner. Write all the compound words you find on the page. Use two compound words in a sentence.

Tech Tip With an adult, find four more compound words online.

How-to Talks

Imagine that you are telling a friend how to get to school from your house. That is a how-to talk. Any time you tell someone how to do something, you are giving a how-to talk.

A how-to talk is a lot like a how-to article. A how-to talk has all the parts of a how-to article. Can you remember what these parts are?

Title

The title of a how-to talk tells what the talk is about. Start your how-to talk by telling your audience the title.

Introduction

The beginning of a how-to talk is the introduction. In the introduction tell your audience what you are going to teach them.

What You Need

During your how-to talk, say what the audience will need for the activity. You might write the What You Need list on a poster and read it to the audience. If you can, show the audience the items they will need.

Steps

Explain the steps to the audience. You might even act out how to do each step. If you can't show the steps to your audience, you might draw pictures. Use time words, such as *first, then,* and *after that.* Time words help listeners follow the steps.

Conclusion

The conclusion is the ending of your how-to talk. You might show what you made. You might tell other ways listeners could do the activity. When you finish, ask if anyone has questions.

Choosing a Topic

Some topics may be good for a how-to article, but they may not be very good for a talk. They may have too many steps. They may be useful, but they may not be very interesting to listeners. For example, explaining how to play a board game may be very long and hard to follow. The information may not be very interesting unless the listeners are planning to play the game.

Some topics may be good if you use pictures or put on a demonstration. For example, if you are explaining how to make an object by doing origami, which is the art of paper folding, it would be a good idea to demonstrate making the object.

ACTIVITY A **Read each topic. Do you think it good for a how-to talk? Explain why or why not.**

1. using a scooter safely
2. how to play chess
3. how to memorize a poem
4. how to play basketball
5. how to jump rope
6. how to ride a skateboard

ACTIVITY B **Read the titles of these how-to talks. For which topics might you act out the steps? For which ones might you draw pictures?**

1. Make Clay Beads
2. How to Do the Butterfly Stroke
3. Starting a School Club
4. Learn to Make Apple and Graham Cracker Sandwiches
5. Tips for Making Paper Boats
6. Playing Chinese Checkers

SPEAKER'S CORNER

Choose a topic for your how-to talk. Make a poster that shows everything your audience will need to complete the activity.

Get Ready

Get the materials that you need for your how-to talk. Then list the steps needed to make or do your topic. Write the steps on note cards. If you are not using a poster to list what readers will need, write another note card with that list. Write one note card each for the introduction and the conclusion. Use the note cards during your how-to talk. They will help you remember what you want to say.

Practice

Practice your how-to talk several times. Use your note cards. Remember to speak clearly. Try not to talk too fast. Show each step slowly. Then practice with a partner. Make sure that your partner can see and hear what you are doing. After you have finished your presentation, discuss these questions with your partner:

- Were my steps easy to understand?
- Did I forget any steps or use unneeded steps?
- Did I forget anything for my What You Need list?
- Was my voice loud enough?

Listening Tips

It is important to be a good listener. Here are some ways to be a good listener.

- Pay attention. Sit quietly.
- Watch what the speaker does. Imagine that you are doing the same thing.
- Wait until the how-to talk is over before asking questions.
- When the speaker has finished, say one thing that you liked about the presentation.

ACTIVITY C Think of something you like to draw. Then teach a partner how to draw the same thing without drawing it yourself.

ACTIVITY D Make a list of the steps you would use to teach someone how to do these everyday activities.

1. washing your hands
2. drawing a picture of a house
3. tying a shoe
4. making a bed
5. blowing a bubble
6. folding a T-shirt

ACTIVITY E Think about how to make your favorite sandwich. Write each step you take when you make that sandwich. Then read through your steps and make a What You Need list.

ACTIVITY F Reread the steps and the What You Need list that you wrote for Activity E. Then practice a how-to talk with a partner on how to make the sandwich. Reread the Listening Tips on page 272. When your partner practices his or her talk, remember to use the Listening Tips.

SPEAKER'S CORNER

Use the poster that you made for the Speaker's Corner on page 271 to practice and present your how-to talk. Practice it with a partner. Think of ways to improve your how-to talk.

Tech Tip Make a podcast of your how-to talk.

Prewriting and Drafting

What do you know how to make or do? Can you fly a kite? Can you make a tasty snack? These can be topics for a how-to article.

Prewriting

Kai's third-grade class was writing how-to articles, so she started by prewriting. Prewriting is what you do before you start writing. Kai knew that this was the time to plan the ideas that would go into her article.

Choosing a Topic

Ideas Kai was having trouble choosing a topic. She decided to make a chart of things she can do.

Kai looked at the chart she made. She was surprised at how much she knows how to do. She asked herself what her classmates might like to learn about. She also asked herself what had been fun for her to learn.

Last summer Kai's older brother, Lono, taught her how to make a time capsule. It had been a lot of fun. Kai couldn't wait until next summer, when she and Lono would open it. She thought that other kids in her class might like to make time capsules too.

Things I Can Do

School	reading adding fractions
Dance and Sports	hula soccer goalie kickball
Arts and Crafts	making a time capsule using watercolors making friendship 　　　bracelets acting in plays
Other Skills	playing the guitar magic tricks making cookies

Your Turn

Make a chart like Kai's to help you think **Voice** of topics. What can you do? How do you have fun? Fill in each column with as many things as you can think of. What things on your list were fun to learn? What would be easy to teach? Choose a topic that seems fun and interesting.

Listing Steps

Kai knew to list all the steps for making the time capsule. She thought about what she and Lono did to make their time capsule.

1. Cover shoe box with construction paper. Write name and date on shoe box. Decorate shoe box.
2. Put fun things in time capsule.
3. Tape up time capsule. Find hiding place for time capsule.

Kai wanted to tell what could go in the time capsule. She and Lono had included coins, stamps, and pictures. She added those things to the second step.

Kai showed her list to Lono. He told her to tell kids how to hide a time capsule. Lono once buried a time capsule. Kai thought the extra tip would be good in the conclusion.

Your Turn

- Make a list of the steps needed to complete the activity you will write about.
- Read the steps again. Did you leave anything out? Are the steps in the right order? Do you see places where you can add information to make the steps clearer?

Organizing Ideas

Kai wanted to make sure that she didn't leave anything out. She wrote the five parts of a how-to article. Then she wrote notes about each part. Sometimes she thought of a question that she should answer. Here are Kai's notes.

Title
  A Buried Surprise
Introduction
  Why would a kid want to make this?
What You Need
  shoe box, construction paper, coins, stamps, pitchers
Steps
  See new list of steps.
Conclusion
  stuff about burying time capsule

Your Turn

- Write the five parts of a how-to article.
- Look at your list of steps. What do you need to add to your What You Need list to complete the steps? What do you want to say in the introduction and the conclusion?
- Write your ideas.

Drafting

A draft is your first chance to put your prewriting notes in order. Kai used the notes she wrote during prewriting to write her first draft. She had written her ideas and steps in the correct parts of a how-to article. She then found that it was easy to write the details. Kai double-spaced her draft so that she would have room to make changes later.

A Buried Surprise

A time capsule is fun to make. George Washington even put one in the cornerstone of the Capitol building. But it has never been found.

<u>What You Need</u>

shoe box	stamps
construction paper	pitchers
coins	tape

<u>Steps</u>

1. Cover the shoe box in construction paper. The box will be the time capsule. Write your name and the date in big letters on the lid. Decerate the box any way that you want. You can ask friends to sign their names, or you can draw pitchers.

2. You can put anything in the time capsule. Put in coins from this year. You can add pretty stamps. You can also place pitchers of you and your friends in the time capsule.

3. Tape the time capsule closed. Then hide it in a closet or under your bed.

You can even put your time capsule in a plastic bag and bury it in your yard. If you do, make a map so that you don't forget where you put it remember to ask an adult to help you bury your time capsule. Don't open your time capsule for a long, long time. Try to wait at least one year!

Your Turn

- Look at your notes.
- Use your notes to write your first draft.
- Remember to double-space your draft so you have room to make corrections later.

Writer's Tip Make sure you use commands in the directions.

Prewriting

Drafting

Content Editing

Revising

Copyediting

Proofreading

Publishing

Content Editing

Kai knew that if she edited her draft for content, the draft would be better. She knew that content editors check to make sure that a reader can understand the article. They also check to make sure that all the important information is included.

Kai used this checklist to content edit her draft.

Kai knew that asking someone else to content edit her draft would be a big help. Kai asked her best friend, Emily. Emily was one of the best readers in the class. Kai knew that Emily would tell her good changes she could make.

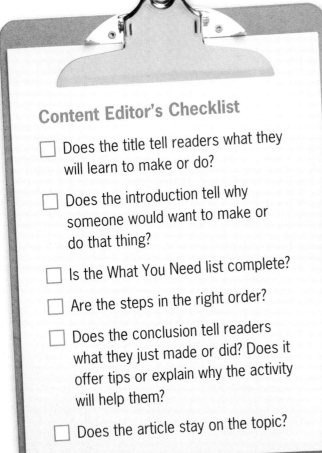

Content Editor's Checklist

- ☐ Does the title tell readers what they will learn to make or do?

- ☐ Does the introduction tell why someone would want to make or do that thing?

- ☐ Is the What You Need list complete?

- ☐ Are the steps in the right order?

- ☐ Does the conclusion tell readers what they just made or did? Does it offer tips or explain why the activity will help them?

- ☐ Does the article stay on the topic?

Emily carefully read Kai's how-to article a few times. She answered the questions on the Content Editor's Checklist about Kai's draft. She also wrote notes about things that she liked in the draft. When Emily had finished, she and Kai met to talk about Emily's ideas.

First, Emily told Kai that making a time capsule sounded like fun. Then Emily showed Kai her ideas.

- The introduction says that making a time capsule is fun. Can you tell kids why it is fun?
- What can kids use to draw on the time capsule? It is not in your What You Need list.
- The steps are easy to follow. I like them.
- I like how you give kids another way of hiding their time capsules.
- I don't think the part about George Washington is about making a time capsule. You should delete it.
- I like how you tell kids what they can put in the time capsule. Maybe they can also put in newspaper articles.
- Can you tell kids what you put in your time capsule?

Kai liked what Emily said about her draft. Emily caught some things that Kai had missed. Even though Kai didn't agree with all Emily's ideas, she knew that her draft would be better because of Emily's help.

Your Turn

- Read your draft and answer the questions on the Content Editor's Checklist.
- Try to answer yes to each question. Don't try to check all the questions at once. Check for one question at a time.
- After you have edited your draft for content, trade drafts with a partner. Give your partner ideas to make the draft better. Be sure that you use the Content Editor's Checklist.
- Talk to your partner about your ideas. Remember to tell your partner what you liked.
- You do not have to make all the changes your partner tells you. But you should think carefully about each one.

Prewriting

Drafting

Content Editing

Revising

Copyediting

Proofreading

Publishing

Revising

This is Kai's revised draft.

Making a Time Capsule
~~A Buried Surprise~~

When you are older, you can open the time capsule and remember what
A time capsule is fun to make. ~~George Washington even put one in~~
it was like when you were in third grade.
~~the cornerstone of the Capitol building. But it has never been found.~~

What You Need

shoe box   stamps

construction paper   pitchers

coins   tape

^markers or crayons   ^news paper articles
Steps

1. Cover the shoe box in construction paper. The box will be the time capsule.

   Write your name and the date in big letters on the lid. Decerate the box

   any way that you want. You can ask friends to sign their names, or you can

   draw pitchers.

2. You can put anything in the time capsule. Put in coins from this year. You can
   News paper articles are good too.
   add pretty stamps. ^You can also place pitchers of you and your friends in the

   time capsule.

3. Tape the time capsule closed. Then hide it in a closet or under your bed.

Prewriting

Drafting

Content Editing

Revising

Copyediting

Proofreading

Publishing

You can even put your time capsule in a plastic bag and bury it in your yard.

If you do, make a map so that you don't forget where you put it remember to ask

an adult to help you bury your time capsule. Don't open your time capsule for a

The longer you wait, the more fun it will be when you open it.

long, long time. Try to wait at least one year!

Look at some things that Kai did to improve her how-to article.

- Kai added a sentence in the introduction. What is it about? Do you think this is a good change?
- She took out the part about George Washington. Why?
- What did Kai add to the What You Need list?
- Kai hadn't even thought about adding newspaper articles. But it was a good idea. What did Kai do?
- Kai decided not to write about what she put in her time capsule. Why not? Do you agree with Kai?
- Can you spot what Emily forgot to check on the checklist?
- Kai liked what Emily said about her conclusion, but she decided to add another sentence to make it more interesting. What did Kai write?

Your Turn

- Use your partner's ideas to revise your draft.
- Read your draft again to see if there is anything else you can improve.
- When you have finished revising, go over the Content Editor's Checklist again. Can you answer yes to each question?

Writer's Tip Make sure that the changes offered by your partner are correct before making them in your draft.

Grammar in Action

There's one punctuation mistake in Kai's draft. Find it and fix it.

Editor's Workshop

Copyediting and Proofreading

Copyediting

Kai thought her draft was pretty good. But she wanted it to be great. Kai used the Copyeditor's Checklist to make sure her

 Sentence Fluency

sentences were complete and that they made sense. She also checked the meanings of words that she was not sure about.

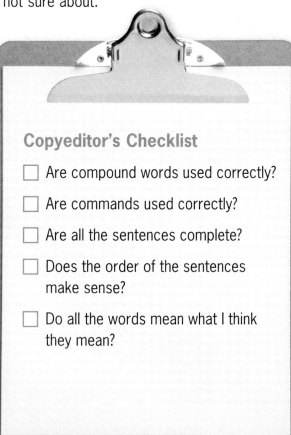

Copyeditor's Checklist

- [ ] Are compound words used correctly?
- [ ] Are commands used correctly?
- [ ] Are all the sentences complete?
- [ ] Does the order of the sentences make sense?
- [ ] Do all the words mean what I think they mean?

Kai read her draft again and tried to answer the questions on the Copyeditor's Checklist.

Word Choice She found a misused word and two words that should have been one compound word. Can you find them?

Kai wasn't sure about the word *pitchers*, so she looked it up in a dictionary. She realized that the word she wanted to use was *pictures*.

Kai also thought that *news paper* might be incorrect. She checked the dictionary and found out that *newspaper* is a compound word.

Your Turn

Read your revised draft carefully. See if you can answer yes to the questions on the Copyeditor's Checklist. Remember to check for one kind of mistake at a time.

Proofreading

Kai knew that good writers proofread their

Conventions work to check for spelling, punctuation, and capitalization. Kai used the Proofreader's Checklist to help her catch these types of mistakes in her revised draft.

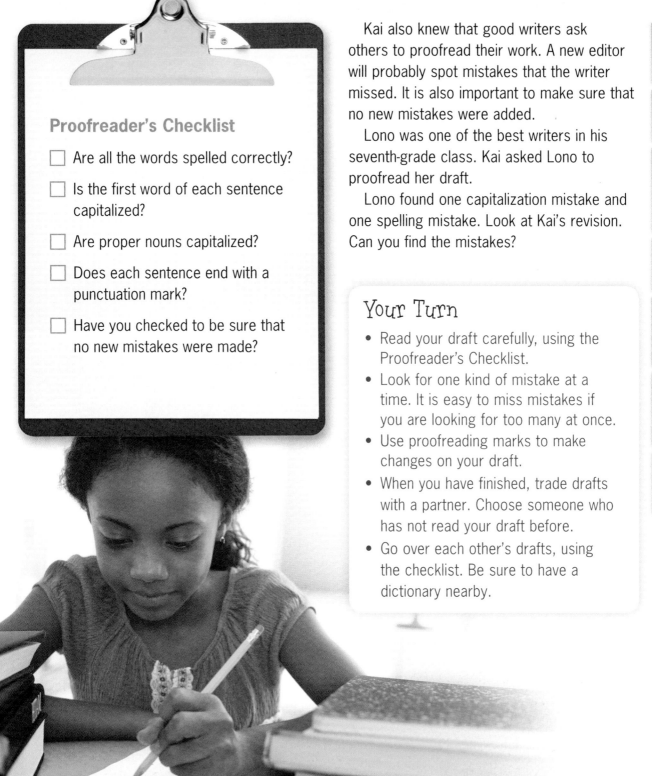

Proofreader's Checklist

- ☐ Are all the words spelled correctly?
- ☐ Is the first word of each sentence capitalized?
- ☐ Are proper nouns capitalized?
- ☐ Does each sentence end with a punctuation mark?
- ☐ Have you checked to be sure that no new mistakes were made?

Kai also knew that good writers ask others to proofread their work. A new editor will probably spot mistakes that the writer missed. It is also important to make sure that no new mistakes were added.

Lono was one of the best writers in his seventh-grade class. Kai asked Lono to proofread her draft.

Lono found one capitalization mistake and one spelling mistake. Look at Kai's revision. Can you find the mistakes?

Your Turn

- Read your draft carefully, using the Proofreader's Checklist.
- Look for one kind of mistake at a time. It is easy to miss mistakes if you are looking for too many at once.
- Use proofreading marks to make changes on your draft.
- When you have finished, trade drafts with a partner. Choose someone who has not read your draft before.
- Go over each other's drafts, using the checklist. Be sure to have a dictionary nearby.

Prewriting
Drafting
Content Editing
Revising
Copyediting
Proofreading
Publishing

Publishing

Publishing is the moment when you decide to share your finished work. You know it is your best work, and you are ready to share it with your audience.

After editing and revising many times, Kai felt that she had done her best. She carefully typed her how-to article on a new sheet of paper.

Making a Time Capsule

A time capsule is fun to make. When you are older, you can open the time capsule and remember what it was like when you were in third grade.

What You Need

shoe box

construction paper

markers or crayons

coins

stamps

newspaper articles

pictures

tape

Steps

1. Cover the shoe box in construction paper. The box will be the time capsule. Write your name and the date in big letters on the lid. Decorate the box any way that you want. You can ask friends to sign their names, or you can draw pictures.

2. You can put anything in the time capsule. Put in coins from this year. You can add pretty stamps. Newspaper articles are good too. You can also place pictures of you and your friends in the time capsule.

3. Tape the time capsule closed. Then hide it in a closet or under your bed.

You can even put your time capsule in a plastic bag and bury it in your yard. If you do, make a map so that you don't forget where you put it. Remember to ask an adult to help you bury your time capsule. Don't open your time capsule for a long, long time. The longer you wait, the more fun it will be when you open it. Try to wait at least one year!

Presentation Publishing is the moment when writers share their finished work. However you publish, be sure the final work is neat and organized. There are lots of ways you can publish your how-to article.

 Film it. Use your how-to article as a script and videotape yourself. You might ask some of your friends to help you.

 Do a PowerPoint presentation of your how-to article. Add clip art for items, such as your materials and the finished product.

 Create a song out of it (like the "Hokey Pokey"). Choose a popular tune and write new lyrics, or create an entirely new how-to song.

 Post it to an online how-to manual. You might also take digital photos of each step and include the images with your article.

Your Turn

Remember, when you publish a how-to article, your goal is to share what you know with others. To publish, follow these steps:

- Make sure you have not left out any important steps.
- Use your best handwriting or a computer to make a final copy of your how-to article.
- Proofread your copy one more time for correct spelling, grammar, capitalization, and punctuation.

Prewriting
Drafting
Content Editing
Revising
Copyediting
Proofreading
Publishing

Descriptions

LiNK

James and the Giant Peach

by Roald Dahl

The garden lay soft and silver in the moonlight. The grass was wet with dew and a million dewdrops were sparkling and twinkling like diamonds around his feet. And now suddenly, the whole place, the whole garden, seemed to be *alive* with magic.

Almost without knowing what he was doing, as though drawn by some powerful magnet, James Henry Trotter started walking slowly toward the giant peach. He climbed over the fence that surrounded it, and stood directly beneath it, staring up at its great bulging sides. He put out a hand and touched it gently with the tip of one finger. It felt soft and warm and slightly furry, like the skin of a baby mouse. He moved a step closer and rubbed his cheek lightly against the soft skin. And then suddenly, while he was doing this, he happened to notice that right beside him and below him, close to the ground, there was a hole in the side of the peach.

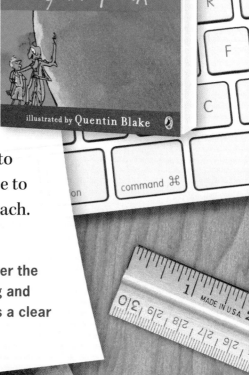

> *James and the Giant Peach* is read by children all over the world. It is a good description because it uses strong and colorful words, it appeals to the senses, and it paints a clear picture for the reader.

Room 405

Henry Jin Yeo

A New Home for Gorillas

The West Haven Nature Park has opened a new gorilla habitat. Planners, gorilla specialists, and construction workers spent two years getting it ready for everyone to enjoy.

At the new habitat, visitors are separated from the animals by a pit that looks like a river canyon. Tangled ivy climbs out of a slow-moving stream at the bottom. The ivy curls around the iron rails where visitors stand. Beyond the pit is the habitat. It was built to be like the dense, wet, jungle home of lowland gorillas. Thick, green plants and knobby roots give baby gorillas places to play. Sprinklers keep the habitat wet and humid. You can even smell the rich jungle plant life. If you stand close enough, you may even feel the mist on your face. Bird calls and animal noises complete the habitat. Listen closely for the tree frog's chirp. At the center of the habitat, a rocky peak rises up for the bravest gorillas to climb.

The new gorilla habitat is a place where the park's 12 gorillas can feel at home. I hope to visit the West Haven Nature Park again soon. It's the best place to see our primate friends.

West Haven Nature Park

What Makes a Good Description?

A description tells about a person, an animal, a place, or an object. Good descriptions form clear pictures in a reader's mind. Great descriptions tell not only how things look but also how they might sound, smell, feel, or even taste. What is the description on page 287 about?

Choosing Words

Choose words carefully. Strong and colorful words make clear pictures in a reader's mind. Pick words that help readers think about sight, sound, smell, touch, and taste.

Read the two descriptions. What words in the second description help you see and feel the gift?

A **The box on the table had silver paper and a red ribbon.**

B **The enormous box on the table was covered in shiny, smooth, silvery paper that sparkled in the light. The box was tied with a bright red, velvety ribbon.**

Audience

Think about who is going to read your description. Will it be your parents or a teacher? Will it be your friends? What does your audience know about what you are describing? Thinking about your audience will help you choose words that they will understand.

ACTIVITY A Which description uses strong and colorful words? Tell which words in the description help you imagine the scene.

1. My Cat

    I really like my cat. She is black and white and very cute. Her name is Tippy. She chases insects. She catches a fly. She doesn't like it, so she spits it out. It flies away.

2. Tippy's Snack

    My cat Tippy is a ball of black and white fur. She likes to leap at flies. Oh, no, she's eaten one! Her pink nose wrinkles, and her mouth opens. The fly hurries out and buzzes away.

ACTIVITY B Replace the underlined word in each sentence with a strong and colorful word. You can use more than one word. Imagine that your classmates are your audience.

1. What a <u>nice</u> view of the mountains!
2. That was a <u>good</u> dinner.
3. We can't burn the leaves because they make a <u>bad</u> smell.
4. The skater <u>moved</u> across the ice.
5. Our new puppy <u>cries</u> at night.
6. My room was <u>clean</u>.
7. The clouds were <u>pretty</u>.
8. I really <u>liked</u> that movie.
9. We saw a <u>large</u> building.
10. The child was <u>happy</u> on the water slide.

LiNK

James and the Giant Peach

The tunnel was damp and murky, and all around him there was the curious bittersweet smell of fresh peach. The floor was soggy under his knees, the walls were wet and sticky, and peach juice was dripping from the ceiling. James opened his mouth and caught some of it on his tongue. It tasted delicious.

Roald Dahl

WRITER'S CORNER

Choose an item in your classroom. It might be a toy, a desk, or your backpack. Then write four sentences describing the item. Use strong and colorful words.

James and the Giant Peach

There was an Old-Green-Grasshopper as large as a large dog sitting on a stool directly across the room from James now. And next to the Old-Green-Grasshopper there was an enormous Spider. And next to the Spider, there was a giant Ladybug with nine black spots on her scarlet shell. . . . On a sofa nearby, reclining comfortably in curled-up positions, there was a Centipede and an Earthworm.

Roald Dahl

A good description gives a picture of what is being described. Using a clear order will help your reader follow your description without getting lost.

When you use time order, you tell about events in the order that they happened. Here is another way to order a description.

Space Order

There are many kinds of space order. When you write a description from top to bottom, from side to side, or from near to far, you are using space order. Space order can help a reader see things the way that you do. Look at these examples of space order.

top to bottom

My cousin Micha has dark, curly hair. He has big, bushy eyebrows like Grandpa's. His eyes are almost black. His nose is just like mine. It is square at the tip. He has the same cheery smile my mom has.

side to side

My collections are on the shelf above my bed. On the left are my comic books. In the middle are my baseball cards. Then there are my dragon models. I keep my bowling trophies on the right side of the shelf.

near to far

The first thing you'll see by the park entrance are some picnic tables. Past the picnic tables are groups of trees. In the middle of all the trees is a duck pond. From there you can see the other end of the park.

What other things might you describe from top to bottom, from side to side, or from near to far?

ACTIVITY C **What kind of space order is used in each of the descriptions below?**

1. Just ahead, the trees grew dense and wild. The pine branches beyond were thick and prickly. I could see a wooden lookout station in the distance.

2. The veil floated around Mara's head like smoke. Her face was hidden. Her white dress was almost blinding. A long train with tiny pearls on the edges flowed behind her.

3. Father Elephant led the colorful circus parade. Mother Elephant gripped his tail with her trunk and followed. Baby Elephant tried to keep up. He held on to his mother's tail and trotted along after them.

4. The entrance hall to the museum was huge. Near the main entrance was a ticket booth. There was a long line of people waiting to buy tickets. Behind them was the information area. It had a big, round desk at which people were sitting. They could answer your questions and give out maps. In the background, towering over all, was a skeleton of a huge dinosaur—a *Tyrannosaurus rex*.

ACTIVITY D **Write a short description of one of the items below. Write the description from top to bottom, from side to side, or from near to far.**

- a birthday cake
- a classroom
- a table full of food
- a snow-covered mountain
- a model train
- a view of the ocean
- a parrot

WRITER'S CORNER

Picture someone you know well. Write five details you could use to describe that person. Then write one sentence for each detail. Put the sentences in space order from top to bottom.

Grammar in Action Use at least two different pronouns in your descriptive sentences.

Writing a Description

A good description helps readers feel like they are part of the story. When you write a description, think about and imagine what you are describing. Use words that help a reader easily follow your description.

Choosing a Topic

The topic of your description is the thing you are describing. Anything that you can see, hear, smell, touch, or taste can be the topic of a description.

Beginning

The beginning of a description tells what you will describe. A good beginning makes the reader want to read more.

Middle

The middle of a description tells about what is being described. In the middle the topic is described using either space order or time order.

Ending

The ending often retells what was said in the beginning and the middle of the description. The ending might explain why the thing being described is important. A good ending might leave the reader with something to think about.

Silverback gorilla

ACTIVITY A Answer the questions below about "A New Home for Gorillas" on page 287.

1. What is the topic?
2. Does the beginning make you want to read more? Why or why not?
3. What words in the middle help paint a clear picture of what is being described?
4. What words appeal to your sense of sight, sound, smell, and touch?
5. What kind of space order is used in the middle?
6. Does the ending make sense? Why or why not?

VEGETABLES

ACTIVITY B Read the description below. Imagine what the market stall looks like and draw a picture of it, using the description as a guide.

The stall at the farmer's market had many boxes of colorful fruits and vegetables. At the left was a large box of peppers in three colors—some dark green, some bright red, and some light yellow. Next was a small box of light green grapes, followed by a small box of nectarines. At the right was a large box of red tomatoes with parts of their dark green stems and vines still attached.

ACTIVITY C Write a short description of a thing such as your favorite toy. Exchange your description with a partner. Read your partner's description and draw it. Then discuss how your drawings compare to the descriptions and the actual things.

WRITER'S CORNER

Look at the middle of "A New Home for Gorillas" on page 287. Write two sentences describing something else that could be in the gorilla habitat.

ACTIVITY D Write two sentences that describe each topic below. Use strong and colorful words that help readers think about each topic.

1. a flock of pigeons
2. a bonfire
3. a newborn baby
4. a racehorse
5. a castle
6. a sunset
7. a firefly
8. a tree
9. a farm
10. a beach
11. a rainy day
12. a birthday party

ACTIVITY E Choose one of the topics from Activity D. Write the beginning of a description of that topic. Remember to tell readers something that will make them want to read more.

ACTIVITY F Read each middle of a description. Name the topic of each.

1. His nose is crooked because of a flying hockey puck years ago. His shoulders are so broad that he looks like he is still wearing his hockey shoulder pads.

2. The banana swims in gooey fudge along the bottom of the dish. Vanilla ice cream melts slowly over the banana, threatening to drown everything. Whipped cream forms three gentle peaks at the top, each holding a shiny, perfect cherry.

3. The smell of bacon frying tickles my nose. I hear the pop of the toaster and the hiss of spattering butter. I know that the sound of cracking eggs is coming next. I am up before the eggs are scrambled.

ACTIVITY G Read the pairs of endings below. Which ending in each pair is stronger? Why do you think so?

1. **a.** My bedroom isn't fancy or neat, but that's OK. It's cozy, colorful, and comfortable. It's filled with lots of my favorite things. When I go into my bedroom, I can relax and be myself.

   b. My bedroom is my favorite room in the house. You could say it's two rooms, actually, because there's also a closet. I keep my clothes in there.

2. **a.** Grandma's gingerbread house makes me hungry. I sometimes want to break off a piece and eat it. Grandma would probably get mad if I did.

   b. Grandma's gingerbread house looks both beautiful and delicious. The candy canes, gumdrops, and peanut brittle somehow form a perfect house. I almost want to stop by for a visit and take a bite while I'm there!

3. **a.** Our backyard garden is an amazing sight. A few little seeds have sprouted into tomatoes, carrots, and beans. I can't wait to eat our homegrown vegetables.

   b. Our backyard garden is full of vegetables, not flowers. The flowers are in the front yard. Flowers are nice to look at, but vegetables are better to eat.

LiNK

James and the Giant Peach

And now the peach had broken out of the garden and was over the edge of the hill, rolling and bouncing down the steep slope at a terrific pace. Faster and faster and faster it went, and the crowds of people who were climbing up the hill suddenly caught sight of this terrible monster plunging down upon them and they screamed and scattered to the right and left as it went hurtling by.

Roald Dahl

WRITER'S CORNER

Choose a middle from Activity F and imagine that you wrote it. Write an ending for it. You might retell what was said in the beginning and the middle, or you might explain why the topic was important.

Sensory Words

People have five senses: sight, sound, smell, taste, and touch. What senses might you use to describe a flower shop?

Descriptions include words that tell what the writer sees, hears, smells, tastes, and feels. These sensory words help the reader imagine what is being described.

Read these two sentences. Both sentences tell what happened. Which sentence helps you imagine the swing?

A **The swing swayed in the wind.**

B **The rusty, old swing creaked and groaned as the wind pushed it about.**

In sentence A the writer writes only about what he or she saw. In sentence B the writer uses more senses to describe the scene. Sentence B forms a clearer picture in the reader's mind.

ACTIVITY A Tell which sense is used to describe the thing in each sentence.

1. Grandpa's homemade ice cream is sweet and nutty.

2. The rooster's ear-splitting crow woke us up at dawn.

3. The spaghetti sauce's spicy scent made my mouth water.

4. Becca buried her face in the soft, warm towels just out of the dryer.

5. The stormy sky was thick with clouds that were gray, purple, and muddy brown.

6. The roaring engine of the huge truck was deafening as it rumbled down the street.

7. The fireworks burst into expanding blooms of red, blue, green, and white in the sky.

8. The lilacs' strong, sweet fragrance spread from the garden into our house.

ACTIVITY B **Match the sensory words in Column A to what the words describe in Column B.**

Column A

1. sour smoke, blue flame, rough wood, sharp crack

2. bumpy walnuts, crunchy vegetables, sweet berries

3. cool metal, creaky steps, swooshing sounds

4. sharp thorns, soft petals, sweet smell, dark red color

5. whistling steam, hot metal, blue flames beneath

6. dusty curtains, smooth glass, tinkling wind chimes, gray screen

Column B

a. a teakettle

b. a slide

c. a salad

d. a window

e. a match

f. a rose

ACTIVITY C **Choose three topics below. Imagine the scene. List at least five sensory words.**

1. a birthday party
2. a carnival
3. a baseball game
4. lunch in the school cafeteria
5. a family reunion
6. a picnic
7. a parade
8. a thunderstorm

WRITER'S CORNER

Choose two senses: sight, sound, smell, taste, and touch. Then choose one of your favorite things, such as a food, a hobby, or a sport. Write two sentences, each using one of the senses you chose. Use strong and colorful words.

ACTIVITY D Which sense is used to describe the thing in each sentence below? Which words give you clues?

1. People always say that Kyle's laugh is like the hee-haw of a donkey.
2. Jo's dress is such a wild shade of red it hurts your eyes to look at it.
3. Sleeping on a featherbed is like cuddling on a cloud.
4. The buttery, salty-sweet scent drew us to the caramel corn.
5. At first Amanda didn't like the tangy flavor of mangos.
6. Gary's pet rabbit's fur was smooth and soft under my fingers.
7. The air in a rain forest can be heavy and humid.
8. The deep red, juicy-looking seeds of the pomegranate seemed tasty.
9. In the garden the perky, yellow tulips waved their heads in the breeze.
10. As we paddled our canoes, the water of the stream whooshed and gurgled over the stones.

LiNK

James and the Giant Peach

A minute later, this brown sticky mess was flowing through every street in the village, oozing under the doors of houses and into people's shops and gardens. Children were wading in it up to their knees, and some were even trying to swim in it, and all of them were sucking it into their mouths in great greedy gulps and shrieking with joy.

Roald Dahl

ACTIVITY E Find the sensory words in the paragraph below.

Bright yellow sunlight blazed through my window. I had overslept again. A sweet, rotten smell came from the garage. I realized that I had not taken the trash to the curb this morning. Boy, was I in trouble! I buried my face in my soft, warm pillow. I wished I could go back to sleep.

ACTIVITY F Complete the paragraph below with sensory words from the word box.

| smoky | buttery | hot | blue | cry |

I like to go to the beach with my family. As soon as we get there, I run across the hot sand and jump into the _____ water. Then I lie on my towel and soak up the _____ sun. I close my eyes and listen to the seagulls _____. When the _____ smell of roasting corn tickles my nose, I know that it is time for lunch. I can't wait for the first _____ bite.

ACTIVITY G Write one sentence that describes each item below. Include as many sensory words as you can.

1. a kitten
2. an old radio
3. fresh-baked bread
4. a new bicycle
5. a band concert
6. a cow
7. a snowstorm
8. a muddy puddle
9. a bouquet of flowers
10. a bowl of soup

ACTIVITY H Look at the words in the word box in Activity F. Write one item that each word might describe. Then write a sentence describing each item you listed. Use the words in the word box in your sentences.

ACTIVITY I Reread the paragraph from Activity F. List your own sensory words for each blank.

WRITER'S CORNER

Imagine a picnic. What do you see, hear, and smell? What can you touch and taste? Write five sentences describing the picnic. Use a different sense in each sentence.

Grammar in Action. Replace the subjects in your sentences with subject pronouns.

Five-Senses Chart

Using sensory words will help you write a clear, interesting description. Sensory words help the reader imagine what you describe.

A five-senses chart can help you remember details about what you are describing. It can also help you think of sensory words that you can use in your description.

Here is a five-senses chart that Elizabeth made on a computer about her favorite snack.

Touch
rough chips
lumpy brown beans
sticky cheese
juicy tomatoes

Sight
yellow tortilla chips
juicy red tomatoes
bright green lettuce
pale orange cheese

Sound
crunchy chips

Taste
sweet tomatoes
tangy cheese
creamy sour cream
spicy salsa

Smell
peppery salsa

Topic:
My Favorite Snack

Elizabeth might have also used a two-column five-senses chart. It might have looked like this.

Topic: My Favorite Snack

Sight	yellow tortilla chips, juicy red tomatoes, bright green lettuce, pale orange cheese
Sound	crunchy chips
Smell	peppery salsa
Taste	sweet tomatoes, tangy cheese, creamy sour cream, spicy salsa
Touch	rough chips, lumpy brown beans, sticky cheese, juicy tomatoes

ACTIVITY A **Look at Elizabeth's charts and answer the questions below.**

1. What is Elizabeth's favorite snack?
2. What did the writer see that was bright green?
3. What sound did the writer hear?
4. What word does the writer use to describe the smell of salsa?
5. What word does the writer use to describe the taste of tomatoes?
6. What word does the writer use to describe how the chips feel?

WRITER'S CORNER

Imagine that you wrote one of Elizabeth's five-senses charts. Write three sentences describing nachos, using the sensory words from the charts.

ACTIVITY B Copy the five-senses chart below. Write the words from the word box where they belong on the chart.

> burnt marshmallows   sparkling lake   prickly grass
> colorful wildflowers   laughing kids   sticky crafts
> sharp pine scent   gritty sand   salty popcorn

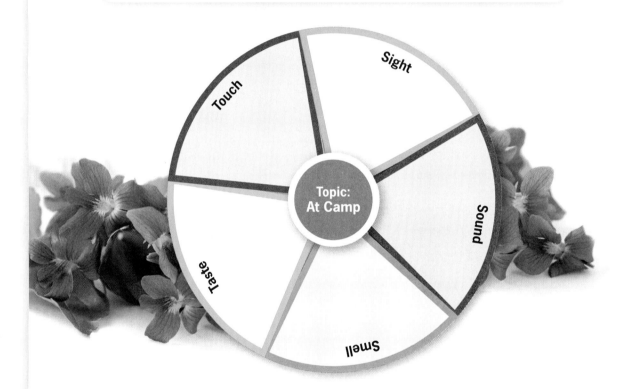

ACTIVITY C Use the words from the word box in Activity B to complete these sentences from a description.

1. As I reached the campfire, I could smell the _____ and feel the _____ brush against my legs.

2. I lay back in my chair beside the _____ and dug my feet into the _____.

3. On my hike I saw the _____ in the fields and breathed in the _____ in the woods.

4. Outside at the picnic tables, _____ were enjoying making _____.

ACTIVITY D Look at the five-senses charts below. Imagine that you went to these places. Write two more items for each sense.

1. Topic: Picnic in the Park

Sight	bright sunshine, fluffy white clouds, pale blue sky
Sound	chirping birds, gently rustling trees
Smell	freshly cut grass, flower blossoms
Taste	tangy grilled chicken, buttery corn, sour lemonade
Touch	soft blanket, cool grass

2. Topic: Bakery

Sight	gleaming glass display cases, pies with glossy brown crusts in crisscross patterns
Sound	chattering of bakery workers, clicking sound of silverware against cups
Smell	smell of freshly baked bread, smell of brewing coffee
Taste	sweet frosting on cakes, tangy blueberry pie
Touch	warm muffin, hot coffee cup

ACTIVITY E Draw a two-column five-senses chart. Think about getting ready for school this morning. What are some things you saw, heard, smelled, tasted, and touched? Use your ideas to fill in the chart.

WRITER'S CORNER

Use your five-senses chart from Activity E. Write a sentence for each sense. Include any new sensory words that come to mind.

Synonyms

Synonyms are words that have the same or almost the same meaning. You probably use synonyms when you speak and write. Here are some pairs of synonyms you might know.

happy	**glad**
talk	**speak**
gift	**present**
store	**shop**
begin	**start**
hunt	**search**
fast	**quick**
big	**large**

Writers use synonyms to make their writing more interesting. They use synonyms to replace words that are used over and over. What are some other synonyms for the word *happy*?

Look at the sentences below. Which sentence in each pair is more interesting?

The runners *ran* across the finish line.

The runners *sprinted* across the finish line.

The giant wore *big* shoes.

The giant wore *enormous* shoes.

ACTIVITY A Match each word in Column A
to its synonym in Column B.

Column A	Column B
1. cry	**a.** kids
2. children	**b.** angry
3. ill	**c.** mend
4. mad	**d.** paste
5. fix	**e.** sick
6. glue	**f.** journey
7. hurt	**g.** damage
8. polite	**h.** weep
9. pale	**i.** colorless
10. trip	**j.** respectful

ACTIVITY B Tell whether the words
in each pair are synonyms.

1. hurry	scary
2. draw	bring
3. smile	grin
4. wide	narrow
5. thin	skinny
6. yummy	tasty
7. teach	guide
8. own	possess
9. grow	expand
10. shout	whisper
11. purchase	buy
12. bright	dull

WRITER'S CORNER

Look at "A New Home for Gorillas" on page 287. List five words that you could replace with synonyms. Then work with a partner to think of a synonym for each word.

Tech Tip With an adult, use an online thesaurus.

ACTIVITY C Use a synonym from the word box to replace each underlined word.

pick	hunt	shop	buddy	kind
chats	gift	giant	rush	carry

1. The <u>nice</u> guard showed us the way out.
2. Did you <u>choose</u> a book about the planets?
3. My parents <u>search</u> for the car keys every morning.
4. My <u>friend</u> Taye won the three-legged race.
5. Mrs. Torres <u>talks</u> with her friends on her front porch.
6. Kylie bought a chess set at a new <u>store</u> on Maple Street.
7. Did you <u>take</u> the garden tools into the house?
8. The <u>huge</u> pumpkin is sure to win first place.
9. There was a little <u>present</u> on my pillow.
10. Guy is always in a <u>hurry</u>.

ACTIVITY D Write a synonym for each word below.

1. see	6. calm	11. quiet
2. glad	7. meal	12. chair
3. yell	8. find	13. rock
4. start	9. fast	14. finish
5. story	10. path	15. hard

ACTIVITY E Read the rhymes below. Complete each rhyme with a correct synonym for the underlined word. Use the words from the word box.

> old   town   like   bright   tiny   delighted   say   rip

1. The city bus goes up and down,
   Then moves on quickly to the next _____.

2. A tear in your paper you don't want to see.
   If you're not careful, a _____ there will be.

3. Shiny stars fill the sky at night.
   They glow in the dark and look so _____.

4. My new baby brother is very small.
   His _____ fingers can't hold a ball.

5. My older sister has a lot to _____.
   She speaks on the phone all day.

6. That table is weak and really _____.
   It's ancient, or so I'm told.

7. I enjoy spinach, and prunes that are stewed.
   Actually, I _____ almost any food!

8. The happy child saw the toys in the store.
   He was so _____ with one that he wanted more.

ACTIVITY F Choose three synonyms you thought of for Activity D. Use each synonym in a sentence.

WRITER'S CORNER

Make a list of five pairs of synonyms. Then work with a partner. Say one of the words in each pair and see whether your partner can think of the synonym you wrote. Try to guess the synonyms your partner wrote.

Oral Descriptions

Imagine that you opened a present and found a walking, talking robot. Suppose that the robot was too big to bring to school. How would you describe it to your friends? If you told your friends about the robot, you would be giving an oral description.

Here are some tips on giving oral descriptions.

- If you are describing something you saw, try to remember what you thought and felt when you first saw it. Use space order to talk about it so that your listeners can imagine it.
- If you are describing something that happened, try to remember how you felt and what you thought both before and after it happened. Use time order to tell what happened so that your listeners can imagine it happening to them.

Remember that a description forms a clear picture in the listener's mind.

Visual Aids

Sometimes when we describe something to someone else, it helps if we show what we are talking about. A picture, drawing, map, or poster that you might show is called a visual aid. Visual aids help your audience imagine what you are describing. Anything that your audience can look at is a visual aid.

Prepare and Practice

Think of something you want to describe. Close your eyes and imagine how it looks or how it happened. Try to remember with all five of your senses. You may want to make a five-senses chart to help you. Write what you remember thinking and feeling. Use what you write to decide what you will say and what order you will use.

After you decide what you will say, try it out. Practice your description many times so that you will remember all you want to say. You might want to write notes on cards to help you remember the most important parts. As you practice, think about these things.

- Speak loudly enough for your audience to hear but do not shout.
- Stand up straight and try not to move around too much.
- Remember to breathe. Try pausing between sentences so you do not talk too fast.

ACTIVITY A Imagine that alien creatures took you to their home planet and gave you a tour. Close your eyes and try to imagine what their planet might be like. Are the rocks purple? Are there bubbles popping in the sky? Are there pools of green lava? Draw a picture of your imaginary alien planet. Then make a list of sensory words that describe your planet.

SPEAKER'S CORNER

Imagine that you were asked to give an oral description of your classroom to a family member. Draw a map of your classroom. Label your visual aid with the important parts of the classroom that you would want to describe.

Tech Tip Use a computer to design your map.

Listening Tips

Practicing can make it easier for you to tell an oral description to an audience. When you are a good listener, you can make it easier for someone else who is talking. Here are some things you can do to be a better listener.

- Listen to hear whether the speaker is talking about something that he or she saw or something that happened.
- Try to figure out whether the speaker is using space order or time order.
- Look at the visual aids the speaker uses to help you imagine.
- Try to imagine what it would feel like to see or do what the speaker is talking about.
- Don't laugh if the speaker makes a mistake.

LiNK

James and the Giant Peach

SMACK! [The peach] hit the water with a colossal splash and sank like a stone. . . . But a few seconds later, it came up again, and this time up it stayed, floating serenely upon the surface of the water. . . . The sun was shining brightly out of a soft blue sky and the day was calm. The giant peach, with the sunlight glinting on its side, was like a massive golden ball sailing upon a silver sea.

Roald Dahl

ACTIVITY B Work with a partner. Choose an animal to describe, but don't tell your partner what it is. Take turns describing what you chose so your partner can guess what it is. Use sensory words so that your partner knows what the animal might look, feel, or sound like. If it has a smell, describe that too.

ACTIVITY C Use the drawing you made for Activity A on page 309 to describe your alien planet to a partner. Point to things in your drawing as you describe them. Use your list of sensory words to tell your partner what you think a person might see, hear, and smell on that planet.

ACTIVITY D Work in small groups. Think of a cartoon character from television or from a movie. Picture the character and try to remember some things that he or she does and says. Then take turns describing your character without saying the character's name. Describe the way the character looks from top to bottom. Describe the way the character sounds or things the character says. After your description ask your classmates to guess who your character is.

ACTIVITY E Think of a chore you do at home for your family, such as washing dishes or dusting. Draw a five-senses chart and write the chore as your topic. Then try to describe your chore, using each sense. Use your chart to help you describe the chore to a partner.

ACTIVITY F Make a list of 10 things in the classroom that you could describe. Trade lists with a partner. Choose items from your partner's list and describe each one. See how quickly your partner can guess each item. Have your partner do the same with your list.

Tech Tip Do a podcast or a video of your oral description.

SPEAKER'S CORNER

Look at the map of your classroom you drew for the Speaker's Corner on page 309. Read the parts you labeled. Then meet with a partner. Pretend that your partner is a family member who has not seen your classroom before. Describe your classroom to your partner. Use sensory words. Try to use more than one sense to describe the classroom.

Writer's Workshop

Prewriting and Drafting

Descriptions can tell about people, places, animals, or objects. A description uses sensory words to form a clear picture in the reader's mind. You will be writing a description of a place that is special to you.

Prewriting

Georgia is a third grader who wrote a description for class. Her teacher asked the class to write descriptions of places that are special to them. Georgia was eager to get started, but first she needed to think of a topic.

Choosing a Topic

 Georgia's teacher gave the class this list to help them think of topics.

- a place that I visit with my family
- an exciting place
- the prettiest place I have ever seen
- a place that makes me calm and peaceful
- a place that I dream about
- a place that amazes me
- a place that scares me

Georgia sat in a quiet corner of the school library and used her teacher's list to help her choose a topic. Here is part of Georgia's list.

a place that makes me calm and peaceful
—window seat at home where I read
a place that I dream about
—beach near Uncle Thad's house
a place that amazes me
—Empire State Building
—lighted fountain in the park
a place that scares me
—empty building on Peeling Street

Georgia decided to write about the window seat at home. She read there almost every day, so she knew it well. There were also lots of things outside the window to describe.

> ## Your Turn
>
> - Use the list Georgia's teacher gave her to help you think of topics for your description.
> - Think of one or more places for each item on the list.
> - When you have finished, circle the place that you most want to write about.

Using a Five-Senses Chart

Georgia decided to use a five-senses chart to  **Organization** help her think of things that appeal to each of her five senses. Here is Georgia's chart.

Topic: My Window Seat

Sight	cars in street, bus, dogs, people, Mr. Deimos
Sound	squeaky snack cart, traffic, barking, airplanes
Smell	popcorn, smoky bus, cut grass
Taste	lemonade
Touch	warm sunlight, smooth glass, curtains tickle my arm

When she was finished, Georgia read her chart. She was surprised by how many senses she could write about by just looking out a window. But she also knew that she needed to stay on the topic. She wanted to write about the taste of lemonade because she drinks lemonade while she reads. But it didn't really fit with what was outside the window. The feel of the smooth glass or the curtains that tickle her arm didn't fit either. She knew she wouldn't be able to use everything in her chart. But by making a chart, she had plenty of ideas to choose from.

Georgia decided that space order would be best for her description. She could describe the things nearest to her window first and the farthest things last.

Your Turn

Make a five-senses chart like Georgia's. When you have finished, look at your chart. Think about how best to organize the details in your description.

Drafting

First, Georgia wrote the beginning of her description. It told what she was going to describe. Then she wrote the middle in space order. She described things nearest to her window first, and she described the things far away last. She finished by writing an ending that told readers to try to find a special place like hers. Here is Georgia's draft.

A Warm, Sunny Spot

My favrite place is a window seat. I love the sights, sounds, and smells outside my window. They get me ready to read my book. The sunlight on the window seat. The street has cars parked along both sides. When I open the window, I smell popcorn from Mr. deimos's snack cart. I hear his bell ringing as he pushes his squeaky cart down my sidewalk. A bus drives by at four o'clock every day. People and dogs play across the street. barking dogs and quiet dogs chase tennis balls in the green grass. The crazy dogs always make me laugh.

After I enjoy what I see, hear, and smell, I am ready to read. It is the perfect way to calm down after a day at school. Everyone should try reading at a window seat.

While Georgia wrote, she tried to use some things she had learned in class about descriptions. She used sensory words to

 Word Choice

make the picture clearer for her audience. She wrote about the things outside her window in space order, starting with the nearest things. She also made sure to write a beginning, a middle, and an ending. She left extra space between lines so she could write changes on her draft later.

Your Turn

- Write the first draft of your description. Make sure that you tell the reader in the beginning what you are describing.
- Use space order to give the reader a clear idea of how things are placed.
- Use sensory words that describe more than just what you see.
- Use your five-senses chart to remind you of different sensory words to put in your description.

Similes

A simile is something you can use to make a

Voice

clearer picture. When you use a simile, you compare things by using either the word *like* or the word *as*.

Imagine you are trying to describe a man at the park. He is wearing a blue sweater. You want to make a clear picture for the reader. What kind of blue is his sweater? Is it blue like a thundercloud? Or is it blue like a blueberry? If you tell your reader that the sweater is blue like a blueberry, you make the picture clearer. You also use a simile.

Editor's Workshop

Content Editing

Georgia was happy with her first draft. But she knew she could make it better. A content editor would check that the ideas in Georgia's description made sense.

Georgia thought it would be best if she had someone else content edit her draft. Armand lived in Georgia's building. He could look out his own window and see the same things as Georgia saw. Armand could make sure that Georgia's description was clear for a reader. Armand used the Content Editor's Checklist below.

Armand read Georgia's description a few times. He even read it once sitting on his own window seat. Armand wrote ideas he had to improve Georgia's draft. Then he met with Georgia to share his ideas.

Content Editor's Checklist

- ☐ Do the title and beginning tell what is being described?

- ☐ Does the middle describe something by using space order?

- ☐ Does the ending leave the reader with something to think about?

- ☐ Are sensory words used to tell what the writer sees, hears, smells, tastes, and feels?

- ☐ Does the description make a clear picture for the audience?

Armand started by saying what he liked about Georgia's description. Armand liked the sensory words that Georgia used, such as *squeaky* and *barking*. He said that he could almost smell the popcorn in Mr. Deimos's snack cart. He also liked that Georgia told readers to try reading at a window seat. He thought that would give readers something to think about when they were finished reading. Then Armand shared these ideas.

- Could you make the beginning grab the reader's attention more? It's also not clear to me which part is the beginning and which part is the middle.

- I can tell you are using space order in your description. But something is out of place. You describe the cars in the street before you finish describing the sidewalk. The sidewalk is closer.

- You use lots of sensory words in your description. But maybe you could say something about the great bread that Mr. Deimos's wife makes at the bakery down the street.

- You should tell your audience that there is a dog park across the street. They probably don't know that.

Georgia thanked Armand for reading her draft. She thought his ideas were helpful. But she wasn't sure she wanted to use all of them. She wanted to think about the ideas and come up with ideas of her own before she revised her draft.

Your Turn

- Read your first draft. Use the Content Editor's Checklist to help make it better.
- Mark your corrections on the draft.
- Trade drafts with a partner and read each other's work.
- Use the Content Editor's Checklist while you read your partner's draft.
- Pay attention to only one question at a time.
- Write ideas you have for making your partner's draft stronger.
- Take turns talking about your drafts. Remember to start by saying what you liked about your partner's draft.

Writer's Tip Write your partner's ideas. Think about each one before you make any changes. Which ideas will make your description clearer and more colorful?

Prewriting

Drafting

Content Editing

Revising

Copyediting

Proofreading

Publishing

Descriptions

Revising

When Georgia revised her draft, it looked like this.

A Warm, Sunny Spot

Everybody likes a special place to read.
My favrite place is a window seat. I love the sights, sounds,
and smells outside my window. They get me ready to read my
book. ¶ The sunlight on the window seat. The street has cars parked
along both sides. When I open the window, I smell popcorn from
Mr. deimos's snack cart. I hear his bell ringing as he pushes his
                              big, smoky   rumbles
squeaky cart down my sidewalk. A bus ~~drives~~ by at four o'clock
                      fill the dog park
every day. People and dogs ~~play~~ across the street. barking dogs and
quiet dogs chase tennis balls in the green grass. The crazy dogs
always make me laugh.

After I enjoy what I see, hear, and smell, I am ready to read. It
is the perfect way to calm down after a day at school. Everyone
should try reading at a window seat.

Here are some things Georgia did to make her description clearer.

- Georgia changed the beginning of her description. What did she do? Why? How does the change help the reader understand the topic?
- Where did Georgia choose to start a new paragraph? Why do you think she did this?
- What information did Georgia add about the people and dogs across the street? How does this change help the reader?
- Georgia decided to move the sentence about the cars in the street to a different place. Why did she make this change? Do you agree with her change? Why or why not?
- Georgia still thought the sentence about the bus could be better. She added two adjectives to describe the bus. What were they?
- Georgia decided to change the word *drives* to a stronger word. What word did she choose? Do you agree with her word choice? Why or why not?
- Armand had said that Georgia should say something about the smell of Mrs. Deimos's bread. But Georgia decided not to make that change. Why do you think she did not make the change?

Georgia read her draft again. She was glad that Armand liked all the sensory words in her description.

Your Turn

- Read the ideas your partner had about ways to change your draft.
- Think about which of those ideas and which of your own ideas you would like to use. Remember that it is up to you whether you want to use your partner's ideas in your draft.
- Revise your draft.
- When you have finished, go over the Content Editor's Checklist again. See if you can answer yes to each question.

Prewriting
Drafting
Content Editing
Revising
Copyediting
Proofreading
Publishing

Copyediting and Proofreading

Copyediting

Georgia liked the content editing changes. She thought her draft was much better. But Georgia knew that by copyediting her draft, she could make the sentences and words stronger. Georgia used this checklist to copyedit her description.

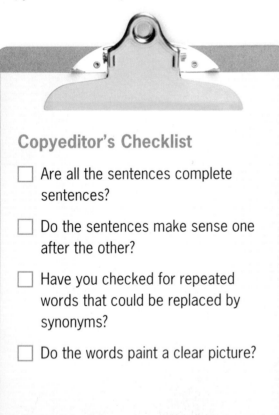

Copyeditor's Checklist

- [ ] Are all the sentences complete sentences?

- [ ] Do the sentences make sense one after the other?

- [ ] Have you checked for repeated words that could be replaced by synonyms?

- [ ] Do the words paint a clear picture?

Georgia checked each question one at a time. She found an incomplete sentence in the second paragraph. Do you see it? Georgia fixed the sentence and added a sensory word to describe what the sunlight felt like. What did she write?

 Sentence Fluency

Georgia also changed the order of some sentences. They didn't follow space order. She thought that it might be clearer if she described the street first, then the bus.

When Georgia checked the third question on the checklist, she saw that she used the word *dogs* five times in one paragraph. She decided to replace a few with synonyms. Which words did Georgia choose to replace the word *dogs*?

Writer's Tip Make sure the synonym or more exact word you use doesn't change the meaning of the sentence.

Your Turn

Read your draft again, using the Copyeditor's Checklist. Remember to check only one question at a time.

Proofreading

Georgia's mom was a professional writer. She would be the perfect person to proofread Georgia's draft. Her mom used the Conventions checklist below. It was similar to the checklist her mom used when she checked for mistakes in her own writing.

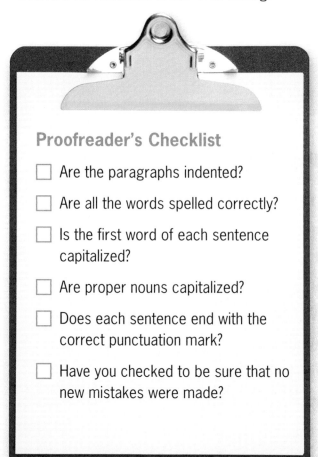

Proofreader's Checklist

- ☐ Are the paragraphs indented?
- ☐ Are all the words spelled correctly?
- ☐ Is the first word of each sentence capitalized?
- ☐ Are proper nouns capitalized?
- ☐ Does each sentence end with the correct punctuation mark?
- ☐ Have you checked to be sure that no new mistakes were made?

Georgia's mom found a sentence that didn't start with a capital letter. She also found a proper noun that needed a capital letter. Can you find the two mistakes in Georgia's draft?

Your Turn

- Use the Proofreader's Checklist to proofread your draft. Check for only one question at a time.
- When you have finished proofreading your description, ask a partner to check your work, using the Proofreader's Checklist.
- Make sure that the changes your partner suggests are correct before you make the changes in your draft.
- Be sure to use a dictionary if you have a question about spelling or capitalization.

Grammar in Action

Georgia's mom found one misspelled word in Georgia's description. Find it and fix it.

Prewriting
Drafting
Content Editing
Revising
Copyediting
Proofreading
Publishing

Publishing

Georgia typed her final draft on her mom's computer. As she typed, she added the proofreading changes. She typed slowly and carefully. She wanted to be sure she didn't make any new mistakes while typing.

Georgia printed out her description. When she brought it to school, her teacher collected the students' descriptions and put them together to make a book.

A Warm, Sunny Spot

Everybody likes a special place to read. My favorite place is a window seat. I love the sights, sounds, and smells outside my window. They get me ready to read my book.

The sunlight on the window seat warms my skin. When I open the window, I smell popcorn from Mr. Deimos's snack cart. I hear his bell ringing as he pushes his squeaky cart down my sidewalk. The street has cars parked along both sides. A big, smoky bus rumbles by at four o'clock every day. People and dogs fill the dog park across the street. Barking hounds and quiet puppies chase tennis balls in the green grass. The crazy dogs always make me laugh.

After I enjoy what I see, hear, and smell, I am ready to read. It is the perfect way to calm down after a day at school. Everyone should try reading at a window seat.

Presentation Publishing is the moment that you turn your work in to your teacher, read it aloud to your classmates, or post it on the bulletin board for others to read. Give these publishing ideas a try.

 Post your description on your classroom's wiki, blog, or Web site. Invite other students to review and comment on your work.

 Create a class magazine. Decorate the margins with small pictures of things representing the descriptions. Work with your classmates to decide on a cover.

 Film it. Videotape the person, place, or thing you described and add music. Narrate your video with your description.

 Submit your description to be published in your school's newspaper or literary magazine.

Whenever you publish your work, your goal is to share your thoughts and experiences with other people.

Your Turn

- Make a final copy of your description by writing it on a clean sheet of paper or by typing it on a computer.
- Make the proofreading changes that you decided to use. Try not to make any new mistakes while you fix the old ones.
- When you have finished your description, draw a picture of it. Read your description again to help you remember everything you will want to put in your picture.

Personal Letters

LiNK **Yours Truly, Goldilocks**

by Alma Flor Ada

Brick House
Woodsy Woods
April 7

Dear Goldilocks,

Thank you, thank you, thank you! The three of us had a great time at your birthday party.

It was a wonderful, wonderful, wonderful party. That is, all three of us think it was wonderful.

As you know, we have had a terrible time building our houses. Now that we are sure that no wolf can blow down our new house, no matter how hard he huffs and puffs, we would like to finally have a house warming party on April twenty-ninth. We would be very happy if you were our special guest. We are also sending invitations to Baby Bear, Little Red Riding Hood, and Peter Rabbit. We look forward to a wonderful day.

Love, love, love your three friends,
Pig One, Pig Two, and Pig Three

> This personal letter has five parts and states one topic at a time.

CHAPTER 4

30 Bailey Road
Park Forest, CA 90317
July 30, 20—

Dear Mr. and Mrs. Ruiz,

    Thank you so much for inviting me to spend last week at your cottage with you and Alicia. It was the best week!

    Before Saturday I had never spent a night away from home. I was a little nervous about being in the country. What if there were weird insects or snakes? Well, there were insects and snakes, but they were interesting and not scary.

    I loved everything we did on the water. I liked swimming in the lake, fishing from the boat, and canoeing to the store. I will never, ever forget the morning we paddled on the lake as the sun came up. I almost tipped the canoe when that big silver fish jumped out of the water to catch a bug. Have you caught any giant fish since I left?

    I hope the rest of your summer is wonderful. Tell Alicia that I can't wait to see her back at school.

Your friend,
Layne

What Makes a Good Personal Letter?

We write and send personal letters to people we know. Personal letters have five parts.

The **heading** of the personal letter gives the address of the writer and the date the letter was written. It goes in the top right-hand corner. A comma goes between the name of the town or city and the state. Another comma goes between the day and the year. A line of space follows the heading.

The **greeting** gives the name of the receiver. It goes on the left side of the letter. The words in the greeting are capitalized except for *and* between two people's names. A comma goes after the greeting.

The **body** is the message of the letter. It is what you want to say to the receiver. In the body each paragraph is indented. Leave an extra line of space below the body.

The **closing** comes after the body. It lines up under the heading. It is where you say good-bye to the receiver. Only the first word is capitalized. A comma goes after the closing.

30 Bailey Road
Park Forest, CA 90317
July 30, 20—

Dear Mr. and Mrs. Ruiz,

    Thank you so much for inviting me to spend last week at your cottage with you and Alicia. It was the best week!

    Before Saturday I had never spent a night away from home. I was a little nervous about being in the country. What if there were weird insects or snakes? Well, there were insects and snakes, but they were interesting and not scary.

    I loved everything we did on the water. I liked swimming in the lake, fishing from the boat, and canoeing to the store. I will never, ever forget the morning we paddled on the lake as the sun came up. I almost tipped the canoe when that big silver fish jumped out of the water to catch a bug. Have you caught any giant fish since I left?

    I hope the rest of your summer is wonderful. Tell Alicia that I can't wait to see her back at school.

Your friend,
Layne

The closing is followed by a **signature**. The signature is your written name.

ACTIVITY A Answer the questions below about the parts of the letter on page 325.

1. What city is Layne from?
2. On what day did Layne write the letter?
3. To whom did she write the letter?
4. Why did Layne write the letter?
5. What message did Layne want Alicia to know?
6. How did Layne say good-bye in the letter?

ACTIVITY B Work with a partner to write the parts of the letter that are missing below.

955 ____(1)____ Lane

Hoffman Lakes, ___(2)___ 61049

___(3)___ 18, 20–

Dear Mrs. ____(4)____,

    Please excuse Jason from class today. He is sick with the chicken pox and cannot come to school. On doctor's orders he will be missing a few days. Please send any work home with his sister, Kelly.

    I hope to see you at the next Open House. I always have a nice time talking with you about your adventures during the summer. You went to Peru this year, right?

____(5)____,

Carol Zeckman

WRITER'S CORNER

Imagine that Layne wrote the letter on page 325 to you and that you would like to invite Layne to your home next summer. Write the heading, the greeting, the closing, and the signature for the letter.

ACTIVITY C Identify the parts of the letter below.

828 North Gunnison St.
Brazil, IL 60313
August 28, 20–

Dear Owen,

How are you doing, brother? How is college? I wanted to tell you that I heard that your favorite band, The Bowling Weevils, is going to be playing here on October 5. I was wondering if you were going to come home.

I hope you are having a good first week at school. Tell me if you are going to go to any football games. If you do, I will look for you on TV.

Yours truly,
Luke

ACTIVITY D Copy the headings, greetings, and closings below. Then add the correct punctuation.

1. Your best friend
2. March 28 20–
3. Dear Henry
4. Baltic ND
5. New Braunfels TX
6. Sincerely
7. Dear Uncle Marcos
8. Love
9. November 12 20–
10. Dear Mr. and Mrs. Hund
11. Des Plaines IL 60178
12. Yours truly

ACTIVITY E The parts of the letter below are mixed up. Rewrite the parts in the correct order.

Monique
    Yesterday I went with my neighbors Kat and Jack to a movie set. Kat works for a famous director. The movie is a big secret, but I can tell you it's about your favorite story.

Dear Leah,

Los Angeles, CA 90211

Your pen pal,

1823 La Casa Drive

October 3, 20–

ACTIVITY F Tell which part of a personal letter each item is from. Then rewrite the item with correct capitalization and punctuation.

1. dear ali.
2. your Grandson
3. did you hear kelly won.
4. may, 23 20–
5. toledo OH 78791
6. dear Kasey johnson
7. 1984 Lisbon avenue
8. best wishes
9. miami fl 33127
10. i will leave for paris in one week.

WRITER'S CORNER

Draw on a sheet of paper boxes where each part of a letter belongs. Then write the heading, greeting, closing, and signature as if you were writing the letter to a friend.

The Body of a Personal Letter

The body of a personal letter is where you write your message. Writing a personal letter is like talking on paper to someone you know.

Purpose

We write personal letters to someone we know. People write personal letters for different reasons. Here are some common reasons.

LiNK

Dear Mother,

There is only room for me to send my love, and some pressed pansies from the root I have been keeping safe in the house for Father to see. I read every morning, try to be good all day, and sing myself to sleep with Father's tune. . . . Everyone is very kind, and we are as happy as we can be without you.

. . . Oh, do come home soon to your loving . . .

LITTLE BETH

- People write personal letters to tell about something that happened to them. The topics can be anything. You might write about your day at school, your summer, or even a coyote you saw in your backyard.
- People write personal letters to share news or to tell a story about someone else. You might write to your grandpa about your sister's first day in acting class.
- People write personal letters to thank someone. On page 325 Layne wrote to Alicia's parents to thank them for letting her stay in their cottage.
- People write personal letters to find out information. You might write to your uncle to see what you need to bring when you go to the basketball championship with him.

ACTIVITY A Pick which of the purposes below are for a personal letter.

1. to tell Aunt Rita you met the mayor of Chicago
2. to ask Luna Restaurant to help with the food drive
3. to talk about baseball with your friend in Miami
4. to tell your aunt that your brother won a swim meet
5. to complain to Street Team that the skateboard you bought from them broke after one ride
6. to thank your cousin for the gift card to your favorite store
7. to ask Paws Place Shelter if you can volunteer
8. to ask your friend what movie she would like to see with you when she visits

ACTIVITY B Read the paragraphs from personal letters below. Decide the purpose of each personal letter.

1. Stephanie, the smartest kid in my class, told me about a new book about cheetahs that fly spaceships. Have you heard about this book? The main character is named Flip the Cheetah, and his friend is Donnie. She said the characters are funny. Do you know who wrote it?

2. Last Friday I had a chance to go to the museum to see the new exhibit about Rome. I got to pretend I was a gladiator in a show they had. Then we saw parts of old statues. You would have loved it, Mandy!

3. I wish you could have seen Kevin at the state spelling bee. He closed his eyes when he spelled each word. He finally won by spelling *individuality* correctly. We are so proud of him!

WRITER'S CORNER

Think of a family member to whom you would like to write a personal letter. Choose a purpose for your letter. Write the purpose and the person to whom you are writing. Then write the heading, greeting, closing, and signature.

Organization of a Personal Letter

A personal letter needs to be organized. In personal letters the writer writes about one topic at a time.

A personal letter will have a different order depending on your purpose.

- If the purpose of your personal letter is to tell a story about yourself or about someone else, write the events in the order they happened.
- If the purpose of your letter is to thank someone, write about one thing at a time. In Layne's letter she talked about many things she liked. But she wrote all her ideas about one thing before she wrote about the next.
- If the purpose of your letter is to find information, explain your questions one at a time. Then write why you want to know the answer.

Dear Pierre,

I am very happy you and I were matched up to be pen pals. You and your family sound very interesting.

In what part of France do you live? I could not find Fayence on my map. . . .

Your pen pal,
Eloise

ACTIVITY C Read the topics for personal letters below. Decide what the best way to organize each topic would be.

1. thanking your sister for the gifts from her vacation to Brazil
2. telling grandma about Dad getting chased by a dog
3. thanking your friend for a sleepover
4. telling your cousin about your first day of dance class
5. asking your friend to help you understand a difficult book
6. telling your grandfather what it was like to watch a dog show
7. asking your pen pal what her country is like
8. thanking your librarian for the books he found for you

ACTIVITY D Choose a topic for a personal letter. Think about the events you want to write about in the body of your letter. Tell the events in the order that they happened.

1. Your day at school
2. A friend's sporting event
3. A day spent with your family
4. A funny pet story

ACTIVITY E The personal letter below has two sentences out of order and two missing parts. Rewrite the letter in the right order. Add the missing parts.

1521 Agatite Ave.

Silvis, MI 90010

September 17, 20—

Thank you for the box of sports supplies, Uncle Andre! I love the baseball bat. The new baseball glove is great too. My old glove is too small for me now. Using a wooden bat is going to be much easier than using a metal one. The tennis racket is going to be great. I can go to tennis camp next summer. My little sister loves basketball, and now she won't bother me so much. Finally, the basketball is going to be fun too. Thank you once again!

Ricardo

ACTIVITY F Write the body of a letter to a new pen pal. Remember to tell your pen pal about yourself. Ask your pen pal at least one question.

WRITER'S CORNER

Organize the personal letter you began in the Writer's Corner on page 331. Choose the organization that best fits the purpose of your letter. Then write the body of your letter.

Grammar in Action. Find one action verb and one being verb in the first sentence of the letter on page 332.

Personal E-Mails

Some e-mails are like personal letters. People write e-mails to keep in touch with friends and family. People often write e-mails to share news and to get information quickly.

E-mails usually have fewer parts than letters you send through the post office.

Address

In an e-mail you need to type the receiver's e-mail address accurately, character by character. Otherwise, the person will not receive it, and the e-mail may bounce back to you.

The e-mail program automatically puts your e-mail address and date at the top of the e-mail. You do not have to type them. You do not have to type your street address at the top of an e-mail.

Subject Line

Subject lines are special to e-mails. They state the main topic of the e-mail in a few words. For example, if you are writing a thank-you e-mail, you might write "Thanks for the gift." Personal e-mails may have several topics, and people may sometimes use general headings such as "Checking in" or "What's new?" or "Touching base."

ACTIVITY A **Read the e-mail and answer the questions.**

To:	martinaginetti@emailcentral.com
From:	lizziesanson@mailboxforme.com
Date:	March 22, 20–
Subject:	My new cat!

Dear Martina,

How are you? How are Aunt Anna and Uncle Will?

I am writing to tell you I got a cat yesterday from the shelter. His name is Leopold. He's a Siamese, and he's one year old.

Right now Leopold seems a little scared in his new home, but he already likes me to pet him. Soon he probably will be very friendly and even sleep in my bed.

I know that you have a cat. Can you suggest any good toys to get for Leopold? How about a cat DVD for my new cat to watch?

Please write back soon.

Your cousin,

Lizzie

1. Who is receiving the e-mail?
2. What is the date of the e-mail?
3. What are the words in the subject line? What is the topic of the e-mail?
4. Look back at page 326. Which part of a personal letter is missing from the e-mail?

ACTIVITY B **Read the subject lines. What is each e-mail about?**

1. See you at the train station on Friday
2. Birthday party!
3. Your recipe for banana bread
4. Amusement park trip

WRITER'S CORNER

Think of a topic for an e-mail that you would like to send a family member or a friend. Write the subject line and the person who will receive the e-mail. Do this for three different topics.

Body of an E-Mail

The body of an e-mail is like the body of a personal letter. E-mails are often written to tell personal stories, to share news, to thank someone, or to ask for information. Look back at page 332 for help on the organization of personal letters. How is the body of the e-mail on page 335 organized?

Closing

The closing of an e-mail is similar to that of personal letters. Some examples are *Your friend, Sincerely,* and *Best wishes.*

Signature

Some e-mail programs have a feature that lets you type your name once and then will automatically include it in your e-mails. Some allow you to include a handwritten copy of your signature. Does your e-mail account have a signature feature? Do you know how to use it?

E-mail Safety

It is important to follow some rules for using e-mail.

- Always get your parent's permission before going online.
- Keep the password for your e-mail account to yourself.
- Do not give out personal information on the Internet. There are people who try to get your personal information and use it for themselves.
- Remember that your e-mail may not stay private.
- Do not open e-mail for which you do not know the sender. Don't be fooled by subject lines such as "Remember me?"
- Do not download attachments from people you don't know. These attachments might have viruses that could harm your computer.

ACTIVITY C Write subject lines for these e-mails.

1. You are writing to your grandmother to tell her that your poem won a prize in a state poetry contest.
2. You are writing to a friend to ask where you can get a special backpack you know she has.
3. You are writing to a friend about your first time hiking.
4. You are writing to an aunt who sent you a book on knights for your birthday.

ACTIVITY D Complete the following e-mail. Then reorder the paragraphs of the body.

PITTSBURGH **PIRATES**

Roberto Clemente outfield

To: daveb@worldwide.com

From: _____ **(1)**

Date: November 11, 20—

Subject: _____ **(2)**

_____ **(3)** ,

Here's what happened. I went to a garage sale with my mom, and I saw an old shoe box filled with baseball cards. I looked through the box carefully. Can you imagine my surprise when I saw a card for Roberto Clemente? And it only cost a dollar. I used some of my allowance to buy it.

The next time you come over, I can show it to you.

I am writing to tell you about my terrific find. I now own a Roberto Clemente baseball card! You know he's my favorite old-time player.

_____ **(4)** ,

_____ **(5)**

WRITER'S CORNER

Think of a topic for an e-mail you want to write to a friend. Write the e-mail, using the correct format.

Compound Subjects

If two or more subjects in a sentence have the same predicate, they form a compound subject.

Chad and Nikki tied for first place.

In this sentence the compound subject is *Chad and Nikki.* You can use compound subjects to add variety to your writing. You can also use compound subjects to combine, or join, short, choppy sentences.

If two sentences have the same predicate, you can combine them.

Matt dug for worms. Curtis dug for worms.

These sentences have different single subjects. They are about two different people, Matt and Curtis. What is the same? The predicate is the same. Matt and Curtis did the same thing. They both *dug for worms.* The two sentences can be combined with the compound subject *Matt and Curtis.*

Matt and Curtis dug for worms.

ACTIVITY A **Find the subject in each sentence.**

1. Kasey and Chris planned a pet circus.
2. Reggie made posters.
3. Mia and Miguel rounded up the pets.
4. The owners trained their pets.
5. Koren announced the acts to the audience.
6. My parrot squawked.
7. The puppies and kittens ran into the crowd.
8. The audience laughed and clapped.

ACTIVITY B Identify the subject in each sentence. Tell whether it is a single subject or a compound subject.

1. Akimi wanted to go skateboarding.
2. The skateboard is black with many decals.
3. Akimi and Rex performed a trick.
4. The children wore helmets.
5. Callie, Josh, and Carlos got to the park late.
6. The boys and girls skated all day.
7. The twins learned a new trick.
8. Everyone had a great time.
9. Kids and adults enjoy the skate park.
10. They can't wait to go again next week.

ACTIVITY C Combine each pair of sentences into one sentence with a compound subject.

1. José played the piano. Kiko played the piano.
2. The pencil fell off the desk. The pen fell off the desk.
3. The mad scientist laughed. His assistant laughed.
4. Beth went to the capital. Uncle George went to the capital.
5. Maria hiked the valley. The guide hiked the valley.
6. Paige washed the car. Her mom washed the car.
7. Ben played soccer. Katie played soccer.
8. The fruit ripened. The vegetables ripened.
9. Emilio moved away. His sister moved away.
10. The flag swayed in the breeze. The branches swayed in the breeze.
11. The glass broke. The vase broke.
12. Tom read a book. Marisol read a book.

WRITER'S CORNER

Read a page from a story that tells about two or more characters. Write three sentences describing where the characters are and what they are doing. Use compound subjects in your sentences.

Grammar in Action. Use at least two helping verbs in your sentences.

More Compound Subjects

Sometimes writers can combine subjects from sentences with different predicates. The predicates have to be close in meaning.

Olivia went upstairs silently. Kari crept upstairs silently.

Both predicates mean about the same thing. To make a sentence with a compound subject, choose one of the predicates to use. Which predicate would you use—*went upstairs silently* or *crept upstairs silently*? Use the predicate that makes a clearer picture.

Olivia and Kari crept upstairs silently.

Crept upstairs silently makes a clearer picture than *went upstairs silently.*

ACTIVITY D Combine each pair of sentences into one sentence with a compound subject.

1. A German shepherd went down the street. A dalmatian streaked down the street.

2. The president stepped out of the airplane. The Secret Service agents got out of the airplane.

3. Kim went across the lake in a kayak. I paddled across the lake in a kayak.

4. At the game Drew yelled a cheer. At the game Cameron and Lucy said a cheer.

5. Terrel went over the high jump. Randy leaped over the high jump.

6. Feng ran by. Ryan sprinted by.

7. Jared cleaned the roller coaster. Steve scrubbed the roller coaster.

8. The Cats were in the playoffs. The Squids played in the playoffs.

ACTIVITY E Choose one of the paragraphs below. Combine short, choppy sentences into longer sentences with compound subjects.

A. Carmen helped set the table. Her brother Tony helped set the table. Aunt Nora arrived at about 6:30. Aunt Julia came at about 6:30. Carmen was happy to see them. Tony was thrilled to see them. The chicken was grilled. The peppers were grilled. The guests enjoyed the tasty dinner. After dinner everyone went for a walk. Then Aunt Nora and Aunt Julia left. Carmen waved good-bye. Tony waved good-bye.

B. The farmer had spilled grain near the barn. The chicken pecked at the grain. The rooster ate the grain. The rooster flew to the roof. The chicken waddled across the yard. The chicks went across the yard. The barn in the yard was red. The wheelbarrow located in the yard was red. The day of work was finished. The chicken went to sleep. The chicks drifted off to sleep.

ACTIVITY F Choose four sets of words below. Use each set in a sentence with a compound subject.

A. squirrels, chipmunks, chattered
B. Jordan, Owen, painted
C. carrots, broccoli, grew
D. shark, seaweed, live
E. astronaut, alien, screamed
F. guide, hikers, photographed

WRITER'S CORNER

Write five sentences about a monster you have read about. Use compound subjects in three of the sentences.

Antonyms

Antonyms are words that have opposite meanings. For example, *little* and *big* are antonyms. These words have opposite meanings of each other. Here are some other antonyms that you might know.

noisy	quiet
good	bad
in	out
happy	sad
thick	thin
first	last
up	down
fast	slow
come	go
weak	strong
messy	neat
forget	remember

Remember that writers use synonyms to make their writing interesting. Writers also use antonyms to make their writing interesting. They use antonyms to show the difference between people or things. What are some more antonyms for the word *good*?

ACTIVITY A Match each word in Column A with its antonym in Column B.

Column A	Column B
1. first	a. full
2. open	b. on
3. sick	c. day
4. new	d. old
5. off	e. closed
6. warm	f. little
7. sharp	g. cool
8. big	h. dull
9. empty	i. healthy
10. night	j. last

ACTIVITY B Tell whether the words in each pair are antonyms.

1. rough	smooth		7. dark	bright
2. above	over		8. many	few
3. nasty	mean		9. straight	crooked
4. hot	cold		10. coarse	rough
5. win	lose		11. wide	broad
6. near	close		12. tame	wild

WRITER'S CORNER

Choose three pairs of antonyms from Activity A. Use each pair of antonyms in a sentence.

ACTIVITY C Complete each sentence with the antonym of the word that is underlined. Use an antonym from the word box.

soft	first	fast	down
old	laugh	last	never

1. December is the <u>last</u> month of the year. January is the _____ month.
2. After Mom put the pictures <u>up</u>, one fell _____.
3. Some pretzels are <u>hard</u>, and some are _____.
4. The tortoise finished the race <u>first</u>, and the hare finished _____.
5. The snail was <u>slow</u>, but the dragonfly was very _____.
6. Dad bought me a <u>new</u> catcher's mitt because my _____ mitt was falling apart.

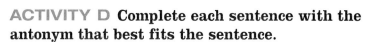

7. My little sister wanted to <u>cry</u> when she fell, so I made funny faces to make her _____.
8. I <u>always</u> set my alarm clock. I _____ oversleep.

ACTIVITY D Complete each sentence with the antonym that best fits the sentence.

1. Be (careful careless) when you cross Main Street.
2. Only a (strong weak) person could carry that box.
3. I found a penny at the (bottom top) of the glass.
4. Please (open close) a new can of cat food for Zeus.
5. The (new old) rusty door hinge squeaked.
6. The (sleepy alert) guard did not notice the burglars.
7. Our car seems (roomy cramped) when all my brothers and sisters are in it.
8. The long, wooden table was (rough smooth), so Dad sanded it.

ACTIVITY E Read these rhymes. Complete each rhyme with an antonym of the word that is underlined. Choose words from the word box.

> in   sad   thin   bad   clean   mean

1. When the weather is <u>good</u>, we don't feel _____.
   When a clown is <u>happy</u>, she isn't _____.

2. When the dog is <u>out</u>, he won't come _____.
   I like my pancakes <u>thick</u>, not _____.

3. When my room looks <u>messy</u>, I need to make it look _____.
   With my friends and family I am <u>nice</u>, not _____.

ACTIVITY F Think of an antonym for each word below. Write the antonym pairs.

1. tall
2. easy
3. late
4. end
5. push

6. whisper
7. here
8. young
9. find
10. wrong

WRITER'S CORNER

How many antonyms can you think of for the words *little*, *nice*, and *slow*? Make a list with at least three antonyms for each word. Then compare your list with a partner's list.

Telephone Conversations

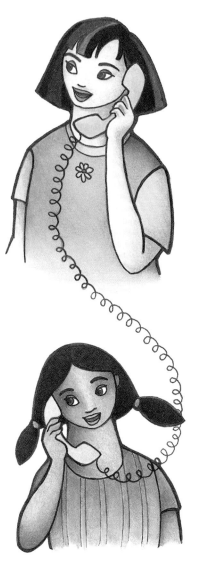

Talking on the telephone is something that you might do every day. You might call someone or someone might call you. You might call a family member to catch up or a friend for help with math homework. A salesperson might call to speak to one of your parents. Your mom's boss might call.

Answering the Telephone

When the telephone rings, answer it right away. Before you answer it, turn down the radio or television. You can also leave a noisy room.

When you answer the phone, start by saying, "Hello." You might also say, "Hello, Peters' residence" or "Leah speaking, who's calling please?" Whatever you say, make sure it is how your parents want you to answer the telephone.

Talking on the Telephone

Be polite to anyone you talk to on the telephone, even if it is someone you don't know. Remember that the person you are talking to can't see you. Speak clearly and use your voice to show how you feel. The person on the other end won't be able to see you frown or smile.

Here are a few things that you need to remember.

- Pay attention to the person you are talking to.
- Don't talk to other people in the room.
- When you have finished, make sure you say good-bye.

ACTIVITY A Choose which sentences are good ways to answer the phone.

1. Hello, this is the Robinson residence.
2. Yeah, it's Jennifer.
3. Hi, Jon and Greta Calo's, how may I help you?
4. Hello, Theresa speaking.
5. Talk to me.
6. Who is this?

ACTIVITY B Tell what you would say in the following telephone conversation with your teacher.

(Telephone rings.)

Student: _____

Teacher: Hi (student's name). This is (teacher's name). I wanted to remind you that you are taking our class hamster home tomorrow. Do you have any questions?

Student: _____

Teacher: Okay. I will see you tomorrow.

Student: _____

Teacher: Good-bye.

ACTIVITY C Practice what you would say in these situations.

1. NoLeaks Roofers call and an adult can't come to the phone.
2. Your best friend calls to talk to you.
3. Your mother is at home, and her best friend calls to talk to her.
4. Your brother's boss at Grow 'em Garden Store calls, and your brother is in the backyard.
5. Your uncle calls to wish your sister a happy birthday. You are not sure if she is home, but your father is home.

Hello?

SPEAKER'S CORNER

Meet with a partner and take turns "calling" each other. Show that you are happy, making a joke, worried, or sad by using only your voice.

Taking a Message

Suppose a caller wants to speak to your older brother. He's at work, and you ask if you can take a message. The caller says yes. What do you do to take a message?

Taking a message depends on what your parents want you to do. If they want only the name and phone number of the caller, that's all you ask for. Taking a message also depends on the caller. If a caller wants to give you a lot of information, write it down. Here are good questions to ask when taking a message.

- Who is calling?
- Who are you calling for?
- What is the message?
- What is your phone number?
- What would be a good time to return your call?

Be sure you have a pencil and paper near the phone. Also make sure to give the message to the person it is for. When you have finished taking a message, thank the caller. Then say good-bye and hang up.

Making a Telephone Call

What do you do when you make a telephone call? The first thing to do is to make sure that you have the right number. If you call the wrong number, don't hang up before saying you're sorry for calling the wrong number.

When someone answers the phone, say, "Hello," and tell who you are. Ask to speak to the person you called for. When that person answers, say, "Hello," and say your name again. If no one answers, leave a message on their voice mail or answering machine. Leave your name, number, and the reason for calling.

ACTIVITY D Pretend you are Cody. Take a message based on the conversation Cody had with Mr. Gonbug. Use the questions from the lesson to help you.

Cody: Hello, this is the Seer residence.

Mr. Gonbug: Hello, this is Mr. Gonbug with Gonbug's Lawn Care. Is Mrs. Seer at home?

Cody: I'm sorry, she can't come to the phone right now. May I take a message?

Mr. Gonbug: Please tell her that Gonbug's Lawn Care will come out at 4:30 instead of 3:30 tomorrow to take care of her lawn.

Cody: What is a phone number where she can reach you?

Mr. Gonbug: The office number is 555-4445.

Cody: What time can she call you back?

Mr. Gonbug: Tell her to call back by noon tomorrow.

Cody: Thank you. I'll give her the message.

Mr. Gonbug: Thank you. Good-bye.

Cody: Good-bye.

ACTIVITY E Pretend that you are calling to speak with your cousin. Have a partner be your uncle or aunt. Practice what you would say to your uncle or aunt in order to speak to your cousin. Then practice leaving a message on an answering machine.

SPEAKER'S CORNER

Prepare a conversation with your partner in which you ask your partner for help with homework. Take turns making the call and answering the call. Practice taking a message and leaving a message on an answering machine.

Tech Tip Videotape or record your conversation.

Writer's Workshop

Prewriting and Drafting

There are many reasons to write thank-you letters. You might thank an uncle for helping you with your homework. You might thank a friend for a birthday present. When you write a thank-you letter, follow these steps.

Prewriting

Prewriting is the time to think about what you want to write. It is also the time to freewrite and to organize your ideas.

Choosing a Topic

Luis is a third grader. Luis's cousin Alejandro sent him a guitar last week. Luis likes playing  the guitar, so he wanted to write Alejandro a letter to thank him. Luis wanted to tell his cousin that the guitar was the best gift he had ever received. He also wanted to tell Alejandro why the guitar was a great gift. Before Luis started writing his letter, he took time to think about what he wanted to write.

Your Turn

Brainstorm a list of people that you know and like. Then think about something you might thank them for. It can be something they did for you or something special they gave you. For example, you might want to thank someone for baking muffins for your class.

Freewriting

Luis freewrote to think of what to write in his letter. He knew that the guitar was the best gift he had ever received. Luis freewrote a list of reasons why he liked the guitar.

It is beautiful.

I was surprised when I got it.

It makes a cool sound.

I sit on the porch and play it.

It has a strap for my shoulder.

It has a picture of a sunset in a desert.

Prewriting

Drafting

Content Editing

Revising

Copyediting

Proofreading

Publishing

Your Turn

Freewrite a list of reasons why you want to thank the person you are writing to. Write until you run out of ideas.

Organizing the Letter

Luis read what he freewrote. He had a lot of reasons for liking his guitar, but he knew

 Organization some reasons were more

important than others. To help organize his letter, he decided to put a number 1 by the most important reason. Then he put a number 2 by the next most important reason. He kept doing this until he had written a number by each reason on his list.

He cut the list into strips and put them in order. His list looked like this.

1. It makes a cool sound.

2. It has a picture of a sunset in a desert.

3. It is beautiful.

4. I sit on the porch and play it.

5. It has a strap for my shoulder.

6. I was surprised when I got it.

Your Turn

Read your own freewriting. Then think about which reasons are most important and number them. If you don't like some reasons, remove them.

Drafting

Drafting is a time to write the first copy of your thank-you letter.

 Voice Luis used his prewriting notes to write his draft. He made sure to use words that sounded like he was talking to Alejandro.

September 28, 20–
1100 Greenwood Lane
Estes Park AZ 80711

Dear Alejandro

There are many things I like about this beautiful guitar, and I want to tell you about them.

I like the guitar because I like the sound it makes. When I strum the guitar, it sounds nice.

Mom likes the picture on the front of the guitar. I like the picture on the front of the guitar. The picture looks like the desert we saw when we came to see you last summer. Sitting on the porch with the guitar is one of my favorite things to do while playing it.

Thank you agan for the guitar. It's the best present anyone has ever given to me.

Your cousin,

Luis

Luis remembered what he and his class talked about to write his thank-you letter. He knew that he should put in all the parts of a personal letter, which are the heading, the greeting, the body, the closing, and the signature. He also knew that he should write the purpose of his letter and keep it well organized.

Your Turn

- Use what you wrote in prewriting to write a draft of your thank-you letter.
- Be sure to include all the parts of the letter in your draft.

Writer's Tip Remember to leave extra space between the lines of your draft so that you can make changes later.

Telling More

When you write your letter, be sure to include

 Word Choice

descriptions that help your readers picture what you are saying. Which of the following sentences tells more about what happened?

- Thank you for helping me the other day.
- Thank you for helping me patch my bike tire last Tuesday.

The second sentence tells more about what happened. It tells what the person did to help and when it was done.

Prewriting
Drafting
Content Editing
Revising
Copyediting
Proofreading
Publishing

Content Editing

Luis knew he had written a good thank-you letter. But he also wanted to make it better. Content editing is a time to make sure that all the ideas in the letter make sense.

To help content edit his letter, Luis asked a classmate, Lexy, to read his draft. Lexy used this Content Editor's Checklist to check Luis's draft.

Content Editor's Checklist

- ☐ Does the beginning of the body give the purpose of the letter?

- ☐ Does the letter tell about one idea at a time?

- ☐ Does the body of the letter describe what the writer is thanking the receiver for?

- ☐ Does the letter have all the parts: the heading, the greeting, the body, the closing, and the signature? Are all the parts in the right place?

Lexy carefully read Luis's draft several times. She wrote her ideas on a sheet of paper. When she was finished content editing, she talked with Luis. She told him that she liked his letter very much. She said that it was nice of his cousin to send him a guitar. She also shared these ideas with Luis.

- The first part of the letter doesn't thank Alejandro for the guitar. I think it should.

- The letter mostly talked about one idea in each paragraph. But the third paragraph seems to be talking about two ideas. Can you make that paragraph two paragraphs instead?

- I know the letter describes the guitar, but I also think it could have more details.

- The date is in the wrong place. It should be moved under the heading.

Luis thanked Lexy for her ideas. He decided to think about her ideas before he made any changes.

Your Turn

- Read your first draft. Use the Content Editor's Checklist to help you improve the draft. Answer each question on the checklist.

- Trade your draft with a partner. Use the Content Editor's Checklist as you edit. Read the draft once for each question on the checklist. Write your ideas as you edit.

- When you have finished, share your notes with your partner. Remember to start by telling your partner what you liked about the letter.

Prewriting

Drafting

Content Editing

Revising

Copyediting

Proofreading

Publishing

Revising

Here is Luis's revised draft with his changes marked on it.

September 28, 20—
1100 Greenwood Lane
Estes Park AZ 80711

Dear Alejandro

Thank you for giving me your beautiful guitar.
There are many things I like about this ~~beautiful~~ guitar, and

I want to tell you about them.

I like the guitar because I like the sound it makes. When I strum

like it is humming to me.
the guitar, it sounds ~~nice.~~

of the desert sunset
Mom likes the picture on the front of the guitar. I like the

picture on the front of the guitar. The picture looks like the desert

we saw when we came to see you last summer. ¶ Sitting on the porch

Mom can hear me
with the guitar is one of my favorite things to do while playing it.
inside the house. She tells me that I play well.
Thank you agan for the guitar. It's the best present anyone has

ever given to me.

Your cousin,

Luis

Luis agreed with most of Lexy's ideas. Here are the changes he made to his draft.

- Luis added a sentence to the first paragraph. What did it say?
- He agreed with Lexy that the third paragraph should be made into two paragraphs. How did he do this?
- Luis thought that he should describe the guitar in more detail. What did he do?
- What change did Luis make to the heading?
- What details did Luis add to his letter?

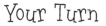

Your Turn

- Use your ideas and your partner's ideas to revise your draft.
- Read your letter again. Use the Content Editor's Checklist to help you think of other ways to improve your letter.

Prewriting
Drafting
Content Editing
Revising
Copyediting
Proofreading
Publishing

Copyediting and Proofreading

Copyediting

Luis made many content changes to his letter. But he knew that he could make his letter better by copyediting it. Copyediting means checking that all the sentences are strong and correct. It also means making sure the words in the letter make sense. Luis used this Copyeditor's Checklist to copyedit his letter.

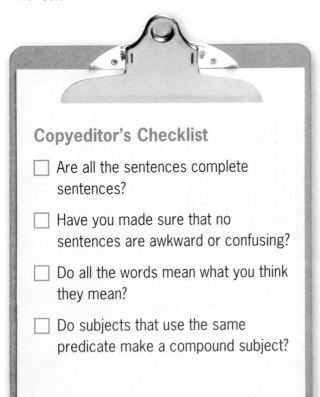

Copyeditor's Checklist

☐ Are all the sentences complete sentences?

☐ Have you made sure that no sentences are awkward or confusing?

☐ Do all the words mean what you think they mean?

☐ Do subjects that use the same predicate make a compound subject?

Luis noticed that the first sentence of his new fourth Sentence Fluency paragraph was confusing. He decided to rewrite the sentence. Look at his revision.

Old Sentence: Sitting on the porch with the guitar is one of my favorite things to do while playing it.

New Sentence: One of my favorite things to do is sit on the porch and play the guitar.

Luis also found two sentences with subjects that had the same predicate. He combined those sentences to make one sentence with a compound subject. Can you find the two sentences that he might have combined?

Your Turn

- Carefully read your letter. Use the Copyeditor's Checklist to edit your draft.
- Be sure to check for one kind of mistake at a time when you copyedit your letter.

Writer's Tip Read your letter aloud to make sure the sentences are not awkward or confusing.

Proofreading

Luis asked Bobby, a boy from his class, to proofread his letter. Because Bobby hadn't

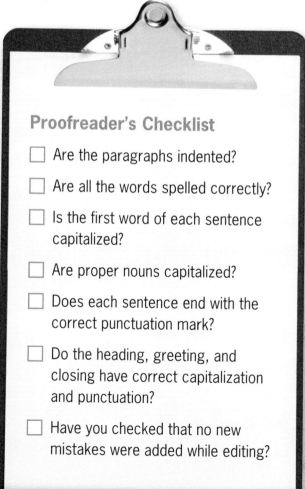 **Conventions**

read the letter, he could find mistakes that Luis might have missed.

Bobby used this Proofreader's Checklist to help him.

Proofreader's Checklist

- ☐ Are the paragraphs indented?
- ☐ Are all the words spelled correctly?
- ☐ Is the first word of each sentence capitalized?
- ☐ Are proper nouns capitalized?
- ☐ Does each sentence end with the correct punctuation mark?
- ☐ Do the heading, greeting, and closing have correct capitalization and punctuation?
- ☐ Have you checked that no new mistakes were added while editing?

Bobby found two places where commas were needed. Can you find them?

Your Turn

- Use the Proofreader's Checklist to proofread your letter.
- Have a partner proofread your letter. Did he or she spot any mistakes that you missed?
- Be sure to check that no new mistakes were added during editing.
- When you proofread, you are more likely to spot mistakes if you check for one kind of mistake at a time.

Grammar in Action

There is a misspelled word in Luis's letter. Find it and fix it.

Prewriting
Drafting
Content Editing
Revising
Copyediting
Proofreading
Publishing

Writer's Workshop

Publishing

Luis carefully wrote the finished draft of his thank-you letter. He also carefully made all the proofreading changes. Publishing his letter meant that he would mail it to his cousin Alejandro. Here is Luis's finished letter.

1100 Greenwood Lane

Estes Park, AZ 80711

September 28, 20—

Dear Alejandro,

Thank you for giving me your beautiful guitar. There are many things I like about this guitar, and I want to tell you about them.

I like the guitar because I like the sound it makes. When I strum the guitar, it sounds like it is humming to me.

Mom and I like the picture of the desert sunset on the front of the guitar. The picture looks like the desert we saw when we came to see you last summer.

One of my favorite things to do is sit on the porch and play the guitar. Mom can hear me inside the house. She tells me that I play well.

Thank you again for the guitar. It's the best present anyone has ever given to me.

Your cousin,

Luis

Presentation There are many ways you can publish your letter. However you decide to publish, make sure the message is clear.

Mail or e-mail your letter. If you mail it, make sure to check the bulleted list at the right. Don't forget to sign your letter.

 Create a class display of all the situations in which people might send a personal letter. Include photos, drawings, and personal experiences.

 Post your letter on your classroom's wiki, blog, or Web site. You can receive comments about your letter and review others' work.

 Post your letter on a bulletin board along with your classmates' letters. Label the display "We Love Letters!"

Your Turn

Getting mail from someone you know can be exciting. A personal letter is like a gift. After your teacher reads your letter, mail it.

Follow these steps to finish your letter.

- Use a computer or a pen and paper to make a final copy of your letter.
- Proofread your letter one more time. Use your computer's spell-checker if you can.
- Write the address on an envelope. Check to make sure the address is correct.
- Fold your letter and place it in the envelope. See below.
- Seal the envelope and put a stamp on it.
- Ask a parent or your teacher to help you mail it.

1

2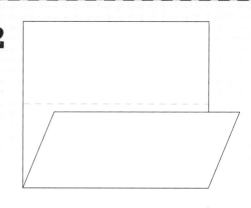

3

Book Reports

LiNK

Dawn Undercover
by Anna Dale

Reviewed by Kristi Olson

Would you love to be a spy? Doesn't it sound so adventurous, so important, and most of all, like a whole lot of fun? That's exactly why 11-year-old Dawn Buckle is so thrilled to be selected as a child spy for the British spying organization, S.H.H. (Strictly Hush-Hush) in the P.S.S.T. division (Pursuit of Scheming Spies and Traitors).

. . . Upon arriving at the P.S.S.T. headquarters, she is introduced to a quirky cast of spy-types who work hard to train her in the ins and outs of spying. . . . It seems that she has been made for spying and now will be put to the test on her first mission. The mission aims to track down a missing spy along with an evil criminal, Murdo Meek.

Dawn Undercover is a fun read with mystery and adventure—all good things a spy novel should possess. The character of Dawn Buckle is highly likeable . . . Though the book feels long at points, the ending is highly satisfying.

> This book report tells who the story is about, what happens in the story, and what the reader thought of the book.

Sarah, Plain and Tall
by Patricia MacLachlan

Book Report by Ethan Sterle

Sarah, Plain and Tall is by Patricia MacLachlan, and it is about a woman who moves to Kansas. She wants to help a farmer raise his children. The story is set on the prairie over 100 years ago.

Jacob Witting puts an ad in a newspaper for a wife and mother. He does this to help his children, Anna and Caleb. Then he gets a letter from a woman in Maine named Sarah Wheaton. She tells him that she is "plain and tall." That is where the title of the book comes from.

Sarah moves to Kansas to stay with the Wittings. Anna and Caleb like Sarah very much. But Jacob acts snobbily to her. Also Sarah is homesick for the ocean where she came from.

Later Sarah says she is going to town alone. Jacob and the children are afraid. They think that she has left for Maine. Jacob learns how much he cares for Sarah. He believes the family has lost her forever.

Sarah, Plain and Tall is a great book, and I think everyone should read it. The book is a little sad because Anna and Caleb's mother had died. But when Sarah wants to be their new mother, it makes the reader happy. The book also makes you think about the way families were in the past and why running a farm was such hard work.

To: Ethan Sterle
From: Matt Hoffman

What Makes a Good Book Report?

Books are like magic carpets. They can take you anywhere you want to go. There is much to see and do in the world of books.

Writing a book report is one way to share what you have read. In a book report, include the title, the author, what the book is about, and what you think of the book. When you write a book report, use language that shows you know the book well. Write your opinions in a way that shows you are sure about how you feel.

Beginning

Book reports start with the title of the book and the name of the author. The title should be complete. The author's name should be spelled correctly.

The beginning of a book report should tell who the story is about. But readers want to know more than just the names of the people or animals in the book. Readers also want to know something about what the people or animals are like.

Sometimes the beginning describes the setting. The setting is when and where the story takes place. If the setting is important to the story, include it in your book report.

Middle

In the middle of a book report, you tell what happens in the story. Book reports tell just enough to make the audience want to read the book. You might tell about a problem a person in the book has, but don't tell how the problem was solved. Telling too much can spoil surprises for the reader. Don't tell the reader how the book ends!

Ending

The ending of a book report is where you tell what you think of the book. You should explain why you think the way you do. This is the place to tell about the parts of the book that you liked. It can also be the place to tell about the parts of the book that you did not like.

ACTIVITY A Answer the questions about the book report on page 363.

1. What is the title of the book?
2. Who wrote the book?
3. What is the setting?
4. Who are the people in the book?
5. What problems do the people have?
6. Why does the author think people will like this book?
7. After reading this book report, would you want to read the book? Why or why not?

ACTIVITY B Tell whether each piece of information below would be found in the beginning, middle, or ending of a book report.

1. A description of a character's problem
2. The title and the author's name
3. The reason why the writer liked or disliked the book
4. The names of the main characters
5. A description of the setting
6. A sentence telling people to read the book

WRITER'S CORNER

Find three books in the library. Write the titles of the books and the authors' names. Carefully check that you spelled the names and the titles correctly.

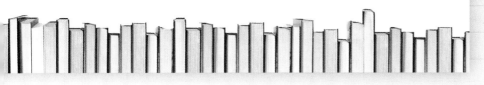

ACTIVITY C Read the following paragraphs from books. Choose one. Work with a partner and describe the time and place as fully as you can. What clue words let you know the setting?

A. A bright light flashed in the playground, and the drum noise burst out louder than ever. It spread all over the sky before curling away into nothingness. Polly Platt, who was easily frightened, bit her lip. Suddenly, there was an enormous cracking sound as though the walls of the school had split open. Bobby Briggs yelled and Polly Platt rushed toward Mr. Salt. But Mr. Salt didn't yell or rush anywhere. No, Mr. Salt smiled.

—*Summer Magic* by Margaret Nash

B. I'm beginning to see that Joe Feather was right not to try and find a way over the mountains for the wagons. They're much steeper than they look from the plains. Right now I'm on a patch of grass. But I can't be sure how the feed will be beyond. Before the sun went down, I checked the way ahead. . . .

In the morning I'll try the horses on one of the slopes and see if they can manage the climb.

—*The Climb* by Roger Carr

C. He took the path along the hedge towards the woods where he and his pals often played, hoping he might find somebody else to fool instead. At the very least, he thought, he could squirt them with his trusty water pistol that bulged from the back pocket of his jeans. But, in fact, what he did find in the middle of the woods made all thoughts of April Fools' Day fly right out of his head.

—*April Aliens* by Rob Childs

ACTIVITY D Read the following parts of book reports. Think about why the writer liked each book. Which book report is the best? Explain why.

1. In the book *Crow Boy* by Taro Yashima, I liked reading about Chibi. He was a young boy. The book was short, so I liked it. You will like reading this book too.

2. Young Ralph S. Mouse is the mouse in *The Mouse and the Motorcycle,* a story by Beverly Cleary. Ralph lives in room 215 of the Mountain View Inn, and people leave behind crumbs for him to eat. One day a boy named Keith stays in room 215. He brings along a toy motorcycle, just the right size for a mouse. Ralph borrows the motorcycle, and he gets trapped in a wastebasket. This story of adventure and friendship was funny. I read all of it without stopping. You probably will too.

3. I really enjoyed reading the book by Laura Ingalls Wilder. Laura's writing style was very clear and easy to follow. The stories she told about her life made me feel as if I was really there. She made me care very much about her and the other characters. The book made me want to learn more about life on the prairie.

LiNK

Into the Land of the Unicorns

by Bruce Coville

After leaping from a church steeple, Cara leaves her familiar world behind and lands in the mysterious land of Luster. At first, she can't believe her fairy tale-like surroundings. This strange, new world seems older than time itself. Filled with wonderful and not-so-wonderful creatures, she is attacked by delvers, rescued by a bearman, and healed by a rebellious young unicorn named Lightfoot . . . Together, Cara and her newfound friends, Lightfoot, Dimblethum, Thomas, and Squijim, must get to the Unicorn Queen before the mysterious person following them.

Reviewed by Tammy L. Currier

WRITER'S CORNER

Think of a story you read recently. Write four sentences telling what you think about the story. Then give two examples from the story to show why you liked it or did not like it.

Grammar in Action. Use at least four adjectives in your sentences. Circle each adjective.

Character and Plot

A character is a person, an animal, or a thing in a story. The plot of a story is what happens in the story.

Character

A character is not just a name in a story. A character is someone who seems real to you. You should be able to close your eyes and see the character and the action. When you write a book report, tell some important things about the character that you learned from the story.

The characters in stories can be kids just like you and your friends. Characters can also be people from times long ago and far away. They can be animals such as Ralph S. Mouse, Ribsy, or the Black Stallion. Characters can even be things like Thomas the Tank Engine, a talking train. Who or what are some of your favorite story characters?

ACTIVITY A Read these sentences from book reports. Give the name of each character. Tell whether the character is a person, an animal, or a thing.

1. On the planet Atara, there are no people or animals, just a robot named FIP-20.

2. Jonathan is a silly 10-year-old boy.

3. One of my favorite parts was when Sally tried to wash the spots off the dog.

4. The part about the dog Tatters being alone and hungry is sad.

5. What happens when Tony the Dinosaur gets a toothache?

6. Mr. Baileymill, a grumpy old man, lives on top of a hill.

7. The best part is when the detectives' robot dog, Ruff, sniffs out a clue in the spider's lair.

8. The story really gets going when Moog, a talking tree, comes lumbering down the road.

9. Peter is a selfish boy who never wants to share his lunch with anyone.

10. When a ladybug named Laura gets swept down the river, she begins an amazing journey.

ACTIVITY B Imagine that the people and animals below are characters in books you have read. Give each character a name and think of three words that describe the character.

1. A neighbor

2. A friend

3. Your favorite animal

4. Your favorite athlete

5. A person in a movie or on TV

6. A wild animal

ACTIVITY C Draw a picture of a character you have read about. Show the character doing something he or she would normally do. At the bottom of the picture, write the name of the character and the book the character comes from.

WRITER'S CORNER

Write four sentences that tell why you like or do not like the character from Activity C.

 With an adult, find and read a book report online.

Plot

When you think about the plot of a story, remember what the characters did. In most stories the characters have a problem that must be solved or a goal they want to reach.

Characters do things in the story to solve their problem. Sometimes villains work against the characters. This can make stories more exciting to read.

The ending of a book tells how the characters solved their problem or whether they reached their goal. A book report should tell only enough of the plot so the reader gets an idea of the beginning and middle of the story. A book report should not tell the ending of the story.

Strange Happenings
by Avi

Tom is so bored he wishes he could sleep all day like his cat Charlie. Suddenly, this unusual feline starts talking to Tom and asks if he really would like to be a cat. Tom thinks he would, so Charlie takes him to a deserted building filled with cats. They are granted an audience with the wizard cat, who transforms Tom into Charlie and vice versa. For Tom, however, the experience isn't quite what he expected it to be.

Reviewed by Robert M. Oksner

ACTIVITY D Read each plot description from two different book reports. Put the events in the order that they happen so they make sense.

1. **Mystery Plot**
   a. You will never believe where they find Queenie!
   b. Then a detective is hired to help find Queenie.
   c. A champion show dog, Queenie, has been stolen from Jenny Clark.
   d. Jenny tells the police about her missing pet.

2. **Adventure Plot**
   a. The Miller family is enjoying a calm day of sailing.
   b. Mr. Miller has to make the decision for his family to stay on the boat or leave it.
   c. The boat is badly damaged, and dark, cold water quickly begins to fill the lower cabin.
   d. Suddenly, the boat hits a reef of sharp coral, and the family hears a loud, crashing noise.

ACTIVITY E The following sentences are from book reports. Which sentences tell about the character's problem? Which sentences tell how a villain tries to make a problem?

1. After that one little fib, life sure becomes harder for Junior!
2. It suddenly came to Emily that she had forgotten the item that no hiker should ever forget, water.
3. Fester can always get Bobo, the funny St. Bernard, into trouble.
4. Though the evil queen throws the key away, Tyrone finally finds it and opens the castle door.
5. Many kids are shy, but Cameron could not speak at all to his teacher.
6. After Antwan found the necklace, his brother hid it from him again.
7. Princess Alice knows that when she misbehaves, Lil will be punished.
8. Robert drove the go-cart to the other side of town during the storm.
9. While Penny was sleeping, her evil twin Margaret made a mess.
10. Jim flies to Europe to rescue his cat Sparks from the evil magicians.

ACTIVITY F Read the following paragraph. Describe what happens. Does the paragraph make you want to read more of the story? Explain why or why not.

Tabitha took a deep breath and walked slowly down the basement stairs. Each step creaked and groaned under her weight. The more she tried to step lightly and quietly, the louder each sound seemed. With only a candle to light her way, Tabitha squinted through the darkness. Shadows jumped and danced across the walls. Then Tabitha felt something brush the back of her neck. She quickly spun around, but the breeze blew out the candle. Now Tabitha was in the cold, damp basement alone and in the dark. What was that odd sound? Was someone or something there? She felt as if she was not alone after all.

WRITER'S CORNER

Choose a book that you have read. Describe its plot in five sentences so that the reader would want to read the book. Think of ways to tell a little about the ending without telling the reader exactly how the book ends.

Grammar in Action. Use at least two subject complements in your plot description. See Section 5.3.

Parts of a Book

Most books have the same parts. Look around your classroom. A textbook, a book about making tree houses, and a book about volcanoes probably have the same parts.

Cover and Spine

The cover has the title of the book and often the author's name. The cover might have a picture or design.

The part of the cover that connects the front and the back is called the spine. The spine often shows the title of the book, the author's name, and the name of the publisher.

Title Page

The title page has the title of the book, the author's name, and sometimes the illustrator's name. It might also have the name of the company that published the book.

Contents Page

The contents page tells the name of each chapter. It also tells the page where the chapter starts.

Glossary

The glossary is a list of important words in the book and what they mean. The words are listed in alphabetical order. A book about volcanoes might have the word *magma* in its glossary. A book that tells a story won't have a glossary.

Index

The index is a list of the topics found in the book. The topics are listed in alphabetical order with the page numbers where the topics can be found.

Page numbers connected with a dash tell readers that the pages between the numbers have information about that topic. If the page numbers are 8–11, you should look on pages 8, 9, 10, and 11.

ACTIVITY A **Match each part of a book in Column A to its description in Column B.**

Column A	Column B
1. index	a. a page with the title and the author's name
2. contents page	b. the outside of a book
3. glossary	c. a list of the chapters and the page numbers on which the chapters start
4. cover	d. a list of a book's topics in alphabetical order with page numbers
5. title page	e. a list of the meanings of important words in a book

ACTIVITY B **Copy a title page from a book in your classroom. Then label each item, using the labels below. Trade your title page with a partner. Check to make sure the labels are in the correct place.**

- Title
- Author's name
- Illustrator's name
- Publisher's name

ACTIVITY C **Find a book that has a glossary. Write three words and their meanings from the glossary. Use each word in a sentence.**

WRITER'S CORNER

Find a book that has an index. What is the title of the book? Who is the author? How many chapters does the book have? Write those facts. Then find an interesting topic from the index and look it up.

ACTIVITY D Use this contents page to answer the questions.

Contents

1. What is this book about?

2. How many chapters are in this book?

3. On what page does Chapter 6 start?

4. On what page does the information about the temperature of Mars start?

5. On what page does the index start?

6. What is the title of Chapter 4?

7. On what pages could you find the meanings of important words in the book?

8. On what page would you begin to look to find out if plants grow on Mars?

9. What chapter starts on page 39?

10. To what page would you turn to learn about flights to Mars?

ACTIVITY E Use this index to answer the questions.

Index

International Space Station, 47–48

magnetic fields, 8–11

Mars rover *Opportunity*, 35–36

Milky Way, 10–13

moons, 43

orbit, 13–14

planets, 2–6

plant life, 17–21

satellites, 43–46

space travel, 30–38

surface, 39–42

temperature, 26–29

1. On which pages would you learn how hot and how cold it is on Mars?
2. What topic is on pages 35–36?
3. Which pages tell about magnetic fields?
4. Which pages tell how long it takes Mars to orbit the sun?
5. On which page does the information about a space station start?
6. On which pages would you learn how many moons Mars has?
7. Which page is the last page to learn about the Milky Way?
8. What is the topic that starts on page 17?
9. On which pages would you learn how people live in outer space?
10. Where could you find what the ground on Mars is like?
11. Which topic appears first in the book—*space travel* or *moons*?
12. Which pages tell about all the planets?
13. Which topic has the greatest number of pages?

WRITER'S CORNER

Imagine you are writing a book about the state you live in. Design a book cover with a picture, the title of the book, and your name.

Tech Tip With an adult, find facts about your state online.

Compound Predicates

Two sentences can often give information about the same subject. When sentences have the same subject, you can join the predicates to make one sentence. Read these sentences. Can you see how they can be joined to make one sentence?

My tabby cat sits in the sun.
My tabby cat watches the birds.

These sentences tell about the same subject—*My tabby cat.* The predicates are different—*sits in the sun* and *watches the birds.* You can make one smooth sentence by joining the predicates with the word *and.*

My tabby cat sits in the sun *and* watches the birds.

Writers use compound predicates so they don't have a row of choppy sentences. Writers often turn short, choppy sentences into smoother sentences by joining predicates.

Look at these sentences. You can join the predicates by using the word *and.*

Babies sleep at night.
Babies cry at night.
Babies sleep *and* cry at night.

ACTIVITY A Each of the following sentences has a compound predicate. Find the two verbs in each compound predicate.

1. An airplane speeds down the runway and lifts off with its nose up.
2. The lion leaped from behind a bush and ran after the zebra.
3. Tim shovels snow in the winter and mows lawns in the summer.
4. Joe argued with his mother and pouted in his room.
5. After the party, I waved good-bye and walked away.
6. My dog, Sparky, rolls over and plays dead.
7. A crow swooped down and landed on the fence.
8. Uncle Roberto wrote and illustrated a children's book.
9. Yolanda moved the chair and set the table.
10. Wendy answered the phone and took the message.
11. The car turned the corner and zoomed away.
12. A hammer pounds nails and pulls them out.
13. Selina thought about the answer and gave it.
14. Ivan moved his chess piece and smiled at me.
15. Dad brought a pot of coffee and poured a cup.

ACTIVITY B Add two different verbs to each sentence to make a compound predicate.

1. The famous ballerina _____ and _____.
2. Miranda _____ her shoe and _____.
3. The fans _____ and _____ for their team.
4. Kyle _____ the car and _____ to the radio.
5. The photographer _____ his camera and _____ pictures of us.

WRITER'S CORNER

Look in a book or a magazine. Find two sentences that have compound predicates. Write the sentences. Then underline each verb.

Grammar in Action, Name the compound predicate in the first sentence of the page 367 excerpt.

ACTIVITY C **Find the predicate in each sentence. Tell whether it is a compound predicate.**

1. Dana and Reese made dinner last night.
2. My two sisters dusted the dining room and set the table.
3. They served salad, steak, and baked potatoes.
4. Every dish looked appealing and tasted delicious.
5. We all laughed and chatted during dinner.
6. Then Dana and Reese looked at each other and made an announcement.
7. Uncle Harry had sold them his old car.
8. Dad choked on his food and turned red as a beet.
9. Reese patted Dad's back and handed him a glass of water.
10. Dad finally got used to the news.

ACTIVITY D **Join each pair of sentences into one sentence with a compound predicate.**

1. The elephant flapped its big ears. The elephant flicked its scruffy tail.
2. Leigh and Cal played basketball after school. Leigh and Cal rode bikes after school.
3. Jim played games at the carnival. Jim rode the roller coaster at the carnival.
4. The lion stretched out on a rock. The lion took a nap.
5. The monkey ate four bananas. The monkey threw the peels over its shoulder.
6. Kiki goes to the mall. Kiki parks in the same spot.
7. Dr. Harmon washed the dishes. Dr. Harmon dried the dishes.
8. Hank bought fresh corn. Hank grilled fresh corn.
9. Rosa made a piñata. Rosa stuffed it with candy.
10. I earned money by babysitting. I spent most of it before I got home.

ACTIVITY E Choose three of the following pairs of verbs. Write a sentence for each pair that uses both verbs as a compound predicate.

A. run, jump

B. chuckle, grin

C. mix, pour

D. study, learn

E. train, perform

F. draw, paint

G. enter, climb

H. wash, scrub

I. paddle, swim

J. camp, hike

ACTIVITY F Choose three of the following topics. For each topic write a sentence with a compound predicate.

A. pets you have known

B. planets and stars

C. homework every day

D. younger brothers or sisters

E. long vacations

F. favorite desserts

G. learning new things

H. keeping a journal

I. chores around the house

J. best friends

WRITER'S CORNER

Work with a partner. Choose one pair of verbs in Activity E that you did not use. Write a sentence that uses the verbs as a compound predicate. Then write another sentence about the same subject. Use a compound predicate in that sentence too.

Prefixes

A prefix is a word part added to the beginning of a word. Prefixes change the meaning of a word. Sometimes a prefix changes the meaning of a word to its opposite. Two common prefixes are *re-* and *un-*.

Re-

Re- is a prefix that means "again." Read the example below. The prefix *re-* is added to the word *paint*.

> **re- + paint = repaint**

Repaint means "to paint again." *Re-* can also mean "back." Read the example below. The prefix *re-* is added to the word *pay*.

> **re- + pay = repay**

Repay means "to pay back." What other words do you know that have the prefix *re-*?

Un-

The prefix *un-* means "not." This prefix usually changes a word's meaning to its opposite. Read the example below.

> **un- + happy = unhappy**

Un- means "not," so *unhappy* means "not happy." *Unhappy* is the opposite of *happy*. What other words do you know that have the prefix *un-*?

ACTIVITY A Find the prefix in each word. Then write the meaning of each word.

1. redo
2. resend
3. unable
4. redraw
5. reappear
6. rewrite
7. unbeaten
8. uncomfortable
9. uncertain
10. rejoin

ACTIVITY B Match the words with prefixes in Column A with their meanings in Column B. Check your answers in a dictionary.

Column A	Column B
1. unbelievable	a. build again
2. unusual	b. not usual
3. reread	c. apply again
4. rebuild	d. not safe
5. unwashed	e. not washed
6. uncertain	f. sell again
7. reapply	g. not remarkable
8. unsafe	h. not believable
9. unremarkable	i. read again
10. resell	j. not certain

ACTIVITY C Choose three words from Column A in Activity B. Use each word in a sentence. Underline the prefix in each word.

WRITER'S CORNER

Find four words with the prefixes *re-* or *un-* in a book you have read. Write what you think the meanings of the words are. Then check your answers in a dictionary.

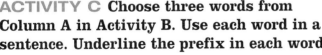

Tech Tip With an adult, use an online dictionary.

ACTIVITY D Complete each sentence with a word from the word box.

unhappy	unbeaten	reheat	unwise
rerun	rewrite	unfortunate	unclog

1. The end of summer makes me _____.
2. Taking a test without studying is _____.
3. When writers _____ a paper, they try to improve it.
4. I missed the TV show, but they will _____ it.
5. The dinner is cold, so I will _____ it.
6. It is _____ that only a few people came to our band concert.
7. The championship team finished the season with an _____ record.
8. Dad spent an hour trying to _____ the bathtub drain.

ACTIVITY E Work with a partner. Complete each sentence with a word that has the prefix *re-* or *un-*. Use a dictionary if you need help.

1. What color would you like to _____ the house?
2. Jamal wrote neatly so that he would not have to _____ his draft.
3. Taking off a coat is much easier when you _____ it.
4. This hot weather is simply _____!
5. No matter how hard I try, I'm _____ to do more than 10 push-ups in a row.
6. My shoelaces were loose, so I had to _____ them.
7. When I arrived at Grandma's house, the first thing I did was _____ my suitcase.
8. I have to _____ the batteries in my flashlight.

ACTIVITY F Choose two of the following topics. Write a sentence about each topic. Use a word with the prefix *re-* or *un-* in each sentence.

A. writing a story

B. wacky inventions

C. sailing around the world

D. an exciting sports match

E. a day you'll never forget

F. your earliest memory

G. your favorite CD

H. something you did to make money

I. something you do well

J. something you'd like to do better

ACTIVITY G Read the sentences below and find the words with the prefixes *re-* or *un-*. Write the meaning of each word. Use a dictionary if you need help.

My family's vacation started early in the morning. After the car was loaded, my mom saw many shirts lying untouched on the bed. She would have to repack two suitcases. She told my dad to unload the car.

First, he had to untie a knot he made to get to the suitcases. Then he had to rearrange things around the suitcases. When Mom opened the suitcases, she was unable to fit anything else in. She decided to just replace the shirts during our trip. We finally pulled out of the driveway around noon!

WRITER'S CORNER

Imagine you are writing a mystery book. Write one paragraph about the plot of your book. Use the words *reappear* and *unknown*.

Oral Book Reports

Have you ever read an interesting book that you wanted to share with friends? Giving an oral book report is one way to tell others about a book that you have read.

Beginning

Begin your talk by stating the name of the book and its author. Bring the book to show to your audience. Give your listeners an idea of what the book is about.

Middle

In the middle of your talk, tell what happens in the book. You may want to read a short part from the book. Reading from the book gives your listeners a chance to hear the words the author uses. Don't give away the ending! Let readers find out for themselves how the book ends.

Ending

End your talk by telling your audience what you thought of the book. You could say that you did not like the book. Or you could say that it was one of your favorites. Make sure that you tell your audience why you liked or did not like the book.

Prepare

After you choose a book for your talk, look through the book and write on note cards the important parts of the plot. If the book has pictures, look at them too. You might show the pictures in your talk.

ACTIVITY A Talk with a partner about books that you have read. Write the titles and authors. Tell your partner what each book is about, who the characters are, and what the setting is. Then talk with your partner about whether or not you liked each book.

ACTIVITY B Talk with a partner about the books you wrote in Activity A. Which book is the most fun to talk about? Which book do you think your class would like to hear about? Choose one of the books for your book report. Then ask your partner to choose a book from his or her list. Tell your partner which book you would be most interested in hearing about.

ACTIVITY C Look through your book to help you remember the story. Write on note cards information about the characters, setting, and plot that you want to share with your listeners. If your book has a contents page, look at it to help you find information in the book. Use the note cards when you give your talk.

ACTIVITY D Look through your book and find a place that you would like to read aloud to your audience. Put a bookmark at the page so you can find it quickly when you give your talk.

SPEAKER'S CORNER

Write on note cards the three best events from the book you chose in Activity B. Then write what you thought of the book. Look through your book to help you remember the characters and the plot.

Tone of Voice

Think about the times you've told your friends or family about something that you really liked. Did you tell people by using a quiet tone of voice? Or did you sound excited by using a lively tone of voice? Which way would make someone interested in what you have to say?

Use your tone of voice to show your feelings about your book. Speak lively, even if you did not like the book. Your audience wants to know what you think.

When you read aloud from your book, speak in a way that shows the mood of the story. Use a more excited voice if you are reading an exciting part. Use a deeper or slower voice if you are reading a spooky part. If you read dialogue from a character, use the tone of voice that you think the character would use.

Practice

Practice giving your talk. Ask a partner to listen to it. Ask your partner for ways to make your talk better. Remember to do these things.

- Introduce the book by telling its title and author. Hold up the book so everyone can see it.
- Speak loudly, clearly, and slowly. Tell your audience about the characters in the book. Tell what the book is about. Use your tone of voice to show your feelings about the book.
- Look at your audience. If you have notes, look at them, but do not simply read them aloud.
- Tell why you liked or did not like the book.

Listening Tips

Listen to your classmates' book reports. You might hear about a book you would want to read. Do these things while you listen.

- Look at the person giving the talk. Pay attention to what he or she is saying.
- Picture the characters and setting in your mind. Think about what happens in the book.
- If you have read the book the speaker is talking about, think about what you liked or didn't like about the book. Does the speaker talk about what you remember? Do you agree with the speaker?
- Don't interrupt the speaker. Wait until he or she is finished before raising your hand to ask a question.

ACTIVITY E Use the library or the Internet to look up information about the author of your book. You might share what you learned about the author during your talk.

ACTIVITY F Think about why you liked or did not like your book. Write on note cards some of the reasons why you feel that way. Use the note cards when you give your talk.

ACTIVITY G Take turns reading to a partner a short part from your book. Do it more than once so you feel comfortable looking up from your book. Ask your partner to suggest ways that you can change the tone of your voice to make it more interesting to your listeners.

SPEAKER'S CORNER

Practice and present the book report you chose in Activity B. Use the tips you learned to help give your talk.

Writer's Workshop

Prewriting and Drafting

Have you ever told someone about a book you liked or about a book you didn't like? Writing a book report is a way to tell many people about a book. In a book report, you share what you thought about the book. If you really enjoyed a book, this is a way to tell other people how much you enjoyed it.

Prewriting

Callie is a third grader who wrote a book report for class. Callie needed to choose a book before she could write her book report. She wanted to pick her book carefully and plan her book report before she started writing.

Choosing a Book

Callie wanted to write a book report about a book that she enjoyed. She thought about the books that she had recently read. Callie

<u>Ideas</u>

wanted to pick a book that no one else in her class had read. She also wanted to pick one that she remembered well.

Callie remembered reading *Abel's Island* by William Steig. Abel, the main character, is a mouse. He has many funny and exciting adventures. Callie thought she would do well writing about this book because she enjoyed thinking about it.

Your Turn

Choose a book that you remember well and that you would like to write about. Or choose a new book that you really want to read now and report on that.

Planning the Book Report

Now that Callie knew what book she was

<u>Organization</u>

going to write about, she started to plan her book report. This is Callie's plan with some information already filled in.

My Plan

- Ⓑ Book Title: <u>Abel's Island</u>
- Ⓑ Author: William Steig
- Ⓑ Main character: Abel
- Ⓑ Setting: A deserted island
- ☐M Plot:

- △E What I thought about the book:

- △E Why I thought that way about the book:

Callie completed the plan. She wrote a circled Ⓑ beside the ideas that would go in the beginning. She then drew a square around an ☐M by the ideas for the middle, and a triangle around an △E by the ideas for the ending. It was easy to see where the information went in the book report. She knew it was now easier to write the first draft of her book report.

Your Turn

- Write a plan like the one that Callie used for her book report.
- Complete the plan with the information about your book.
- Talk with a partner about the parts that will go into your book report.

Drafting

Now it was time for Callie to write her draft. She used her plan from prewriting to help her. First, she wrote a beginning to tell about Abel and the setting of the book. Then she wrote in the middle what happens to Abel. Callie made sure not to give away the ending of the book. She finished the book report with an ending that told what she thought about *Abel's Island*.

Abel's Island
by William Steig

Abel's Island by William Steig is a wonderful book. It is a story about Abel Flint the mouse. The book is set in 1904 on a desserted island and Abel is a spoiled mouse who is trying to get home to his wife. Abel is on a picnic by a river with his new wife, Amanda. I thought the story of Abel was something that people could like if they have spent a lot of time on their own in the country.

When he chases it because Amanda's scarf blows away. He falls into the river. He is swept downstream, and he washes up on an island. He hopes to be saved, but that doesn't happen. He must learn to live alone on an island about 12,000 tails long. It is just like if I measured my house using my own feet! Abel is used to the comforts of home. But on the island he has adventures just trying to do everyday things. He has to find a place to live! He also has to find food to eat. He has to try not to be eaten himself. To make things harder. Through many adventures Abel learns to live in nature. Slowly he starts to try to find a way to get home to Amanda.

Abel's Island is filled with exciting adventures. I won't forget the funny characters. They made me laugh because they are animals that talk, dress, and act like people. I couldn't stop reading about how Abel fights so hard to live so he can see Amanda again.

Prewriting

Drafting

Content Editing

Revising

Copyediting

Proofreading

Publishing

Your Turn

- Write the first draft of your book report. Make sure to start with the title of the book and the name of the author.
- Write the beginning. Tell the reader about the main characters and the setting of the book. The setting of the book tells the reader when and where the story happens.
- Write the middle of the book report. Tell the reader what happens, but don't give too much away.
- Write the ending. Write what you thought about the book. Give examples in your book report to show whether or not you liked the book.

Writer's Tip When you write your book report, leave extra space between the lines. That way you will have room to make changes later.

Using Examples

In your book report, support what you say. If something is sad, explain why it is sad, using examples from the book. If something is funny, tell why you think it is. In Callie's book report, she said that the book is funny. She shows why it is funny by saying that the animals acted like people.

Content Editing

Callie wanted to make her draft better. She knew that there were parts of her report she didn't like. She hoped that she would improve her book report by editing it for content.

Callie thought it would be a good idea to ask someone she trusted to content edit her book report. Callie decided to ask Selma. She is a friend of Callie's who lives nearby. Selma would check whether the ideas made sense. She used the Content Editor's Checklist.

Content Editor's Checklist

☐ Does the writing stay on the topic?

☐ Are the characters and setting introduced in the beginning?

☐ Is the plot discussed in the middle?

☐ Did you make sure not to give away the ending of the book?

☐ Does the ending tell what you think of the book?

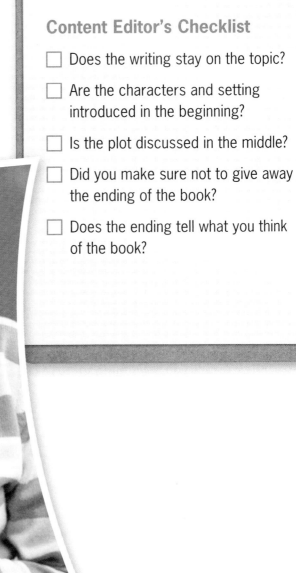

Selma told Callie that she liked the way that the main character and the setting were introduced in the beginning. This would help the reader understand the part about the plot in the middle. Then Selma told Callie these ideas.

- You have information about the plot in the beginning. It should be in the middle.
- The last sentence of the beginning is interesting, but it is what you think about the book. That sentence should be in the ending.
- The part about measuring your house with your feet was funny, but off the topic. It was not a part of the book.
- Why don't you say how Abel starts to find a way to get home to Amanda?

Callie thanked Selma for her help. She was glad Selma liked her book report. But she wasn't sure she was going to use all of Selma's ideas.

Writer's Tip Remember to write your partner's ideas. Think about each one. Make the changes that will make your book report more useful for your readers.

Your Turn

- Work with a partner and read each other's book reports.
- Pay attention to one question in the checklist at a time.
- When you have finished, take turns talking about each other's drafts.

Prewriting

Drafting

Content Editing

Revising

Copyediting

Proofreading

Publishing

Revising

This is how Callie revised her draft.

Abel's Island
by William Steig

Abel's Island by William Steig is a wonderful book. It is a story about Abel Flint the mouse. The book is set in 1904 on a desserted island and Abel is a spoiled mouse who is trying to get home to his wife. ~~Abel is on a picnic by a river with his new wife, Amanda.~~ ~~I thought the story of Abel was something that people could like if they have spent a lot of time on their own in the country.~~ When he chases it because Amanda's scarf blows away. He falls into the river. He is swept downstream, and he washes up on an island. He hopes to be saved, but that doesn't happen. He must learn to live alone on an island about 12,000 tails long. ~~It is just like if I measured my house using my own feet!~~ Abel is used to the comforts of home. But on the island he has adventures just trying to do everyday things. He has to find a place to live! He also has to find food to eat. He has to try not to be eaten himself. To make things harder. Through many adventures Abel learns to live in nature. Slowly he starts to try to find a way to get home to Amanda.

Prewriting

Drafting

Content Editing

Revising

Copyediting

Proofreading

Publishing

Abel's Island is filled with exciting adventures. I won't forget the funny characters. They made me laugh because they are animals that talk, dress, and act like people. I couldn't stop reading about how Abel fights so hard to live so he can see Amanda again. The book makes you think about what people can do if they want something badly enough.

Here are some things that Callie did to improve her book report.

- Callie agreed that the sentence about the plot didn't belong in the beginning. Where did she move the sentence?
- What did Callie do to the last sentence of the beginning? Do you agree with this change?
- Callie took out the part about measuring her house. Why?

As Callie looked at her book report again, she saw that her ending didn't seem complete. Callie thought about adding how Abel tries to find a way home. But she kept it out because it would give away the ending of the book. Callie ⬩•⬩ Voice wanted her ending to tell how she felt about the book. What did Callie do?

Your Turn

- Use your ideas and your content editor's ideas to revise your draft.
- Look at the Content Editor's Checklist again. Answer each question while reading your book report.

Copyediting and Proofreading

Copyediting

Callie knew that her book report was much stronger. Selma suggested that Callie copyedit her book report. By copyediting, Callie could check whether all the sentences and words were used correctly. Callie used this checklist to copyedit her book report.

Copyeditor's Checklist

☐ Are all the sentences complete sentences?

☐ Do the sentences make sense?

☐ Do the sentences make sense one after the other?

☐ Are compound predicates used correctly?

☐ Have exact words been used?

Callie found three sentences that she thought needed some work. The third sentence in the first paragraph seemed too long.

👀 Sentence Fluency

When she read it again, she realized that the sentence was about both the character and the setting. She wanted to make a sentence about each. What could Callie do with the sentence?

The next problem was the second sentence of the second paragraph. Callie didn't think the sentence made sense. How could she fix it?

Finally, Callie found an incomplete sentence near the end of the second paragraph. Can you find it? How would you fix it?

Your Turn

Copyedit your book report. Look for

👀 Word Choice

only one kind of mistake at a time. If you have problems with a sentence or word, ask someone for help. Look for ways to make your words and sentences clearer.

Proofreading

Callie asked her cousin, Ezra to proofread

her book report. Ezra checked for spelling, capitalization, and punctuation. He also checked to see that the paragraphs were indented. This is the checklist that Ezra used.

Proofreader's Checklist

☐ Are the paragraphs indented?

☐ Are all the words spelled correctly?

☐ Are proper nouns capitalized?

☐ Does each sentence end with the correct punctuation mark?

☐ Have you checked to be sure that no new mistakes were added while editing?

Ezra proofread Callie's book report. He told Callie that she shouldn't use an exclamation point for the sentence "He has to find a place to live." Ezra and Callie agreed that the sentence and the sentences around it didn't show a strong enough feeling to need an exclamation point.

Callie thanked Ezra and then checked her book report again.

Your Turn

- Use the Proofreader's Checklist to proofread your draft.
- Ask a partner to use the checklist to check your work.
- Remind your partner to check for only one kind of mistake at a time.
- Make sure that the changes from your partner are correct.

Grammar in Action

There is a tricky spelling mistake in Callie's book report. Find it and fix it.

Publishing

Publishing is sharing your work with an audience. Callie carefully typed the final draft of her book report. Since she wrote a book report, she knew that many people would be reading it to learn about the book. Callie liked the book *Abel's Island*. Reading it had made her want to learn more about mice, so she included some pictures and facts about mice with her book report.

Presentation

Abel's Island
by William Steig

Book Report by Callie O'Sullivan

Abel's Island by William Steig is a wonderful book. It is a story about Abel Flint the mouse. The book is set in 1904 on a deserted island. Abel is a spoiled mouse who is trying to get home to his wife.

Abel is on a picnic by a river with his new wife, Amanda. When Amanda's scarf blows away, he chases it. He falls into the river. He is swept downstream, and he washes up on an island. He hopes to be saved, but that doesn't happen. He must learn to live alone on an island about 12,000 tails long. Abel is used to the comforts of home. But on the island he has adventures just trying to do everyday things. He has to find a place to live. He also has to find food to eat. To make things harder, he has to try not to be eaten himself. Through many adventures Abel learns to live in nature. Slowly he starts to try to find a way to get home to Amanda.

Abel's Island is filled with exciting adventures. I won't forget the funny characters. They made me laugh because they are animals that talk, dress, and act like people. I couldn't stop reading about how Abel fights so hard to live so he can see Amanda again. The book makes you think about what people can do if they want something badly enough.

There are many ways you can publish your book report.

 Post your report to a Web site that publishes children's book reports. Work with an adult to find an appropriate site and share your report with the world.

 Make a classroom newsletter. Include all of your classmates' book reports so that the class can learn about books they might be interested in.

 Mail or e-mail your report to a local newspaper or to a children's magazine. If it gets printed, be sure to save a copy or two for your scrapbook.

 Make a poster with a picture and facts about what you have read. Display your book report and your poster.

Whenever you publish your work, your goal is to share your thoughts and experiences with other people.

Your Turn

- Make a clean, final copy of your book report. Add the changes from proofreading.
- Be careful making this final copy. Write it on a clean sheet of paper or type it on a computer.
- People are going to read this book report to see whether or not they want to read the book. If you want people to follow your opinion, your book report will have to be written well.
- When you have finished, choose one thing from the story to read more about. If your book is set in the rain forest, you might choose to read about the Amazon rain forest.

Persuasive Writing

LiNK

Drinking Water: Bottled or From the Tap?

National Geographic Kids, February 14, 2008
by Catherine Clarke Fox

Plastic bottles use a lot of fossil fuels and pollute the environment. . . . In order to make all these bottles, manufacturers use 17 million barrels of crude oil. That's enough oil to keep a million cars going for twelve months.

. . . Some people drink bottled water because they think it is better for them than water out of the tap, but that's not true. In the United States, local governments make sure water from the faucet is safe. There is also growing concern that chemicals in the bottles themselves may leach into the water.

People love the convenience of bottled water. But maybe if they realized the problems it causes, they would try drinking from a glass at home or carrying water in a refillable steel container instead of plastic.

> This is a good example of persuasive writing. It gives clearly explained reasons why the reader should agree with the writer. It also tells the reader what to do if he or she agrees.

Faster Library Computers

by Jeb Nealson

Have you ever worked on a computer at the Quincy Public Library? You search the Internet for the information you need, but then you give up waiting for the Web site to appear on your screen. These computers are slow. Quincy has extra money in its budget to spend at the library. I believe the money should go to creating a new computer lab.

More and more people are relying on the library's computers for information. They come here to check the Internet for news and to get e-mail from their family and friends. Adding faster computers would give people who don't have computers a way to use the Internet.

The librarians want new computers too. Computers make it easier to find books. The electronic catalog the library has now is slow and hard to figure out. Most libraries have updated computers with faster, easy-to-use electronic catalogs. They are also easier to update.

The citizens of Quincy want and need new computers at the library. If you want new computers there too, please go to the next town meeting.

What Makes Good Persuasive Writing?

Persuasive writing asks readers to believe something or to do something. A letter to the editor of a newspaper is an example of persuasive writing. The article on page 401 was written to persuade readers that the library needs a new computer lab.

Topic

A persuasive article needs to have a topic. The topic is what you want the reader to believe or do. Imagine that you want your parents to buy you a new computer. You could write a persuasive article to get your parents to agree. The topic of your article might be why it is a good idea for your parents to buy the computer.

Reasons

Reasons help your audience understand why they should do something. When you write a persuasive article, give at least two reasons why people should agree with you. For example, computers help kids learn by giving them practice in reading and writing. Kids can also play learning games. If you give your audience good reasons, they might agree with you.

Research

When you write a persuasive article, you should know a lot about your topic. You need to give reasons for your readers to agree with you. Research can help you find the reasons. For an article about buying a computer, you might read on the Internet about ways computers can help kids learn. Or you might ask a teacher how computers help kids learn. The more you know about your topic, the more willing your audience will be to agree with you.

ACTIVITY A **Answer these questions about the article on page 401.**

1. What is the topic?
2. What does Jeb ask people to do in the ending of his letter?
3. Why does Jeb think the library needs new computers?
4. Imagine Jeb wrote that the town should add computers so he could play video games. Why do you think his audience might not agree?
5. If you lived in Jeb's town, would you go to the town meeting? Why or why not?

ACTIVITY B **Read each topic and decide if you agree or disagree. Choose three topics. Then write one sentence about each topic to tell why you agree or disagree.**

1. making the school day longer
2. eight o'clock bedtime
3. no hats in school
4. dogs being the best pets
5. no chewing gum in class
6. having year-round school
7. using cell phones at school
8. taking a second language
9. summer being the best season
10. no homework on Fridays
11. having more field trips
12. a computer for each student

WRITER'S CORNER

Look at the article on page 401. Work with a partner. Write two more reasons why people might disagree with the topic of the article.

Grammar in Action. Include two adverbs in your reason. Review Section 6.1.

Why Exercise Is Cool

It feels good to have a strong, flexible body that can do all the activities you enjoy—like running, jumping, and playing with your friends. It's also fun to be good at something, like scoring a basket, hitting a home run, or perfecting a dive.

But you may not know that exercising can actually put you in a better mood. When you exercise, your brain releases a chemical called **endorphins** (say: en-**dor**-funz), which may make you feel happier. It's just another reason why exercise is cool!

Mary L. Gavin, M.D., kidshealth.org

Audience

When you think of reasons, keep in mind who is going to read your article. Who will be your audience? Think of reasons that interest them. For example, what reasons would interest your parents if you asked them to buy you a computer? Your parents might not agree if you said that you wanted a computer to e-mail your friends. But they might agree if you said that a computer would help you with your homework.

ACTIVITY C Tell which sentences are asking you to believe something or to do something.

1. I like my cousin's cottage in Michigan.
2. Many people may disagree, but recess is an important part of the school day.
3. We have no choice but to vote Mel Ross out of office for stealing money from the city.
4. Margaret's goldfish is more of a red color.
5. Kids should be allowed to decorate their bedrooms any way they want.
6. Do clowns scare you as much as they scare me?
7. Let Homer play for the baseball team because he tries hard.
8. Come and support the high school band as they try for their third state championship.

ACTIVITY D Match each topic in Column A to an audience in Column B.

Column A

1. I should have a later bedtime.
2. The public library should have more DVDs.
3. Everybody in our school should play this video game.
4. Schools should allow soft-drink machines.

Column B

a. friends
b. parents
c. school board
d. librarian

ACTIVITY E Choose one of the following topics. Work with a partner to write two reasons for someone to agree with the topic.

A. Students should not have to do any homework.
B. Summer vacation should be longer than three months.
C. All students should wear school uniforms.
D. Third graders should decide how much TV they watch.
E. Students should not be able to sit wherever they want in class.
F. Students should not receive grades for their work.
G. No students should be allowed at parent-teacher conferences.

WRITER'S CORNER

Write three topics that you have strong feelings about. After each topic write a sentence explaining why it is important to you.

Beginning, Middle, and Ending

Most kinds of writing need a beginning, a middle, and an ending. In persuasive writing each part has a special job to do.

Beginning

The beginning of a persuasive article has a topic sentence. The topic sentence tells exactly what the topic is. It tells readers what you want them to do or to think. Look at this topic sentence.

A swimming pool at school would help students in many ways.

Middle

The middle gives the reader reasons to agree with you. Write more than one sentence to support each reason. Clearly explained reasons are more likely to persuade a reader. Look at this reason from a persuasive article.

A swimming pool will help students become healthier.

This is a good reason. But it could be explained better.

A swimming pool will give students a fun way to exercise. Exercise will help keep students healthy.

Give each reason its own paragraph. Let the reader clearly see each reason you give.

Ending

The ending retells the topic of a persuasive article. Remind the reader what you want him or her to believe or to do. Try to say it in a different way. You might say what the reader can do to change things if he or she agrees with you. Use opinion words such as *should, ought, must,* or *believe* to show that you feel strongly about your topic.

This sentence tells the reader what to do if he or she agrees that there should be a swimming pool at school.

If you believe that a swimming pool at school is a good idea, you should write a letter to Principal Pak today.

ACTIVITY A Read this list of questions. Choose three questions you feel strongly about. Decide what you believe about each one. Write a topic sentence for it.

A. Should every student have a computer at school?

B. Should people on bicycles have to wear helmets?

C. Should there be bowling alleys in schools?

D. Should students be able to wear in-line skates in school?

E. Should schools be open on Saturdays?

F. Should students be able to attend online school?

G. Should students be allowed to bring pets to school?

WRITER'S CORNER

Imagine that you are writing a persuasive article about going to school all year long. Your topic sentence is "Students should not have to go to school all year long." Write two reasons why readers should agree with your topic sentence.

Tech Tip Graph a survey of your classmates' reasons.

ACTIVITY B Read this persuasive article. Find the topic sentence. Then tell the two reasons the writer uses to persuade readers. Tell what sentence gives readers something to do if they agree with the writer.

It's 12:00, and the bell rings. Everybody marches into the lunchroom. The lunchroom worker puts gravy on a square of mystery meat. Something green and slimy is supposed to be a vegetable. We need a change. Kids should decide what gets served in the lunchroom.

Most kids don't get to make grown-up decisions. Their families or the school decides what they eat. If kids get to decide what is served at lunch, they will get practice making grown-up decisions.

It could also be a chance to learn. Kids could learn more about food. They could find out where vegetables grow. They could find out about different kinds of fruits and grains.

Everyone agrees that our school lunches are bad. Instead of just buying different food, we should let students decide what to eat. If you think this is a good idea, go to Mrs. Silva's classroom and sign my petition.

LiNK

School Lunches

The typical school lunch is still higher in fat than it should be, according to a recent study. That doesn't mean you shouldn't buy your lunch, it just means you might want to give the cafeteria menu a closer look. Read the cafeteria menu the night before. Knowing what's for lunch beforehand will let you know if you want to eat it! Bring home a copy of the menu or figure out how to find it on the school website.

kidshealth.org

ACTIVITY C Read these reasons why people should recycle. Tell which reasons you think are good reasons.

1. We're running out of room for trash. Recycling helps keep trash out of landfills.

2. Recycling is something that cool movie stars do. I want to be like my favorite movie stars.

3. Recycling turns trash into new stuff. I think it's a good idea.

4. Recycling can save more of our natural resources. When you recycle, people can cut down fewer trees, forests, and jungles.

ACTIVITY D Match each topic sentence in Column A with two reasons that support it in Column B.

Column A

1. Hurting pets should be a serious crime.
2. People should get free medicine when they need it.
3. Students should not have to go to recess.
4. The school day should be longer.

Column B

a. Giving medicine to people who need it would mean fewer sick people passing their germs around.

b. Pets are best friends for some people. Hurting a pet is like hurting someone's best friend.

c. Some students like drawing pictures inside better than playing outside.

d. Some countries already give free medicine to people. It works well in those countries.

e. A longer school day would give teachers more time to help with schoolwork.

f. Some students can get hurt playing at recess.

g. Other countries have longer school days. Students in those countries score high on tests.

h. People who hurt pets might hurt people too.

WRITER'S CORNER

Choose a topic sentence from Activity D. Write an ending for a persuasive article on that topic.

Idea Webs

If you get lost, a map can help you find where you are. When you are writing, you can use a map to find where your ideas are. We call this kind of map an idea web. An idea web looks a little like a spider web. It helps catch all your ideas.

Making an Idea Web

This is Jason's idea web for a persuasive article.

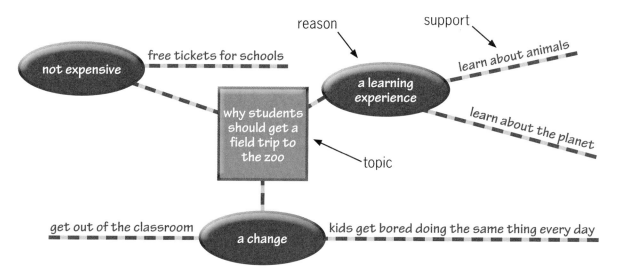

To get started, Jason wrote his topic. Then he drew a square around it. The topic of his article was why students should get a field trip to the zoo.

He wrote his reasons around the topic and drew ovals around each one. Then he drew lines from his topic to each of his reasons. He drew lines off of each reason. He wrote on each line ideas to support that reason.

ACTIVITY A **Answer these questions about Jason's idea web on page 410.**

1. What are the three reasons students should get a field trip to the zoo?

2. What are two ideas that support the reason that going to the zoo would be a good learning experience?

3. Which reason do you think is best? Why?

ACTIVITY B **Use the following to make your own idea webs.**

1. **Topic A: why I deserve more allowance**

   Reason 1: I do more chores now.
   Support: sweep porch
   Support: do breakfast dishes
   Support: clean my room once a week

   Reason 2: Jamie got a raise.
   Support: be fair to your children
   Support: consider what each chore is worth

   Reason 3: The cost of everything has risen.
   Support: can't afford gum anymore
   Support: want to be able to buy things for myself

2. **Topic B: why living in the city is the best**

   Reason 1: many things to see and do
   Support: visit museums and stores
   Support: see monuments and play in big parks
   Support: plays, concerts, and sporting events

   Reason 2: many places to eat
   Support: try different kinds of food
   Support: find a restaurant for any occasion

   Reason 3: easy to get around
   Support: buses going anywhere
   Support: many trains and taxis

WRITER'S CORNER

Write three sentences that tell how you think an idea web can help you improve your writing. Share your sentences with a partner.

Phrases or Sentences

When you make an idea web, it is OK if you do not write complete sentences. You can write phrases, or groups of words. You can use only important words and not worry about capital letters or periods. Or you can write in complete sentences if you choose.

ACTIVITY C Copy this idea web. Fill in the missing blanks and ovals with your own ideas.

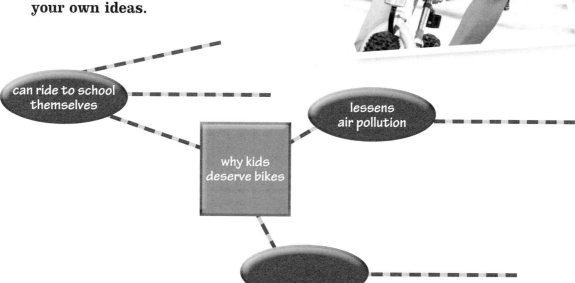

ACTIVITY D These sentences are topics and reasons to be used in a persuasive article. Rewrite each sentence as a phrase, or group of words, to put in an idea web.

1. Topic: Kids should spend at least an hour a day outside.
   Reason 1: Exercise is good for everyone.
   Reason 2: There are lots of fun games to play outside.

2. Topic: Parents and kids should shop for clothes together.
   Reason 1: Parents don't know all the latest fashions.
   Reason 2: Kids should try on the clothes to see if they fit.

ACTIVITY E Each set of phrases is from an idea web. Identify which phrase is the topic, the reason, and the support.

1. a. better math scores
   b. will do better in school
   c. why kids should have calculators

2. a. why bedtime should be later
   b. homework harder in third grade
   c. will have more time for homework

3. a. will always know what time it is
   b. won't be late for school
   c. why all kids should have watches

4. a. teamwork good for building trust
   b. why gym class should teach soccer
   c. will teach kids teamwork

ACTIVITY F Choose one of the topics below. Make an idea web for the topic.

A. why the school day should be shorter

B. why the school day should be longer

C. why every kid should have a pet

D. why kids should not have pets

E. why students should be able to use calculators for math tests

F. why students should not be able to use calculators for math tests

G. why the school gym should be open all summer

H. why the school gym should not be open all summer

WRITER'S CORNER

Use the idea web you made in Activity F to write the middle of a persuasive article.

Compound Sentences

You can join two sentences to make a compound sentence by using words such as *and, or*, and *but*. These words are called conjunctions. Compound sentences can make your writing more interesting. Can you find the compound sentence below?

One musician played a bass. Another musician played a trumpet.

One musician played a bass, and another musician played a trumpet.

Making a Compound Sentence

Sometimes you might find two sentences in your writing that are related to each other. Do these three things to join two sentences into one compound sentence.

- Change the period after the first sentence to a comma.
- Choose the word that best fits between the sentences. Use *and, or,* or *but.* Put that word after the comma.
- Change the capital letter at the beginning of the second sentence to a small letter. If the first word is the word *I* or a proper noun, don't change it. A proper noun and the word *I* always begin with a capital letter.

Check that both sentences are complete before you join them. Also be sure that the ideas go together. It's possible to join any two sentences, but not all sentences belong together as a compound sentence.

ACTIVITY A Read these compound sentences. Tell which conjunction was used to make the compound sentence: *and, or,* or *but.*

1. Tyler bought baseball cards, and Milo bought comic books.
2. Milo paid with dollar bills, but Tyler paid with quarters.
3. The clerk gave Milo his change, and he stuffed it in his pocket.
4. Milo and Tyler could take the bus home, or they could walk.
5. It started raining, and Milo and Tyler took the bus.
6. Tyler thought the bus smelled funny, and Milo agreed.
7. Milo could go to Tyler's house, or he could go home.
8. Tyler wanted Milo to stay, but Milo decided to leave.

ACTIVITY B Find the mistake in each compound sentence. Look for correct punctuation marks and capital letters.

1. All of the Casos play musical instruments and they play tennis too.
2. I like big dogs, but The little ones scare me.
3. The clowns ran out of the tent, And the lions ran after them.
4. My best friend is a magician. but he is not a very good one.
5. Stevie the Mole is a character in a book but I wish he were real.
6. Evan has a pet iguana, but sam doesn't like it.
7. We were late but Mom made us change our clothes.
8. The horn sounded to start the game and, John scored a goal right away.
9. I can buy a new bike, Or I can keep saving my money.
10. Remove the roast from the oven, but, be sure to use pot holders.

WRITER'S CORNER

Write one sentence about something you did after school yesterday. Then write a sentence about something you did after that. Rewrite the two sentences as a compound sentence using the word *and.*

Conjunctions

Conjunctions have different meanings. When you write a compound sentence, be sure to use the correct conjunction. Here is how you can use some conjunctions.

CONJUNCTIONS

and	shows how two things are the same or belong together
	Judy will wash the dishes, *and* I will dry.
but	shows how two things are different
	Max plays the piano, *but* Keene plays the guitar.
or	shows that one of two things might happen
	Tamera can go to the zoo, *or* she can go to the museum.

ACTIVITY C Use the conjunction in parentheses to combine each pair of sentences into a compound sentence.

1. You painted the wall a pretty color. You missed a spot. (but)

2. Tito is taking a bus to the mall. Renaldo is riding his bike. (and)

3. The skate park is closed. I don't want to go home. (but)

4. Jada likes Mexican food. She might eat all these tacos. (and)

5. Oranges can be sweet. Oranges can be sour. (or)

6. I want to go to the monkey house. My sister doesn't like monkeys. (but)

7. Roberta is learning math. Jake is learning science. (and)

ACTIVITY D Complete these compound sentences.

1. Teresa draws pictures at the table, and _____.

2. _____, but Allen wants to go home.

3. Jesse's car has a flat tire, and _____.

4. _____, or you can see a movie.

5. Ivan and Tess want to buy that dollhouse, but _____.

6. _____, but Uncle Gilberto lost his fishing pole.

7. Elaine found a skunk in her yard, and _____.

8. Frieda can go camping this weekend, or _____.

9. I had planned to go sailing, but _____.

10. Michael got on his bike, and _____.

ACTIVITY E Write a sentence that contains the conjunction _and, or,_ or _but_ to connect each pair of sentences.

1. Kim read the map. Keith drove the truck.

2. Jerry can swim in the lake. He can hike the trails.

3. My family will visit the country. We will go to the city.

4. Kara must take the test. She will study with Lucy.

5. The author read from his book. He talked about the characters.

6. We wanted to have a picnic. It rained all afternoon.

7. Levi's sister will dance on the stage. She will design the programs.

8. Mrs. White planted bushes on the side of the house. They grew up to her window.

9. Melissa broke her foot. The doctor put it in a cast.

10. The phone was ringing loudly. I could not answer it.

WRITER'S CORNER

Write one compound sentence using each of these conjunctions: _and, or,_ and _but._

Grammar in Action. Find the compound sentence in the page 416 excerpt. Name the conjunction.

Suffixes

A prefix is a word part that you can add to the beginning of a base word to change its meaning. A suffix is a word part that you can add to the end of a base word to change its meaning. It is useful to learn suffixes. Knowing suffixes can help you figure out what words mean.

-er

One suffix is -er. If you add -er to the end of the word *teach,* it changes the meaning of the word. Look at the example below. *Teach* is the base word, and -er is the suffix.

teach + -er = teacher

Each suffix has its own meaning. The suffix -er means "one who." So when you add -er to the end of the word *teach,* you change it to mean "one who teaches." A teacher is "a person who teaches." Many words use this suffix. A *farmer* is a person who farms. A *painter* is a person who paints. Can you think of other words that use the suffix -er?

-less

Another suffix is -less. Can you think of words that end with the suffix -less? What do you think this suffix means?

One example is the word *hopeless.* The word *hopeless* means "without hope." The suffix -less means "without."

ACTIVITY A Find the suffix in each word.

1. binder
2. helpless
3. careless
4. thoughtless

5. seller
6. brainless
7. timeless
8. leader

9. trainer
10. climber
11. doubtless
12. buyer

ACTIVITY B These words have the suffix *-er* or the suffix *-less*. What does each word mean?

1. player
2. windless
3. shoeless
4. singer
5. cleaner
6. painter

7. wordless
8. thoughtless
9. drifter
10. sender
11. pitcher
12. endless

ACTIVITY C Add the suffix –er or –less to the base word in parentheses to correctly complete each sentence.

1. The owner fed the tiny _____ puppy. (help)
2. Wishing for a chance to take the test again was _____. (hope)
3. Coach Bill is a very good batting _____. (teach)
4. The _____ started her day planting flowers. (work)
5. My _____ coin was just an old, rusty piece of metal. (worth)
6. A _____ looked at the blueprints for the new library. (build)
7. The losing _____ called to the champion for a rematch. (play)
8. All the food we ate at the party was bland and _____. (taste)

WRITER'S CORNER

Write a sentence using one of the words from Activity A. Underline the base word in the word you used. Then write another sentence using just the base word.

Grammar in Action. Find the word with the suffix -er in the page 400 excerpt.

ACTIVITY D Write a word with the suffix *-er* or the suffix *-less* to fit each definition.

1. without hair
2. person who follows
3. person who farms
4. without hope
5. without color
6. without speech
7. person who teaches
8. person who owns
9. person who supports
10. without noise
11. person who reports
12. person who builds

ACTIVITY E Complete each sentence with an *-er* or *-less* word from the word box.

| singer | buyer | trainer | skinless | spotless |

1. He learned to tread water from a swimming _____.
2. Colby is looking for a _____ for her old tuba.
3. Jacob only eats _____ chicken.
4. With such a beautiful voice, she should be a _____.
5. Have you noticed that Austin's bedroom is always _____?

ACTIVITY F Complete each sentence with a word that has the suffix *-er* or *-less*.

1. If you have a _____ cat, you can see the wrinkles that are usually covered by fur.
2. Dozens of _____ make their way up Mt. Everest every year.
3. It's a _____ movie that never seems to get old.
4. The _____ dusted the desks and swept the floor.
5. The clear blue sky was _____ and full of sunlight.
6. He is such a _____ worker that I've never seen him take a break.
7. The _____ didn't have enough money to pay for the Oriental rug.
8. If it weren't for _____, students would have recess all day.
9. Without his Super Power Bands, the hero was _____.
10. I wonder which _____ is giving the speech.
11. Jennie is a great soccer _____.
12. At recess we played follow the _____.
13. The _____ threw a fast ball.
14. The doctor promised the shot would be _____.
15. A sailboat won't go anywhere on a _____ day.
16. Meg spilled the milk all over the table because she was _____.

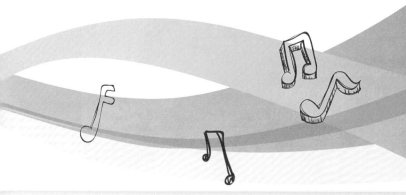

WRITER'S CORNER

Write five sentences using the words from the word box in Activity E.

Persuasive Speeches

You can hear persuasive speech any time you turn on the TV. A commercial is a kind of persuasive speech. The people who make the commercials are trying to persuade you to buy something. Do you have a favorite commercial? What do you like about it?

Audience

When people make commercials, they have an audience in mind. Have you ever noticed that commercials for toys almost always have kids in them? That's because the audience for those commercials is kids.

When you give a persuasive speech, you should keep your audience in mind. Who will be listening to you? How old is your audience? Will they be interested in your topic?

Voice and Body Language

Speak calmly when you are trying to persuade people. Try not to use sounds and words such as *um, uh,* and *you know.* Stand straight. Use your hands to make what you are saying come alive.

Visual Aids

When you give a persuasive speech, include visual aids such as pictures, charts, or maps. You can also use objects. Even costumes can be good visual aids.

ACTIVITY A Match the things in Column A to the possible audience in Column B.

Column A

1. swing set
2. prom clothes
3. car rental company
4. mustache comb
5. perfume

Column B

a. men
b. kids
c. grown-ups
d. women
e. teenagers

ACTIVITY B Imagine you are talking to each audience below. Use your voice and body language to persuade your audience to agree with you.

1. **Audience:** friend
   Topic: You want to go to a different movie than your friend does.

2. **Audience:** brother or sister
   Topic: You want to switch after-school chores.

3. **Audience:** neighbor
   Topic: You want him or her to be your team's new soccer coach.

4. **Audience:** teacher
   Topic: You want to learn more about dinosaurs.

ACTIVITY C Imagine you are trying to persuade an audience to do the following things. Name a visual aid that you think would help you get your message across.

1. Add a crossing guard near the school.
2. Create a dog park in your neighborhood.
3. Assign a special day to honor the person your school is named after.
4. Visit a nearby large city.
5. Play a new sport in gym class.

SPEAKER'S CORNER

Imagine you invented something for kids your age, such as a flying bicycle. What is it called? What does it look like? What does it do? Write a four-sentence description of your invention. Then talk about it with a partner.

Being an Active Listener

When you listen to persuasive speech, be an active listener. Think about whether you agree with the speaker. Keep these things in mind for active listening.

- Think about whether the speaker's reasons are true.
- Decide if you agree with the speaker.
- Politely ask the speaker questions if you don't understand something.

ACTIVITY D Work with a partner. Take turns reading each of these sentences in different ways. First, read the sentence in a calm voice. Then read the sentence the way you might if you wanted to persuade someone to agree with you. Practice using your hands with each reading.

1. We should change the way our desks are arranged.
2. We should not have to wear uniforms to school.
3. Our class should go on more field trips.
4. We should have no homework.
5. We should have different kinds of food at lunchtime.
6. Science is one of the most important subjects.
7. We should have a two-hour lunch on Wednesdays.
8. First graders can learn a lot from third graders.
9. There should be a TV in the lunchroom.
10. We should have 15 minutes each day to read whatever we want.

ACTIVITY E Think of something that you use or like. List reasons why someone should buy it. Then meet with a partner. Tell your reasons. Here are some things you might talk about.

- toys
- clothes
- video games
- cereal
- books

ACTIVITY F Imagine that you are making a commercial for the thing you invented for the Speaker's Corner on page 423. List two visual aids that you might use in an oral presentation about your invention. Discuss with a partner how you might use the visual aids in your commercial.

ACTIVITY G Write a commercial for your invention. Tell the reasons people should buy it. Try to use at least one of the visual aids that you listed in Activity F.

SPEAKER'S CORNER

Practice with a partner the commercial that you wrote in Activity G. Then give your partner helpful feedback about his or her commercial. Present your commercial to your classmates. Talk about what you liked about each commercial.

Tech Tip Videotape the commercial for your new invention.

Writer's Workshop

Prewriting and Drafting

People write persuasive articles when they want someone to agree with them. What do you want people to agree with you about? Is it something that others might disagree with? How might you persuade them to agree with you?

Prewriting

Prewriting is the time you plan what you are going to say in a persuasive article. Read about how Jake, a third grader, planned his persuasive article.

Choosing a Topic

When Jake was in second grade, his sister Amelia took him to a special Earth Day event.
 He learned about the importance of recycling.
Now Jake wants to help the environment. Amelia said that he should start a recycling program at his school. To do that, Jake would need a lot of help. So he wrote a persuasive article to send to his town newspaper.

Your Turn

Choose your own topic. Think about something you want people to do. You might look back through this chapter, or you might ask your family for ideas. Make a list of topics that you find interesting.

Ask yourself these questions to help you decide which topic to choose:
- What do I want to happen?
- Will some people disagree with me?
- What do I know about my topic?
- Can I find out more about my topic?

Researching the Topic

Jake had learned a lot about recycling when he went to the Earth Day event. But he wanted to know more. So he did some research at the library, using books, magazines, and the Internet.

Jake found out that many things can be recycled. He learned that recycling paper saves trees from being cut down. He took notes on some of the things he learned.

Jake called the Brownsville Recycling Center. He was able to find out information about how to start a recycling program. Jake thought he might be able to use the information in his article.

Your Turn

- Write the things that you know about your topic.
- Do research online or in the library.
- Read articles and Web sites about your topic.
- If you read something that might make your persuasive article stronger, write it on a note card. You might be able to use the information in your article.

Writer's Tip Idea webs can help you organize your thoughts and research.

Organizing Ideas

Jake's head was buzzing with ideas. He wasn't sure where to start his article. So  Jake made an idea web to help organize his thoughts. Look at Jake's idea web below.

Your Turn

- Make your own idea web. Write the topic of your article in the square.
- Write your reasons in ovals around your topic.
- Write ideas that support your reasons.

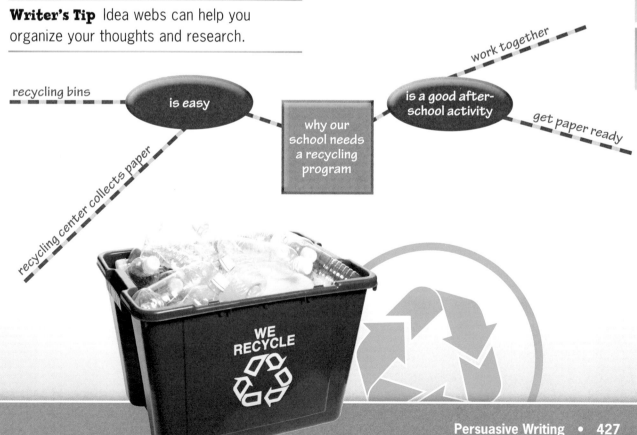

recycling bins

is easy

recycling center collects paper

why our school needs a recycling program

work together

is a good after-school activity

get paper ready

WE RECYCLE

Prewriting

Drafting

Content Editing

Revising

Copyediting

Proofreading

Publishing

Drafting

Jake carefully looked over his prewriting notes and his idea web. Then he used his notes and idea web to write his persuasive article.

Why Brownsville Grade School Needs a Recycling Program

Every week Americans throw away a lot of paper. That's like throwing away trees. These trees are homes for animals. They also clean the air we breathe. Trees are very important. We should all do our part to protect our trees. Brownsville Grade School can do its part by starting a recycling program.

Recycling paper is very easy. We would have to put recycling bins around the school. Students and teachrs can put all the paper that they might throw away into the bins. the Brownsville Recycling Center will collect the paper every friday.

Recycling is also a good after-school activity. Students and teachrs can work together to bag up the paper and get it ready to be picked up. One ton of recycled paper saves 3,700 pounds of lumber and 7,000 gallons of water. That's like saving at least 7 trees from being cut down.

Your Turn

Use your notes and your idea web to write your draft. As you write, remember the following points.

- Write a clear topic sentence in the beginning.
- Make sure that you have at least two reasons that tell why people should agree with your topic sentence. Write each reason in a separate paragraph.
- Say what your topic is again in the ending. If you can, tell your audience what you want them to do.
- Remember to leave extra space between the lines of your draft. That way you can make changes later.

Respecting Your Audience

You probably believe strongly in your topic.

 **Voice**

You might use strong words when you write your reasons. But not everyone will agree with you. Remember, when you write a persuasive article, you want to persuade people to agree with you. You don't want to make them angry. So choose your words carefully. Don't use words like *stupid, silly,* or *crazy.* You want your personality to shine through, but you should also respect your audience.

Editor's Workshop

Content Editing

Jake liked what he had written so far. But he wanted his article for the newspaper to be his best work. He didn't want to have mistakes for the whole town to read!

Jake knew that the first thing he should do was content edit his draft. By content editing, he would be sure that the ideas in his draft made sense. He used this checklist to content edit his draft.

Content Editor's Checklist

- [ ] Does the beginning have a clear topic sentence?

- [ ] Does the middle include at least two reasons that are well supported?

- [ ] Are the reasons clear and fully explained?

- [ ] Does the ending retell what the topic is?

- [ ] Are opinion words used?

Jake read over his draft carefully, answering each question on the checklist. He knew that if the ideas in his draft were clear, he would have a better chance of persuading people to agree with him.

Then Jake asked his friend Charlie to content edit his draft. Jake knew that Charlie was good at content editing. He also knew that Charlie would make good suggestions for making the draft better.

Writer's Tip Try to put yourself in the reader's place. Imagine that you don't know anything about the topic. That will help you figure out what to add and what might be confusing.

Charlie read Jake's draft carefully. He used the Content Editor's Checklist to edit the draft. He wrote a list of his comments so he wouldn't forget any of his ideas.

When Charlie was finished, he and Jake met to talk about the draft. Here are Charlie's comments.

- Your topic sentence is good. But maybe in the beginning you should take out the stuff about trees being homes for animals and cleaning the air.
- The first reason in the middle looks OK. But people might wonder what the school will need to buy. The school might not have the money.

- You should explain your second reason more. Why would kids want to recycle after school?
- The stuff about recycling in the ending is good. But you didn't retell what your topic is. And you didn't use any opinion words to show how strongly you feel.

Jake liked what Charlie said about the draft. The article would be better because of Charlie's help.

Your Turn

- Content edit your draft.
- Trade drafts with a partner. Use the Content's Editor's Checklist to give your partner ideas to make the draft better.
- When you have finished, meet with your partner to talk about your ideas.
- When it is your turn to share your ideas, remember to use polite words.
- Think carefully about each of your partner's ideas before you decide if you will use them. You do not have to use all the ideas. It is up to you to decide what will make your writing better.

Prewriting

Drafting

Content Editing

Revising

Copyediting

Proofreading

Publishing

Revising

Here is Jake's revised draft.

Why Brownsville Grade School Needs a Recycling Program

Every week Americans throw away a lot of paper. That's like throwing away trees. ~~These trees are homes for animals. They also clean the air we breathe.~~ Trees are very important. We should all do our part to protect our trees. Brownsville Grade School can do its part by starting a recycling program.

Recycling paper is very easy. ~~We would have to put~~ All need to do is buy recycling bins to put around the school. Students and teachrs can put all the paper that they might throw away into the bins. the Brownsville Recycling Center will collect the paper every friday. It won't cost the school any money to have the paper collected.

Recycling is also a good after-school activity. Students and teachrs can work together to bag up the paper and get it ready to be picked up. One ton of recycled paper saves 3,700 pounds of lumber and 7,000 gallons of water. That's like saving at least 7 trees from being cut down. This will be a good way for kids to make friends who are interested in helping our planet. We should start a recycling program. We must do our part to help save our trees.

Jake made a lot of changes after he met with Charlie. Look at some of the things he did to improve his persuasive article.

- Jake liked the facts about trees being homes for animals and cleaning the air. But he thought Charlie was right. They made the beginning confusing. What did Jake do?

- He agreed that people might wonder what the school would need to buy. So he called the recycling center. How did Jake use this new information?

- Jake thought about Charlie's suggestion to explain the second reason more. He added a sentence. What is it about?

- He also added two sentences to the ending. Do you think they make the ending stronger? Why or why not?

- Jake also included opinion words. Which ones? Why?

Jake was happy with the changes that he had made. He thanked Charlie for his help.

Your Turn

- Use your partner's suggestions to revise your draft.
- Read your draft again and look for more ways to improve it.
- Try to answer the questions on the Content Editor's Checklist again. Can you answer yes to each question?

Prewriting

Drafting

Content Editing

Revising

Copyediting

Proofreading

Publishing

Copyediting and Proofreading

Copyediting

Jake was sure that the ideas in his article were good. Now he wanted to make sure that the sentences were complete and that they made sense. He also wanted to make sure Word Choice that all the words were used correctly. So he decided to copyedit his draft. He used this Copyeditor's Checklist.

Jake read his draft again and answered the questions on the Copyeditor's Checklist. He found in his beginning two sentences he could Sentence Fluency join to make a compound sentence. Can you guess which sentences he joined?

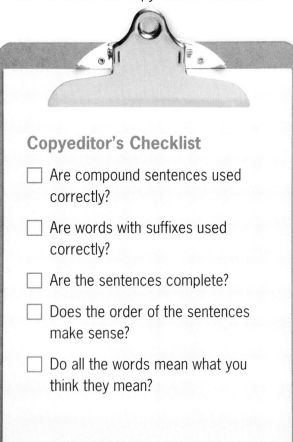

Copyeditor's Checklist

- [ ] Are compound sentences used correctly?
- [ ] Are words with suffixes used correctly?
- [ ] Are the sentences complete?
- [ ] Does the order of the sentences make sense?
- [ ] Do all the words mean what you think they mean?

Your Turn

- Read your revised draft carefully.
- Can you join any sentences to make compound sentences?
- Have you used words with suffixes correctly?
- Make sure that you can answer yes to all the questions on the checklist.

Proofreading

Jake wanted people to take his persuasive article seriously. If his article had mistakes

 Conventions

in spelling, capitalization, or punctuation, people wouldn't take him seriously. Jake used the Proofreader's Checklist to catch these kinds of mistakes. He also checked to make sure that he hadn't left out anything when he revised his article.

Jake knew that a different proofreader would spot mistakes that he missed. Jake asked his teacher, Mrs. Wu, to proofread his draft. Mrs. Wu found one capitalization mistake and one word misspelled several times. Can you find these mistakes?

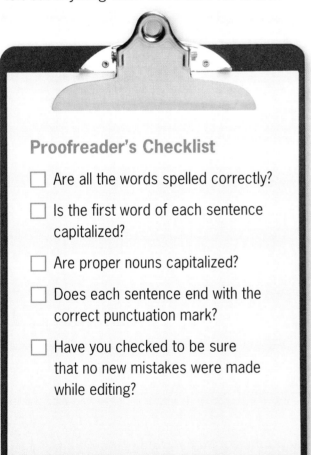

Proofreader's Checklist

☐ Are all the words spelled correctly?

☐ Is the first word of each sentence capitalized?

☐ Are proper nouns capitalized?

☐ Does each sentence end with the correct punctuation mark?

☐ Have you checked to be sure that no new mistakes were made while editing?

Your Turn

- Read your draft carefully, using the Proofreader's Checklist.
- Look for only one kind of mistake at a time.
- Use the proofreading marks from page 245 to mark changes on your draft.
- When you have finished, trade drafts with a new partner. Go over each other's drafts, using the checklist.
- Use a dictionary to look up any words that might be misspelled or used incorrectly.

Grammar in Action

Jake used an incorrect suffix twice. Find it and fix it.

Prewriting
Drafting
Content Editing
Revising
Copyediting
Proofreading
Publishing

Publishing

Jake typed the final copy. He checked his final copy one more time. He used the Proofreader's Checklist to make sure that he didn't make any new mistakes while he typed. Here is Jake's final persuasive article.

Why Brownsville Grade School Needs a Recycling Program

Every week Americans throw away a lot of paper. That's like throwing away trees. Trees are very important, so we should all do our part to protect them. Brownsville Grade School can do its part by starting a recycling program.

Recycling paper is very easy. All we need to do is buy recycling bins to put around the school. Students and teachers can put all the paper that they might throw away into the bins. The Brownsville Recycling Center will collect the paper every Friday. It won't cost the school any money to have the paper collected.

Recycling is also a good after-school activity. Students and teachers can work together to bag up the paper and get it ready to be picked up. This will be a good way for kids to make friends who are interested in helping our planet.

One ton of recycled paper saves 3700 pounds of lumber and 7,000 gallons of water. That's like saving at least 7 trees from being cut down. We should start a recycling program. We must do our part to help save our trees.

Jake sent his persuasive article to the newspaper. A few days later it was published in the newspaper. He was glad that he had taken the time to write his persuasive article.

Whenever you publish your work, your goal is to share your thoughts and

 Presentation

experiences with other people. There are many ways you can publish your persuasive article.

 Post the articles on a class bulletin board. Include photos or drawings of your subject.

 Submit your article to the class or school newspaper. Perhaps include a survey for students to give their opinion on the topic.

 Mail your article to someone who might be able to help your cause, such as your mayor, senator, or governor.

 Post your article to a Web site that publishes student writing. Work with an adult to find a site and share your article with the world.

Your Turn

Publishing is exciting for writers. Publishing means that an audience will see the writer's article for the first time. A strong final copy will be more likely to persuade your audience.

- Make sure that your work is its best before you publish it.
- Write or type your article carefully.
- Check your final copy one last time, using the Proofreader's Checklist.

Prewriting

Drafting

Content Editing

Revising

Copyediting

Proofreading

Publishing

Creative Writing

LiNK **Fly Away Home**

by Eve Bunting

My dad and I live in an airport. That's because we don't have a home and the airport is better than the streets. We are careful not to get caught.

. . . Dad and I try not to get noticed. We stay among the crowds. We change airlines.

"Delta, TWA, Northwest, we love them all," Dad says.

He and I wear blue jeans and blue T-shirts and blue jackets. . . . Not to be noticed is to look like nobody at all.

Once we saw a woman pushing a metal cart full of stuff. She wore a long, dirty coat and she lay down across a row of seats in front of Continental Gate 6. The cart, dirty coat, the lying down were all noticeable. Security moved her out real fast.

> *Fly Away Home* is a good example of realistic fiction. It has characters that readers care about, and there is a problem the characters need to solve.

Super Spy

by Giada Michaelson

Keenan's dad was a spy. Keenan was sure of it. His dad always wore a black suit and tie to work. His huge watch had lots of gears and buttons. Keenan was sure it was a spy watch. And his dad went bowling by himself every Friday. But half the time he forgot his bowling ball! Keenan just knew he was meeting with other spies. Keenan had to find out the truth.

One Friday Keenan raised his arms and yawned. "I'm tired. I'm going to go to bed early tonight."

"It's only seven o'clock!" his father said.

Keenan shrugged. "I'm a growing boy."

He shut off his bedroom light. He changed into dark clothes. He slipped out the window. The door of his dad's van was open. Keenan climbed in and hid in back under a blanket.

A little while later, his dad got in. Then the van rumbled into the night. Keenan smiled under the blanket. "Bowling! Ha! We'll see," he whispered to himself.

When the van stopped, Keenan peeked out. His dad went through a glass door and up a staircase. The staircase was lit by one lightbulb. It sure didn't look like a bowling alley!

Keenan tiptoed up the creaky stairs. Strange music came from behind a closed door. Keenan burst through the door. There was his dad! Dancing? In a line of people? "Keenan!" his dad shouted. "What are you doing here?"

Keenan's dad explained during the drive home. He was taking dancing lessons. He wanted to surprise Keenan's mom, who was a great dancer. He was going to dance with her at a family costume party. Keenan looked at his dark clothes.

"I guess I know what my costume will be," he said. "A super spy!"

What Makes Good Realistic Fiction?

Fiction is a made-up story. Realistic fiction tells about people and events that could be real, even though they are not. Adventure stories and mysteries can be realistic fiction. But they are realistic only if they could really happen. Realistic fiction could be about a boy sneaking into a circus tent to find his missing dog. If he discovered that talking lizards run the circus, the story would not be realistic fiction.

Characters

The characters in realistic fiction are usually people. They might be teachers, singers, or taxi drivers. The character that the story is about is called the main character. Sometimes there is a group of main characters. Who is the main character in the story on page 439?

Setting

The setting is the time and place of the story. The setting might be a backyard or an airport in China. The setting also includes the time. Realistic fiction takes place in the past or in the present.

Some stories could happen almost anywhere. Other stories need a special setting. A story that happens at a baseball diamond will be different from a story that happens in a jungle. Some characters will fit with one setting but not with another.

Problem

Fiction is interesting when characters have a problem they need to solve. One character might need to learn to do a flying judo kick for a contest. Another might have a noisy pet that bothers the neighbors. Another might be trapped in a snowstorm. What is the main character's problem in the story on page 439?

Readers become interested because they want to see how the character solves the problem. A story about a character walking to school might be boring. But if the character has to get past a bully to get there, then the story gets interesting.

ACTIVITY A Write a sentence describing a realistic character you might find in each of these settings. Be sure to give your character a name.

1. in a cornfield
2. at a swimming pool
3. at a toy store after it is closed
4. in an airplane over Montana
5. at a pond in the woods
6. in a rose garden at sunrise
7. at a parade on Thanksgiving Day
8. in an elevator going to the top of a skyscraper
9. on the soccer field during the championship game
10. in a dunk tank at the school carnival
11. in a bike race
12. at a pet shop

WRITER'S CORNER

Think of a fiction book you have read. Then write four sentences to describe the setting and one character.

Grammar in Action Include one sentence that expresses a strong feeling. Circle all the end punctuation.

Fly Away Home

Everything in the airport is
on the move—passengers,
pilots, flight attendants,
cleaners with their brooms.
Jets roar in, close to the
windows. Other jets roar
out. Luggage bounces down
chutes, escalators glide up
and down, disappearing
under floors. Everyone's going
somewhere except Dad and
me. We stay.

Eve Bunting

Plot

The plot is what happens in a story. It tells
what the characters do to solve a problem.
A plot is the events that happen in the
beginning, middle, and ending of a story.

The beginning of a story tells the
reader about the characters and the
setting. The plot begins when the
characters face a problem that they must
solve. Readers will be interested if they
know what the problem is right away.

The middle tells what the characters
do to solve their problem. The middle can
be one paragraph or many paragraphs. It
can have one event or many events. One
event usually leads to the next.

The ending of the story tells whether the characters solved
their problem. It finishes the story. Sometimes it tells what
happens to the characters after the problem is solved.

ACTIVITY B **Write three sentences telling what might
happen next in these plot descriptions. Choose something that
might happen in realistic fiction.**

1. Austin sees a white monkey loose in the monkey house at the zoo.
   He tells his parents, but they don't see the monkey. Then he sees
   a brown monkey. It peeks its head out from a trash can. He tells a
   zookeeper, but the zookeeper doesn't see the monkey either.

2. Sydney hears a strange machine noise from her neighbor's house
   one night. She goes to her neighbor's yard. A bright light shines in
   the basement. She hears her neighbor whistling in the basement.
   Then the machine noise roars again.

3. All day long the new student stared at Deborah. Once, the student
   tried to get her attention, but Deborah's friend Maria caught her
   attention first. At last the new student found Deborah at the end of
   the school day. "I think this is yours," the student said.

4. As Kyle leaves for school, he notices a big hole that has been dug under the top step to his house. He knows that the hole wasn't there the day before. He is running late, so he doesn't have time to tell his mom about it. Kyle thinks about the hole all day at school. When he gets home, his dog runs out to greet him, but immediately turns around and starts barking at the hole.

ACTIVITY C Answer these questions about the story on page 439.

1. Who are the characters in the story?
2. What is Keenan's problem in the story?
3. How do you know the story is realistic fiction?
4. What are the events in the middle of the plot?

ACTIVITY D Tell which of these you think would make a good problem for a realistic story. Explain your answers.

1. Kelven gets a real dragon for his birthday.
2. Teresa has a treasure map and wants to find the treasure.
3. Fergus is riding a school bus that starts to fly.
4. Jude loses her mother's new cell phone.
5. Michael is trying to win a pie-eating contest.
6. Holly is throwing a surprise birthday party for her mom.
7. Lyle moves away to another town.
8. David finds a lost unicorn in his backyard.
9. Jason's grandfather leaves him a crystal ball that lets him see the future.
10. Elizabeth discovers that she is locked in her school for the night.

Bearded dragon

WRITER'S CORNER

Pick one character you made up for Activity A on page 441. Imagine what that character's life is like. Write three sentences about a problem that character might have to solve.

Characters

In realistic fiction, readers care about the main characters. You can help readers care about your characters by telling what the characters are like.

Appearance

Readers can picture your characters when you tell how they look. Does your character have curly hair or straight hair? Does your character wear smelly, old sneakers or shiny, new boots? Readers like to know how the characters in a story look. Good descriptions can help readers picture the characters more clearly.

Dialogue

Dialogue is what the characters say in a story. Dialogue also tells readers about the characters. A character who is excited talks differently than a character who is nervous. What is Ava's mood in these examples?

> **"Yippee! School is closed today!" Ava shouted.**
>
> **"Oh, no, school is closed today," Ava groaned.**

One line of dialogue shows Ava is happy that school is closed. The other example shows she is sad that school is closed.

ACTIVITY A Think of a character you might like to put in a story. Decide if it is a boy or a girl. Give your character a name. Then write answers for these questions about your character.

1. Where does your character live?
2. What kinds of books does your character read?
3. What is your character's hobby?
4. How old is your character?
5. How does your character dress for school?
6. What is your character's favorite food?
7. What is something your character might say?
8. Who lives with your character?
9. Where does your character like to visit?
10. What three words best describe your character's appearance?

ACTIVITY B Write one sentence each character might say.

1. Mrs. Charles, a school bus driver with loud children on her bus
2. Timeka, a girl who is lost in the woods
3. Hanna, a third grader about to play a piano concert
4. Mr. Conner, a teacher who is surprised with a gift from his class
5. Kasey, a fifth grader about to win a big prize
6. Horace, a firefighter trying to get a cat out of a tree
7. Delia, an older sister who dares her brother to knock on a door
8. Gina, a first grader meeting her baby brother for the first time
9. Mrs. Day, a principal who sees an older student crying by her locker
10. Jay, a boy greeting his dog who has just been sprayed by a skunk

WRITER'S CORNER

Write three sentences that describe the appearance of the character you thought of for Activity A.

Actions

Readers learn about characters from the things they do. Different characters might choose different ways to solve a problem. Suppose that a character needs money for a new comic book. What are some different ways he or she could get the money? What would you think about that character, based on the way he or she got the money?

Characters might also act differently when something happens. Suppose that a boy falls off his bike in front of two characters. One character might walk away. Another character might try to help. What would you think about each of these characters?

Fly Away Home

Once a little brown bird got into the main terminal and couldn't get out. It fluttered in the high, hollow spaces. It threw itself at the glass, fell panting on the floor, flew to a tall, metal girder, and perched there, exhausted.

Eve Bunting

ACTIVITY C **Pick one character from the word box. Then answer the questions about that character.**

police officer	bank robber	librarian

1. Your character is trapped in an elevator with a woman and her young daughter. What does your character say?

2. Your character finds a wallet at the beach. What does your character do?

3. Your character needs money for a new car. How does your character get the money?

4. Your character goes to the video store, but the movie your character wanted isn't there. What does your character do?

5. Your character is asked to give money to help buy new equipment at the local school. What does your character say and give if anything?

ACTIVITY D **Read the story beginning below. Then answer the questions.**

Kari did not want to live at her Aunt Lynn's farm for two months. Kari was a city girl. She was used to cars and buses. She was used to people and noise. She liked having stores she could walk to. Working on a quiet farm was not her idea of a summer vacation.

"You'll love it once you get used to it," Kari's father promised. "My sister and I had a lot of fun growing up there."

Kari packed her jeans and T-shirts in her suitcase. She put her long brown hair in a ponytail and then took one last look around her room. She put on her ripped green jacket with the army patches. Then she slid her sunglasses over her brown eyes. "Let's get this over with," she groaned at the mirror.

Kari reluctantly got into the car with her father. She put her earphones in right away. She crossed her arms over her chest. There was silence in the car for over an hour. "I can come home if I hate it, right?" Kari finally asked.

Her father looked at Kari and smiled. "Give this a little time. You won't hate it," he replied. "You'll see."

1. Who is the main character?

2. What do you know about Kari's appearance?

3. Is there dialogue in the story? Who says it?

4. What lines of dialogue tell you that Kari doesn't want to go to the farm?

5. What actions tell you that Kari is angry about going to the farm?

WRITER'S CORNER

Think about the character you described in the Writer's Corner on page 445. Write four sentences about what that character would do if he or she was going on a long trip.

Dialogue

Dialogue lets readers know the exact words a character says. Which of these is dialogue? Which is more interesting?

Mr. Fielding told the kids to get out of his barn.

"Hey! You get out of my barn right now!" Mr. Fielding shouted.

Using Dialogue

Quotation marks show which words a character said. A dialogue tag tells the reader which character said the words. Can you tell which part of the example sentence above was spoken by a character? Which part is the dialogue tag?

There are three rules to remember when writing dialogue.

- Spoken words have quotation marks before and after the words.
- The first word of each spoken part is capitalized.
- Spoken words are separated from the dialogue tag by a comma. If the dialogue tag comes first, the comma goes after it.

Jared said, "But we lost our ball in your barn!"

If the spoken part comes first, the comma goes after the last word before the quotation marks.

"I guess I'll help you kids find your ball," Mr. Fielding said.

The third rule changes with questions and exclamations. A character's question ends with a question mark, not a comma. An exclamation ends with an exclamation point.

"Do you see it in that horse stall?" Jared asked.

"What a beautiful horse!" Maya exclaimed.

Readers can follow dialogue better if you write a new paragraph for each speaker. Every time a different character speaks, indent the sentence and start it on a new line.

ACTIVITY A Rewrite the sentences. Add the missing quotation marks around the dialogue.

1. Airplanes fly over my house all night long, Jerome said.
2. Julianna asked, Where are my shoes?
3. Karl yelled, Someone just stole my bike!
4. Lexi is short for Alexis, the girl explained.
5. Someone in the audience stood and said, This show stinks!
6. Jeanne says that she is going home after school, said Veronica.

ACTIVITY B Rewrite the sentences. Add the missing quotation marks to the dialogue. Add capital letters where they are needed.

1. Gary said, this book is about a family in Alaska.
2. he is looking out a window at the hospital, she whispered.
3. He stood up and said, let's head for that hill.
4. She asked, what's the big idea?
5. the fishing is great today, the old captain said.
6. Her brother shouted, now this is a party!
7. did you bring your lunch? asked Ashley.
8. Pat cried, she's going to trip over her shoelace!
9. Craig asked, what time is it?
10. Ming whispered, who wants to go first?

WRITER'S CORNER

Write two lines of dialogue you remember from a book or movie. Be sure to use dialogue tags to tell who said each line. Have a partner check that you followed all three rules for writing dialogue.

Tech Tip With an adult, research your book or movie online.

Creative Writing • 449

Fly Away Home

"Don't stop trying," I told [the bird] silently. "Don't! You can get out!"

For days the bird flew around, dragging one wing. And then it found the instant when a sliding door was open and slipped through. I watched it rise. Its wing seemed OK.

"Fly, bird," I whispered. "Fly away home!"

Though I couldn't hear it, I knew it was singing. Nothing made me as happy as that bird.

Eve Bunting

Dialogue Tags

Dialogue tags tell who spoke a line of dialogue. Dialogue tags can also tell how the character spoke the line.

> **"It's just a grass stain," said Maria.**
>
> **"A grass stain doesn't come out!" Tori shouted.**

The dialogue tags *said Maria* and *Tori shouted* tell you who said that dialogue. The second example also tells that Tori shouted when she spoke. Dialogue tags can tell a reader how a character is feeling. Each example below tells a different feeling by using dialogue tags.

> **"This is not mine," Robbie said.**
>
> **"This is not mine," Robbie sobbed.**
>
> **"This is not mine!" Robbie shouted.**
>
> **"This is not mine," Robbie whispered.**

Dialogue tags help readers learn more about the characters. Dialogue tags also keep readers interested in the story. Follow the "just right" rule about using the word *said*. Don't use *said* too many times or too few. If everyone in your story is screaming and shouting and crying, your story won't seem realistic.

ACTIVITY C Rewrite this dialogue, using correct punctuation and capitalization.

Tippy gave her little brother a dirty look. get out of my bedroom she growled.

but I like being in here Malcolm wailed.

Tippy said you are such a pain.

I'll play any game you want Malcolm begged.

Tippy felt sorry for her brother. fine, let's play checkers she said and smiled at him.

ACTIVITY D Rewrite these sentences as dialogue.

EXAMPLE **Silvio said that he was going to be late for soccer practice.**

"I'm going to be late for soccer practice," Silvio said.

1. Mrs. Donovan told her class to stop giggling.
2. The clerk asked the kids not to skate in the store.
3. Jackie asked her friend to come to her party.
4. Marco told his sister to get off his bike.
5. Anamaria said she hates her red shirt.
6. Darcy told her brother she was coming home soon.
7. Bindi said she scraped her knee.
8. Mr. Britt told the dog to get out of his garden.
9. Jill asked the librarian to show her a book.

ACTIVITY E Rewrite each line of dialogue. Make up a character name for each line. Add a dialogue tag to tell how each line is said.

1. "Does this water taste strange?"
2. "I guess we'll just go home early."
3. "That was the best movie I ever saw!"
4. "Our picnic is ruined."
5. "This package is for you and me."
6. "Bedtime is nine o'clock and no later."
7. "Jump in! The water isn't cold at all!"
8. "I can't find my homework!"
9. "May I please go with you?"
10. "Don't put your dirty shoes on the couch!"

WRITER'S CORNER

Imagine that your teacher brought a llama to class. Write three sentences of dialogue your classmates might say.

Grammar in Action. Remember to use commas correctly in direct address. See Section 7.7.

Contractions

A contraction is a short way to write two words. The words are joined into one word with an apostrophe. The apostrophe replaces the letters that are left out.

it + is = it's

The words *it* and *is* are joined to make the contraction *it's*. An apostrophe takes the place of the letter *i*.

do + not = don't

The words *do* and *not* are joined to make the contraction *don't*. Which letter is replaced by the apostrophe?

Look at this contraction.

let's

Which two words are joined to make *let's*? What letter is replaced by the apostrophe?

Here are some contractions with *am, are,* and *is.*

I + am = I'm	**she + is = she's**
you + are = you're	**we + are = we're**
he + is = he's	**they + are = they're**

Here are some contractions with *have.* In these contractions an apostrophe replaces the two letters *h* and *a.*

I + have = I've	**we + have = we've**
you + have = you've	**they + have = they've**

Let's ride that roller coaster!

I'm not sure. It looks scary.

We'll have fun! You'll see.

Contractions make your writing sound more like the way people talk. Contractions can help you write dialogue that sounds real.

ACTIVITY A Write the missing word that makes up each contraction.

1. she + _____ = she's

2. we + have = _____

3. _____ + have = you've

4. I + have = _____

5. _____ + are = they're

6. we + are = _____

7. they + _____ = they've

8. _____ + am = I'm

9. _____ + is = he's

10. you + _____ = you're

ACTIVITY B Answer each riddle in a complete sentence. Use the contractions *I'm*, *we're*, or *she's* in each answer.

1. She sees animals and acrobats. Where is she?

2. I hear the crowd yell, "Home run!" Where am I?

3. We see books, desks, and friends. Where are we?

4. She swims and builds sand castles. Where is she?

5. We see shelves of fruits, vegetables, and cereal boxes. Where are we?

6. I ride roller coasters and bumper cars. Where am I?

WRITER'S CORNER

Pick two contractions from Activity A. Write two sentences. Use one contraction in each sentence.

Grammar in Action. Review the correct use of apostrophes in Section 7.9.

Here are some contractions with *not*.

can't	**don't**	**won't**
couldn't	**shouldn't**	**wouldn't**

The word *won't* is a contraction with *not*. But it is different from the others. The word *won't* is a contraction of *will* and *not*.

Here are some contractions with *will*.

I'll	**she'll**	**he'll**
we'll	**you'll**	**they'll**

ACTIVITY C **Rewrite the sentences. Use contractions to make these sentences sound more like the way people talk.**

1. Is not Jamal at camp this week?
2. Are not all the visitors gone yet?
3. Were not the stones nice and smooth?
4. Is not this a good night for stories?
5. Was not the boat rocking on the waves?
6. You will see lots of stars here.
7. The hikers are not camping in cabins.
8. Some children could not swim.

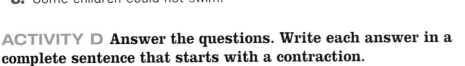

ACTIVITY D **Answer the questions. Write each answer in a complete sentence that starts with a contraction.**

1. He is tall with a long neck and eats leaves from trees. What is he?
2. She is able to jump and carries her baby in a pouch. What is she?
3. They are legless and slither on the ground. What are they?
4. We are furry, eat bananas, and swing through trees. What are we?
5. She is fierce and white and lives near the North Pole. What is she?
6. He is a colorful bird who can talk. What is he?
7. They are using their trunks to spray water in the air. What are they?

ACTIVITY E Match each word group in Column A with its contraction in Column B.

Column A	Column B
1. do not	**a.** we'll
2. I am	**b.** won't
3. we are	**c.** you're
4. we have	**d.** don't
5. they are	**e.** hasn't
6. could not	**f.** I'm
7. has not	**g.** we've
8. we will	**h.** couldn't
9. will not	**i.** they're
10. you are	**j.** we're

LiNK

Fly Away Home

"Will we ever have our own apartment again?" I ask Dad. I'd like it to be the way it was, before Mom died.

"Maybe we will," he says. "If I can find more work. If we can save some money." He rubs my head. "It's nice right here, though, isn't it, Andrew? It's warm. It's safe. And the price is right."

But I know he's trying all the time to find us a place.

Eve Bunting

ACTIVITY F Identify the two words in each sentence that can form a contraction. Then tell the contraction they form.

1. Kati will not climb the tree in her backyard.
2. "I am afraid," she said.
3. Whiskers, her cat, should not climb the tree.
4. "Do not go near that tree!" Kati tells Whiskers.
5. However, Whiskers could not resist chasing the squirrel up the tree.
6. Kati did not see Whiskers at first.
7. Then she would not let Whiskers be alone in the tree.
8. "I guess we will just climb this tree together," laughed Kati.

WRITER'S CORNER

Look at the story on page 439. Copy one sentence of dialogue that uses a contraction. What are the words that make up the contraction you found? Rewrite the sentence, using the two words instead of the contractions. Read both sentences aloud. Can you hear the difference?

Lines That Rhyme

Poetry is writing that expresses feelings or ideas in a special way. Poets use the sounds of words to create feelings in the reader. Do you have a favorite poem? Why do you like it?

Rhyme

Many poems rhyme. Words that rhyme start with different sounds but end with the same sound. Look at the example below.

share	*rhymes with*	hair
		care
		stare
		bear
		wear
		tear

Can you think of other words that rhyme with *share*?

Poets make patterns of rhyme in their poems. One way is to have the last word of each line rhyme with the last word of another line. Read this poem by Rachel Field.

In the morning very early,
That's the time I love to go
Barefoot where the fern grows curly
And grass is cool between each toe.

In this poem every other line rhymes.

ACTIVITY A Match each word in Column A to its rhyming word in Column B.

Column A	Column B
1. creep	**a.** bed
2. hop	**b.** guest
3. care	**c.** stalk
4. walk	**d.** leap
5. said	**e.** wiggle
6. jiggle	**f.** share
7. test	**g.** plop

ACTIVITY B Complete each sentence with a word that rhymes with the underlined word in the sentence above.

1. Peacocks squawk.
Parrots _____.

2. Panthers hunt.
Piglets _____.

3. Gerbils wiggle.
Kids _____.

4. Tigers roar.
Eagles _____.

5. Toddlers fall.
Babies _____.

6. Lions track.
Ducks _____.

7. Monkeys swing.
Canaries _____.

WRITER'S CORNER

Look at Activity B. Think of other ways that animals move and act. Write two rhyming words that compare the animals.

Rhyming Couplets

A rhyming couplet is two lines of a poem that rhyme at the end. Read the poem below.

Late for Dinner

Ms. Seal was late, tripped on her shoelace.

Mr. Seal ate, kept stuffing his face.

There was nothing left of the famous fish bake.

But Ms. Seal ate sea scallop dessert cake.

In "Late for Dinner," the last words of the first two lines rhyme. The word *shoelace* rhymes with *face*. These lines together are a rhyming couplet. This poem has two rhyming couplets. What rhyming words are used in the second rhyming couplet?

ACTIVITY C Complete each rhyming couplet. Choose a word from the word box that rhymes with each underlined word.

> book   hill   tree   dad

1. A duck with an orange <u>bill</u>
   Came running over the _____.

2. In the yard the big oak _____
   Provides a lot of shade for <u>me</u>.

3. In the doorway stood my _____
   Uh-oh, he looks very <u>mad</u>!

4. While fishing in the leafy <u>brook</u>
   My brother found a golden _____.

ACTIVITY D The following lines of poetry are mixed up. Match each line to its rhyme to form three pairs of rhyming couplets.

Last night I had a wonderful dream,

My little brother is a pest.

Time to clean, I guess!

It's because he knows that I'm the best.

of chocolate cake and vanilla ice cream.

My bedroom is quite a mess.

ACTIVITY E Choose three of the following word pairs. Then write rhyming couplets using each word pair.

wonder/thunder	bark/shark
taste/paste	ditch/pitch
drum/plum	broken/spoken
dwell/shell	win/spin
candle/handle	sail/pail
doubt/shout	sour/power

ACTIVITY F Write a rhyming couplet about each of these subjects.

1. A farmer
2. A hairdresser
3. A veterinarian
4. A firefighter
5. A mail carrier
6. A dog groomer

WRITER'S CORNER

Write a poem that uses three rhyming couplets. The poem might be about how you feel. It might be about something that you like or someone that you care about.

Tech Tip With an adult, search for rhyming words online.

Skits

A skit is a story acted out in front of
an audience. A skit has characters, a
problem, and a plot. A skit also has
dialogue. The audience watches the
actors in the skit. The actors move and
talk as the characters would. The audience
watches the skit to find out what happens.

Characters and Problems

A skit is mostly dialogue. Each character talks in a
different way. If you think about your characters
first, it will be easier to write dialogue for them.

Decide which characters you want in your skit.
Then write notes about your characters.

- Write the characters' names.
- Draw or write what the characters look like.
- Write how the characters act.

When you know the characters, you can think
about a problem for the skit. What kind of trouble
can these characters get into? Sometimes the problem can
be between the characters. Sometimes it can be a problem the
characters have to work together to solve.

You might have an idea for a story's problem before you have
an idea for the characters. Think about the problem for your
story. What kind of characters might have that problem? Then
write notes about your characters.

Plot

The plot is what happens in a skit. The beginning of the skit tells the audience what the problem is. The middle tells what the characters do to solve their problem. In skits the characters talk to one another about their problems. The listeners can hear about the problems and become interested in the story.

Sometimes the characters talk about what is happening in the skit. For example, if the characters are going into a spooky cave, they might talk about how spooky the cave is. The characters can also crawl or bend the way they would in a cave. Using your imagination, you can make your characters go anywhere.

The ending will show how the characters solve their problem. Write dialogue that lets them talk about what happened. When you have finished your skit, take a bow!

ACTIVITY A **Read these character notes. Write a problem this character might have in a skit.**

Name: Cuba Delmore

Appearance: Cuba is tall. He has short black hair. His eyes are brown. He wears a red cap when it is cold. His white shoes are clean. His favorite shirt is blue and gray with black buttons. At school he always wears a big silver watch his sister gave him.

What the character is like: Cuba is clumsy. He trips on things a lot. When he trips, his face turns red. If he falls on someone, he always says he is sorry. He is a good student. He plays the piano. His favorite game is chess.

SPEAKER'S CORNER

Look at the problem you wrote for Cuba in Activity A. Write three lines of dialogue that you think Cuba might say in a skit.

Writing a Skit

Skits are written for the actors to read. The written skit will help the actors know what to say and do when they perform. Dialogue for a skit is written differently than in a story. It looks like this.

Cuba: Hey guys, look at this caterpillar!

Martha: That's gross, Cuba.

Cuba: It's orange and fat. Boy, is it climbing fast!

Write the name of the character who is speaking. Put a colon after the name. Then write what the character says.

Read your plot and character notes before you write dialogue for your characters. Be sure that the dialogue tells the audience what is happening in the skit.

Rehearse

When actors rehearse, they practice the skit together. Practice your skit. Try saying lines in different ways. Talk about what kinds of gestures and actions the characters might use. In the example above, Cuba might point at the caterpillar. He might wrinkle his nose, or he might do both.

When you decide how the characters will act, rehearse a few times. Try different ways of doing the skit. You might want to have a friend watch your skit before you perform for an audience. Your friend can tell you if something is confusing in the skit.

Think about costumes you might use. What would your characters wear? You can also use props. A book, a phone, or a chair could all be props. Using these props will make your skit more interesting.

Listening Tips

Skits can be fun to watch. You can see people become the characters in the skit. You can imagine where the characters are. You can see how they solve their problems. Here are some tips for watching a skit.

- Do not talk during the skit.
- Think about whether the story could really happen. Would you act the way the characters do?
- Laugh at the funny parts. But don't laugh if someone makes a mistake. Think about how you would feel if people laughed at your mistakes.
- When the skit is over, clap to show that you enjoyed it.

ACTIVITY B Find five lines of dialogue in a book. Write the dialogue as a skit. Write the names of the characters at the top. Describe the characters. Then write their dialogue like the example on page 462. Practice reading your dialogue with a partner.

ACTIVITY C Imagine you got a package in the mail. You open the package. The thing inside makes you feel mad, scared, happy, or amazed. Pick one feeling. Without using words, act out opening the package for a partner. Use gestures and actions only. See if your partner can guess how you felt when you opened the package.

SPEAKER'S CORNER

Work in small groups. Make up characters for each member of your group. Write dialogue for all the characters. Then perform your skit for the class.

Record or videotape your rehearsal for review.

Prewriting and Drafting

Have you ever read a story or seen a movie about kids like you? Did you think the characters could be real? Were you interested in what happened to the characters? Realistic fiction has characters, settings, and plots that could be real, even though they are not.

Prewriting

Before writing realistic fiction, many writers brainstorm ideas. When writers brainstorm, they jot down ideas about the characters, the setting, and the plot. A good way to start brainstorming is to ask, what if? Did you ever wonder, What if *this* happened? For example, what if a lion got loose in a big city?

Brainstorming

Riley is a third grader. Her grandmother likes hearing the stories that Riley writes.

 **Ideas** Riley wanted to write a new story for her grandmother. She began by brainstorming a list of characters. When she had finished, she read her list. She liked the name Lauren, so she decided that her main character would be a girl named Lauren.

Next, Riley brainstormed ideas for a plot. She had many ideas, but one interested her more than the others. She asked herself, What if Lauren had a little brother who gave her a problem? Riley thought more about what kind of problem Lauren's brother could give her. She decided that Lauren would fight with her brother over a clubhouse. That would be a good problem for her character to solve.

Your Turn

Take some time to brainstorm ideas. Start by listing possible characters, settings, and problems. If you get stuck, you can ask yourself the following questions:

- What setting would be fun to write about? A big city? A small town? A desert? An island? Which setting might lead to an interesting character or problem?
- What characters would be fun to write about? Are any of the characters like you? Are any like your best friend? What is special about these characters?
- What will happen in the story? What is the problem that must be solved?

Prewriting

Drafting

Content Editing

Revising

Copyediting

Proofreading

Publishing

Planning the Story

Riley thought she had some good ideas.

 Organization She decided to plan her story. She added more about the setting, the plot, and each character. Here is Riley's plan.

Setting: In Lauren's backyard. The clubhouse is under a tree.

Characters:
Lauren—smart, 8 years old, long red hair, green eyes, freckles
Caleb—Lauren's brother, crafty, 6 years old, short red hair, brown eyes
Cady—Lauren's best friend, helpful, 8 years old, dark hair, glasses

Problem: Caleb takes over Lauren's clubhouse.

Plot:
1. Lauren and her dad build the clubhouse.
2. Caleb takes over Lauren's clubhouse.
3. Lauren and Cady make the clubhouse seem like a giant spider lives inside
4. Caleb gets scared and runs from the clubhouse.

Ending: Lauren's trick works. Caleb never goes back to the clubhouse.

Your Turn

- Make a plan like Riley's. Write about the setting and what it looks like. Then list the characters and write about each one. You might give their ages and describe their appearance.

- Write some things that might happen in the story. What do the characters do to solve their problems?

- Finally, describe the ending. What happens after the characters solve their problems?

Writer's Tip It is OK if your ideas change as you plan your story. Change the setting if it seems dull. Add or take out characters if it makes the story better.

Drafting

Riley used her plan to write her first draft. As she wrote, she thought of new details and ideas to include. Riley used colorful words like *huge*, *ugly*, and *fuzzy*.

👀 Word Choice

She decided to leave some ideas from her plan out of her story. Here is Riley's first draft.

The Clubhouse

Lauren and her dad built a clubhouse. Lauren was eight years old. She had red hair and green eyes. She had freckles. Lauren's clubhouse would be a place where she could hang out with her friends. She could also get away from her little brother, Caleb.

But the day Lauren was ready to move in, there was a problem Caleb had already moved his stuff into the clubhouse.

Lauren told her best friend, Cady, that she was angry at Caleb.

Lauren had a plan. Caleb was afraid of spiders. So one day Lauren and Cady sat under the tree in the backyard. They knew that Caleb could hear them. Lauren told Cady that a huge, ugly spider lived in the clubhouse. Lauren explained that the spider had spun a web in the corner of the clubhouse. It had big, fuzzy legs and ate anything that came near it.

Lauren knew that Caleb heard every word. Lauren and Cady waited

Prewriting

Drafting

Content Editing

Revising

Copyediting

Proofreading

Publishing

until dark. Then they hid under the window of the clubhouse. They waited until Caleb went inside the clubhouse. Then Lauren sprayed silly string through the window at the back of Caleb's neck. A moment later Caleb ran out of the clubhouse, shouting that there was a giant spider inside.

Lauren finally had the clubhouse all to herself.

Your Turn

- Use your plan to help write your first draft.
- Add details as you write. Give more information about the characters and the setting.
- Include dialogue to bring your characters to life.
- Be sure that the events in your story make sense. Time order can help you be sure one event leads to the next.
- Use colorful words in your descriptions to make your story more interesting.

Something's Not Right

Sometimes you can make a story interesting by making something not right. You can put things together that don't seem to belong together.

You probably wouldn't find a soccer coach lost in a desert. But that could be an interesting beginning for a story. The reader would want to know how the soccer coach got there. The reader will want to know how the soccer coach is going to get out.

You can make something not right with a character too. You can describe a character wearing a dirty, ripped jacket and no shoes. Then you can tell that he's really a millionaire. Why is he dressed like that? The reader will

 Voice

want to know. If you are excited about your characters and story, it will come through for your readers.

Editor's Workshop

Content Editing

Riley was happy with her story. She liked writing about Lauren. She also liked how Lauren solved her problem.

Riley knew that she could make her story better. The day after she wrote her draft, she read her story again. She read it aloud to hear how it sounded. Then she used this Content Editor's Checklist to edit her draft.

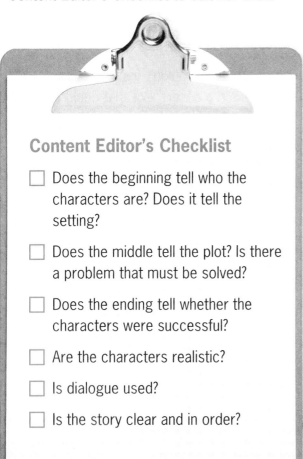

Content Editor's Checklist

☐ Does the beginning tell who the characters are? Does it tell the setting?

☐ Does the middle tell the plot? Is there a problem that must be solved?

☐ Does the ending tell whether the characters were successful?

☐ Are the characters realistic?

☐ Is dialogue used?

☐ Is the story clear and in order?

Using the checklist, Riley wrote ways she might improve her draft. But she knew that a different reader could help her with content editing. She decided to take her draft to the writing center at school. High school students there helped younger kids with reading and writing. Evan, one of the high school students, offered to content edit Riley's story.

Evan read Riley's story a few times. First, he wrote things he liked about the story. He used the checklist and wrote his suggestions. Then he and Riley talked about her draft.

Evan really liked the story. He told Riley that Lauren's problem got him interested. He also liked Lauren's trick to get Caleb out of the clubhouse. Evan thought that the characters were realistic. He told Riley that the order of the story was clear. Then he shared the following comments with Riley.

- You don't need a description of what Lauren looks like. You tell the reader a lot about her through what she does.

- Where is this story set? You don't say in the beginning.

- In the middle you say that Lauren and Cady sit under the tree. Where was Caleb? How do they know that Caleb can hear them?
- Maybe you should add a description of Cady.
- The ending tells whether Lauren is successful. But maybe you could add something about Caleb. Readers might wonder whether he goes back to the clubhouse again.
- You don't have any dialogue. Dialogue might help readers learn more about the characters. Dialogue can make the story seem more real.

Riley thanked Evan for his help. Then Riley went through her story again to decide which of Evan's suggestions she would use.

Your Turn

- Read your draft again. Make sure that all the parts of realistic fiction are included. Then see if there are other ways you might improve your draft.
- Trade drafts with a classmate. Use the checklist to make suggestions about your partner's draft. Remember to write some things that you like about the story. Then take turns talking about your stories with your partner.
- Think about your partner's comments. Use the ideas that you think will make your draft better.

Prewriting

Drafting

Content Editing

Revising

Copyediting

Proofreading

Publishing

Revising

Read Riley's revised draft. Notice how she marked her changes.

Creepy-Crawly

The ^ Clubhouse

in the backyard

Lauren and her dad built a clubhouse. ~~Lauren was eight years old. She had red hair and green eyes. She had freckles.~~ Lauren's clubhouse would be a place where she could hang out with her friends. She could also get away from her little brother, Caleb.

But the day Lauren was ready to move in, there was a problem Caleb had already moved his stuff into the clubhouse.

"He did'nt even help build it! And now he thinks it's his."

^ Lauren told her best friend, Cady, ~~that she was angry at Caleb.~~

Lauren had a plan. Caleb was afraid of spiders. So one day Lauren and

Caleb was in the clubhouse.

Cady sat under the tree in the backyard. ^ They knew that Caleb could hear

Lauren said, "Cady, I'm scared of the huge spider in the clubhouse."

them. ~~Lauren told Cady that a huge, ugly spider lived in the clubhouse.~~

"I did see a large spider web in the corner," Cady said. Lauren said, "yes, it has big,

~~Lauren explained that the spider had spun a web in the corner of the~~

fuzzy legs and it eats anything that comes near it."

~~clubhouse. It had big, fuzzy legs and ate anything that came near it.~~

Lauren knew that Caleb heard every word. Lauren and Cady waited

Prewriting

Drafting

Content Editing

Revising

Copyediting

Proofreading

Publishing

until dark. Then they hid under the window of the clubhouse. They waited

until Caleb went inside the clubhouse. Then Lauren sprayed silly string

through the window at the back of Caleb's neck. A moment later Caleb ran

out of the clubhouse, shouting that there was a giant spider inside.

Caleb never went near the clubhouse again.

ᴧLauren finally had the clubhouse all to herself.

Riley used a lot of Evan's ideas. She also found some other ways to make her story better. Here is what Riley did.

- Riley took out the description of what Lauren looks like. Why?
- She added information about the setting. What did she write?
- What information about Caleb did Riley add to the fourth paragraph? Why do you think she did this?
- Riley decided not to add a description of Cady. A description of Cady would not add anything to the story. Do you agree or disagree? Why?
- Riley added a sentence about Caleb to the ending. What did she add? Why?
- What dialogue did Riley add to the story? Do you like what she added? Why?
- Riley changed the title of her story. What is the new title? Do you like it better than the old title? Why or why not?

Your Turn

- Think about your content editor's ideas. Choose the ideas that you think will make your story better.
- Mark the changes neatly on your draft.
- When you have finished, read your draft again.
- Check your draft against the Content Editor's Checklist. Can you answer yes to each question?

Copyediting and Proofreading

Copyediting

Riley thought that her story was better because of her revisions. She especially liked the dialogue that she added.

Now Riley wanted to make sure that the sentences were clear and correct. Riley read her story aloud.

Sentence Fluency

Reading aloud would help her hear places in the story that sounded choppy. As she read aloud, she heard that she used Lauren's name a lot. She changed *Lauren* to *she* in one place. Then she read her story, using the Copyeditor's Checklist.

Riley saw that she should have capitalized *yes* when Lauren spoke back. She also remembered that she should have put Lauren's and Cady's dialogue into separate paragraphs when she revised.

Copyeditor's Checklist

☐ Does the dialogue include correct capitalization and punctuation? Is each speaker's dialogue in a separate paragraph?

☐ Are contractions used correctly?

☐ Are all the sentences complete?

☐ Does the order of the sentences make sense?

☐ Do all the words mean what you think they mean?

Your Turn

- Read your draft again, using the Copyeditor's Checklist.
- Make sure that you can answer yes to each question on the checklist.

Writer's Tip Read your story aloud as you copyedit.

Proofreading

Riley had worked hard on her story. Content editing and copyediting had made the story much better. Now Riley had to do proofreading.

Riley knew that a new reader would catch mistakes that she might have missed. So she asked her best friend, Olivia, to proofread her draft. Olivia was good at spelling and grammar. Plus she liked to read Riley's stories. Olivia used this Proofreader's Checklist as she read Riley's story.

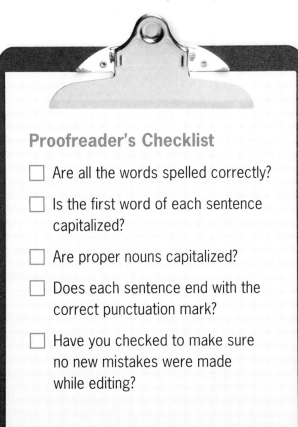

Conventions

Proofreader's Checklist

- [ ] Are all the words spelled correctly?
- [ ] Is the first word of each sentence capitalized?
- [ ] Are proper nouns capitalized?
- [ ] Does each sentence end with the correct punctuation mark?
- [ ] Have you checked to make sure no new mistakes were made while editing?

Olivia read Riley's story several times. She found one contraction spelled incorrectly. Can you find it and correct it?

Your Turn

Read your draft and answer the questions on the Proofreader's Checklist. Remember to check for mistakes that you may have added as you revised your draft.

Next, trade drafts with a partner. Proofread each other's stories. Use the Proofreader's Checklist and answer the questions about your partner's draft. Then talk to your partner about what you found.

Grammar in Action

Riley forgot to add end punctuation to one of her sentences. Find it and fix it.

Publishing

After all her hard work, Riley was excited to publish her story. She printed out her story. Then she mailed it to her grandmother. Her grandmother thought it was great! Here is Riley's final copy.

The Creepy-Crawly Clubhouse

Lauren and her dad built a clubhouse in the backyard. Lauren's clubhouse would be a place where she could hang out with her friends. She could also get away from her little brother, Caleb.

But the day Lauren was ready to move in, there was a problem. Caleb had already moved his stuff into the clubhouse.

"He didn't even help build it! And now he thinks it's his," Lauren told her best friend, Cady.

Lauren had a plan. Caleb was afraid of spiders. So one day Lauren and Cady sat under the tree in the backyard. Caleb was in the clubhouse. They knew that Caleb could hear them.

Lauren said, "Cady, I'm scared of the huge spider in the clubhouse."

"I did see a large spider web in the corner," Cady said.

Lauren said, "Yes, it has big, fuzzy legs and eats anything that comes near it."

Lauren knew that Caleb heard every word. Lauren and Cady waited until dark. Then they hid under the window of the clubhouse. They waited until Caleb went inside the clubhouse. Then Lauren sprayed silly string through the window at the back of Caleb's neck. A moment later Caleb ran out of the clubhouse, shouting that there was a giant spider inside.

Caleb never went near the clubhouse again. Lauren finally had the clubhouse all to herself.

Whenever you publish your work, your goal is

 Presentation to share your thoughts and experiences with other people. There are many ways you can publish your story.

 Create a book. Decorate the margins with small pictures that illustrate the story. You might choose to print the title and your name on a separate cover page and illustrate it with a scene from your story.

 Film it. Ask friends to take parts and paint scenery. Add music. Do the narration as you film it.

 Ask your school librarian if the book you created could be a checkout book for a limited time.

 Create a classroom "Realistic Fiction" banner decorated with pictures of characters from the stories. Display the stories below the banner.

Your Turn

- Read your story one more time. If you typed your story on a computer, use the spell-checker to look for spelling mistakes. Make sure you have not added new mistakes as you revised.

- Check your title again. Does it still fit the story? If not, revise it.

- Use your best handwriting or a computer to make a final copy of your story.

- If you liked writing this story, think about writing more on your own. There are a lot of characters just waiting for you to tell their stories!

Prewriting
Drafting
Content Editing
Revising
Copyediting
Proofreading
Publishing

Lauren's Creepy-Crawly Clubhouse

Research Reports

LiNK

Mountains

by Seymour Simon

Mountain ranges do not arise just anyplace. Most are formed when *plates,* giant pieces of the earth's crust, push and pull against each other. The United States, Canada, Mexico, and part of the North Atlantic Ocean are on the North American plate. The Rockies and the coast ranges of the western United States and Canada were formed where the North American plate pushed against the Pacific plate.

The Mid-Atlantic Ridge, a 12,000-mile-long underwater mountain chain that stretches the length of the Atlantic Ocean, was formed where the North American plate pulled away from the Eurasian plate and the African plate. The islands of Iceland and Surtsey are actually the tops of volcanic mountain peaks reaching above the surface of the ocean, which covers most of the Mid-Atlantic Ridge.

> The book *Mountains* has many characteristics of a research report. It contains facts from reliable sources and is written in an organized way.

The Callimico Monkey

by Hector Regalado

If you are traveling in the rain forests of South America, be sure to look up at the trees. You might hear the sounds of Callimico monkeys talking to one another. *Callimico* means "beautiful little monkey." These small, lovable monkeys are fascinating creatures that live in groups and are omnivores.

Callimicos are found in the rain forests of Peru, Ecuador, Brazil, Colombia, and Bolivia. They live in groups of about six family members. Each group usually has one male, some females, and their babies. All the monkeys in the group stay close together. They are always within 50 feet of one another. Some scientists believe they do this for protection. The rain forest can be a dangerous place for small animals, and there's safety in numbers.

A Callimico weighs just two ounces at birth, which is small enough to fit in your hand. Mothers care for babies for the first few weeks. Later, other monkeys in the group help with baby care. Under the care of the group, Callimicos can grow to a weight of about one pound.

An adult Callimico is about nine inches tall, and its tail grows to about 12 inches long. Callimicos have thick, soft fur and a short mane on top of their heads. Callimicos are omnivorous. This means they eat both plants and animals. Callimicos mostly eat insects, but they also eat fruit, tree gum, and sap. They have also been known to eat snakes.

Callimicos are beautiful and interesting animals. Our own human families can learn more about these beautiful little families of monkeys by visiting them at the zoo.

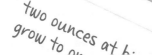
two ounces at b:
grow to a

477

What Makes a Good Research Report?

A research report is a kind of writing that gives facts about one topic. A research report uses formal language.

Topic

Choose a topic that you can find facts about in a library. Your topic should be narrow enough to cover in one or two pages. The topic "sea animals" is too broad. The topic "bottle-nosed dolphins" is better.

Introduction

The introduction of the report should grab the reader's attention and tell about the topic. The topic is stated in a topic sentence. In the report on page 477, the topic sentence comes at the end of the first paragraph.

Body

The body of a research report gives details about the topic. The information comes from different sources. Details that are alike are grouped together in paragraphs.

Conclusion

The conclusion is at the end of the report. The conclusion sums up the information in the report. The conclusion also contains a comment about the topic.

Research

When writers do research, they first gather information from different sources. A source is any book, magazine, newspaper, encyclopedia, or Web site in which you can find information for your report.

After writers do research, they organize the facts and write them in their own words. Writing facts in your own words shows that you understand what you are reading.

ACTIVITY A Decide whether each idea below makes a good topic for a research report. Explain your answers.

1. my trip to the museum
2. the history of Europe
3. coral reefs
4. John Quincy Adams
5. mammals
6. the cotton plant
7. the invention of the airplane
8. the future of space travel
9. the parts of the eye
10. my favorite band's latest album

LiNK

Magnets

A magnet works because of a natural force called magnetism. Magnetism is a force that you cannot see. . . . The force of magnetism pushes and pulls, causing a magnet to pull some metal objects. . . . Magnets also can push or pull other magnets. Each magnet has a magnetic field around it. This is the area where the force of magnetism can affect objects.

Jason Cooper

WRITER'S CORNER

Write two facts that you know about the weather. Be sure to write complete sentences.

Grammar in Action. After you write your weather facts, underline the subjects and circle the predicates.

ACTIVITY B Read each research topic below. Choose the best topic sentence for a report about that topic.

1. **whitetail deer**
   a. Whitetail deer are well-known, large mammals in North America.
   b. I like deer, especially the whitetail deer.
   c. Bambi is the cutest whitetail deer.

2. **red pandas**
   a. I have a stuffed panda at home.
   b. Red pandas are shy animals that live in Nepal, Burma, and central China.
   c. There is a really good documentary about red pandas that everyone should watch.

3. **orcas**
   a. Orcas are warm-blooded mammals and one of the largest members of the dolphin family.
   b. Shamu is an orca.
   c. We had to do a report about animals, so I chose orcas.

4. **cairn terriers**
   a. Cairn terriers are dogs.
   b. I saw a cairn terrier at the park the other day and decided I want one.
   c. Cairn terriers are courageous and smart dogs that make great companions.

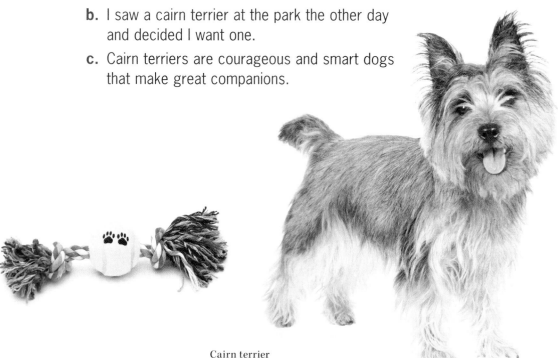

Cairn terrier

ACTIVITY C Choose the best ending sentence that would be in a conclusion about each topic below. Tell why you chose that sentence.

1. **whitetail deer**
   a. Whitetail deer change colors in the fall.
   b. Whitetail deer can run very fast.
   c. Watch for these beautiful creatures in a field near you.

2. **red pandas**
   a. The red panda is a beautiful creature, and we should all do our part to save it.
   b. Red pandas live in forests and mountains.
   c. I really want to see a red panda.

3. **orcas**
   a. Orcas have teeth like sharp cones.
   b. Orcas are one of the most majestic creatures in the sea.
   c. Orcas are not fish, but are large mammals.

4. **cairn terriers**
   a. Cairn terriers are funny and furry.
   b. Now that I know so much about them, I want a cairn terrier as a pet.
   c. Cairn terriers are lovable creatures.

Red panda

WRITER'S CORNER

Write the name of a country that you would like to know more about. List three questions that you might research about that country.

Tech Tip With an adult, research your country online.

Facts and Notes

After choosing a topic for your research report, you will need to find information about it. Your classroom and your school library are good places to start. If you need more information, go to your local library and do research on the Internet.

Finding Facts

Nonfiction Books

Nonfiction books are about real people, things, and events. Nonfiction books are usually about one topic. For example, a book about tigers would probably cover all the different kinds of tigers. It would discuss where tigers live, what they eat, and how they act toward one another.

Encyclopedias

Encyclopedias contain information about many different topics. For example, there would be an entry for "Tiger." The information would probably be more general than what you would find in a book about tigers.

Magazines

Magazine articles usually have the latest information about a topic. For example, a magazine article about tigers might tell about new ideas that scientists have about what tigers eat. Or the article might tell about new places in the wild where tigers have been seen.

Internet

You can search the Internet to find information about your topic. If you don't know how to use a computer, ask the librarian for help.

Be careful when choosing Web sites to use in your research. Not all the information on the Internet is correct. Look for sites written by experts or organizations. A site written by another student might not have the best facts. Ask an adult if you are not sure whether a Web site is reliable.

Be sure to tell your teacher or parents if you are doing research on the Internet. Never give information about yourself without first asking your teacher or parents.

ACTIVITY A **Read each topic. Choose which two sources would have good information for a research report about that topic. Then tell why the third source would not have good information.**

1. Los Angeles, California
    a. an encyclopedia, volume *C*
    b. the book *American Cities Travel Guide*
    c. *Surfer* magazine

2. tarantula
    a. the movie *Spiders from Mars*
    b. the Web site www.spiders.edu
    c. the book *The Life of Spiders*

3. the sun
    a. the book *Solar Flares Explained*
    b. the magazine *Astronomy Today*
    c. a student's Web site about the sun

WRITER'S CORNER

With an adult find information on the Internet about one of the planets. Write three Web site addresses that contain information about that planet. Then write one fact from each site.

Taking Notes

As you find facts in your sources, write them on note cards. Use your own words to write your notes. Write one fact on each note card. Also write the title of the source, the page number, and the author. Think about the information you are reading.

A note card might look like this.

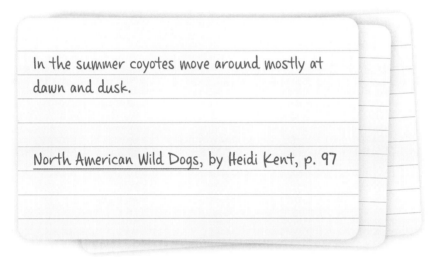

In the summer coyotes move around mostly at dawn and dusk.

North American Wild Dogs, by Heidi Kent, p. 97

Organizing Notes

After you have taken notes from your sources, you should put them in order. One way to organize your note cards is to put them into piles.

Suppose the topic of your report is the mongoose. You might want to make three separate piles of note cards. The first pile could be about what the mongoose looks like. The second pile could tell where it lives. The third pile could describe what the mongoose eats.

ACTIVITY B **Choose an animal that interests you. Use an encyclopedia to find out one fact about the animal. Write the fact on a note card in your own words. Write the name, the volume, and the page number of the encyclopedia.**

ACTIVITY C Look in two nonfiction books to find information about the animal that you chose in Activity B. Write three facts on separate note cards. Find facts about what your animal looks like, where it lives, and what it eats. Write on the note card the source for each fact.

ACTIVITY D Go to one of the Web sites below to find facts about the animal that you chose in Activity B. Make note cards about what your animal looks like, where it lives, and what it eats. For each fact write the Web site address you used as the source.

Phoenix Zoo
www.phoenixzoo.org

Kids' Planet ESPECIES Animal Fact Sheets
www.kidsplanet.org

SeaWorld/Busch Gardens
www.seaworld.org

Western North Carolina Nature Center
www.wildwnc.org

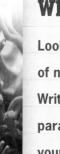

ACTIVITY E Gather all the note cards that you wrote. Arrange them into three piles: what your animal looks like, where it lives, and what it eats.

Crested gecko

Maroon clown fish and anemone

WRITER'S CORNER

Look over one of your piles of note cards from Activity E. Write a five-sentence paragraph using the facts in your notes.

Library Skills

How Libraries Are Organized

Finding useful information is a big part of writing a research report. Your school library and local library are good places to look for information.

Knowing how libraries are organized can help you find the information you need. Libraries separate fiction books from nonfiction books.

Fiction Books

Fiction books are organized alphabetically by the last name of the author.

Nonfiction Books

Nonfiction books are organized by subject, or what they are about. For example, books about whales can usually be found together in the same area of the library.

Reference Books

Reference books help you find information about different people, places, things, and events. Dictionaries, encyclopedias, and atlases are kinds of reference books.

Searching for Books

When searching for a book in a library, the first place to look is the library catalog. The library catalog is a complete list of all the books in a certain library or a group of libraries. The library catalog tells you exactly where to find the books you need. There are three ways that you can search for books in a library: by the title, by the author's name, and by the subject.

ACTIVITY A **Tell whether each book is a fiction book, a nonfiction book, or a reference book.**

1. *Trees of North America*
2. *World Book*
3. *The Mousewife*
4. *The Civil War*
5. *Encyclopaedia Britannica*
6. *Prehistoric Animals*
7. *The Adventures of Liam Leprechaun*
8. *Webster's New World Student's Dictionary*
9. *The Life and Times of George Washington*
10. *Atlas of the World*
11. *Mr. and Mrs. Moonbeam*
12. *The Planets*

ACTIVITY B **Read the book cover below. Then answer the questions.**

1. What is the title of the book?
2. Who is the author of the book?
3. What is the subject of the book?

WRITER'S CORNER

Go to the library with a partner and find the following: two fiction books, two nonfiction books, and two reference books. Write all six titles.

Electronic Catalogs

Although card catalogs are still used in some libraries, most libraries have electronic catalogs. You use a computer to search for books on electronic catalogs.

You usually start your search by typing a title, an author, or a subject into a search box. For a research report, type your topic into the box. Then click on a menu to tell the computer that you are looking for a subject. Press "Enter" or "Return" on the keyboard or click the button on the screen that starts the search.

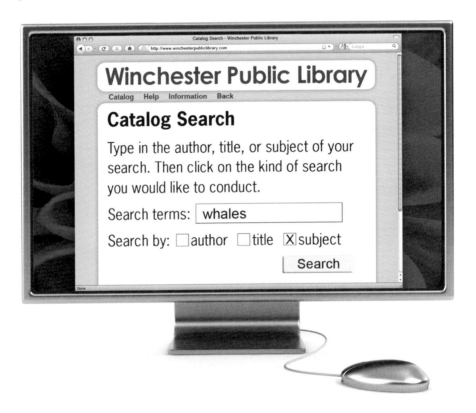

The computer will look for books about your topic and list them on the screen. Sometimes you may have to click on a book title to get more information about it. The screen will show the book's title, its author, and its call number. Sometimes electronic catalogs include a brief description of the book.

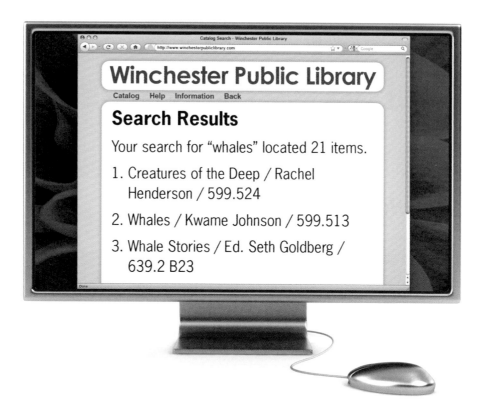

Call Numbers

Every nonfiction book has a call number. The call number is like an address. It tells where the book can be found. Use the call number to find the books that you need.

Write the call numbers, authors, and titles of the books you want. Ask the librarian to help you find the books.

ACTIVITY C Choose three of the following topics. Use a library catalog to find one book about each topic. If you need help, ask a librarian.

outer space	Native Americans
American Revolution	glaciers
dinosaurs	whales
tornadoes	China

WRITER'S CORNER

Look at the books you found for Activity C. Write each book's title, the author's name, and the book's call number. Then write two facts from each book.

Revising Sentences

When you revise a sentence, you change words and combine ideas to improve your writing.

Exact Words

One way to make your sentences more interesting is to use exact words. Read the following sentences. Notice how the sentence becomes more interesting with a few changes.

The horse ran home.

1. Change to tell what kind of horse.

   The mare ran home.
   The pinto ran home.

2. Change to tell how the horse ran.

   The mare galloped home.
   The pinto trotted home.

3. Change to describe where the horse ran.

   The mare galloped into the corral.
   The pinto trotted into its stall.

4. Use colorful adjectives and adverbs.

   The runaway mare galloped into the muddy corral.
   The shivering pinto gladly trotted into its cozy stall.

In each example the writer used exact nouns, stronger verbs, and colorful adjectives and adverbs to revise the sentence.

ACTIVITY A Read the following sentences. The first sentence is the original sentence. The second is the revised sentence. Tell what the writer did to revise each sentence.

EXAMPLE **The third graders put on a show.**

The hardworking third graders put on a dazzling talent show.

used colorful adjectives

1. We saw many trees.

   We gazed at many redwoods.

2. Our family rode a train through a redwood forest.

   Our family rode an old, rickety train through a redwood forest.

3. Our guide said that some trees get to be 300 feet tall.

   Our guide said that some trees grow to be 300 feet tall.

4. Kenny did gymnastics, and Calvin jumped on the trampoline.

   Kenny performed gymnastics, and Calvin tumbled on the trampoline.

5. When the movie ended, everyone clapped.

   When the thrilling adventure movie ended, everyone clapped loudly.

ACTIVITY B Write an exact noun or a stronger verb in place of each underlined word. Add colorful adjectives and adverbs to make the sentences more interesting.

1. Jennifer <u>laughed</u> when she saw me water the plastic plant.

2. The <u>dog</u> rolled around in the mud.

3. The dish <u>broke</u> into pieces.

4. Mom put her necklace into a <u>box</u>.

5. The penguin <u>walked</u> toward the man.

WRITER'S CORNER

Look through a piece of your past writing. Find sentences that can be improved by using exact words. Revise those sentences.

Tech Tip   With an adult, use an online thesaurus.

Combining Sentences

Too many short sentences together will make your writing sound choppy. That's why good writers write sentences of different lengths. One way to make sentences longer is by combining them.

You can use the word *and* to combine subjects or predicates. You can also use the word *and* to combine two short sentences that give information about the same idea. Read these examples. Notice how sentence parts can be combined.

> **Mules are dependable. They are sure-footed.**
>
> **Mules are dependable *and* sure-footed.**

And is not the only word that you can use to combine sentences. The word *but* can be used to combine two different ideas.

> **Mustangs are wild horses. Mustangs can be trained.**
>
> **Mustangs are wild horses, *but* they can be trained.**

The word *or* is used to show a choice.

> **I can ride with an English saddle. I can ride with a Western saddle too.**
>
> **I can ride with an English saddle *or* a Western saddle.**

ACTIVITY C In each item below, the first two sentences are choppy. The third sentence is a revision of those two sentences. Tell whether the writer combined subjects, predicates, or sentences in each.

1. Dale read funny poems. Christa read funny poems.
   Dale and Christa read funny poems.

2. Nancy played the piano. Ron played his drums.
   Nancy played the piano, and Ron played his drums.

3. Eve sang a song. Eve danced at the same time.
   Eve sang a song and danced at the same time.

ACTIVITY D Combine each of the following pairs of short sentences into a longer sentence.

1. I can ride the bus. I can drive my car.
2. Erin played the violin. Charlie played the violin.
3. The road was bumpy. The road had many turns.
4. I combed Ginger's mane. I combed her tangled tail too.
5. I could buy a new hat. I could buy new boots instead.
6. Harry returned the screwdriver. He returned the nails.
7. Pam sees the sailboat on the water. She cannot see Rich steering the sailboat.
8. We put the party favors away. We put the games away.
9. Jenny biked home. Gretchen biked home.
10. Write the address on the envelope. Put a stamp on the envelope.

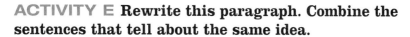

ACTIVITY E Rewrite this paragraph. Combine the sentences that tell about the same idea.

The Fun Fair had finally begun. Everyone was excited. Kim worked at the popcorn booth. Mrs. Carter grilled hot dogs. Linda sold raffle tickets. Mr. Palmer organized a softball game. All the students had a chance to play. By the end of the day, we were tired. Everyone was ready to go home.

WRITER'S CORNER

Write two sentences about a carnival or fair. Trade your sentences with a partner. Combine your partner's sentences into one longer sentence.

Homophones

Homophones are words that sound alike but are spelled differently and have different meanings.

Here are some pairs of homophones:

deer/dear	meet/meat	ate/eight
be/bee	our/hour	here/hear
threw/through	write/right	your/you're
night/knight	plane/plain	son/sun

When you use homophones, make sure that you use the correct spellings.

Often you will know which spelling to use because you have seen the words before in your reading. If you aren't sure which spelling is correct, look up the words in a dictionary.

ACTIVITY A Tell which word is correct in each sentence.

1. The baby (deer dear) ran across the road.

2. Lions eat (meet meat).

3. Spiders have (ate eight) legs.

4. The (be bee) flew from flower to flower.

5. (Our Hour) class went on a field trip.

6. The coach (threw through) the ball to the player.

7. Turn (write right) when you get to the corner.

8. I (here hear) music playing from that house.

9. The woman's (son sun) bought her a new car.

10. We will board the (plain plane) in a few minutes.

ACTIVITY B Use a homophone in parentheses in place of the underlined word or words.

1. Jenna <u>pitched</u> the ball over the fence. (threw through)
2. The sun felt warm on my <u>uncovered</u> feet. (bear bare)
3. Let's <u>print</u> a report about eagles. (write right)
4. <u>You are</u> coming with me. (Your You're)
5. I am my parents' first <u>male child</u>. (son sun)
6. Owls don't hunt until <u>after sunset</u>. (night knight)
7. The startled bird <u>fluttered</u> away. (flu flew)
8. The burned toast had a <u>bad</u> smell. (foul fowl)
9. A <u>rabbit</u> hopped in the garden. (hair hare)
10. I had to <u>stop</u> and <u>watch</u>. (pause paws) (stair stare)

ACTIVITY C Choose the correct words from the word box to complete each sentence.

here	hour	ate	meat	knight	right	you're
hear	our	eight	meet	night	write	your

1. Ed can _____ with his left hand or his _____ hand.
2. I can _____ you whispering way over _____.
3. _____ wearing _____ new shoes today.
4. They _____ breakfast today at _____ o'clock.
5. We have one _____ before _____ train leaves.
6. You can _____ the butcher when we buy our _____.
7. The _____ put on his armor and rode off into the _____.

WRITER'S CORNER

Use a dictionary to look up the following homophones: *to, too,* and *two.* Use each word in a sentence that shows what it means.

ACTIVITY D Complete each sentence with the correct homophone from the word box.

steal	cent	hare	doe	creak
steel	scent	hair	dough	creek

1. The bridge we crossed was made of _____.
2. In the fable the tortoise beats the _____.
3. A _____ is a female deer.
4. The stairs in the old house began to _____.
5. A skunk's _____ is easy to recognize.
6. Pizza crust is made out of _____.
7. A penny is worth one _____.
8. The raccoon will _____ the apple from the picnic table.
9. Marcy can get her _____ cut and styled tomorrow.
10. We put our feet in the cool _____.

ACTIVITY E Complete each pair of sentences with the correct homophones. Use a dictionary if you need help.

1. (bough/bow)
   a. That tree has a strong _____.
   b. The ship's _____ cuts into the water.
2. (fur/fir)
   a. The campers slept under a _____ tree.
   b. A thick coat of _____ keeps a bear warm.
3. (yoke/yolk)
   a. The oxen were held by the _____ of the plow.
   b. Mix the egg _____ with the milk.

ACTIVITY F Match each homophone in Column A with its definition in Column B. Use a dictionary if you need help.

Column A	Column B
1. wait	**a.** listened to
2. weight	**b.** shelters made from cloth
3. tense	**c.** paddle
4. tents	**d.** heaviness
5. oar	**e.** stay
6. ore	**f.** group of animals
7. heard	**g.** rocks dug from the ground
8. herd	**h.** nervous
9. weak	**i.** seven days
10. week	**j.** not strong

ACTIVITY G The paragraph below includes several incorrect homophones. Rewrite the paragraph, using the correct homophones.

Today I cent a package to my grandma. It was a little statue of a baby dear and its mother. I walked to the post office to male it. The postal worker said that I should right my address on the package. She said the package would be put on a plain that evening and flown to Reno, where Grandma lives. I can't weight until she sees it!

LINK

Beacons of Light

Today, at many lighthouse sites, foghorns give off warnings. Each foghorn has its own special sound and number of blasts. The *diaphone*, one of the best foghorns, uses compressed air to give off two tones, a high-pitched screech and a low grunt. The high sound can be heard for seven miles. The low tone travels farther. Lighthouses also use radio beacons to send warning signals.

Gail Gibbons

WRITER'S CORNER

Work with a partner to write a short poem using homophones. Use any of the homophones in this lesson. Use any other homophones that you can think of.

Grammar in Action Find the homophones in the excerpt on this page.

Oral Biographies

An oral biography is a researched talk about the life of a famous person. The talk can be about almost anyone, but it should be about someone that you can research. For example, you can give a report about Abraham Lincoln or Martin Luther King Jr.

Keep these things in mind as you prepare your oral biography.

Research

After you have chosen a person for your oral biography, you should start researching that person's life. You will need to use your school or local library to find sources, just as you do for a written research report.

Use your own words to tell about your subject, or the person you are talking about. Using your own words shows that you understand the sources you used in your research.

Prepare

To prepare your report, gather information about your subject's life. Write your notes on note cards.

The next step is to organize your notes. One way to organize them is to put them into separate piles. One pile might be about the early years of the subject's life. A second pile might cover the middle years, and a third pile might be about the later years. A fourth pile might be about what we should remember about this person. Use your piles to plan the introduction, body, and conclusion of your biography.

"I have a dream . . ."

Dr. Martin Luther King Jr.

Visual Aids and Audio Aids

If possible, use visual aids, such as pictures and photos, to make your report livelier. Your audience will want to know what the person you're talking about looks like.

You can also play audio recordings or videos to help your audience get to know your subject. For example, if you are giving a report on President John F. Kennedy, you might want to play an audio recording of one of his speeches.

President John F. Kennedy

ACTIVITY A Choose a subject for your oral biography. If you need help thinking of ideas, look in your social studies book for famous people.

ACTIVITY B Look in the library for information about the subject for your oral biography. Write on a separate note card each fact that you learn. When you have finished, organize your note cards into piles. Think of an interesting introduction and a memorable conclusion for your report.

ACTIVITY C Think about visual aids that will help your audience understand your subject better. Make a list of pictures, videos, and audio recordings you want to include in your oral biography. Check with an adult to see if you need permission to use these visual aids and audio aids.

SPEAKER'S CORNER

Tell a partner at least five facts that you learned about the subject of your oral biography. Talk about which facts seem most interesting. Decide what other facts about the subject might be interesting to know.

Practice

When you have written your note cards, practice giving your talk. Look at your notes to remind you what to say. Look up at the audience. Make your voice sound lively. Sound interested in your subject.

Find an audience to listen to your talk. Family members make good listeners. You can also take turns listening and speaking to classmates.

Speaking Tips

Here are some tips to make your oral biography go smoothly.

- Give your speech in front of a mirror before you give it to an audience. Know your information well enough to avoid pausing and using fillers such as "uh" and "um." Being familiar with your presentation will build your confidence.
- Make sure that everyone can hear you. Always talk loudly enough and clearly enough so that people who are sitting in the back can understand what you are saying.
- Speaking in front of others can be a little scary. Pick out two or three friendly faces around the room and pretend that you are speaking only to them.

- Move your hands to make a point if you need to. Use a lively voice to keep your listeners interested.

Remember that giving an oral biography is like any other skill. The more you do it, the easier it gets.

Listening Tips

Show the speaker the same courtesy that you want when you give your oral biography.

- Be quiet while others are giving their talks. If you speak, you will disturb the speaker and the other people in the audience.
- Pay attention to the speaker.
- Listen to the talk for interesting parts of the biography. Listen for something in the talk that makes you want to know more about that person.
- Take notes while you listen to the speaker. Use these notes to ask questions about the subject when the speaker is finished giving the talk.
- Save your questions until the end of the talk. Raise your hand to ask your questions.

ACTIVITY D Use a recorder or video camera to record yourself presenting your oral biography. Listen to or watch your presentation. Look for places where you think you can improve your oral biography.

SPEAKER'S CORNER

Present your oral biography to your class. Use your visual aids or audio aids and your notes.

Writer's Workshop

Prewriting and Drafting

When you are interested in a topic, do you try to learn more about it? Writing a research report is a way to learn more about something you are interested in. It is also a way to share what you have learned with others.

Prewriting

Adil is a third grader. His class decided to make an encyclopedia. The encyclopedia would be made up of research reports.

Adil needed a topic to research before he could write a report. He would take time to choose a topic, research it, and organize the facts and ideas he found.

Choosing a Topic

Adil wanted to choose a topic he was interested in. He didn't want to get bored while he was researching his topic.

Adil was born in India. He and his parents moved to the United States when he was a baby. There were many pictures and statues of elephants in his home. He was curious about the animals, so he decided to research them. Adil did know one fact already. He knew that the elephants in the pictures were Asian elephants.

Your Turn

- Think of topics that interest you. You might research an animal, a famous person, a special place, or an important event.
- Think of topics that you already know something about. Write a list of topics that interest you or that you know something about.
- Choose the topic that seems most interesting to you.

Researching

Adil went to the local library after school. He found in an encyclopedia information about Asian elephants. He also found books and Web sites about Asian elephants.

With the books and Web sites, Adil had many sources. He decided to look at the information that was most recent. He made sure the Web sites he used were from reliable sources. He used only Web sites from zoos.

Your Turn

- Find sources that give information about your topic.
- Check in an encyclopedia for information about your topic. Don't rely on only one book or article. Instead, look in many different books and articles.
- Use the index and contents page of a book to search for information you need.
- You can also check Web sites for information. Ask your teacher or the librarian if the Web site has reliable information.

Using Note Cards

Adil began to find facts from his sources. After he found a fact he thought might be interesting, he wrote it on a note card. Adil wrote the facts in his own words. Then he made sure to write at the bottom of each card the name of the source and the author.

Here is a note card that Adil wrote about the eating habits of Asian elephants.

Adil had written many note cards. He decided to organize them into separate piles.

 Organization Some were about how the elephants live or what they eat. Others were about why the elephants are endangered. He had note cards with other ideas too.

Your Turn

- Begin taking notes from your sources. Write on note cards facts you find interesting. Put only one fact on each note card.
- Remember to include at the bottom of the card the title of the source, the author, and the page number.
- Place the note cards in piles with other note cards about the same ideas.
- Put aside any note cards that don't fit with any of the other cards.

eats 330 to 350 pounds of food each day

Large Animals by Maxine Orwell, p.55

Prewriting
Drafting
Content Editing
Revising
Copyediting
Proofreading
Publishing

Drafting

Now it was time for Adil to write his draft. He used the note cards he wrote during prewriting to help him. First, he wrote a title. Then he wrote an introduction that gives some general information about the Asian elephant. Next, he wrote the body. In the body Adil included information that he learned from his research. Adil finished his report with a conclusion.

The Asian Elephant

The Asian elephant lives in India, Srilanka, and Sumatra. Asian elephants are amazing creatures. They are intelligent. They are strong. But they are also endangered. This means that there are not many Asian elephants left. They need to be protected so that we all can enjoy them.

Asian elephants are endangered. The mane reason is that they are losing their forest home. People need more land. They cut down the forests that the elephants live in. There is another problem. Elephants are getting in trouble with people because elephants eat peoples crops. But some people are working to protect the Asian elephant. Large areas of forest are being saved. These are places for the elephants to live without fences or cages.

Asian elephants are large animals. They need to eat a lot of food. They will wash it all down with up to 30 gallons of water. In one day an Asian elephant will eat up to 350 pounds of food. How does all of that food and water get into the elephant. It uses its trunk. The trunk has a "finger" it uses like a hook. Not only are elephants interesting, but they are also smart. They can dig for food by using their tusks. They can talk to one another using their own language.

The Asian elephant is a special animal. It is smart and strong and can do amazing things. There are good ideas for how to protect it. But Asian elephants also need people to come up with new ideas to help them. I like Asian elephants.

Prewriting

Drafting

Content Editing

Revising

Copyediting

Proofreading

Publishing

Your Turn

- Write the first draft of your research report. First, write a title. Next, write your introduction. In your introduction tell your reader the topic of the research report. Give some general information about your topic.
- Write the body of the research report. This is where you present the information

  ◦◦ Voice

  you found. Be sure to use your own words and write with a confident voice. Group similar ideas together in the body.
- For the conclusion, sum up the information in the report. Also write a comment about your topic.
- When you write your research report, leave extra space between the lines. That way you will have room to make changes later.

Writer's Tip Catch the reader's attention with an interesting fact or question about the topic.

Content Editing

Now that Adil had finished his first draft, he wanted to make it better. He hoped to improve his research report by content editing.

Content Editor's Checklist

☐ Does the writing stay on the topic?

☐ Does the introduction state the topic and catch the reader's attention?

☐ Is the information in the body organized?

☐ Are there supporting facts?

☐ Does the conclusion sum up the topic and end with a comment?

Adil asked his classmate Henry to content edit his research report. Henry would check whether Adil's ideas made sense. Henry used the Content Editor's Checklist.

Henry read Adil's research report. He told Adil that he enjoyed learning about the Asian elephant. He said that he really liked learning about the "finger" on the end of the trunk. He had never heard of that before. Then Henry made these suggestions.

- The facts in the third paragraph are interesting, but the information about the elephants' tusks and how elephants talk doesn't fit with the rest of the ideas. The rest of the paragraph is about what they eat and how they use their trunk.

- Your report needs a more interesting introduction. Maybe you can add a fact or a question.

- It would be better to read about the elephants before reading about the problems that the elephants are having.
- It would be good to know more facts. How tall and how heavy are these elephants?
- The conclusion sums up the topic, but it doesn't include a comment on the topic. The last sentence is just your opinion.

Adil thanked Henry for his help. Adil liked what Henry said, but he didn't know if he agreed with everything. Adil needed to think about each idea before deciding to use it.

Your Turn

- Work with a partner and read each other's research reports. Pay attention to only one question on the checklist at a time. When you have finished, take turns talking about each other's drafts.
- Think about each of your partner's ideas. Make only the changes that seem right to you. You did the research, so you know the information best.

Prewriting

Drafting

Content Editing

Revising

Copyediting

Proofreading

Publishing

Revising

This is how Adil decided to revise his research report.

The Asian Elephant

Did you know that elephants live in other places besides Africa?

^The Asian elephant lives in India, Srilanka, and Sumatra. Asian elephants are amazing creatures. They are intelligent. They are strong. But they are also endangered. This means that there are not many Asian elephants left. They need to be protected so that we all can enjoy them.

Asian elephants are endangered. The mane reason is that they are losing their forest home. People need more land. They cut down the forests that the elephants live in. There is another problem. Elephants are getting in trouble with people because elephants eat peoples crops. But some people are working to protect the Asian elephant. Large areas of forest are being saved. These are places for the elephants to live without fences or cages.

Some are as tall as 10 feet. Some are as heavy as 11,000 pounds.

Asian elephants are large animals.^They need to eat a lot of food. They will wash it all down with up to 30 gallons of water. In one day an Asian elephant will eat up to 350 pounds of food. How does all of that food and water get into the elephant. It uses its trunk. The trunk has a "finger" it uses like a hook. Not only are elephants interesting, but they are also smart. They can dig for food by using their tusks. They can talk to one another using their own language.

The Asian elephant is a special animal. It is smart and strong and can do amazing things. There are good ideas for how to protect it. But Asian elephants also need people to come up with new ideas to help them. ~~I like Asian elephants.~~

We must care for them before they are gone forever.

Here are some things that Adil did to improve his research report.

- Adil left in the two sentences about tusks and language. Why do you think he did this?
- He wrote a new sentence in the introduction. What kind of sentence did he write? Does it grab your attention? Why or why not?
- What did Adil do to the order of the two body paragraphs? Why?
- What new information did Adil add to the body? Do you think it's a good change? Why or why not?
- Adil wrote a new sentence in the conclusion. What did the sentence say?

Adil felt that he had learned a lot about the Asian elephant. He thought that other people would be interested in his topic too.

Your Turn

- Use your ideas and your content editor's ideas to revise your draft.
- Use the Content Editor's Checklist to check your draft again.

Prewriting

Drafting

Content Editing

Revising

Copyediting

Proofreading

Publishing

Copyediting and Proofreading

Copyediting

Adil knew that his revisions had made his draft stronger. Now he needed to copyedit his research report. He wanted to check whether ~~Word Choice~~ all the sentences and words were clear and correct. Adil used this checklist to copyedit his research report.

Copyeditor's Checklist

☐ Are all the sentences complete sentences?

☐ Do the sentences make sense?

☐ Do the sentences make sense one after the other?

☐ If sentences were combined, was it done correctly?

☐ Are all the words used correctly?

Adil decided to combine two sentences in the first paragraph to make the writing flow better. He wrote a new sentence, *They are intelligent and strong.* He also combined the sentences about how tall and heavy the elephants are. Can you explain how?

Adil found a sentence about what the elephants eat that he thought was out of ~~Sentence Fluency~~ order. It made sense first to talk about how much food elephants ate and then to say that they drank a lot of water. Adil moved the two sentences about food next to each other.

Grammar in Action

Adil found that he had used a word that was the homophone of the word he really wanted to use. Can you find it? What word should Adil have used?

Prewriting

Drafting

Content Editing

Revising

Copyediting

Proofreading

Publishing

Your Turn

- Copyedit your research report, using the Copyeditor's Checklist.
- Look for only one kind of mistake at a time.
- Pay special attention to words that are homophones.
- Try to make your sentences different lengths by combining them. Be sure your sentences still make sense.

Proofreading

Adil wanted someone to proofread his research report before he wrote a final draft. Adil decided to ask his Aunt Kamala. Here is the checklist that Aunt Kamala used.

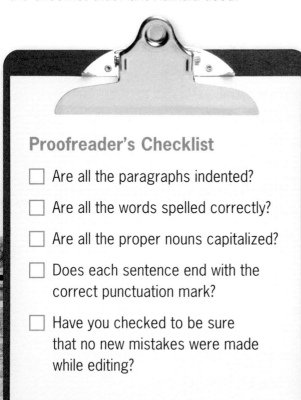

Proofreader's Checklist

☐ Are all the paragraphs indented?

☐ Are all the words spelled correctly?

☐ Are all the proper nouns capitalized?

☐ Does each sentence end with the correct punctuation mark?

☐ Have you checked to be sure that no new mistakes were made while editing?

Aunt Kamala proofread Adil's research report. She found that the name of the country  Conventions Sri Lanka was spelled wrong. She told Adil that he needed to put a space between *Sri* and *lanka*. She also told him that he needed to capitalize the *L* in *Lanka*.

Aunt Kamala found that Adil had used a punctuation mark incorrectly. In the new second paragraph, one of the sentences asks a question but ends with a period. Can you find it?

In the new third paragraph, Aunt Kamala added an apostrophe. The word *peoples* needed an apostrophe. Can you explain why?

Your Turn

- Use the Proofreader's Checklist to proofread your draft.
- Trade drafts with a partner and proofread each other's drafts, using the Proofreader's Checklist.
- Check for one type of mistake at a time.
- Read over your draft again to make sure that none of the changes added a new mistake to your research report.

Writer's Tip Be sure you agree with each change you get from your proofreader.

Publishing

Adil worked on the final copy of his research report. He made sure to add his proofreading changes while writing. Here is Adil's finished research report.

Adil included a picture of an Asian elephant, and he made a map showing where Asian elephants live. He then presented his

 **Presentation**

research report to the class. The class put together all the reports and pictures in their encyclopedia.

The Asian Elephant

Did you know that elephants live in other places besides Africa? The Asian elephant lives in India, Sri Lanka, and Sumatra. Asian elephants are amazing creatures. They are intelligent and strong. But they are also endangered. This means that there are not many Asian elephants left. They need to be protected so that we all can enjoy them.

Asian elephants are large animals. Some are as tall as 10 feet and as heavy as 11,000 pounds. They need to eat a lot of food. In one day an Asian elephant will eat up to 350 pounds of food. They will wash it all down with up to 30 gallons of water. How does all of that food and water get into the elephant? It uses its trunk. The trunk has a "finger" it uses like a hook. Not only are elephants interesting, but they are also smart. They can dig for food by using their tusks. They can talk to one another using their own language.

Asian elephants are endangered. The main reason is that they are losing their forest home. People need more land. They cut down the forests that the elephants live in. There is another problem. Elephants are getting in trouble with people because elephants eat people's crops. But some people are working to protect the Asian elephant. Large areas of forest are being saved. These are places for the elephants to live without fences or cages.

The Asian elephant is a special animal. It is smart and strong and can do amazing things. There are good ideas for how to protect it. But Asian elephants also need people to come up with new ideas to help them. We must care for them before they are gone forever.

Whenever you publish your work, your goal is to share your thoughts and experiences with other people. There are many ways you can publish your research report. However you decide to publish, make sure the message is clear.

 Submit your report to an online magazine or newspaper that publishes student work. Add photos or illustrations that support your topic.

 Film it. Make your own documentary. Narrate the report with a backdrop of photos, music, and illustrations. Interview someone who can add information to your topic.

 Create a class encyclopedia by combining all the research reports under a single cover. Arrange the reports in alphabetical order and create a contents page.

 Have your class encyclopedia on hand for Parents' Night. You might wish to present it as a PowerPoint presentation.

Your Turn

- Make a clean, final copy of your research report. Be careful copying or typing your report.
- Find visual aids that go with your research report. You can use pictures that you find or draw. You might make charts that show your research. If your report is about a certain place, you might want to include a map that shows the location.

Common Proofreading Marks

Use these proofreading marks to mark changes when you proofread.
Remember to use a colored pencil to make your changes.

Symbol	Meaning	Example
¶	begin new paragraph	over. ¶Begin a new
◡	close up space	close u p space
∧	insert	students ∧think *should*
ℒ	delete, omit	that the the book
/	make lowercase	/Mathematics
∿	reverse letters	reverse letters
≡	capitalize	washington
∨∨ ∨∨	add quotation marks	I am, I said.
⊙	add period	Marta drank tea ⊙

Making a Time Capsule

A Buried Surprise

A time capsule is fun to make. George Washington even put one in
it was like when you were in third grade.
the cornerstone of the Capitol building. But it has never been found.

When you are older, you can open the time capsule and remember what

What You Need

Grammar and Mechanics Handbook

Grammar

Adjectives

An adjective points out or describes a noun.

Adjectives That Compare

Adjectives can be used to make comparisons. To compare two people, places, or things, -er is often added to an adjective. To compare three or more people, places, or things, -est is often added to an adjective.

A horse is **taller** than a deer.
A moose is **bigger** than a horse.
An elephant is the **largest** land animal.

Some adjectives that compare have special forms.

Vanilla ice cream is **good**.
Strawberry ice cream is **better** than vanilla.
Chocolate ice cream is the **best** flavor of all.

The girl had a **bad** cold on Sunday.
The cold was **worse** on Monday.
It was the **worst** cold she'd ever had.

Adjectives That Tell How Many

Some adjectives tell how many or about how many.

Only **six** members came to the meeting.
A **few** members were sick.

Some adjectives tell numerical order.

I finished reading the **sixth** chapter.

Articles

Articles point out nouns. *The, a,* and *an* are articles. *The* points out a specific person, place, or thing. *A* and *an* point out any one of a group of people, places, or things. Use *a* before a consonant sound and *an* before a vowel sound.

> **The** man ate **a** peach and **an** apple.

Demonstrative Adjectives

Demonstrative adjectives point out or tell about a specific person, place, or thing. The demonstrative adjectives are *this, that, these,* and *those.*

	Singular	Plural
Near	**This** flower is red.	**These** bushes are tall.
Far	**That** flower is yellow.	**Those** bushes are short.

Descriptive Adjectives

A descriptive adjective tells more about a noun. It can tell how something looks, tastes, sounds, feels, or smells. It can tell about size, color, shape, or weight.

A descriptive adjective often comes before the noun it describes.

> A **tall** tree stood beside the **red** barn.

A descriptive adjective can follow a being verb as a subject complement. It describes the subject of the sentence.

> The tree is **tall**.   The barn was **red**.

Possessive Adjectives

A possessive adjective shows who or what owns something. A possessive adjective is used before a noun. The possessive adjectives are *my, your, his, her, its, our,* and *their.*

> I have **my** camera, and Lucy has **her** cell phone.

Proper Adjectives

Proper adjectives are formed from proper nouns. A proper adjective begins with a capital letter.

When we went to Mexico, I ate **Mexican** food.

Adverbs

An adverb tells more about a verb. Many adverbs end in *ly*.

Some adverbs tell when or how often an action takes place.

I went to the mall **yesterday**. I **sometimes** go to the toy store.

Some adverbs tell where an action takes place.

I went **outside** after dinner. I played **there** until it was dark.

Some adverbs tell how an action takes place.

My new skateboard goes **fast**. I ride it **gracefully**.

Negative Words

Some adverbs form negative ideas. Use *not, n't* for *not* in a contraction, or *never* to express a negative idea. Do not use more than one negative word in a sentence.

He will **not** be ready on time. He **can't** find his sneakers.
He **never** remembers where he left them.

Contractions

A contraction is a short way to write some words. An apostrophe (') is used to show where one or more letters have been left out of a word. Many contractions are formed with the word *not*.

do not = don't
cannot = can't
was not = wasn't
will not = won't

Coordinating Conjunctions

A coordinating conjunction joins two words or groups of words. The words *and, but,* and *or* are coordinating conjunctions.

My dad **and** I went to the pool. I can swim **but** not dive.
The pool is never too hot **or** crowded.

Nouns

A noun is a word that names a person, a place, or a thing.

Collective Nouns

A collective noun names a group of people or things.

My **class** saw a **herd** of buffalo.

Common Nouns

A common noun names any one member of a group of people, places, or things.

My **cousin** saw a **dog** run down the **street**.

Plural Nouns

A plural noun names more than one person, place, or thing.

The **boys** have some **puppies** and some **fish**.

Possessive Nouns

The possessive form of a noun shows possession or ownership.

A singular possessive noun shows that one person owns something. To form the singular possessive, add an apostrophe (') and the letter *s* to a singular noun.

friend	friend**'s** book report
baby	baby**'s** bottle
Tess	Tess**'s** soccer ball
woman	woman**'s** purse

A plural possessive noun shows that more than one person owns something. To form the regular plural possessive, add an apostrophe (') after the plural form of the noun.

friends	friends' book reports
babies	babies' bottles
the Smiths	the Smiths' house

To form the plural possessive of an irregular noun, add an apostrophe and s ('s) after the plural form.

| women | women's purses |
| mice | mice's cheese |

Proper Nouns
A proper noun names a particular person, place, or thing. A proper noun begins with a capital letter.

Meg saw **Shadow** run down **Pine Street**.

Singular Nouns
A singular noun names one person, place, or thing.

The **girl** has a **kite** and a **skateboard**.

Predicates

The predicate of a sentence tells what the subject is or does.

Complete Predicates
The complete predicate of a sentence is the simple predicate and any words that go with it.

Tom **rode his new bike**.

Compound Predicates
Two predicates joined by *and, but,* or *or* form a compound predicate.

Karen **got a glass and poured some milk**.

Simple Predicates

The simple predicate of a sentence is a verb, a word or words that express an action or a state of being.

The boys **ran** noisily down the street.   They **were** happy.

Pronouns

A pronoun is a word that takes the place of a noun.

Personal Pronouns

A personal pronoun refers to the person speaking or to the person or thing that is spoken to or about. In this sentence *I* is the person speaking, *you* is the person spoken to, and *them* are the people spoken about.

I heard **you** calling **them**.

Object Pronouns

An object pronoun is used after an action verb. The object pronouns are *me, you, him, her, it, us,* and *them.* An object pronoun can be part of a compound object.

Karen will help **them**.   Chris will help **her** and **me**.

Possessive Pronouns

A possessive pronoun shows who or what owns something. A possessive pronoun takes the place of a noun. It takes the place of the owner and the thing that is owned. The possessive pronouns are *mine, yours, his, hers, its, ours,* and *theirs.*

My cap is here, and **your cap** is over there.
Mine is here, and **yours** is over there.

Subject Pronouns

A subject pronoun can be used as the subject of a sentence. The subject pronouns are *I, you, he, she, it, we,* and *they.* A subject pronoun can be part of a compound subject.

She is a great tennis player. **She** and **I** play tennis often.
She and **Tom** like to play video games.

Sentences

A sentence is a group of words that expresses a complete thought. Every sentence has a subject and a predicate. Every sentence begins with a capital letter.

Commands

A command is a sentence that tells what to do. The subject of a command is *you*. The subject is not stated in most commands. A command ends with a period (.).

> Please wear your jacket.

Compound Sentences

Two sentences joined by a comma and *and, but,* or *or* form a compound sentence.

> Ming is eating, but Lili is sleeping.

Exclamations

An exclamation is a sentence that shows strong or sudden emotion. An exclamation ends with an exclamation point (!).

> How cold it is today!

Questions

A question is a sentence that asks something. A question ends with a question mark (?). A question often starts with a question word. Some question words are *who, when, where, what, why,* and *how.*

> Are you ready?   Where is your jacket?

Statements

A statement is a sentence that tells something. A statement ends with a period (.).

> Your jacket is in the closet.

Subject Complements

A subject complement is an adjective that comes after a being verb in a sentence. A subject complement describes or tells more about the subject. Two or more subject complements can be joined by *and, but,* or *or* to form a compound subject complement.

The sky is **blue**.　　　　The clouds are **white** and **fluffy**.

Subjects

The subject of a sentence is who or what the sentence is about. The subject can be a noun or a pronoun.

Complete Subjects
The complete subject is the simple subject and the words that describe it or give more information about it.

The little gray kitten is playing.

Compound Subjects
Two or more subjects joined by *and* or *or* form a compound subject.

Bob and **Lisa** went to the movies. **Nora** or **I** will sweep the floor.

Simple Subjects
The simple subject is the noun or pronoun that a sentence tells about.

His little **dog** likes to chase the ball.　　　**It** runs very fast.

Tense

The tense of a verb shows when the action takes place.

Future Tense
The future tense tells about something that will happen in the future.

One way to form the future tense is with a form of the helping verb *be* plus *going to* plus the present form of a verb.

I **am going to make** toast.   Dad **is going to butter** it.

They **are going to eat** it.

Another way to form the future tense is with the helping verb *will* and the present form of a verb.

We **will go** to the museum. The guide **will explain** the exhibits.

Past Progressive Tense

The past progressive tense tells what was happening in the past. This tense is formed with *was* or *were* and the present participle of a verb.

I **was feeding** the cat.   My parents **were reading**.

Present Progressive Tense

The present progressive tense tells what is happening now. The present progressive tense is formed with *am, is,* or *are* and the present participle of a verb.

We **are watching** TV.   I **am eating** popcorn.

My sister **is drinking** juice.

Simple Past Tense

The simple past tense tells about something that happened in the past. The past part of a verb is used for the past tense.

We **cooked** breakfast this morning.   Mom **fried** the eggs.

We **drank** orange juice.

Simple Present Tense

The simple present tense tells about something that is always true or something that happens again and again. The present part of a verb is used for the present tense. If the subject is a singular noun or *he, she,* or *it, -s* or *-es* must be added to the verb.

Prairie dogs **live** where it's dry.

A prairie dog **digs** a burrow to live in.

Verbs

A verb shows action or state of being. See TENSE.

Action Verbs

An action verb tells what someone or something does.

The girl **sings**.   Dogs **bark**.

Being Verbs

A being verb shows what someone or something is. Being verbs do not express action.

The girl **is** happy.   The dog **was** hungry.

Helping Verbs

A verb can have more than one word. A helping verb is a verb added before the main verb that helps make the meaning clear.

We **will** go to the movie.   We **might** buy some popcorn.

Irregular Verbs

The past and the past participle of irregular verbs are not formed by adding -*d* or -*ed.*

Present	Past	Past Participle
sing	sang	sung
send	sent	sent
write	wrote	written

Principal Parts

A verb has four principal parts: present, present participle, past, and past participle. The present participle is formed by adding -*ing* to the present. The past and the past participle of regular verbs are formed by adding -*d* or -*ed* to the present.

Present	Present Participle	Past	Past Participle
walk	walking	walked	walked
rake	raking	raked	raked

The present participle is often used with forms of the helping verb *be*.

We **are walking** to school. Carla **was raking** leaves.

The past participle is often used with forms of the helping verb *have*.

We **have walked** this way before.
She **has raked** the whole backyard.

Regular Verbs

The past and the past participle of regular verbs are formed by adding *-d* or *-ed* to the present.

Present	Past	Past Participle
jump	jumped	jumped
glue	glued	glued

Mechanics

Capitalization

Use a capital letter to begin the first word in a sentence.

Tomorrow is my birthday.

Use a capital letter to begin the names of people and pets.

Aunt **P**eg let me play with her ferret, **N**ibbles.

Use a capital letter to begin the names of streets, cities, states, and countries.

I live on **R**oscoe **S**treet. My cousin lives in **G**uadalajara, **M**exico.

Use a capital letter to begin the names of days, months, and holidays.

Veteran's **D**ay is on **W**ednesday, **N**ovember 11.

Use a capital letter to begin a proper adjective.

I like to eat **C**hinese food.

Use a capital letter to begin personal titles.

Mrs. Novak

Dr. Ramirez

Governor Charles Royce

Use a capital letter to begin the important words in the title of a book or poem. The first and last words of a title are always capitalized.

The **S**ecret **G**arden

"**S**ing a **S**ong of **C**ities"

The personal pronoun *I* is always a capital letter.

Punctuation

Apostrophes

Use an apostrophe to form possessive nouns.

Keisha's skateboard
the children's lunches
the horses' stalls

Use an apostrophe to replace the letters left out in a contraction.

didn't   can't   wasn't

Commas

Use a comma to separate the words in a series.

Mark, Anton, and Cara made the scenery.
They hammered, sawed, and nailed.

Use a comma or commas to separate a name in direct address.

Carl, will you help me?
Do you think, Keshawn, that we will finish today?

Use a comma when two short sentences are combined in a compound sentence.

Dad will heat the soup, and I will make the salad.
Dad likes noodle soup, but I like bean soup.

Use a comma to separate the names of a city and state.

She comes from Philadelphia, Pennsylvania.

Use a comma or commas to separate a direct quotation from the rest of the sentence.

"Hey," called Mario, "where are you going?"
"I'm going to the movies," Juana answered.

Exclamation Points

Use an exclamation point after an exclamation.

We won the game!

Periods

Use a period after a statement or a command.

The cat is hungry.

Please feed it.

Use a period after most abbreviations.

Sun.	Sept.	Mrs.
Ave.	gal.	Gov.

Question Marks

Use a question mark after a question.

Where are you going?

Quotation Marks

Use quotation marks to show the exact words a person says.

Nicole said, "I can't find my markers."

"Where," asked her mother, "did you leave them?"

Use quotation marks around the title of a poem. Underline the title of a book.

"Paul Revere's Ride"

<u>Dawn Undercover</u>

Index

Acknowledgments

Literature

Excerpt and cover from *Yours Truly, Goldilocks* by Alma Flor Ada. Text Copyright © 1998 by Alma Flor Ada. Reprinted by permission of Aladdin Paperbacks, an imprint of Simon & Schuster Children's Publishing Division.

Review of *Bats at the Library* used by permission of Katie Harvey. www.katiesliteraturelounge.blogspot.com

Excerpt from "Be a Fit Kid." Kidshealth.org. Copyright © 1995–2009 The Nemours Foundation. All rights reserved. Used by permission.

Excerpt and cover from *Fly Away Home* by Eve Bunting. Text copyright © 1991 by Eve Bunting. Published by Clarion Books, an imprint of Houghton Mifflin Company. All rights reserved.

Excerpt from *The Climb* by Roger Carr. Copyright © 2007. Reprinted by permission of Sundance/Newbridge LLC.

Excerpt from *April Aliens* by Rob Childs. Reprinted by permission of Harcourt Education, United Kingdom.

"Cheesy Quesadillas" from *The Kids' Multicultural Cookbook.* Copyright © 1995 by author Deanna F. Cook. Used by permission of Williamson Books, an imprint of Ideals Publication.

Excerpt from *Magnets* by Jason Cooper. Copyright © 2003 Rourke Publishing LLC. Used by permission.

Excerpt and cover from *James and the Giant Peach* by Roald Dahl. Copyright © 1961 by Roald Dahl. Text copyright renewed 1989 by Roald Dahl. Used by permission of Alfred A. Knopf, an imprint of Random House Children's Books, a division of Random House, Inc.

Review of *Dawn Undercover* used by permission of Kidsread.com. Copyright © 1998–2009 by Kidsread.com. All rights reserved.

Excerpt from "Drinking Water: Bottled or From the Tap?" *National Geographic Kids.* February 2008. Copyright © 2008 by National Geographic Society. Used by permission.

Excerpt from *Beacons of Light: Lighthouses* by Gail Gibbons. Copyright © 1990 by Gail Gibbons. Published by William Morrow & Company. All rights reserved. Used by permission.

Excerpt from *Easy Art Fun! Do-It-Yourself Crafts for Beginning Readers* by Jill Frankel Hauser. Copyright © 2002 by Jill Frankel Hauser. Used by permission of Williamson Books, an imprint of Ideals Publication.

Review of *Into the Land of the Unicorns* used by permission of Kidsread.com. Copyright © 1998–2009 by Kidsread.com. All rights reserved.

Excerpt from *Learning How: Karate* by Jane Mersky Leder. Copyright © 1992 by Bancroft-Sage Publishing. Used by permission.

Excerpt from *How to Write a Letter* by Florence D. Mischel. Copyright © 1957, 1988. Published by Franklin Watts. All rights reserved.

Excerpt from *Summer Magic (With a Pinch of Salt)* by Margaret Nash. Reprinted by permission of Harcourt Education, United Kingdom.

Excerpt and cover from *Water Buffalo Days* by Huynh Quang Nhuong. Copyright © 1997 by Huynh Quang Nhuong. Used by permission of HarperCollins Publishers.

Excerpt from "School Lunches." Kidshealth.org. Copyright © 1995–2009 The Nemours Foundation. All rights reserved. Used by permission.

Excerpt from *Mountains* by Seymour Simon. Copyright © 1994 by Seymour Simon. Published by William Morrow & Company. All rights reserved. Used by permission.

Review of *Strange Happenings* used by permission of Kidsread.com. Copyright © 1998–2009 by Kidsread.com. All rights reserved.

Excerpt from "Why Exercise Is Cool." Kidshealth.org. Copyright © 1995–2009 The Nemours Foundation. All rights reserved. Used by permission.

All other excerpts come from public-domain sources, including Project Gutenberg.

Art and Photography

When there is more than one picture on a page, credits are supplied in sequence, left to right, top to bottom. Page positions are abbreviated as follows: **(t)** top, **(c)** center, **(b)** bottom, **(l)** left, **(r)** right.

Photos and illustrations not acknowledged are either owned by Loyola Press or from royalty-free sources including but not limited to Alamy, Art Resource, Big Stock, Bridgeman, Corbis/ Veer, Dreamstime, Fotosearch, Getty Images, Northwind Images, Photoedit, Smithsonian, Wikipedia. Loyola Press has made every effort to locate the copyright holders for the cited works used in this publication and to make full acknowledgment for their use. In the case of any omissions, the Publisher will be pleased to make suitable acknowledgments in future editions.

Frontmatter: vii(bl) Phil Martin Photography.

iStockphoto, Frontmatter: iii, iv, vi, vii **Section 1:** 9, 10, 11, 15, 21, 26 **Section 2:** 32, 33, 36–39, 44–49 **Section 3:** 57, 58, 65, 66, 68, 69 **Section 4:** 75, 77, 79, 80, 82, 85, 86–88, 92, 104 **Section 5:** 113, 114, 116, 117, 120, 122, 124–126 **Section 6:** 137, 138, 142, 143, 152, 153, 156 **Section 7:** 167, 169, 171, 178, 182 **Section 8:** 187, 199, 202, 206, 207 **Chapter 1:** 210, 211, 222, 225, 226, 233, 235, 236, 238, 239, 241, 243, 247 **Chapter 2:** 248, 249, 251, 252, 260, 261, 267, 268 **Chapter 3:** 286, 287, 290, 292, 293, 303, 309, 311–313, 318 **Chapter 4:** 325, 327–330, 332, 333, 335, 338, 340, 341, 343–345, 349 **Chapter 5:** 362, 375, 379, 383, 385 **Chapter 6:** 400, 401, 402, 403, 413–415, 420 429, 433, 437 **Chapter 7:** 438, 440, 443, 451, 457, 462, 463 **Chapter 8:** 479, 481, 485, 492 493, 496, 502

Jupiterimages Unlimited, Frontmatter: iii–vii **Section 1:** 12–15, 17, 18, 19, 20, 22, 23 **Section 2:** 28, 29, 31, 35–37, 40–44, 52 **Section 3:** 54–56, 60–63, 66, 67 **Section 4:** 74, 76, 78, 80, 81, 83, 84, 86–91, 93–105, 108 **Section 5:** 110–112, 114–125, 127–130, 134 **Section 6:** 136, 138–142, 144–152, 156 **Section 7:** 158, 160–167, 170–179 **Section 8:** 184–186, 189–201, 203–205

Section 2: 30, Time & Life Pictures/Getty Images. **Section 3: 59(b)** Bettmann/Corbis. **Section 7: 159,** Herb Scharfman/ Bettmann/Corbis. **Chapter 1: 219** Anni Betts. **237** Claire Joyce. **Chapter 2: 257(bl)** Greg Kuepfer. **270** Anni Betts. **Chapter 4: 331(t)** Anni Betts. **337** Bettmann/Corbis. **346** Anni Betts. **351(l)** Phil Martin Photography. **353(l)** Phil Martin Photography. **355(r)** Phil Martin Photography. **357(b)** Phil Martin Photography. **Chapter 5: 391** Anni Betts. **393** Anni Betts. **395** Anni Betts. **397** Anni Betts. **Chapter 7: 454** Anni Betts. **469(t)** Anni Betts. **Chapter 8: 487** Anni Betts. **499** President of the United States John Fitzgerald Kennedy, 1961–1963. Portrait photograph distributed by the White House.

Common Proofreading Marks

Use these proofreading marks to mark changes when you proofread. Remember to use a colored pencil to make your changes.

Symbol	Meaning	Example
¶	begin new paragraph	over. ¶Begin a new
‿	close up space	close u͡p space
∧	insert	students ∧think ~~should~~
℘	delete, omit	that the ~~the~~ book
/	lowercase letter	/Mathematics
∽	letters are reversed	letters are reve∽rsed
≡	capitalize	washington
⌄" ⌄"	quotation	⌄"I am,⌄" I said.
⊙	add period	Marta drank tea ⊙